Lecture Notes in Computer Science 10094

Viktória Zsók · Zoltán Porkoláb ·
Zoltán Horváth (Eds.)

Central European Functional Programming School

6th Summer School, CEFP 2015
Budapest, Hungary, July 6–10, 2015
Revised Selected Papers

Springer

Editors
Viktória Zsók
Eötvös Loránd University
Budapest, Hungary

Zoltán Porkoláb
Eötvös Loránd University
Budapest, Hungary

Zoltán Horváth
Eötvös Loránd University
Budapest, Hungary

ISSN 0302-9743 ISSN 1611-3349 (electronic)
Lecture Notes in Computer Science
ISBN 978-3-030-28345-2 ISBN 978-3-030-28346-9 (eBook)
https://doi.org/10.1007/978-3-030-28346-9

LNCS Sublibrary: SL1 – Theoretical Computer Science and General Issues

Cover illustration: Algorithmic principle of convolution, shown in the 2-dimensional case with a 5-point stencil (left) and a 9-point stencil (right). LNCS 10094, p. 230. Used with permission

This Springer imprint is published by the registered company Springer Nature Switzerland AG
The registered company address is: Gewerbestrasse 11, 6330 Cham, Switzerland

Preface

This volume presents the revised lecture notes of selected talks given at the 6th Central European Functional Programming School (CEFP 2015), held during July 6–10, in Budapest, Hungary and organized by the Eötvös Loránd University, Faculty of Informatics.

The summer school was organized in the spirit of intensive programmes. CEFP involves a large number of students, researchers, and teachers from across Europe.

The intensive programme offered a creative, inspiring environment for presentations and for the exchange of ideas on new specific programming topics. The lectures covered a wide range of functional programming and C++ programming subjects.

We are very grateful to the lecturers and researchers for the time and effort they devoted to their talks and lecture notes. The lecture notes were each carefully checked by reviewers selected from experts. The papers were revised by the lecturers based on reviews. The last paper of the volume is a selected paper of the PhD Workshop organized for the participants of the summer school.

We would like to express our gratitude for the work of all the members of the Programme Committee and the Organizing Committee.

March 2019

Viktória Zsók
Zoltán Porkoláb
Zoltán Horváth

Contents

Watch Out for that Tree! A Tutorial on Shortcut Deforestation 1
João Paulo Fernandes, Jácome Cunha, João Saraiva, and Alberto Pardo

Functional Reactive Programming in C++ 42
Ivan Čukić

Immutables in C++: Language Foundation for Functional Programming. 75
Zoltán Porkoláb

Programming in a Functional Style in C++ 111
Rainer Grimm

Functional, Reactive Web Programming in F# 137
Adam Granicz and Loic Denuziere

Functional Languages in Design of Coloured Petri Nets Models 161
Štefan Korečko

Single Assignment C (SAC): The Compilation Technology Perspective 207
Clemens Grelck

Type-Safe Functions and Tasks in a Shallow Embedded DSL for Microprocessors. 283
Pieter Koopman and Rinus Plasmeijer

Static and Dynamic Visualisations of Monadic Programs 341
Jurriën Stutterheim, Peter Achten, and Rinus Plasmeijer

Analyzing Scale-Free Properties in Erlang and Scala 380
Gábor Oláh, Gergely Nagy, and Zoltán Porkoláb

Author Index 395

Watch Out for that Tree! A Tutorial on Shortcut Deforestation

João Paulo Fernandes[1(✉)], Jácome Cunha[2], João Saraiva[3], and Alberto Pardo[4]

[1] CISUC, Universidade de Coimbra, Coimbra, Portugal
jpf@dei.uc.pt
[2] NOVA LINCS, Universidade do Minho, Braga, Portugal
jacome@di.uminho.pt
[3] HASLab/INESC TEC, Universidade do Minho, Braga, Portugal
saraiva@di.uminho.pt
[4] Universidad de la República, Montevideo, Uruguay
pardo@fing.edu.uy

Abstract. Functional programmers are strong enthusiasts of modular solutions to programming problems. Since software characteristics such as readability or maintainability are often directly proportional to modularity, this programming style naturally contributes to the beauty of functional programs. Unfortunately, in return of this beauty we often sacrifice efficiency: modular programs rely, at runtime, on the creation, use and elimination of intermediate data structures to connect its components. In this tutorial paper, we study an advanced technique that attempts to retain the best of this two worlds: (i) it allows programmers to implement beautiful, modular programs (ii) it shows how to transform such programs, in a way that can be incorporated in a compiler, into programs that do not construct any intermediate structure.

1 Introduction

Functional programming languages are a natural setting for the development of modular programs. Features common in functional programming languages, like polymorphism, higher-order functions and lazy evaluation are ingredients particularly suitable to develop software in a modular way. In such a setting, a software engineering develops her/his software by combining a set of simple, reusable, and off-the-shelf library of generic components into more complex (and possibly reusable) software. Indeed, already in Hughes (1984) it is stressed that modularity is a fundamental reason contributing to successful programming, hence the expressive power and relevance of functional languages.

Let us consider, for example, that we wish to define a function, named *trail*, to compute the last n lines of a given text. The naive programmer will solve this problem by defining from scratch all that functionality in a single, monolithic function. Although such a function may be correct and may have an efficient execution time, it may be harder to define and to understand. In a modular

V. Zsók et al. (Eds.): CEFP 2015, LNCS 10094, pp. 1–41, 2019.
https://doi.org/10.1007/978-3-030-28346-9_1

setting programmers tend to solve these problems by re-using simpler functions and to combine them in order to solve the problem under consideration.

For example, *trail* may be defined in an elegant way as follows:

$$trail :: Int \rightarrow Text \rightarrow Text$$
$$trail\ n\ t = (unlines \circ reverse \circ take\ n \circ reverse \circ lines)\ t$$

where several simple, well known, and well understood library functions are reused, namely, function *lines* that breaks a text in (a list containing) the lines that constitute it, function *reverse* that inverts the order of the elements in a list, function *take n* that selects the first n elements of a list, and function *unlines* that implements the inverse behavior of *lines*. Such functions are easily combined by using another reusable, higher-order construction: function composition, denoted by $\circ$.[1]

However, such a setting may also entail a drawback: as it encourages a compositional style of programming where non-trivial solutions are constructed composing simple functions, intermediate structures need to be constructed to serve as connectors of such functions.

In *trail*, for example, function *lines* produces a list of strings which is used by *reverse* to construct another list, which then feeds *take n*, and so on.

In practical terms, constructing, traversing and destroying these data structures may degrade the performance of the resulting implementations. And, in fact, the naive programmer surely agrees that the modular solution is more elegant, concise, and easy to understand, but may still be convinced that his monolithic solution is better simply because it may be more efficient!

In this tutorial we will study concrete settings where this drawback can be avoided. For this, we rely on a program transformation technique, usually referred to as program deforestation or program fusion (Wadler 1990; Gill et al. 1993), which is based on a certain set of calculation laws that can merge computations and thus avoid the construction of intermediate data structures. By the application of this technique a program $h = f \circ g$ is then transformed into an equivalent program that does not construct any intermediate structure.

In this tutorial we study a particular approach to the fusion technique known as shortcut fusion (Gill et al. 1993; Takano and Meijer 1995; Fernandes et al. 2007). The laws we present assume that it is possible to express the functions f and g, that occur in a composition $f \circ g$, in terms of well-known, higher-order, recursion patterns. As we will see later, while the applicability of such laws is certainly not universal, the fact is that the state of the art in shortcut fusion techniques can already deal with an extensive set of programs.

A remarkable observation that can be made about the programs that we calculate is that they often rely on either higher-order functions or on lazyness to be executed. So, these constructions, that Hughes (1984) identified as being essential to modularity, are in fact not only useful to increase modularity, but

[1] Program composition $(f \circ g)\ x$ is interpreted as $f\ (g\ x)$, and is left associative, i.e., $f \circ g \circ h = (f \circ g) \circ h$.

they can also be explored for reasoning about modular programs, including to increase their efficiency.

This Paper is Organized as Follows. In Sect. 2 we introduce the programming language that is used in the examples throughout the paper, that is, Haskell, and review the concepts of that language that are necessary to follow our materials. In Sect. 3, we present concrete shortcut fusion rules that are used to achieve deforestation of intermediate structures in small examples that are also introduced. These rules are concrete instances of generic ones, whose definition we present in Sect. 4. In Sect. 5 we study the application of fusion rules to a realistic example, and in Sect. 6 we conclude the paper.

2 A Gentle Introduction to Haskell

In this tutorial, all the code that we present is written in the Haskell programming language (Peyton Jones et al. 1999; Peyton Jones 2003). Haskell is a modern, polymorphic, statically-typed, lazy, and pure functional programming language.

In this section, we introduce the constructions that are necessary for the reader to follow our tutorial. While some familiarity with functional programming is expected, we hope that the reader does not need to be proficient in Haskell to understand such materials.

Haskell provides a series of predefined types such as *Int* (typifying natural numbers), *Float* (typifying floating point numbers) or *Char* (typifying single characters), and natural solutions to well known problems can readily be expressed. This is the case of the following (recursive) implementation of *factorial*, that directly follows from its mathematical definition:

$$\begin{array}{l} \mathit{factorial} :: \mathit{Int} \rightarrow \mathit{Int} \\ \mathit{factorial}\ 0 = 1 \\ \mathit{factorial}\ n = n * \mathit{factorial}\ (n-1) \end{array}$$

In Haskell, type judgments are of the form $e :: \tau$ and state that an expression e has type τ. In the case of *factorial* the type $\mathit{Int} \rightarrow \mathit{Int}$ indicates that it is a function from integers to integers.

Besides working with predefined types, we also have ways of constructing more complex data-types based on existent ones (either provided by Haskell itself or defined by the user). Indeed, in its prelude Haskell already defines (polymorphic) lists as:

$$\mathbf{data}\ [a] = [\,]\ |\ a : [a]$$

A concrete list of elements of type a, which is of type $[a]$, is then either empty, $[\,]$, or it has an element of type a followed by a list $[a]$. By polymorphic we mean that we are able of creating a list of any type, which is achieved by instantiating the type variable a with that type. For example, the type *String* is simply defined as,[2]

$$\textbf{type}\ String = [\,Char\,]$$

and concrete lists can easily be defined:

$$l_1 :: String$$
$$l_1 = [\,\texttt{'c'}, \texttt{'e'}, \texttt{'f'}, \texttt{'p'}\,]$$

$$l_2 :: [\,Int\,]$$
$$l_2 = [2, 0, 1, 5]$$

For clarity, we have explicitly annotated l_1 and l_2 with their corresponding types (l_1 is a lisf of characters, or a *String*, and l_2 is a list on integers), but this is not strictly necessary. The definitions of l_1 e l_2 are simply syntactic sugar for the following definitions:

$$l_1 = \texttt{'c'} : \texttt{'e'} : \texttt{'f'} : \texttt{'p'} : [\,]$$

$$l_2 = 2 : 0 : 1 : 5 : [\,]$$

Notice that the operator : for constructing lists (usually pronounced cons) is an infix operator. It can be turned into a prefix operator by using parenthesis, i.e., by writing (:). Hence, $5 : [\,]$ and $(:)\ 5\ [\,]$ are equivalent expressions. The same can be done with any other infix operator.

This means that l_1 and l_2 can also be expressed as:

$$l_1 = (:)\ \texttt{'c'}\ ((:)\ \texttt{'e'}\ ((:)\ \texttt{'f'}\ ((:)\ \texttt{'p'}\ [\,])))$$

$$l_2 = (:)\ 2\ ((:)\ 0\ ((:)\ 1\ ((:)\ 5\ [\,])))$$

In this paper, we will use all these different notations for lists interchangeably.

Regarding l_1, and since it is a string, it could alternatively have been defined as:

$$l_1 = \texttt{"cefp"}$$

Regarding the manipulation of lists, we normally use its constructors [] and (:) to pattern match on a given list. Indeed, a function f defined as:

$$f\ [\,] = f_1$$
$$f\ (h : t) = f_2$$

[2] Note that type synonyms are declared with the keyword **type** and that new datatypes are declared with **data**.

defines that its behavior on an empty list is that of f_1 and that its behavior on a list whose first element is h and whose tail is t is that of f_2. Of course, h and t can be used in the definition of f_2.

As an example, we may define the following function to compute the sum of all elements in a list of integers.[3]

$$\begin{aligned}&\mathit{sum}\ [\,] = 0\\&\mathit{sum}\ (h : t) = h + \mathit{sum}\ t\end{aligned}$$

Regarding this implementation, already in 1990 Hughes pinpointed that only the value 0 and the operation + are specific to the computation of *sum*. Indeed, if we replace 0 by 1 and + by $*$ in the above definition, we obtain a function that multiplies all the elements in a list of integers:

$$\begin{aligned}&\mathit{product}\ [\,] = 1\\&\mathit{product}\ (h : t) = h * \mathit{product}\ t\end{aligned}$$

This suggests that abstract/generic patterns for processing lists are useful. And in fact all modern functional languages allow the definition of such patterns relying on the concept of higher-order functions.

In Haskell functions are first-class citizens, in the sense that they can be passed as arguments to other functions and they can be the result produced by other functions. With this possibility in mind, we may define a well-know pattern named *fold*:[4]

$$\begin{aligned}&\mathit{fold} :: (b, (a, b) \rightarrow b) \rightarrow [a] \rightarrow b\\&\mathit{fold}\ (\mathit{nil}, \mathit{cons}) = f\\&\quad \textbf{where}\ f\ [\,] = \mathit{nil}\\&\qquad\qquad f\ (x : xs) = \mathit{cons}\ (x, f\ xs)\end{aligned}$$

With this pattern at hand, we may now give unified, modular, definitions for *sum* and *product*:[5]

$$\mathit{sum} = \mathit{fold}\ (0, \mathit{uncurry}\ (+))$$

$$\mathit{product} = \mathit{fold}\ (1, \mathit{uncurry}\ (*))$$

[3] This function is actually included in the Haskell *Prelude*.

[4] This definition of *fold* slightly differs from the definition of $\mathit{foldr} :: (a \rightarrow b \rightarrow b) \rightarrow b \rightarrow [a] \rightarrow b$ provided by Haskell, in that we rely on uncurried functions and we have changed the order of the expected arguments. We give this definition here as it will simplify our presentation later.
Also, for simplicity, we have omitted an argument on both sides of the equation $\mathit{fold}\ (\mathit{nil}, \mathit{cons}) = f$, that could have equally been given the definition $\mathit{fold}\ (\mathit{nil}, \mathit{cons})\ l = f\ l$.

[5] *uncurry* takes a function $f :: a \rightarrow b \rightarrow c$ and produces a function $f' :: (a, b) \rightarrow c$.

Exercise 1. Implement a function $sort :: [Float] \rightarrow [Float]$ that sorts all the elements in a list of floating point numbers. For this, you can rely on function $insert :: Float \rightarrow [Float] \rightarrow [Float]$ that inserts a number in a list whose elements are in ascending order so that the ordering is preserved.

$$
\begin{aligned}
&insert :: Float \rightarrow [Float] \rightarrow [Float] \\
&insert\ n\ [\,] = [n] \\
&insert\ n\ (h : t) = \mathbf{if}\ (n < h) \\
&\qquad\qquad\qquad\qquad \mathbf{then}\ n : h : t \\
&\qquad\qquad\qquad\qquad \mathbf{else}\ h : insert\ n\ t
\end{aligned}
$$

(a) Propose a(n explicitly) recursive solution for *sort*.

(b) Re-implement your previous solution in terms of a *fold*. □

Now, suppose that we want to increment all elements of a list of integers by a given number:

$$
\begin{aligned}
&increment :: ([Int], Int) \rightarrow [Int] \\
&increment\ ([\,], \_) = [\,] \\
&increment\ (h : t, z) = (h + z) : increment\ (t, z)
\end{aligned}
$$

Just by looking at the types involved, we may see that it is not possible to express *increment* in terms of a *fold*. Indeed, *fold* allows us to define functions of type $[a] \rightarrow b$, while *increment* is of type $([Int], Int) \rightarrow Int$, and it is not possible to match $[a]$ with $([Int], Int)$.

Still, the *fold* pattern can be generalized in many ways, one of them to deal with functions of type $([a], z) \rightarrow b$. For this we may define a new pattern, called *pfold*, that also traverses a list in a systematic fashion, but does so taking into account the additional parameter of type z:

$$
\begin{aligned}
&pfold :: (z \rightarrow b, ((a, b), z) \rightarrow b) \rightarrow ([a], z) \rightarrow b \\
&pfold\ (hnil, hcons) = p \\
&\quad \mathbf{where}\ p\ ([\,], z) \quad = hnil\ z \\
&\qquad\qquad\ p\ (a : as, z) = hcons\ ((a, p\ (as, z)), z)
\end{aligned}
$$

Now, we are in conditions to give *increment* a modular definition, as we have done for *sum* and *product*:

$$
\begin{aligned}
&increment = pfold\ (hnil, hcons) \\
&\quad \mathbf{where}\ hnil\ \_ = [\,] \\
&\qquad\qquad\ hcons\ ((h, r), z) = (h + z) : r
\end{aligned}
$$

Besides working with lists, in this tutorial we will often need to use binary trees, whose elements are in their leaves and are of type integer. For this purpose, we may define the following Haskell data-type:

$$\begin{aligned}&\textbf{data}\ \mathit{LeafTree} = \mathit{Leaf}\ \mathit{Int}\\ &\qquad\qquad\qquad\ \mid \mathit{Fork}\ (\mathit{LeafTree}, \mathit{LeafTree})\end{aligned}$$

Similarly to what we have defined for lists, we may now define *fold* and *pfold* for leaf trees, that we will name fold_T and pfold_T, respectively.

$$\begin{aligned}&\mathit{fold}_T :: (\mathit{Int} \to a, (a, a) \to a) \to \mathit{LeafTree} \to a\\ &\mathit{fold}_T\ (h_1, h_2) = f_T\\ &\quad \textbf{where}\ f_T\ (\mathit{Leaf}\ n) = h_1\ n\\ &\qquad\qquad\ f_T\ (\mathit{Fork}\ (l, r)) = h_2\ (f_T\ l, f_T\ r)\\ &\mathit{pfold}_T :: ((\mathit{Int}, z) \to a, ((a, a), z) \to a) \to (\mathit{LeafTree}, z) \to a\\ &\mathit{pfold}_T\ (h_1, h_2) = p_T\\ &\quad \textbf{where}\ p_T\ (\mathit{Leaf}\ n, z) = h_1\ (n, z)\\ &\qquad\qquad\ p_T\ (\mathit{Fork}\ (l, r), z) = h_2\ ((p_T\ (l, z), p_T\ (r, z)), z)\end{aligned}$$

And we can express the recursive function *tmin*, that computes the minimum value of a tree,[6]

$$\begin{aligned}&\mathit{tmin} :: \mathit{LeafTree} \to \mathit{Int}\\ &\mathit{tmin}\ (\mathit{Leaf}\ n) = n\\ &\mathit{tmin}\ (\mathit{Fork}\ (l, r)) = \mathit{min}\ (\mathit{tmin}\ l)\ (\mathit{tmin}\ r)\end{aligned}$$

in terms of a fold for leaf trees:

$$\mathit{tmin} = \mathit{fold}_T\ (\mathit{id}, \mathit{uncurry}\ \mathit{min})$$

Similarly, we can express the recursive function *replace*, that places a concrete value in all the leaves of a tree:

$$\begin{aligned}&\mathit{replace} :: (\mathit{LeafTree}, \mathit{Int}) \to \mathit{LeafTree}\\ &\mathit{replace}\ (\mathit{Leaf}\ n, m) = \mathit{Leaf}\ m\\ &\mathit{replace}\ (\mathit{Fork}\ (l, r), m) = \mathit{Fork}\ (\mathit{replace}\ (l, m), \mathit{replace}\ (r, m))\end{aligned}$$

in terms of a pfold for leaf trees:

$$\mathit{replace} = \mathit{pfold}_T\ (\mathit{Leaf} \circ \pi_2, \mathit{Fork} \circ \pi_1)$$

---

[6] Given two numbers, *min* will compute the minimum of both numbers.

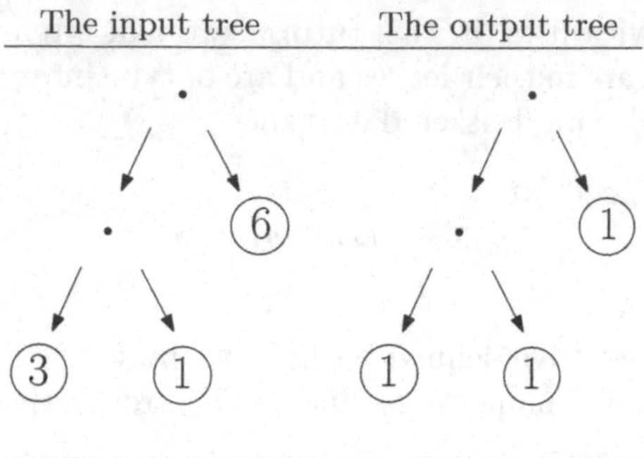

Fig. 1. An example of the use of *repmin*.

In the above implementation, we have used functions π_1 and π_2, whose (type-parametric) definition is as follows:

$$\pi_1 :: (a, b) \to a$$
$$\pi_1\ (a, b) = a$$

$$\pi_2 :: (a, b) \to b$$
$$\pi_2\ (a, b) = b$$

Now, suppose that we want to construct a function that replaces all the leaves in a leaf tree by the minimum leaf of that tree, a problem widely know as *repmin* (Bird 1984). An example of this transformation is given in Fig. 1.

We may combine the above implementations of *replace* and *tmin* in a simple way to obtain a solution to *repmin*:

$$repmin\ t = replace\ (t, tmin\ t)$$

Regarding this implementation, Bird (1984) notices that t is traversed twice, and that in a lazy functional language this is not strictly necessary. In fact, Bird shows how to remove this multiple traversals by deriving circular programs from programs such as *repmin*.

Circular programs hold circular definitions, in which arguments in a function call depend on results of that same call. That is, they contain definitions such as:

$$(..., x, ...) = f\ (..., x, ...)$$

From the above *repmin* definition, Bird derives the following circular program:[7]

[7] In order to make it easier for the reader to identify circular definitions, we frame the occurrences of variables that induce them (m in this case).

$$
\begin{aligned}
&\mathit{repmin}\ t = \mathit{nt} \\
&\quad \textbf{where}\ (\mathit{nt}, \boxed{\mathrm{m}}) = \mathit{repm}\ t \\
&\qquad\quad \mathit{repm}\ (\mathit{Leaf}\ n) = (\mathit{Leaf}\ \boxed{\mathrm{m}}, n) \\
&\qquad\quad \mathit{repm}\ (\mathit{Fork}\ (l, r)) = \textbf{let}\ (l', n_1) = \mathit{repm}\ l \\
&\qquad\qquad\qquad\qquad\qquad\qquad\quad (r', n_2) = \mathit{repm}\ r \\
&\qquad\qquad\qquad\qquad\qquad\quad \textbf{in}\ (\mathit{Fork}\ (l', r'), \mathit{min}\ n_1\ n_2)
\end{aligned}
$$

Although this circular definition seems to induce both a cycle and non-termination of this program, the fact is that using a *lazy* language, the *lazy* evaluation machinery is able to determine, at runtime, the right order to evaluate this circular definition. This reinforces the power of lazy evaluation strategy.

Deriving circular programs, however, is not the only way to eliminate multiple traversals of data structures. In particular, the straightforward *repmin* solution shown earlier may also be transformed, by the application of a well-known technique called lambda-abstraction (Pettorossi and Skowron 1987), into a higher-order program.
This reinforces the power of higher-order features, and as a result, we obtain[8]:

$$
\begin{aligned}
&\mathit{transform}\ t = \mathit{nt}\ m \\
&\quad \textbf{where}\ (\mathit{nt}, m) = \mathit{repm}\ t \\
&\qquad\quad \mathit{repm}\ (\mathit{Leaf}\ n) = (\lambda z \rightarrow \mathit{Leaf}\ z, n) \\
&\qquad\quad \mathit{repm}\ (\mathit{Fork}\ (l, r)) = \textbf{let}\ (l', n_1) = \mathit{repm}\ l \\
&\qquad\qquad\qquad\qquad\qquad\qquad\quad (r', n_2) = \mathit{repm}\ r \\
&\qquad\qquad\qquad\qquad\qquad\quad \textbf{in}\ (\lambda z \rightarrow \mathit{Fork}\ (l'\ z, r'\ z), \mathit{min}\ n_1\ n_2)
\end{aligned}
$$

Regarding this new version of *repmin*, we may notice that it is a higher-order program, since *nt*, the first component of the result produced by the call *repm t*, is now a function. Later, *nt* is applied to *m*, the second component of the result produced by that same call, therefore producing the desired tree result. Thus, this version does not perform multiple traversals.

3 Shortcut Fusion

Having introduced the concepts of Haskell that are necessary to understand the remainder of this paper, in this section we introduce shortcut fusion by example.

We start by introducing simple programming problems whose solutions can be expressed as programs that rely on intermediate structures. That is, we consider programs such as:

$$
\begin{aligned}
&\mathit{prog} :: a \rightarrow c \\
&\mathit{prog} = \mathit{cons} \circ \mathit{prod}
\end{aligned}
$$

[8] In the program, we use two anonymous functions that are defined using the symbol λ. Defining $\lambda m \rightarrow \mathit{Leaf}\ m$, for example, is equivalent to defining $g\ m = \mathit{Leaf}\ m$.

Then, we present specific shortcut fusion rules that are applicable to each such example.

In Sect. 3.1, we demonstrate with programs whose producer and consumer functions are of type $prod :: a \to b$ and $cons :: b \to c$, respectively.

In Sect. 3.2, we extend the applicability of such rules, considering programs whose producer and consumer functions are of type $prod :: a \to (b, z)$ and $cons :: (b, z) \to c$, respectively.

3.1 Standard Shortcut Fusion

In order to illustrate how deforestation can be achieved in practice, let us start by considering an alternative to the *factorial* implementation given in Sect. 2.

For a given, assumed positive, number n, this alternative creates a list with all the integers from n down to 1:

$$
\begin{aligned}
&down :: Int \to [Int] \\
&down\ 0 = [\,] \\
&down\ n = n : down\ (n-1)
\end{aligned}
$$

The elements of such a list then need to be multiplied, which can be achieved with function *product* that we have also already seen earlier:

$$
\begin{aligned}
&product :: [Int] \to Int \\
&product\ [\,] = 1 \\
&product\ (h : t) = h * product\ t
\end{aligned}
$$

Now, in order to implement *factorial* it suffices to combine these functions appropriately:

$$
\begin{aligned}
&factorial :: Int \to Int \\
&factorial\ n = product\ (down\ n)
\end{aligned}
$$

which is equivalent to:

$$factorial\ n = (product \circ down)\ n$$

or simply:

$$factorial = product \circ down$$

While this implementation is equivalent to the original one, it is creating an intermediate list of numbers which is clearly not necessary, and this affects its running performance. Of course, in this simple example, the original solution is at least as simple to implement as this alternative one, but in general, decomposing a problem in the sub-problems that constitute it contributes to increasing modularity and facilitates the programming and debugging tasks.

Regarding the above implementation of *factorial*, we see that if we ask for the value of *factorial* 0, an empty list is produced by *down*, which is replaced by the value 1, as defined in *product*. Similarly, we see that for *factorial* n, the list $n : down\ (n-1)$ is created which is later transformed into the expression $n * product\ (down\ (n-1))$. So, in this simple example, we can straightforwardly reason about the definition of a version of *factorial* that does not construct the intermediate list.

In order to derive this more efficient version of *factorial* in a systematic way we may proceed using shortcut fusion, and namely the *fold/build* rule (Gill et al. 1993; Takano and Meijer 1995; Gill 1996) that can be stated for the case when a list is the intermediate structure used to compose two functions:

Law 1 (FOLD/BUILD RULE FOR LISTS)

$$fold\ (h_1, h_2) \circ build\ g = g\ (h_1, h_2)$$

where

$build :: (\forall\ b\ .\ (b, (a, b) \rightarrow b) \rightarrow c \rightarrow b) \rightarrow c \rightarrow [a]$
$build\ g = g\ ([\,], uncurry\ (:))$

Function *build* allows us to abstract from the concrete list constructors that are used to build the intermediate structure. This abstraction is realized in function g. In this way, and given that $fold\ (h_1, h_2)$ replaces, in a list, all the occurrences of $[\,]$ by h_1 and all the occurrences of $(:)$ by h_2, deforestation proceeds by anticipating this replacement. This is precisely what is achieved in the definition $g\ (h_1, h_2)$.

In order to apply Law 1 to *factorial*, we first need to express *down* in terms of *build* and *product* in terms of *fold*:

$$
\begin{aligned}
& product = fold\ (1, uncurry\ (*)) \\
& down = build\ g \\
& \quad \textbf{where}\ g\ (nil, cons)\ 0 = nil \\
& \quad \phantom{\textbf{where}}\ g\ (nil, cons)\ n = cons\ (n, g\ (nil, cons)\ (n-1))
\end{aligned}
$$

We then follow a simple equational reasoning to obtain:

$$
\begin{aligned}
& factorial \\
= & \quad \{\ \text{definition of } factorial\ \} \\
& product \circ down \\
= & \quad \{\ \text{definition of } product \text{ and } down\ \} \\
& fold\ (1, uncurry\ (*)) \circ build\ g \\
= & \quad \{\ \text{Law 1}\ \} \\
& g\ (1, uncurry\ (*))
\end{aligned}
$$

Finally, by inlining the above definition, we obtain the original formulation of *factorial*:

$$\begin{aligned} \mathit{factorial}\ 0 &= g\ (1, \mathit{uncurry}\ (*))\ 0 \\ &= 1 \\ \mathit{factorial}\ n &= g\ (1, \mathit{uncurry}\ (*))\ n \\ &= \mathit{uncurry}\ (*)\ (n, \mathit{factorial}\ (n-1)) \\ &= n * \mathit{factorial}\ (n-1) \end{aligned}$$

In the following exercise, we encourage the reader to apply Law 1 to another concrete example.

Exercise 2. Imagine that you are given the list of grades (the scale is $[0\,..\,10]$) obtained by a set of students in an university course, such as:

$$l = [(6,8),(4,5),(9,7)]$$

Each pair holds the grades of a particular student; its first component holds the grade obtained by the student in the exam, and its second component the grade obtained in the project.

Implement a function $\mathit{average} :: [(\mathit{Float}, \mathit{Float})] \to [\mathit{Float}]$ that computes the average of the grades obtained by each student. As an example, $\mathit{average}\ l$ is expected to produce the list $[7.0, 4.5, 8.0]$.

(a) Propose a(n explicitly) recursive solution for *average*.
(b) Re-implement your previous solution in terms of a *build*.
(c) Obtain a function $\mathit{sort}_{avgs} :: [(\mathit{Float}, \mathit{Float})] \to [\mathit{Float}]$ simply by composing functions *sort* (from Exercise 1) and *average*.
(d) Notice that function sort_{avgs} relies on an intermediate structure of type $[\mathit{Float}]$, which can be eliminated. Apply Law 1 to obtain a deforested program, say dsort_{avgs} that is equivalent to sort_{avgs}. □

Law 1 deals specifically with programs such as *factorial*, that rely on an intermediate list to convey results between the producer and the consumer functions.

A similar reasoning can, however, be made for programs relying on arbitrary data types as intermediate structures. This is, for example, the case of programs that need to construct an intermediate *LeafTree*, and Law 2, as follows, deals precisely with such type of programs.

Law 2 (FOLD/BUILD RULE FOR LEAF TREES)

$$\mathit{fold}_T\ (h_1, h_2) \circ \mathit{build}_T\ g = g\ (h_1, h_2)$$

where

$$\begin{aligned} &\mathit{build}_T :: (\forall\ a\ .\ (\mathit{Int} \to a, (a, a) \to a) \to c \to a) \to c \to \mathit{LeafTree} \\ &\mathit{build}_T\ g = g\ (\mathit{Leaf}, \mathit{Fork}) \end{aligned}$$

As an example, we can use this law to fuse the following program, that computes the minimum value of a *mirrored* leaf tree.

$$tmm = tmin \circ mirror$$

$$\begin{aligned}
&mirror :: LeafTree \to LeafTree\\
&mirror\ (Leaf\ n) = Leaf\ n\\
&mirror\ (Fork\ (l, r)) = Fork\ (mirror\ r, mirror\ l)
\end{aligned}$$

Since we had already expressed *tmin* in terms of $fold_T$ in Sect. 2, as

$$tmin = fold_T\ (id, uncurry\ min)$$

we now need to express *mirror* in terms of $build_T$:

$$\begin{aligned}
&mirror = build_T\ g\\
&\quad \textbf{where}\ g\ (leaf, fork)\ (Leaf\ n) = leaf\ n\\
&\qquad\qquad g\ (leaf, fork)\ (Fork\ (l, r)) = fork\ (g\ (leaf, fork)\ r,\\
&\qquad\qquad\qquad\qquad\qquad\qquad\qquad\qquad g\ (leaf, fork)\ l)
\end{aligned}$$

Finally, by Law 2 we have that

$$tmm = g\ (id, uncurry\ min)$$

Inlining, we have

$$\begin{aligned}
&tmm\ (Leaf\ n) = n\\
&tmm\ (Fork\ (l, r)) = min\ (tmm\ r)\ (tmm\ l)
\end{aligned}$$

As expected, this function does not construct the intermediate mirror tree.

3.2 Extended Shortcut Fusion

In this section, we move on to study shortcut fusion for programs defined as the composition of two functions that, besides an intermediate structure, need to communicate using an additional parameter. That is, we focus on programs such as $prog = cons \circ prod$, where $prod :: a \to (b, z)$ and $cons :: (b, z) \to c$.

We start by deriving circular programs from such type of function compositions and then we derive higher-order programs from the same programs.

We illustrate with examples relying on intermediate structures of type *LeafTree* only. This is because a realistic example based on intermediate lists will be given in Sect. 5.

Deriving Circular Programs. We start by introducing a new law, whose generic version was originally provided by Fernandes et al. (2007), and which is similar to Law 2. This law, however, applies to the extended form of function compositions we are now considering.

Law 3 (PFOLD/BUILDP RULE FOR LEAF TREES)[9]

$$\begin{aligned} &\mathit{pfold}_T\ (h_1, h_2) \circ \mathit{buildp}_T\ g\ \$\ c = v \\ &\quad \textbf{where}\ (v, \boxed{z}) = g\ (k_1, k_2)\ c \\ &\qquad\quad k_1\ n = h_1\ (n, \boxed{z}) \\ &\qquad\quad k_2\ (l, r) = h_2\ ((l, r), \boxed{z}) \end{aligned}$$

where

$$\mathit{buildp}_T :: (\forall\ a\ .\ (\mathit{Int} \to a, (a, a) \to a) \to c \to (a, z)) \to c \to (\mathit{LeafTree}, z)$$
$$\mathit{buildp}_T\ g = g\ (\mathit{Leaf}, \mathit{Fork})$$

Notice that the consumer is now assumed to be given in terms of a buildp_T and that the consumer function is now expected to be given as a *pfold*. This is precisely to accommodate the additional parameter of type z.

To illustrate the application of this law in practice, recall the *repmin* problem that was introduced in Sect. 2 and its initial solution:

$$\mathit{repmin}\ t = \mathit{replace}\ (t, \mathit{tmin}\ t)$$

An alternative solution to such problem can be given by an explicit composition of two functions, where the first computes the minimum of a tree and the second replaces all leaf values by such minimum:[10]

$$\mathit{transform} :: \mathit{LeafTree} \to \mathit{LeafTree}$$
$$\mathit{transform} = \mathit{replace} \circ \mathit{tmint}$$

where

$$\mathit{tmint} :: \mathit{LeafTree} \to (\mathit{LeafTree}, \mathit{Int})$$
$$\mathit{tmint}\ (\mathit{Leaf}\ n) = (\mathit{Leaf}\ n, n)$$
$$\mathit{tmint}\ (\mathit{Fork}\ (l, r)) = (\mathit{Fork}\ (l', r'), \mathit{min}\ n_1\ n_2)$$

---

[9] We have used $(\$) :: (a \to b) \to a \to b$ in the expression $\mathit{pfold}_T\ (h_1, h_2) \circ \mathit{buildp}_T\ g\ \$\ c$ to avoid the use of parenthesis. The same expression could be defined as $(\mathit{pfold}_T\ (h_1, h_2) \circ \mathit{buildp}_T\ g)\ c$.

[10] Here, we needed to introduce an explicit function composition since one is needed in order to apply the rule. In practice, intermediate structures need to be more informative that the input ones, so the latter *must* be *bigger* than the former, and we are *forced* to define and manipulate intermediate structures. This means that solutions as function compositions are natural ones.

$$\begin{aligned} \textbf{where}\ (l',\ n_1) &= \mathit{tmint}\ l \\ (r',\ n_2) &= \mathit{tmint}\ r \end{aligned}$$

and *replace* remains unchanged:

$$\begin{aligned} &\mathit{replace} :: (\mathit{LeafTree}, \mathit{Int}) \to \mathit{LeafTree} \\ &\mathit{replace}\ (\mathit{Leaf}\ n, m) = \mathit{Leaf}\ m \\ &\mathit{replace}\ (\mathit{Fork}\ (l, r), m) = \mathit{Fork}\ (\mathit{replace}\ (l, m), \mathit{replace}\ (r, m)) \end{aligned}$$

To apply the rule, first we have to express *replace* and *tmint* in terms of pfold_T and buildp_T for leaf trees, respectively:

$$\mathit{replace} = \mathit{pfold}_T\ (\mathit{Leaf} \circ \pi_2, \mathit{Fork} \circ \pi_1)$$

$$\begin{aligned} &\mathit{tmint} = \mathit{buildp}_T\ g \\ &\quad \textbf{where}\ g\ (\mathit{leaf}, \mathit{fork})\ (\mathit{Leaf}\ n) = (\mathit{leaf}\ n, n) \\ &\qquad\quad g\ (\mathit{leaf}, \mathit{fork})\ (\mathit{Fork}\ (l, r)) = \textbf{let}\ (l', n_1) = g\ (\mathit{leaf}, \mathit{fork})\ l \\ &\qquad\qquad\qquad\qquad\qquad\qquad\qquad\quad (r', n_2) = g\ (\mathit{leaf}, \mathit{fork})\ r \\ &\qquad\qquad\qquad\qquad\qquad\qquad\quad \textbf{in}\ (\mathit{fork}\ (l', r'), \mathit{min}\ n_1\ n_2) \end{aligned}$$

Therefore, by applying Law 3 we get:

$$\begin{aligned} &\mathit{transform}\ t = \mathit{nt} \\ &\quad \textbf{where}\ (\mathit{nt}, \boxed{\mathrm{m}}) = g\ (k_1, k_2)\ t \\ &\qquad\quad k_1\ \_ = \mathit{Leaf}\ \boxed{\mathrm{m}} \\ &\qquad\quad k_2\ (l, r) = \mathit{Fork}\ (l, r) \end{aligned}$$

Inlining, we obtain the definition we showed previously in Sect. 2:

$$\begin{aligned} &\mathit{repmin}\ t = \mathit{nt} \\ &\quad \textbf{where}\ (\mathit{nt}, \boxed{\mathrm{m}}) = \mathit{repm}\ t \\ &\qquad\quad \mathit{repm}\ (\mathit{Leaf}\ n) = (\mathit{Leaf}\ \boxed{\mathrm{m}}, n) \\ &\qquad\quad \mathit{repm}\ (\mathit{Fork}\ (l, r)) = \textbf{let}\ (l', n_1) = \mathit{repm}\ l \\ &\qquad\qquad\qquad\qquad\qquad\qquad\quad (r', n_2) = \mathit{repm}\ r \\ &\qquad\qquad\qquad\qquad\qquad\quad \textbf{in}\ (\mathit{Fork}\ (l', r'), \mathit{min}\ n_1\ n_2) \end{aligned}$$

Next, we propose another concrete example where Law 3 is applicable.

Exercise 3. Our goal is to implement a function $\mathit{transform} = \mathit{add} \circ \mathit{convert}$, that takes a list of integers and produces a balanced leaf tree whose elements are the elements of the input list incremented by their sum. So, if the input list is $[1, 2, 3]$ we want to produce a balanced leaf tree whose elements are 7, 8 and 9.

(a) Implement a function $convert :: [Int] \rightarrow (LeafTree, Int)$ that produces a height-balanced leaf tree containing all the elements of a list. Function *convert* must also produce the sum of all elements of the list.
(b) Implement a function $add :: (LeafTree, Int) \rightarrow LeafTree$ that adds to all the elements of a leaf tree a given number.
(c) Write *convert* in terms of $buildp_T$ and *add* in terms of $pfold_T$.
(d) Apply Law 3 to derive a circular program that does not construct the intermediate leaf tree. □

Deriving Higher-Order Programs. Next, we introduce a new law, Law 4, that applies to the same type of programs as Law 3, but that instead of deriving circular programs derives higher-order ones. The specific case of this law that deals with programs relying on intermediate lists instead of leaf trees was originally given by Voigtländer (2008) and its generic formulation was later given by Pardo et al. (2009).

Law 4 (HIGHER-ORDER PFOLD/BUILDP RULE FOR LEAF TREES)

$$\begin{aligned} &pfold_T\ (h_1, h_2) \circ buildp_T\ g\ \$\ c = f\ z \\ &\quad \textbf{where}\ (f, z) = g\ (\varphi_{h_1}, \varphi_{h_2})\ c \\ &\qquad\qquad \varphi_{h_1}\ n = \lambda z \rightarrow h_1\ (n, z) \\ &\qquad\qquad \varphi_{h_2}\ (l, r) = \lambda z \rightarrow h_2\ ((l\ z, r\ z), z) \end{aligned}$$

where

$$\begin{aligned} &buildp_T :: (\forall\ a\ .\ (Int \rightarrow a, (a, a) \rightarrow a) \rightarrow c \rightarrow (a, z)) \rightarrow c \rightarrow (LeafTree, z) \\ &buildp_T\ g = g\ (Leaf, Fork) \end{aligned}$$

To see an example of the application of Law 4, we consider again the straightforward solution to the *repmin* problem:

$$transform = replace \circ tmint$$

$$replace = pfold_T\ (Leaf \circ \pi_2, Fork \circ \pi_1)$$

$$\begin{aligned} &tmint = buildp_T\ g \\ &\quad \textbf{where}\ g\ (leaf, fork)\ (Leaf\ n) = (leaf\ n, n) \\ &\qquad\quad g\ (leaf, fork)\ (Fork\ (l, r)) = \textbf{let}\ (l', n_1) = g\ (leaf, fork)\ l \\ &\qquad\qquad\qquad\qquad\qquad\qquad\qquad\quad (r', n_2) = g\ (leaf, fork)\ r \\ &\qquad\qquad\qquad\qquad\qquad\qquad\quad \textbf{in}\ (fork\ (l', r'), min\ n_1\ n_2) \end{aligned}$$

In order to apply Law 4 to *transform*, we need the expressions of φ_{h_1} and φ_{h_2}. For φ_{h_1}, we have that:

$$
\begin{aligned}
& \varphi_{h_1}\ n \\
= & \quad \{ \text{ definition of } \varphi_{h_1} \text{ in Law 4 } \} \\
& \lambda z \to h_1\ (n, z) \\
= & \quad \{ \text{ definition of } h_1 \ \} \\
& \lambda z \to (\mathit{Leaf} \circ \pi_2)\ (n, z) \\
= & \quad \{ \text{ definition of function composition, definition of } \pi_2 \ \} \\
& \lambda z \to \mathit{Leaf}\ z
\end{aligned}
$$

and similarly for φ_{h_2}, we obtain that $\varphi_{h_2}\ (l, r) = \lambda z \to \mathit{Fork}\ (l\ z, r\ z)$.

Then, by direct application of Law 4 to *transform*, we obtain:

$$
\begin{aligned}
& \mathit{transform}\ t = nt\ m \\
& \quad \textbf{where}\ (nt, m) = g\ (\varphi_{h_1}, \varphi_{h_2})
\end{aligned}
$$

Inlining the above definition, we obtain the higher-order solution to *repmin* that we had already presented in Sect. 2:

$$
\begin{aligned}
& \mathit{transform}\ t = nt\ m \\
& \quad \textbf{where}\ (nt, m) = \mathit{repm}\ t \\
& \qquad \mathit{repm}\ (\mathit{Leaf}\ n) = (\lambda z \to \mathit{Leaf}\ z, n) \\
& \qquad \mathit{repm}\ (\mathit{Fork}\ (l, r)) = \textbf{let}\ (l', n_1) = \mathit{repm}\ l \\
& \qquad \qquad \qquad \qquad \qquad \quad\ \ (r', n_2) = \mathit{repm}\ r \\
& \qquad \qquad \qquad \qquad \qquad \textbf{in}\ (\lambda z \to \mathit{Fork}\ (l'\ z, r'\ z), \mathit{min}\ n_1\ n_2)
\end{aligned}
$$

Exercise 4. Recall the solution to $\mathit{transform} = \mathit{add} \circ \mathit{convert}$ of Exercise 3.

(a) Apply Law 4 to derive a higher-order program that does not construct the intermediate leaf tree. □

4 Generalized Shortcut Fusion

In the previous section, we have used concrete examples to demonstrate the applicability and interest of different types of shortcut fusion rules. In this section, we show that the concrete rules we have introduced before can actually be given uniform, generic formulations, that are applied to a wide range of programs characterized in terms of certain program schemes. The generic formulations of the rules described here are parametric in the structure of the intermediate data-type involved in the function composition to be transformed.

Throughout the section we shall assume we are working in the context of a lazy functional language with a *cpo* (Complete Partial Order) semantics, in which types are interpreted as pointed cpos (complete partial orders with a least element $\bot$) and functions are interpreted as continuous functions between pointed cpos.

While this semantics closely resembles the semantics of Haskell, for now we do not consider lifted cpos. That is, unlike the semantics of Haskell, we do not consider lifted products and function spaces. The precise implications of these semantics differences are studied in Sect. 4.5.

As usual, a function f is said to be *strict* if it preserves the least element, i.e. $f \perp = \perp$.

4.1 Data-Types

The structure of data-types can be captured using the concept of a *functor*. A functor consists of two components: a type constructor F, and a function $map_F :: (a \to b) \to (F\ a \to F\ b)$, which preserves identities and compositions:

$$map_F\ id = id \tag{1}$$

$$map_F\ (f \circ g) = map_F\ f \circ map_F\ g \tag{2}$$

A standard example of a functor is that formed by the list type constructor and the well-known *map* function, which applies a function to the elements of a list, building a new list with the results.

$$
\begin{aligned}
&map && :: (a \to b) \to [a] \to [b] \\
&map\ f\ [\,] && = [\,] \\
&map\ f\ (a : as) && = f\ a : map\ f\ as
\end{aligned}
$$

Another example of a functor is the product functor, which is a case of a bifunctor, a functor on two arguments. On types its action is given by the type constructor for pairs. On functions its action is defined by:

$$
\begin{aligned}
&(\times) :: (a \to c) \to (b \to d) \to (a, b) \to (c, d) \\
&(f\ \times\ g)\ (a, b) = (f\ a, g\ b)
\end{aligned}
$$

Semantically, we assume that pairs are interpreted as the cartesian product of the corresponding cpos. Associated with the product we can define the following functions, corresponding to the projections and the split function:

$$
\begin{aligned}
&\pi_1 :: (a, b) \to a \\
&\pi_1\ (a, b) = a
\end{aligned}
$$

$$
\begin{aligned}
&\pi_2 :: (a, b) \to b \\
&\pi_2\ (a, b) = b
\end{aligned}
$$

$$
\begin{aligned}
&(\vartriangle) :: (c \to a) \to (c \to b) \to c \to (a, b) \\
&(f \vartriangle g)\ c = (f\ c, g\ c)
\end{aligned}
$$

Among other properties, it holds that

$$f \circ \pi_1 = \pi_1 \circ (f \times g) \tag{3}$$
$$g \circ \pi_2 = \pi_2 \circ (f \times g) \tag{4}$$
$$f = ((\pi_1 \circ f) \vartriangle (\pi_2 \circ f)) \tag{5}$$

Another case of a bifunctor is the sum functor, which corresponds to the disjoint union of types. Semantically, we assume that sums are interpreted as the separated sum of the corresponding cpos.

$\textbf{data}\ a + b = \mathit{Left}\ a \mid \mathit{Right}\ b$

$(+) :: (a \to c) \to (b \to d) \to (a + b) \to (c + d)$
$(f + g)\ (\mathit{Left}\ a) = \mathit{Left}\ (f\ a)$
$(f + g)\ (\mathit{Right}\ b) = \mathit{Right}\ (g\ b)$

Associated with the sum we can define the case analysis function, which has the property of being strict in its argument of type $a + b$:

$(\triangledown) :: (a \to c) \to (b \to c) \to (a + b) \to c$
$(f \triangledown g)\ (\mathit{Left}\ a) = f\ a$
$(f \triangledown g)\ (\mathit{Right}\ b) = g\ b$

Product and sum can be generalized to n components in the obvious way.

We consider declarations of data-types of the form[11]:

$$\textbf{data}\ \tau\ (\alpha_1, \cdots, \alpha_m) = C_1\ (\tau_{1,1}, \cdots, \tau_{1,k_1})\ \mid \cdots \mid\ C_n\ (\tau_{n,1}, \cdots, \tau_{n,k_n})$$

where each $\tau_{i,j}$ is restricted to be a constant type (like *Int* or *Char*), a type variable α_t, a type constructor D applied to a type $\tau'_{i,j}$ or $\tau\ (\alpha_1, \cdots, \alpha_m)$ itself. Data-types of this form are usually called regular. The derivation of a functor that captures the structure of the data-type essentially proceeds as follows: alternatives are regarded as sums ($\mid$ is replaced by $+$) and constructors C_i are omitted. Every $\tau_{i,j}$ that consists of a type variable α_t or of a constant type remain unchanged and occurrences of $\tau\ (\alpha_1, \cdots, \alpha_m)$ are substituted by a type variable a in every $\tau_{i,j}$. In addition, the unit type () is placed in the positions corresponding to constant constructors (like e.g. the empty list constructor). As a result, we obtain the following type constructor F:

$$F\,a = (\sigma_{1,1}, \cdots, \sigma_{1,k_1}) + \cdots + (\sigma_{n,1}, \cdots, \sigma_{n,k_n})$$

where $\sigma_{i,j} = \tau_{i,j}[\tau\ (\alpha_1, \cdots, \alpha_m) := a]$ [12]. The body of the corresponding mapping function $map_F :: (a \to b) \to (F\ a \to F\ b)$ is similar to that of $F\ a$, with the

[11] For simplicity we shall assume that constructors in a data-type declaration are declared uncurried.

[12] By $s[t := a]$ we denote the replacement of every occurrence of t by a in s.

difference that the occurrences of the type variable a are replaced by a function $f :: a \to b$:

$$map_F f = g_{1,1} \times \cdots \times g_{1,k_1} + \cdots + g_{n,1} \times \cdots \times g_{n,k_n}$$

with

$$g_{i,j} = \begin{cases} f & \text{if } \sigma_{i,j} = a \\ id & \text{if } \sigma_{i,j} = t, \text{ for some type } t \\ & \text{or } \sigma_{i,j} = a', \text{ for some type variable } a' \text{ other than } a \\ map_D\ g'_{i,j} & \text{if } \sigma_{i,j} = D\ \sigma'_{i,j} \end{cases}$$

where map_D represents the map function $map_D :: (a \to b) \to (D\ a \to D\ b)$ corresponding to the type constructor D.

For example, for the type of leaf trees

$$\begin{aligned} &\textbf{data}\ \mathit{LeafTree} = \mathit{Leaf}\ \mathit{Int} \\ &\qquad\qquad\qquad\ \mid \mathit{Fork}\ (\mathit{LeafTree}, \mathit{LeafTree}) \end{aligned}$$

we can derive a functor T given by

$$T\ a = \mathit{Int} + (a, a)$$

$$\begin{aligned} &map_T \ :: (a \to b) \to (T\ a \to T\ b) \\ &map_T\ f = id + f \times f \end{aligned}$$

The functor that captures the structure of the list data-type needs to reflect the presence of the type parameter:

$$L_a\ b = () + (a, b)$$

$$\begin{aligned} &map_{L_a} \ :: (b \to c) \to (L_a\ b \to L_a\ c) \\ &map_{L_a}\ f = id + id \times f \end{aligned}$$

This functor reflects the fact that lists have two constructors: one is a constant and the other is a binary operation.

Every recursive data-type is then understood as the least fixed point of the functor F that captures its structure, i.e. as the least solution to the equation $\tau \cong F\ \tau$. We will denote the type corresponding to the least solution as μF. The isomorphism between μF and $F\ \mu F$ is provided by the strict functions $in_F :: F\ \mu F \to \mu F$ and $out_F :: \mu F \to F\ \mu F$, each other inverse. Function in_F packs the constructors of the data-type while function out_F packs its destructors. Further details can be found in (Abramsky and Jung 1994; Gibbons 2002).

For instance, in the case of leaf trees we have that $\mu T = \mathit{LeafTree}$ and

$$in_T :: T\ \mathit{LeafTree} \to \mathit{LeafTree}$$

$$in_T = Leaf \triangledown Fork$$

$$\begin{aligned}
&out_T :: LeafTree \rightarrow T\ LeafTree \\
&out_T\ (Leaf\ n) = Left\ n \\
&out_T\ (Fork\ (l, r)) = Right\ (l, r)
\end{aligned}$$

4.2 Fold

Fold (Bird and de Moor 1997; Gibbons 2002) is a pattern of recursion that captures function definitions by structural recursion. The best known example of fold is its definition for lists, which corresponds to the *foldr* operator (Bird 1998).

Given a functor F and a function $h :: F\ a \rightarrow a$, *fold* (also called *catamorphism*), denoted by $fold\ h :: \mu F \rightarrow a$, is defined as the least function f that satisfies the following equation:

$$f \circ in_F = h \circ map_F\ f$$

Because out_F is the inverse of in_F, this is the same as:

$$\begin{aligned}
&fold \quad :: (F\ a \rightarrow a) \rightarrow \mu F \rightarrow a \\
&fold\ h = h \circ map_F\ (fold\ h) \circ out_F
\end{aligned}$$

A function $h :: F\ a \rightarrow a$ is called an *F-algebra*[13]. The functor F plays the role of the signature of the algebra, as it encodes the information about the operations of the algebra. The type a is called the carrier of the algebra. An *F-homomorphism* between two algebras $h :: F\ a \rightarrow a$ and $k :: F\ b \rightarrow b$ is a function $f :: a \rightarrow b$ between the carriers that commutes with the operations. This is specified by the condition $f \circ h = k \circ map_F\ f$. Notice that $fold\ h$ is a homomorphism between the algebras in_F and h.

The concrete instance of *fold* for the case when $F = T$ and $\mu F = LeafTree$ is given by the definition we had already presented in Sect. 2:

$$\begin{aligned}
&fold_T :: (Int \rightarrow a, (a, a) \rightarrow a) \rightarrow LeafTree \rightarrow a \\
&fold_T\ (h_1, h_2) = f_T \\
&\quad \textbf{where}\ f_T\ (Leaf\ n) = h_1\ n \\
&\qquad\qquad f_T\ (Fork\ (l, r)) = h_2\ (f_T\ l, f_T\ r)
\end{aligned}$$

In the same way, the concrete instance of *fold* for the case when $F = L_a$ and $\mu F = [a]$ is the definition we had also given in Sect. 2:

[13] When showing specific instances of fold for concrete data-types, we will write the operations in an algebra $h_1 \triangledown \cdots \triangledown h_n$ in a tuple $(h_1, \ldots, h_n)$.

$$
\begin{aligned}
&\textit{fold} :: (b, (a, b) \to b) \to [a] \to b \\
&\textit{fold}\ (\textit{nil}, \textit{cons}) = f \\
&\quad \textbf{where}\ f\ [\,] = \textit{nil} \\
&\qquad\qquad f\ (x : xs) = \textit{cons}\ (x, f\ xs)
\end{aligned}
$$

Notice that, for simplicity, we are overloading *fold* both as the name of the generic recursion pattern and its instance for lists. This will also be the case for other constructions given in this paper, but it should be clear from every context whether we are referring to the generic or the specific case.

4.3 The Fold/Build Rule

Fold enjoys many algebraic laws that are useful for program transformation (Augusteijn 1998). A well-known example is *shortcut fusion* (Gill et al. 1993; Gill 1996; Takano and Meijer 1995) (also known as the *fold/build* rule), which is an instance of a free theorem (Wadler 1989).

Law 5 (FOLD/BUILD RULE) *For h strict,*

$$
\begin{array}{c}
g :: \forall\ a\ .\ (F\ a \to a) \to c \to a \\
\Rightarrow \\
\textit{fold}\ h \circ \textit{build}\ g = g\ h
\end{array}
$$

where

$$
\begin{aligned}
&\textit{build} :: (\forall\ a\ .\ (F\ a \to a) \to c \to a) \to c \to \mu F \\
&\textit{build}\ g = g\ \textit{in}_F
\end{aligned}
$$

Laws 1 and 2, that we have presented in Sect. 3.1 are particular instances of Law 5. In that section, when we presented their formulation, notice that the assumption about the strictness of the algebra disappears. This is because every algebra $h_1 \triangledown h_2$ is strict as so is every case analysis.

In the same line of reasoning, we can state another fusion law for a slightly different producer function:

Law 6 (FOLD/BUILDP RULE) *For h strict,*

$$
\begin{array}{c}
g :: \forall\ a\ .\ (F\ a \to a) \to c \to (a, z) \\
\Rightarrow \\
(\textit{fold}\ h\ \times\ \textit{id}) \circ \textit{buildp}\ g = g\ h
\end{array}
$$

where

$$
\begin{aligned}
&\textit{buildp} :: (\forall\ a\ .\ (F\ a \to a) \to c \to (a, z)) \to c \to (\mu F, z) \\
&\textit{buildp}\ g = g\ \textit{in}_F
\end{aligned}
$$

For example, the instance of this law for leaf trees is the following:

$$(fold_T\ (h_1, h_2)\ \times\ id) \circ buildp_T\ g = g\ (h_1, h_2) \qquad (6)$$

where

$$\begin{aligned}
& buildp_T :: (\forall\ a\ .\ (Int \to a, (a, a) \to a) \to c \to (a, z)) \\
& \qquad\qquad \to c \to (LeafTree, z) \\
& buildp_T\ g = g\ (Leaf, Fork)
\end{aligned}$$

The assumption about the strictness of the algebra disappears by the same reason as for (2).

To see an example of the application of this law, consider the program *ssqm*: it replaces every leaf in a tree by its square while computing the minimum value of the tree; later, it sums all the (squared) elements of an input tree.

$$\begin{aligned}
& ssqm :: LeafTree \to (Int, Int) \\
& ssqm = (sumt\ \times\ id) \circ gentsqmin
\end{aligned}$$

$$\begin{aligned}
& sumt :: LeafTree \to Int \\
& sumt\ (Leaf\ n) = n \\
& sumt\ (Fork\ (l, r)) = sumt\ l + sumt\ r
\end{aligned}$$

$$\begin{aligned}
& gentsqmin :: LeafTree \to (LeafTree, Int) \\
& gentsqmin\ (Leaf\ n) = (Leaf\ (n * n), n) \\
& gentsqmin\ (Fork\ (l, r)) = \textbf{let}\ (l', n_1) = gentsqmin\ l \\
& \qquad\qquad\qquad\qquad\qquad\quad\ (r', n_2) = gentsqmin\ r \\
& \qquad\qquad\qquad\qquad\qquad \textbf{in}\ (Fork\ (l', r'), min\ n_1\ n_2)
\end{aligned}$$

To apply Law (6) we have to express *sumt* as a fold and *gentsqmin* in terms of $buildp_T$:

$$\begin{aligned}
& sumt \qquad\ = fold_T\ (id, uncurry\ (+)) \\
& gentsqmin = buildp_T\ g \\
& \quad \textbf{where}\ g\ (leaf, fork)\ (Leaf\ n) = (leaf\ (n * n), n) \\
& \qquad\qquad g\ (leaf, fork)\ (Fork\ (l, r)) = \textbf{let}\ (l', n_1) = g\ (leaf, fork)\ l \\
& \qquad\qquad\qquad\qquad\qquad\qquad\qquad\qquad (r', n_2) = g\ (leaf, fork)\ r \\
& \qquad\qquad\qquad\qquad\qquad\qquad\qquad \textbf{in}\ (fork\ (l', r'), min\ n_1\ n_2)
\end{aligned}$$

Hence, by (6), we have

$$ssqm = g\ (id, uncurry\ (+))$$

Inlining, we obtain

$$\begin{aligned}
&ssqm\ (Leaf\ n) = (n * n, n)\\
&ssqm\ (Fork\ (l, r)) = \mathbf{let}\ (s_1, n_1) = ssqm\ l\\
&\qquad\qquad\qquad\qquad\quad (s_2, n_2) = ssqm\ r\\
&\qquad\qquad\qquad\quad \mathbf{in}\ (s_1 + s_2, min\ n_1\ n_2)
\end{aligned}$$

Finally, the following property is an immediate consequence of Law 6.

Law 7 *For any strict h,*

$$g :: \forall\, a\,.\,(F\ a \to a) \to c \to (a, z)$$

$$\Rightarrow$$

$$\pi_2 \circ g\ in_F = \pi_2 \circ g\ h$$

This property states that the construction of the second component of the pair returned by g is independent of the particular algebra that g carries; it only depends on the input value of type c. This is a consequence of the polymorphic type of g and the fact that the second component of its result is of a fixed type z.

4.4 Fold with Parameters

Some recursive functions use context information in the form of constant parameters for their computation. The aim of this section is to analyze the definition of structurally recursive functions of the form $f :: (\mu F, z) \to a$, where the type z represents the context information. Our interest in these functions is because our method will assume that consumers are functions of this kind.

Functions of this form can be defined in different ways. One alternative consists of fixing the value of the parameter and performing recursion on the other. Definitions of this kind can be given in terms of a fold:

$$\begin{aligned}
&f :: (\mu F, z) \to a\\
&f\ (t, z) = fold\ h\ t
\end{aligned}$$

such that the context information contained in z may eventually be used in the algebra h. This is the case of, for example, the function *replace*:

$$\begin{aligned}
&replace :: (LeafTree, Int) \to LeafTree\\
&replace\ (Leaf\ n, m) = Leaf\ m\\
&replace\ (Fork\ (l, r), m) = Fork\ (replace\ (l, m), replace\ (r, m))
\end{aligned}$$

which can be defined as:

$$replace\ (t, m) = fold_T\ (\lambda n \to Leaf\ m, Fork)\ t$$

Another alternative is the use of currying, which gives a function of type $\mu F \to (z \to a)$. The curried version can then be defined as a higher-order fold. For instance, in the case of *replace* it holds that

$$curry\ replace = fold_T\ (\lambda n \to Leaf, \lambda(f, f') \to Fork \circ (f \vartriangle f'))$$

This is an alternative we will study in detail in Sect. 4.6.

A third alternative is to define the function $f :: (\mu F, z) \to a$ in terms of a program scheme, called *pfold* (Pardo 2001, 2002), which, unlike fold, is able to manipulate constant and recursive arguments simultaneously. The definition of pfold relies on the concept of *strength* of a functor F, which is a polymorphic function:

$$\tau^F :: (F\ a, z) \to F\ (a, z)$$

that satisfies the coherence axioms:

$$map_F\ \pi_1 \circ \tau^F = \pi_1$$
$$map_F\ \alpha \circ \tau^F = \tau^F \circ (\tau^F \times id) \circ \alpha$$

where $\alpha :: (a, (b, c)) \to ((a, b), c)$ is the product associativity (see (Pardo 2002; Cockett and Spencer 1991; Cockett and Fukushima 1992) for further details). The strength distributes the value of type z to the variable positions (positions of type a) of the functor. For instance, the strength corresponding to functor T is given by:

$$\tau^T :: (T\ a, z) \to T\ (a, z)$$
$$\tau^T\ (Left\ n, z) = Left\ n$$
$$\tau^T\ (Right\ (a, a'), z) = Right\ ((a, z), (a', z))$$

In the definition of pfold the strength of the underlying functor plays an important role as it represents the distribution of the context information contained in the constant parameters to the recursive calls.

Given a functor F and a function $h :: (F\ \ a, z) \to a$, *pfold*, denoted by *pfold* $h :: (\mu F, z) \to a$, is defined as the least function f that satisfies the following equation:

$$f \circ (in_F \times id) = h \circ (((map_F\ f \circ \tau^F) \vartriangle \pi_2))$$

Observe that now function h also accepts the value of the parameter. It is a function of the form $(h_1 \triangledown \ \ldots\ \triangledown h_n) \circ d$ where each $h_i :: (F_i\ \ a, z) \to a$ if $F\ a = F_1\ a + \cdots + F_n\ a$, and $d :: (x_1 + \cdots + x_n, z) \to (x_1, z) + \cdots + (x_n, z)$ is the distribution of product over sum. When showing specific instances of pfold we will simply write the tuple of functions $(h_1, \ldots, h_n)$ instead of h.

The following equation shows one of the possible relationships between pfold and fold.

$$pfold\ h\ (t, z) = fold\ k\ t\ \textbf{where}\ k_i\ x = h_i\ (x, z) \tag{7}$$

Like fold, pfold satisfies a set of algebraic laws. We do not show any of them here as they are not necessary for the calculational work presented in this thesis. The interested reader may consult (Pardo 2001, 2002).

4.5 The Pfold/Buildp Rule

In this section, we present a generic formulation of a transformation rule that takes compositions of the form $cons \circ prod$, where a producer $prod :: a \to (t, z)$ is followed by a consumer $cons :: (t, z) \to b$, and returns an equivalent deforested circular program that performs a single traversal over the input value.

The rule, which was first introduced in Fernandes et al. (2007) and further studied in Fernandes (2009) and Pardo et al. (2011), makes some natural assumptions about *cons* and *prod*: t is a recursive data-type μF, the consumer *cons* is defined by structural recursion on t, and the intermediate value of type z is taken as a constant parameter by *cons*. In addition, it is required that *prod* is a "good producer", in the sense that it is possible to express it as the instance of a polymorphic function by abstracting out the constructors of the type t from the body of *prod*. In other words, *prod* should be expressed in terms of the *buildp* function corresponding to the type t. The fact that the consumer *cons* is assumed to be structurally recursive leads us to consider that it is given by a pfold. In summary, the rule is applied to compositions of the form: $pfold\ h \circ buildp\ g$.

Law 8 (PFOLD/BUILDP RULE)
For any $h = (h_1 \triangledown \ \dots \ \triangledown h_n) \circ d$,[14]

$$
\begin{array}{l}
g :: \forall\ a\ .\ (F\ a \to a) \to c \to (a, z) \\
\Rightarrow \\
pfold\ h \circ buildp\ g\ \$\ c \\
= v \\
\textbf{where}\ (v, \boxed{z}) = g\ k\ c \\
\qquad\qquad k = k_1 \triangledown \ \dots \ \triangledown k_n \\
\qquad\qquad k_i\ \bar{x} = h_i\ (\bar{x}, \boxed{z})
\end{array}
$$

Semantics of the Pfold/Buildp Rule. According to Danielsson et al. (2006), Law 8 is morally correct *only*, in Haskell. In fact, the formal proof of our rule, that the interested reader may consult in (Fernandes 2009; Pardo et al. 2011), relies on surjective pairing (Law (5)). However, (5) is not valid in Haskell: though it holds for defined values, it fails when the result of function g is undefined, because $\bot$ is different from $(\bot, \bot)$ as a consequence of lifted products. Therefore, (5) is morally correct *only* and, in the same sense, so is our rule.

[14] We denote by $\bar{x}$ a tuple of values $(x_1, \cdots, x_{r_i})$.

Following our work, Voigtländer (2008) performed a rigorous study on various shortcut fusion rules, for languages like Haskell. In particular, the author presents semantic and pragmatic considerations on Law 8. As a first result, pre-conditions are added to our rule, so that its total correctness can be established.

The definition of Law 8 becomes:

Law 9 (HASKELL VALID PFOLD/BUILDP RULE)
For any $h = (h_1 \triangledown \ldots \triangledown h_n) \circ d,\ \forall\, i \in \{1,..,n\}\ .\ h_i\ ((\bot,...,\bot),\bot) \neq \bot$

$$g :: \forall\, a\ .\ (F\ a \rightarrow a) \rightarrow c \rightarrow (a, z)$$
$$\Rightarrow$$
$$\begin{aligned}&pfold\ h \circ buildp\ g\ \$\ c\\ &= v\\ &\textbf{where}\ (v, \boxed{z}) = g\ k\ c\\ &\qquad k = k_1 \triangledown \ldots \triangledown k_n\\ &\qquad k_i\ \bar{x} = h_i\ (\bar{x}, \boxed{z})\end{aligned}$$

It is now possible to prove total correctness of Law 9 Voigtländer (2008). However, although Law 9 is the one that guarantees totally correct transformations, in the semantics of Haskell, it is somewhat *pessimistic*.

By this we mean that even if the newly added pre-condition is violated, it does not necessarily imply that the Law gets broken. In fact, Voigtländer (2008) presents an example where such pre-condition is violated, causing no harm in the calculated equivalent program. We review here such an example.

Consider the following programming problem: from the initial part of an input list before a certain predicate holds for the first time, return those elements that are repeated afterwards. The specification of a natural solution to this problem is as follows:

```
repeatedAfter :: Eq b ⇒ (b → Bool) → [b] → [b]
repeatedAfter p bs = (pfilter elem) ∘ (splitWhen p) $ bs

pfilter :: (b → z → Bool) → ([b], z) → [b]
pfilter _ ([], _) = []
pfilter p (b : bs, z) = let bs' = pfilter p (bs, z)
                        in if p b z
                           then b : bs'
                           else bs'

splitWhen :: (b → Bool) → [b] → ([b], [b])
splitWhen p bs
  = case bs of [] → ([], bs)
               b : bs' → if p b
                         then ([], bs)
                         else let (xs, ys) = splitWhen p bs'
                              in (b : xs, ys)
```

This definition uses a list as the intermediate structure that serves the purpose of gluing the two composed functions. This intermediate list can be eliminated using Law 8. However, in order to apply that law to the *repeatedAfter* program, *pfilter* and *splitWhen p* must first be given in terms of pfold and buildp for lists (the type of the intermediate structure), respectively. The definition of pfold and buildp for lists is as follows.

```
buildp :: (∀ b . (b, (a, b) → b) → c → (b, z)) → c → ([a], z)
buildp g = g ([], uncurry (:))

pfold :: (z → b, ((a, b), z) → b) → ([a], z) → b
pfold (hnil, hcons) = p_L
  where p_L ([], z)     = hnil z
        p_L (a : as, z) = hcons ((a, p_L (as, z)), z)
```

Now, we write *pfilter* and *splitWhen p* in terms of them:

```
splitWhen p = buildp go
  where go (nil, cons) bs
          = case bs of []  → (nil, bs)
                       b : bs' → if p b
                                 then (nil, bs)
                                 else let (xs, ys)
                                            = go (nil, cons) bs'
                                      in (cons (b, xs), ys)

pfilter p = pfold (hnil, hcons)
  where hnil _ = []
        hcons ((b, bs), z) = if (p b z) then (b : bs) else bs
```

Regarding this example, we may notice that $hcons\ ((\bot, \bot), \bot) = \bot$, given that (**if** *elem* $\bot$ $\bot$ **then** $\bot : \bot$ **else** $\bot$) equals $\bot$. This means that the precondition $\forall\ i\ .\ h_i\ ((\bot, ..., \bot), \bot) \neq \bot$, newly added to Law 8, fails. However, it is still possible to use Law 8 to calculate a correct circular program equivalent to the *repeatedAfter* program presented earlier:

```
repeatedAfter p bs = a
  where (a, [z]) = go' bs
        go' bs = case bs of [] → ([], bs)
                            b : bs' → if p b
                                      then ([], bs)
                                      else let (xs, ys) = go' bs'
                                           in (if elem b [z]
                                               then b : xs
                                               else xs, ys)
```

It is in this sense that we say Law 9 is *pessimistic*. However, this Law is the most general one can present, so far, in terms of total correctness.

In the next section, we will present an alternative way to transform compositions between pfold and buildp such that, instead of circular programs, higher-order programs are obtained as result. A good thing about the new transformation is that its total correctness can be established defining fewer pre-conditions than the ones defined in Law 9.

4.6 The Higher-Order Pfold/Buildp Rule

In the previous section, we have presented the generic formulation of a calculation rule for deriving circular programs. There exists, however, an alternative way to transform compositions between *pfold* and *buildp*. Indeed, in this section we derive higher-order programs from such compositions, instead of the circular programs we derived before.

The alternative transformation presented in this section is based on the fact that every *pfold* can be expressed in terms of a higher-order fold: For $h :: (F\ a, z) \to a$,

$$pfold\ h = apply \circ (fold\ \varphi_h \times id) \tag{8}$$

where $\varphi_h :: F\ (z \to a) \to (z \to a)$ is given by

$$\varphi_h = curry\ (h \circ ((map_F\ apply \circ \tau^F) \vartriangle \pi_2))$$

and $apply :: (a \to b, a) \to b$ by $apply\ (f, x) = f\ x$. Therefore, $fold\ \varphi_h :: \mu F \to (z \to a)$ is the curried version of $pfold\ h$.

With this relationship at hand we can state the following shortcut fusion law, which is the instance to our context of a more general program transformation technique called lambda abstraction (Pettorossi and Skowron 1987). The specific case of this law when lists are the intermediate structure was introduced by Voigtländer (2008) and its generic formulation was given in Pardo et al. (2009).

Law 10 (HIGHER-ORDER PFOLD/BUILDP) *For left-strict h,*[15]

$$pfold\ h \circ buildp\ g = apply \circ g\ \varphi_h$$

Like in the derivation of circular programs, $g\ \varphi_h$ returns a pair, but now composed of a function of type $z \to a$ and an object of type z. The final result then corresponds to the application of the function to the object. That is,

$$pfold\ h\ (buildp\ g\ c) = \textbf{let}\ (f, z) = g\ \varphi_h\ c\ \textbf{in}\ f\ z$$

[15] By left-strict we mean strict on the first argument, that is, $h\ (\bot, z) = \bot$.

5 Algol 68 Scope Rules

In Sect. 3 we have applied concrete fusion rules to small, but illustrative examples, and in Sect. 4 we have shown that such rules can be given generic definitions. In this section, we consider the application of shortcut fusion to a real example: the Algol 68 scope rules. These rules are used, for example, in the Eli system[16] (Kastens et al. 1998; Waite et al. 2007) to define a generic component for the name analysis task of a compiler.

The problem we consider is as follows: we wish to construct a program to deal with the scope rules of a block structured language, the Algol 68. In this language a definition of an identifier x is visible in the smallest enclosing block, with the exception of local blocks that also contain a definition of x. In this case, the definition of x in the local scope hides the definition in the global one. In a block an identifier may be declared at most once. We shall analyze these scope rules via our favorite (toy) language: the *Block* language, which consists of programs of the following form:

$$
\begin{array}{l}
[\,\textbf{use}\ y; \textbf{decl}\ x; \\
\quad [\textbf{decl}\ y; \textbf{use}\ y; \textbf{use}\ w;\,] \\
\ \textbf{decl}\ x; \textbf{decl}\ y;\,]
\end{array}
$$

In Haskell we may define the following data-types to represent *Block* programs.

$$
\begin{array}{lcl}
\textbf{type}\ \mathit{Prog} = [\mathit{It}] & \qquad & \textbf{data}\ \mathit{It} = \mathit{Use}\ \mathit{Var} \\
 & & \qquad\quad \mid \mathit{Decl}\ \mathit{Var} \\
\textbf{type}\ \mathit{Var} = \mathit{String} & & \qquad\quad \mid \mathit{Block}\ \mathit{Prog}\quad .
\end{array}
$$

Such programs describe the basic block-structure found in many languages, with the peculiarity however that declarations of identifiers may also occur after their first use (but in the same level or in an outer one). According to these rules the above program contains two errors: at the outer level, the variable x has been declared twice and the use of the variable w, at the inner level, has no binding occurrence at all.

We aim to develop a program that analyses *Block* programs and computes a list containing the identifiers which do not obey to the rules of the language. In order to make the problem more interesting, and also to make it easier to detect which identifiers are being incorrectly used in a *Block* program, we require that the list of invalid identifiers follows the sequential structure of the input program. Thus, the semantic meaning of processing the example sentence is $[w, x]$.

Because we allow a *use-before-declare* discipline, a conventional implementation of the required analysis naturally leads to a program which traverses the abstract syntax tree twice: once for accumulating the declarations of identifiers

[16] A well known compiler generator toolbox.

and constructing the environment, and once for checking the uses of identifiers, according to the computed environment. The uniqueness of names can be detected in the first traversal: for each newly encountered declaration it is checked whether that identifier has already been declared at the current level. In this case an error message is computed. Of course the identifier might have been declared at a global level. Thus we need to distinguish between identifiers declared at different levels. We use the level of a block to achieve this. The environment is a partial function mapping an identifier to its level of declaration:

$$\textbf{type}\ \mathit{Env} = [(\mathit{Var}, \mathit{Int})]$$

Semantic errors resulting from duplicate definitions are then computed during the first traversal of a block and errors resulting from missing declarations in the second one. In a straightforward implementation of this program, this strategy has two important effects: the first is that a *"gluing"* data structure has to be defined and constructed to pass explicitly the detected errors from the first to the second traversal, in order to compute the final list of errors in the desired order; the second is that, in order to be able to compute the missing declarations of a block, the implementation has to explicitly pass (using, again, an intermediate structure), from the first traversal of a block to its second traversal, the names of the variables that are used in it.

Observe also that the environment computed for a block and used for processing the use-occurrences is the global environment for its nested blocks. Thus, only during the second traversal of a block (*i.e.*, after collecting all its declarations) the program actually begins the traversals of its nested blocks; as a consequence the computations related to first and second traversals are intermingled. Furthermore, the information on its nested blocks (the instructions they define and the blocks' level) has to be explicitly passed from the first to the second traversal of a block. This is also achieved by defining and constructing an intermediate data structure. In order to pass the necessary information from the first to the second traversal of a block, we define the following intermediate data structure:

$$\textbf{type}\ \mathit{Prog}_2 = [\mathit{It}_2] \qquad \textbf{data}\ \mathit{It}_2 = \mathit{Block}_2\ (\mathit{Int}, \mathit{Prog}) \mid \mathit{Dupl}_2\ \mathit{Var} \mid \mathit{Use}_2\ \mathit{Var}$$

Errors resulting from duplicate declarations, computed in the first traversal, are passed to the second, using constructor Dupl_2. The level of a nested block, as well as the instructions it defines, are passed to the second traversal using constructor Block_2's pair containing an integer and a sequence of instructions.

According to the strategy defined earlier, computing the semantic errors that occur in a block sentence consists of:

$$\mathit{semantics} :: \mathit{Prog} \to [\mathit{Var}]$$
$$\mathit{semantics} = \mathit{missing} \circ (\mathit{duplicate}\ 0\ [\,])$$

The function *duplicate* detects duplicate variable declarations by collecting all the declarations occurring in a block. It is defined as follows:

$$
\begin{aligned}
&\mathit{duplicate} :: \mathit{Int} \to \mathit{Env} \to \mathit{Prog} \to (\mathit{Prog}_2, \mathit{Env})\\
&\mathit{duplicate}\ \mathit{lev}\ \mathit{ds}\ [\,] = ([\,], \mathit{ds})\\[1ex]
&\mathit{duplicate}\ \mathit{lev}\ \mathit{ds}\ (\mathit{Use}\ \mathit{var} : \mathit{its})\\
&\quad = \textbf{let}\ (\mathit{its}_2, \mathit{ds}') = \mathit{duplicate}\ \mathit{lev}\ \mathit{ds}\ \mathit{its}\\
&\quad\quad \textbf{in}\ \ (\mathit{Use}_2\ \mathit{var} : \mathit{its}_2, \mathit{ds}')\\[1ex]
&\mathit{duplicate}\ \mathit{lev}\ \mathit{ds}\ (\mathit{Decl}\ \mathit{var} : \mathit{its})\\
&\quad = \textbf{let}\ (\mathit{its}_2, \mathit{ds}') = \mathit{duplicate}\ \mathit{lev}\ ((\mathit{var}, \mathit{lev}) : \mathit{ds})\ \mathit{its}\\
&\quad\quad \textbf{in if}\ ((\mathit{var}, \mathit{lev}) \in \mathit{ds})\ \textbf{then}\ (\mathit{Dupl}_2\ \mathit{var} : \mathit{its}_2, \mathit{ds}')\ \textbf{else}\ (\mathit{its}_2, \mathit{ds}')\\
&\mathit{duplicate}\ \mathit{lev}\ \mathit{ds}\ (\mathit{Block}\ \mathit{nested} : \mathit{its})\\
&\quad = \textbf{let}\ (\mathit{its}_2, \mathit{ds}') = \mathit{duplicate}\ \mathit{lev}\ \mathit{ds}\ \mathit{its}\\
&\quad\quad \textbf{in}\ \ (\mathit{Block}_2\ (\mathit{lev} + 1, \mathit{nested}) : \mathit{its}_2, \mathit{ds}')
\end{aligned}
$$

Besides detecting the invalid declarations, the *duplicate* function also computes a data structure, of type Prog_2, that is later traversed in order to detect variables that are used without being declared. This detection is performed by function *missing*, that is defined such as:

$$
\begin{aligned}
&\mathit{missing} :: (\mathit{Prog}_2, \mathit{Env}) \to [\,\mathit{Var}]\\
&\mathit{missing}\ ([\,], \_) = [\,]\\[1ex]
&\mathit{missing}\ (\mathit{Use}_2\ \mathit{var} : \mathit{its}_2, \mathit{env})\\
&\quad = \textbf{let}\ \mathit{errs} = \mathit{missing}\ (\mathit{its}_2, \mathit{env})\\
&\quad\quad \textbf{in if}\ (\mathit{var} \in \mathit{map}\ \pi_1\ \mathit{env})\ \textbf{then}\ \mathit{errs}\ \textbf{else}\ \mathit{var} : \mathit{errs}\\
&\mathit{missing}\ (\mathit{Dupl}_2\ \mathit{var} : \mathit{its}_2, \mathit{env})\\
&\quad = \mathit{var} : \mathit{missing}\ (\mathit{its}_2, \mathit{env})\\[1ex]
&\mathit{missing}\ (\mathit{Block}_2\ (\mathit{lev}, \mathit{its}) : \mathit{its}_2, \mathit{env})\\
&\quad = \textbf{let}\ \mathit{errs}_1 = \mathit{missing} \circ (\mathit{duplicate}\ \mathit{lev}\ \mathit{env})\ \$\ \mathit{its}\\
&\quad\quad\quad\quad \mathit{errs}_2 = \mathit{missing}\ (\mathit{its}_2, \mathit{env})\\
&\quad\quad \textbf{in}\ \mathit{errs}_1 +\!\!+\ \mathit{errs}_2
\end{aligned}
$$

The construction and traversal of an intermediate data structure, however, is not essential to implement the semantic analysis described. Indeed, in the next section we will transform *semantics* into an equivalent program that does not construct any intermediate structure.

5.1 Calculating a Circular Program

In this section, we calculate a circular program equivalent to the *semantics* program presented in the previous section. In our calculation, we will use the specific instance of Law 8 for the case when the intermediate structure gluing the consumer and producer functions is a list:

Law 11 (PFOLD/BUILDP RULE FOR LISTS)

$$
\begin{array}{l}
pfold\ (hnil, hcons) \circ buildp\ g\ \$\ c \\
\quad = v \\
\quad \textbf{where}\ (v, \boxed{z}) = g\ (knil, kcons)\ c \\
\qquad\qquad knil = hnil\ \boxed{z} \\
\qquad\qquad kcons\ (x, y) = hcons\ ((x, y), \boxed{z})
\end{array}
$$

where the schemes *pfold* and *buildp* have already been defined as:

$$
\begin{array}{l}
buildp :: (\forall\ b\ .\ (b, (a, b) \to b) \to c \to (b, z)) \to c \to ([\,a\,], z) \\
buildp\ g = g\ ([\,], uncurry\ (:))
\end{array}
$$

$$
\begin{array}{l}
pfold :: (z \to b, ((a, b), z) \to b) \to ([\,a\,], z) \to b \\
pfold\ (hnil, hcons) = p_L \\
\quad \textbf{where}\ p_L\ ([\,], z) \qquad = hnil\ z \\
\qquad\qquad p_L\ (a : as, z) = hcons\ ((a, p_L\ (as, z)), z)
\end{array}
$$

Now, if we write *missing* in terms of *pfold*,

$$
\begin{array}{l}
missing = pfold\ (hnil, hcons) \\
\quad \textbf{where}\ hnil\ \_ = [\,] \\
\qquad hcons\ ((Use_2\ var, errs), env) \\
\qquad\quad = \textbf{if}\ (var \in map\ \pi_1\ env)\ \textbf{then}\ errs\ \textbf{else}\ var : errs \\
\\
\qquad hcons\ ((Dupl_2\ var, errs), env) \\
\qquad\quad = var : errs \\
\\
\qquad hcons\ ((Block_2\ (lev, its), errs), env) \\
\qquad\quad = \textbf{let}\ errs_1 = missing \circ (duplicate\ lev\ env)\ \$\ its \\
\qquad\qquad \textbf{in}\ errs_1 +\!\!+\ errs
\end{array}
$$

and *duplicate* in terms of *buildp*,

$$
\begin{array}{l}
duplicate\ lev\ ds = buildp\ (g\ lev\ ds) \\
\quad \textbf{where}\ g\ lev\ ds\ (nil, cons)\ [\,] = (nil, ds) \\
\\
\qquad g\ lev\ ds\ (nil, cons)\ (Use\ var : its) \\
\qquad\quad = \textbf{let}\ (its_2, ds') = g\ lev\ ds\ (nil, cons)\ its \\
\qquad\qquad \textbf{in}\ \ (cons\ (Use_2\ var, its_2), ds')
\end{array}
$$

$$
\begin{array}{l}
g\ lev\ ds\ (nil, cons)\ (Decl\ var : its) \\
\quad = \textbf{let}\ (its_2, ds') = g\ lev\ ((var, lev) : ds)\ (nil, cons)\ its \\
\quad\quad \textbf{in}\ \textbf{if}\ ((var, lev) \in ds)\ \textbf{then}\ (cons\ (Dupl_2\ var, its_2), ds')\ \textbf{else}\ (its_2, ds') \\
g\ lev\ ds\ (nil, cons)\ (Block\ nested : its) \\
\quad = \textbf{let}\ (its_2, ds') = g\ lev\ ds\ (nil, cons)\ its \\
\quad\quad \textbf{in}\ \ (cons\ (Block_2\ (lev + 1, nested), its_2), ds')
\end{array}
$$

we can apply Law 11 to the program $semantics = missing \circ (duplicate\ 0\ [\,])$, since this program has just been expressed as an explicit composition between a *pfold* and a *buildp*. We obtain a deforested circular definition, which, when inlined, gives the following program:

$$
\begin{array}{l}
semantics\ p = errs \\
\quad \textbf{where} \\
\quad\quad (errs, \boxed{\text{env}}) = gk\ 0\ [\,]\ p \\
\quad\quad gk\ lev\ ds\ [\,] = ([\,], ds) \\
\quad\quad gk\ lev\ ds\ (Use\ var : its) \\
\quad\quad\quad = \textbf{let}\ (errs, ds') = gk\ lev\ ds\ its \\
\quad\quad\quad\quad \textbf{in}\ (\textbf{if}\ (var \in map\ \pi_1\ \boxed{\text{env}})\ \textbf{then}\ errs\ \textbf{else}\ var : errs, ds') \\
\quad\quad gk\ lev\ ds\ (Decl\ var : its) \\
\quad\quad\quad = \textbf{let}\ (errs, ds') = gk\ lev\ ((var, lev) : ds)\ its \\
\quad\quad\quad\quad \textbf{in}\ \textbf{if}\ ((var, lev) \in ds)\ \textbf{then}\ (var : errs, ds')\ \textbf{else}\ (errs, ds') \\
\quad\quad gk\ lev\ ds\ (Block\ nested : its) \\
\quad\quad\quad = \textbf{let}\ (errs_2, ds') = gk\ lev\ ds\ its \\
\quad\quad\quad\quad \textbf{in}\ (\textbf{let}\ errs_1 = missing \circ (duplicate\ (lev + 1)\ \boxed{\text{env}})\ \$\ nested \\
\quad\quad\quad\quad\quad \textbf{in}\ errs_1 +\!\!+\ errs_2, ds')
\end{array}
$$

We may notice that the above program is a circular one: the environment of a *Block* program (variable *env*) is being computed at the same time it is being used. The introduction of this circularity made it possible to eliminate some intermediate structures that occurred in the program we started with: the intermediate list of instructions that was computed in order to glue the two traversals of the outermost level of a *Block* sentence has been eliminated by application of Law 11. We may also notice, however, that, for nested blocks:

$$
\begin{array}{l}
gk\ lev\ ds\ (Block\ nested : its) \\
\quad = \textbf{let}\ (errs_2, ds') = gk\ lev\ ds\ its \\
\quad\quad \textbf{in}\ (\textbf{let}\ errs_1 = missing \circ (duplicate\ (lev + 1)\ env)\ \$\ nested \\
\quad\quad\quad \textbf{in}\ errs_1 +\!\!+\ errs_2, ds')
\end{array}
$$

an intermediate structure is still being used in order to glue functions *missing* and *duplicate* together. This intermediate structure can easily be eliminated, since we have already expressed function *missing* in terms of *pfold*, and function *duplicate* in terms of *buildp*. Therefore, by direct application of Law 11 to the above function composition, we obtain:

$$\begin{aligned}
&gk\ lev\ ds\ (Block\ nested : its)\\
&\quad = \mathbf{let}\ (errs_2, ds') = gk\ lev\ ds\ its\\
&\qquad \mathbf{in}\ (\mathbf{let}\ (errs_1, \boxed{env_2}) = g\ (lev+1)\ env\ (knil, kcons)\ nested\\
&\qquad\qquad \mathbf{where}\ knil = hnil\ \boxed{env_2}\\
&\qquad\qquad\qquad\quad kcons\ x = hcons\ (x, \boxed{env_2})\\
&\qquad\quad \mathbf{in}\ errs_1 \mathbin{+\!\!+} errs_2, ds')
\end{aligned}$$

Again, we could inline the definition of function g into a new function, for example, into function gk'. However, the definition of gk' would exactly match the definition of gk, except for the fact that where gk searched for variable declarations in environment env, gk' needs to search them in environment env_2.

In order to use the same function for both gk and gk', we add an extra argument to function gk. This argument will make it possible to use circular definitions to pass the appropriate environment variable to the appropriate block of instructions (the top level block or a nested one).

We should notice that, in general, this extra effort is not necessary. In this particular example, this manipulation effort was made since it is possible to calculate two circular definitions from the straightforward solution and both circular functions share almost the same definition. In all other cases, inlining the calculated circular program is enough to derive an elegant and efficient *lazy* program from a function composition between a pfold and a buildp.

We finally obtain the program:

$$\begin{aligned}
&semantics\ p = errs\\
&\quad \mathbf{where}\ (errs, \boxed{\text{env}}) = gk\ 0\ [\,]\ \boxed{\text{env}}\ p\\
&\qquad\qquad gk\ lev\ ds\ env\ [\,] = ([\,], ds)\\
&\qquad\qquad gk\ lev\ ds\ env\ (Use\ var : its)\\
&\qquad\qquad\quad = \mathbf{let}\ (errs, ds') = gk\ lev\ ds\ env\ its\\
&\qquad\qquad\qquad \mathbf{in}\ (\mathbf{if}\ (var \in map\ \pi_1\ env)\ \mathbf{then}\ errs\ \mathbf{else}\ var : errs, ds')\\
&\qquad\qquad gk\ lev\ ds\ env\ (Decl\ var : its)\\
&\qquad\qquad\quad = \mathbf{let}\ (errs, ds') = gk\ lev\ ((var, lev) : ds)\ env\ its\\
&\qquad\qquad\qquad \mathbf{in}\ \mathbf{if}\ ((var, lev) \in ds)\ \mathbf{then}\ (var : errs, ds')\ \mathbf{else}\ (errs, ds')\\
&\qquad\qquad gk\ lev\ ds\ env\ (Block\ nested : its)\\
&\qquad\qquad\quad = \mathbf{let}\ (errs_2, ds') = gk\ lev\ ds\ env\ its\\
&\qquad\qquad\qquad \mathbf{in}\ (\mathbf{let}\ (errs_1, \boxed{env_2}) = gk\ (lev+1)\ env\ \boxed{env_2}\ nested
\end{aligned}$$

$$\textbf{in } errs_1 ++ errs_2, ds')$$

Regarding the above program, we may notice that it has two circular definitions. One such definition occurs in the *semantics* function, and makes it possible for the environment of the outer level of a block program to be used while still being constructed. For the example sentence that we have considered before,

$$\begin{array}{l}[\textbf{use } y; \textbf{decl } x;\\ \quad [\textbf{decl } y; \textbf{use } y; \textbf{use } w;]\\ \textbf{decl } x; \textbf{decl } y;]\end{array}$$

this circularity makes the environment `[("x",0),("x",0),("y",0)]` available to the function that traverses the outer block. The other circular definition, occurring in the last definition of function *gk*, is used so that, for every traversal of a nested sequence of instructions, its environment may readily be used. This means that the function traversing the nested block in the above example sentence may use the environment `[("x",0),("x",0),("y",0),("y",1)]` even though it still needs to be constructed.

The introduction of these circularities, by the application of our calculational method, completely eliminated the intermediate lists of instructions that were used in the straightforward *semantics* solution we started with. Furthermore, the derivation of this circular program made it possible to obtain a *semantics* program that computes the list of errors that occur in a *Block* program by traversing it only once.

5.2 Calculating a Higher-Order Program

In this section we study the application of Law 10 to the *semantics* program given earlier:

$$semantics = missing \circ (duplicate\ 0\ [\,])$$

As we have stated, this definition constructs an intermediate list of instructions, that again we would like to eliminate with fusion. For this purpose, we will now use the specific instance of Law 10 for the case where the intermediate structure is a list:

Law 12 (HIGHER-ORDER PFOLD/BUILDP FOR LISTS)

$$pfold\ (hnil, hcons) \circ buildp\ g = apply \circ g\ (\varphi_{hnil}, \varphi_{hcons})$$

where $(\varphi_{hnil}, \varphi_{hcons})$ is the algebra of the higher-order fold which corresponds to the curried version of *pfold* (*hnil*, *hcons*).

We have already expressed function *missing* in terms of *pfold*,

$$missing = pfold\ (hnil, hcons)$$

$$
\begin{array}{l}
\textbf{where } hnil\ \_ = [\,] \\
\qquad hcons\ ((Use_2\ var, errs), env) \\
\qquad\quad = \textbf{if } (var \in map\ \pi_1\ env)\ \textbf{then } errs\ \textbf{else } var : errs \\
\\
\qquad hcons\ ((Dupl_2\ var, errs), env) \\
\qquad\quad = var : errs \\
\\
\qquad hcons\ ((Block_2\ (lev, its), errs), env) \\
\qquad\quad = \textbf{let } errs_1 = missing \circ (duplicate\ lev\ env)\ \$\ its \\
\qquad\qquad \textbf{in } errs_1 +\!\!+\ errs
\end{array}
$$

and function *duplicate* in terms of *buildp*.

$$
\begin{array}{l}
duplicate\ lev\ ds = buildp\ (g\ lev\ ds) \\
\quad \textbf{where } g\ lev\ ds\ (nil, cons)\ [\,] = (nil, ds) \\
\\
\qquad g\ lev\ ds\ (nil, cons)\ (Use\ var : its) \\
\qquad\quad = \textbf{let } (its_2, ds') = g\ lev\ ds\ (nil, cons)\ its \\
\qquad\qquad \textbf{in } (cons\ (Use_2\ var, its_2), ds') \\
\\
\qquad g\ lev\ ds\ (nil, cons)\ (Decl\ var : its) \\
\qquad\quad = \textbf{let } (its_2, ds') = g\ lev\ ((var, lev) : ds)\ (nil, cons)\ its \\
\qquad\qquad \textbf{in if } ((var, lev) \in ds)\ \textbf{then } (cons\ (Dupl_2\ var, its_2), ds') \\
\qquad\qquad\qquad\qquad\qquad\qquad\qquad \textbf{else } (its_2, ds') \\
\\
\qquad g\ lev\ ds\ (nil, cons)\ (Block\ nested : its) \\
\qquad\quad = \textbf{let } (its_2, ds') = g\ lev\ ds\ (nil, cons)\ its \\
\qquad\qquad \textbf{in } (cons\ (Block_2\ (lev + 1, nested), its_2), ds')
\end{array}
$$

Therefore, in order to apply Law 12 to the *semantics* program, we now only need the expression of the algebra $(\varphi_{hnil}, \varphi_{hcons})$ of the curried version of *missing*:

$$
\begin{array}{l}
missing_{ho} = fold\ (\varphi_{hnil}, \varphi_{hcons}) \\
\quad \textbf{where } \varphi_{hnil} = \backslash\_ \rightarrow [\,] \\
\\
\qquad \varphi_{hcons}\ (Use_2\ var, ferrs) \\
\qquad\quad = \lambda env \rightarrow \textbf{if } (var \in map\ \pi_1\ env)\ \textbf{then } ferrs\ env \\
\qquad\qquad\qquad\qquad\qquad\qquad\qquad\qquad \textbf{else } var : (ferrs\ env) \\
\\
\qquad \varphi_{hcons}\ (Dupl_2\ var, ferrs) \\
\qquad\quad = \lambda env \rightarrow var : (ferrs\ env) \\
\\
\qquad \varphi_{hcons}\ (Block_2\ (lev, its), ferrs) \\
\qquad\quad = \lambda env \rightarrow \textbf{let } errs_1 = missing \circ (duplicate\ lev\ env)\ \$\ its \\
\qquad\qquad\qquad\qquad \textbf{in } errs_1 +\!\!+\ (ferrs\ env)
\end{array}
$$

After inlining the definition that we calculate by directly applying Law 12 to the *semantics* program, we obtain the program presented in the next page.

$$
\begin{array}{l}
\mathit{semantics}\ p = \mathit{ferrs}\ \mathit{env} \\
\quad \textbf{where}\ (\mathit{ferrs}, \mathit{env}) = g_{\varphi}\ 0\ []\ p \\
\qquad\qquad g_{\varphi}\ \mathit{lev}\ \mathit{ds}\ [] = (\lambda \mathit{env} \rightarrow [], \mathit{ds}) \\
\\
\qquad\qquad g_{\varphi}\ \mathit{lev}\ \mathit{ds}\ (\mathit{Use}\ \mathit{var} : \mathit{its}) \\
\qquad\qquad\quad = \textbf{let}\ (\mathit{ferrs}, \mathit{ds}') = g_{\varphi}\ \mathit{lev}\ \mathit{ds}\ \mathit{its} \\
\qquad\qquad\qquad \textbf{in}\ (\lambda \mathit{env} \rightarrow \textbf{if}\ \mathit{var} \in \mathit{map}\ \pi_1\ \mathit{env} \\
\qquad\qquad\qquad\qquad\qquad\qquad \textbf{then}\ \mathit{ferrs}\ \mathit{env} \\
\qquad\qquad\qquad\qquad\qquad\qquad \textbf{else}\ \mathit{var} : (\mathit{ferrs}\ \mathit{env}), \mathit{ds}') \\
\qquad\qquad g_{\varphi}\ \mathit{lev}\ \mathit{ds}\ (\mathit{Decl}\ \mathit{var} : \mathit{its}) \\
\qquad\qquad\quad = \textbf{let}\ (\mathit{ferrs}, \mathit{ds}') = g_{\varphi}\ \mathit{lev}\ ((\mathit{var}, \mathit{lev}) : \mathit{ds})\ \mathit{its} \\
\qquad\qquad\qquad \textbf{in}\ \textbf{if}\ ((\mathit{var}, \mathit{lev}) \in \mathit{ds}) \\
\qquad\qquad\qquad\quad \textbf{then}\ (\lambda \mathit{env} \rightarrow \mathit{var} : (\mathit{ferrs}\ \mathit{env}), \mathit{ds}') \\
\qquad\qquad\qquad\quad \textbf{else}\ (\mathit{ferrs}, \mathit{ds}') \\
\qquad\qquad g_{\varphi}\ \mathit{lev}\ \mathit{ds}\ (\mathit{Block}\ \mathit{nested} : \mathit{its}) \\
\qquad\qquad\quad = \textbf{let}\ (\mathit{ferrs}_2, \mathit{ds}') = g_{\varphi}\ \mathit{lev}\ \mathit{ds}\ \mathit{its} \\
\qquad\qquad\qquad \textbf{in}\ (\lambda \mathit{env} \rightarrow \textbf{let}\ \mathit{errs}_1 = \mathit{missing} \\
\qquad\qquad\qquad\qquad\qquad\qquad\qquad\qquad \circ\ (\mathit{duplicate}\ (\mathit{lev} + 1) \\
\qquad\qquad\qquad\qquad\qquad\qquad\qquad\qquad\qquad\quad \mathit{env})\ \$\ \mathit{nested} \\
\qquad\qquad\qquad\qquad\qquad\quad \textbf{in}\ \mathit{errs}_1 +\!\!+\ \mathit{ferrs}_2\ \mathit{env}, \mathit{ds}')
\end{array}
$$

Notice that the first component of the result produced by the call $g_{\varphi}\ 0\ []\ p$ is now a function, instead of a concrete value. When this function is applied to *env*, it produces the list of variables that do not obey to the semantic rules of the language. The program we have calculated is, therefore, a higher-order program.

Regarding the above program, we may notice that it maintains the construction of an intermediate structure. This situation already occurred in Sect. 5.1. Again, an intermediate structure is constructed whenever a nested sequence of instructions is traversed, in the definition presented next.

$$
\begin{array}{l}
g_{\varphi}\ \mathit{lev}\ \mathit{ds}\ (\mathit{Block}\ \mathit{nested} : \mathit{its}) \\
\quad = \textbf{let}\ (\mathit{ferrs}_2, \mathit{ds}') = g_{\varphi}\ \mathit{lev}\ \mathit{ds}\ \mathit{its} \\
\qquad \textbf{in}\ (\lambda \mathit{env} \rightarrow \textbf{let}\ \mathit{errs}_1 = \mathit{missing} \circ (\mathit{duplicate}\ (\mathit{lev} + 1)\ \mathit{env})\ \$\ \mathit{nested} \\
\qquad\qquad\qquad\quad \textbf{in}\ \mathit{errs}_1 +\!\!+\ \mathit{ferrs}_2\ \mathit{env}, \mathit{ds}')
\end{array}
$$

The $\mathit{missing} \circ \mathit{duplicate}$ composition in the above definition, however, may be eliminated by direct application of Law 12. This is due to the fact that functions *missing* and *duplicate* have already been expressed in terms of the appropriate program schemes. We obtain:

$$
\begin{aligned}
& g_{\varphi}\ \mathit{lev}\ \mathit{ds}\ (\mathit{Block}\ \mathit{nested} : \mathit{its}) \\
& \quad = \mathbf{let}\ (\mathit{ferrs}_2, \mathit{ds}') = g_{\varphi}\ \mathit{lev}\ \mathit{ds}\ \mathit{its} \\
& \qquad \mathbf{in}\ (\lambda \mathit{env} \rightarrow \mathbf{let}\ (\mathit{ferrs}_1, \mathit{env}_1) = g_{\varphi}\ (\mathit{lev} + 1)\ \mathit{env}\ \mathit{nested} \\
& \qquad\qquad\qquad\qquad \mathbf{in}\ \mathit{ferrs}_1\ \mathit{env}_1 +\!\!+\ \mathit{ferrs}_2\ \mathit{env}, \mathit{ds}')
\end{aligned}
$$

The higher-order version of *semantics* that we calculate in this section, by applying Law 12, twice, to the original *semantics* program avoids the construction of any intermediate structure. Furthermore, in this program, the appropriate (local or global) environment is passed to the correct block of instructions. Notice that, in order for this to happen, it was not necessary to post-process the calculated program, as it was in Sect. 5.1. The execution of the higher-order *semantics* program is not restricted to a lazy execution setting. Recall that the intermediate structure free program that we calculated in Sect. 5.1 may only be executed in a lazy setting: it holds two circular definitions.

6 Conclusions

In this tutorial, we revised a systematic technique for the deforestation of intermediate data structures. These data structures enable a compositional style of programming, which contributes to an increased modularity, but their use may degrade the overall running efficiency of the resulting implementations.

As programmers, we would always like to deal with modular programs, but as software users we favour runtime performance. In the context of this tutorial, this opens up two questions:

1. *Is it possible to automatically derive the programs we have manually calculated here?*
   This derivation is indeed possible, for example within the Glasgow Haskell Compiler (GHC), using rewrite rules (RULES pragma). For the reader interested in further details, we suggest (Fernandes 2009).
2. *How do the types of programs we calculate here compare in terms of runtime performance?*
   This issue is particularly relevant for the circular and higher-order programs we have calculated, and we have in the past performed a first attempt on such comparison (Fernandes 2009). While in the examples we considered, higher-order programs as we propose to calculate in Sect. 5.2 were the most efficient, it would be interesting to conduct a detailed and representative benchmark to assess whether this observation holds in general.

In this tutorial, we have focused on programs consisting of the composition of two functions. Recently, we have however followed a similar approach to derive shortcut fusion rules that apply to programs consisting of an arbitrary number of function compositions (Pardo et al. 2013).

Here, we have also focused on the practical and pragmatical aspects of the fusion rules that were studied. In this line, we have chosen not to present their formal proofs, that the interested reader may obtain in (Fernandes 2009; Pardo et al. 2011).

As we have highlighted before, in the techniques we revise, lazy evaluation and higher-order programming are crucial.

References

Abramsky, S., Jung, A.: Domain Theory. In: Handbook of Logic in Computer Science, pp. 1–168. Clarendon Press (1994)

Augusteijn, L.: Sorting morphisms. In: Swierstra, S.D., Oliveira, J.N., Henriques, P.R. (eds.) AFP 1998. LNCS, vol. 1608, pp. 1–27. Springer, Heidelberg (1999). https://doi.org/10.1007/10704973_1

Bird, R.: Using circular programs to eliminate multiple traversals of data. Acta Informatica **21**, 239–250 (1984)

Bird, R.: Introduction to Functional Programming using Haskell, 2nd edn. Prentice-Hall, UK (1998)

Bird, R., de Moor, O.: Algebra of Programming. Prentice-Hall Inernational Series in Computer Science, vol. 100. Prentice-Hall, Upper Saddle River (1997)

Cockett, R., Fukushima, T.: About Charity. Technical Report 92/480/18, University of Calgary, June 1992

Cockett, R., Spencer, D.: Strong Categorical Datatypes I. In: Seely, R.A.C., (ed.) International Meeting on Category Theory 1991. Canadian Mathematical Society Conference Proceedings, vol. 13, pp. 141–169 (1991)

Danielsson, N.A., Hughes, J., Jansson, P., Gibbons, J.: Fast and loose reasoning is morally correct. In: Conference Record of the 33rd ACM SIGPLAN-SIGACT Symposium on Principles of Programming Languages, POPL 2006, pp. 206–217. ACM, New York (2006)

Fernandes, J.P.: Design, Implementation and Calculation of Circular Programs. PhD thesis, Deparment of Informatics, University of Minho, Portugal (2009)

Fernandes, J.P., Pardo, A., Saraiva, J.: A shortcut fusion rule for circular program calculation. In: Proceedings of the ACM SIGPLAN Haskell Workshop, Haskell 2007, pp. 95–106. ACM Press, New York (2007)

Gibbons, J.: Calculating functional programs. In: Backhouse, R., Crole, R., Gibbons, J. (eds.) Algebraic and Coalgebraic Methods in the Mathematics of Program Construction. LNCS, vol. 2297, pp. 151–203. Springer, Heidelberg (2002). https://doi.org/10.1007/3-540-47797-7_5

Gill, A.: Cheap deforestation for non-strict functional languages. PhD thesis, Department of Computing Science, University of Glasgow, UK (1996)

Gill, A., Launchbury, J., Jones, S.L.P.: A short cut to deforestation. In: Conference on Functional Programming Languages and Computer Architecture, pp. 223–232, June 1993

Hughes, J.: Why functional programming matters. Comput. J. **32**, 98–107 (1984)

Kastens, U., Pfahler, P., Jung, M.: The eli system. In: Koskimies, K. (ed.) CC 1998. LNCS, vol. 1383, pp. 294–297. Springer, Heidelberg (1998). https://doi.org/10.1007/BFb0026439

Pardo, A.: A calculational approach to recursive programs with effects. PhD thesis, Technische Universität Darmstadt, October 2001

Pardo, A.: Generic Accumulations. In: IFIP WG2.1 Working Conference on Generic Programming, Dagstuhl, Germany, July 2002

Pardo, A., Fernandes, J.P., Saraiva, J.: Shortcut fusion rules for the derivation of circular and higher-order monadic programs. In: Proceedings of the 2009 ACM SIGPLAN Symposium on Partial Evaluation and Program Manipulation, PEPM 2009, pp. 81–90. ACM Press (2009)

Pardo, A., Fernandes, J.P., Saraiva, J.: Shortcut fusion rules for the derivation of circular and higher-order programs. Higher-Order Symb. Comput. **24**(1–2), 115–149 (2011). ISSN 1388-3690

Pardo, A., Fernandes, J.P., Saraiva, J.: Multiple intermediate structure deforestation by shortcut fusion. In: Du Bois, A.R., Trinder, P. (eds.) SBLP 2013. LNCS, vol. 8129, pp. 120–134. Springer, Heidelberg (2013). https://doi.org/10.1007/978-3-642-40922-6_9

Pettorossi, A., Skowron, A.: The lambda abstraction strategy for program derivation. In: Fundamenta Informaticae XII, pp. 541–561 (1987)

Jones, S.P. (ed.) Haskell 98 Language and Libraries: The Revised Report. Cambridge University Press (2003). Also in Journal of Functional Programming, 13(1)

Jones, S.P., Hughes, J., Augustsson, L., et al.: Report on the programming language Haskell 98. Technical report, February 1999

Takano, A., Meijer, E.: Shortcut deforestation in calculational form. In: Proceedings of Conference on Functional Programming Languages and Computer Architecture, pp. 306–313. ACM Press (1995)

Voigtländer, J.: Semantics and pragmatics of new shortcut fusion rules. In: Garrigue, J., Hermenegildo, M.V. (eds.) FLOPS 2008. LNCS, vol. 4989, pp. 163–179. Springer, Heidelberg (2008). https://doi.org/10.1007/978-3-540-78969-7_13

Wadler, P.: Theorems for free! In: 4th International Conference on Functional Programming and Computer Architecture, London (1989)

Wadler, P.: Deforestation: transforming programs to eliminate trees. Theoret. Comput. Sci. **73**, 231–248 (1990)

Waite, W., Kastens, U., Sloane, A.M.: Generating Software from Specifications. Jones and Bartlett Publishers Inc, USA (2007)

Functional Reactive Programming in C++

Ivan Čukić(✉)

Faculty of Mathematics, University of Belgrade,
Studentski Trg 16, 11100 Belgrade, Serbia
ivan@math.rs

Abstract. Reactive programming is a relatively new discipline that teaches how to design and develop complex systems through the notion of data-flow. The main idea is that the system, and its components, are able to receive signals, and to react to them in some way. The signals can be seen as streams of messages that we can transform using the usual monadic functions (map, bind, filter, etc.) and that we can easily direct through our system.

Reactive programming removes the usual complexity of explicitly dealing with the shared mutable state, manual synchronization with mutexes, and alike.

We are presenting an approach for implementing reactive systems in the C++ programming language, by creating abstractions over the commonly used methods for achieving concurrency, like callbacks and signals and slots.

1 Introduction

Modern software systems tend to require different components that execute simultaneously. Be it a simple GUI application that needs to process system events while waiting for the user response, a multi-threaded application that performs complex calculations, or a multi-client network server that processes multiple requests at the same time.

Since the terminology is not fully standardized, in this paper we are using the term *concurrency* to mean that different tasks are being executed at the same time, as opposed to *parallelism* which will mean that the same function is running at the same time on different data sets.

In a concurrent environment, functional programming patterns allow us to make more robust and less error-prone systems. A significant fraction of software bugs happen due to programmers not being able to fully understand all the possible states their code can be in. In a concurrent environment, this lack of understanding and the issues that arise from it are greatly amplified [4].

The usual approach (in the imperative languages) of dealing with concurrency is through using plain threads and mutexes.

The problems with plain threads are numerous. The main problem is that the threads are not composable [11]. It is impossible to tell whether another

V. Zsók et al. (Eds.): CEFP 2015, LNCS 10094, pp. 42–74, 2019.
https://doi.org/10.1007/978-3-030-28346-9_2

library or a function you are calling creates new threads by itself. This can lead to creating many more threads than the system can effectively handle, and the thread that called said function just sleeps until it gets the result.

Another issue is that the concurrency can not be disabled. When you use plain threads, the program logic usually becomes dependent on different code paths running at the same time. In that case, it is not easy to modify the code to run on a single thread which could be useful in a number of scenarios, especially for testing and debugging purposes.

There is also the problem that there is no standard way to return values from one thread to the caller. It usually involves using a shared variable and manual synchronization through locks.

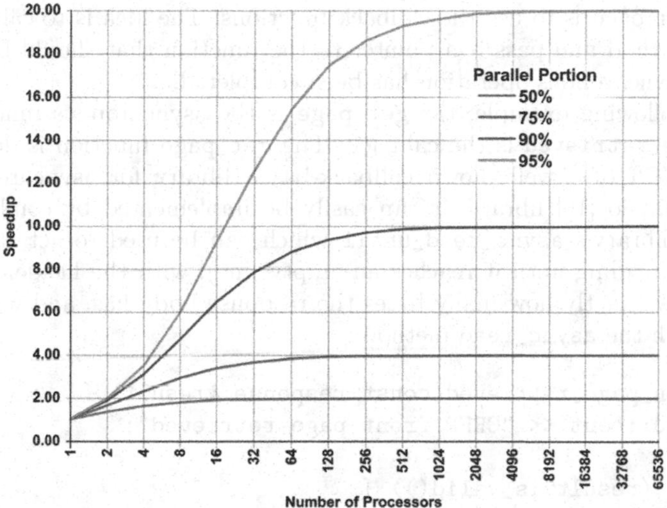

Fig. 1. Amdahl's Law

When we want to achieve higher levels of parallelism, we tend to throw raw power at it, by improving CPUs clocks and adding new cores. According to the Amdahl's Law [13], this is not sufficient since the speed of the program will not double by doubling the number of cores we execute it on. For example, it claims that if only 5% of your code is serialized (95% is parallelized) you can achieve the speedup of only 20 times by running it on 65536 CPU cores (Fig. 1).

In a discussion on recursive mutexes, David Butenhof noted that this basic synchronization primitive should have been called "the bottleneck" [3] instead of creating a "cute acronym" for it (from **mut**ual **ex**clusion). Bottlenecks are useful at times, sometimes indispensable – but they're never good.

These problems all lead to decrease in program speed. Most threads just end up waiting for the results of other computations to be sent to them. Yet, the operating system still has to do all the book-keeping and context-switching to manage all those threads, which is just bureaucracy that takes the CPU time from the actual program that needs to be executed.

2 Asynchronous Functions

Instead of using raw threads and mutexes, we need to create an abstraction that can be used to execute something asynchronously, and to send us the result of the operation back.

There are a few common approaches for achieving this in C++.

2.1 Calls and Callbacks

The first approach is to use the callback functions. The idea is to call an asynchronous method and pass it a pointer to the function that should be invoked when the asynchronous operation has been completed.

In the following example, the `get_page` is the asynchronous function, and the `on_page_retrieved` is the callback. The `get_page` function is designed to follow the API of a well-known callback-based library for asynchronous I/O – the Boost.Asio [10] library. It can easily be implemented by combining the Boost.Asio library's `async_read_until` which can be used to get the request headers (by reading until it reaches an empty line); with the header retrieved, we will know exactly how many bytes the response body has, and we will able to get it with the `async_read` method.

```
void on_page_retrieved(const response &result) {
    std::cout << "CEFP front page retrieved";

    if (result.is_valid()) {
        std::cout << "Success: " << result.body();
    } else {
        std::cout << "Error retrieving the page\n";
    }
}

void get_cefp() {
    get_page("http://people.inf.elte.hu/cefp/",
             on_page_retrieved);

    std::cout << "Sent the request\n";
}
```

It is important to note that the `get_page` call will not block the execution of the rest of `get_cefp` method, so the user will see the `"Sent the request"` message before the actual request is fulfilled.

2.2 Signals and Slots

Another often used approach to dealing with asynchrony are signals and slots.

In general, the signals and slots system is a simple communication mechanism between different objects. Signal is used to emit a message, and a slot receives it.

Lets consider mouse events in an application. Buttons in the user interface are objects that send a `clicked` signal when the user clicks them. We will use the syntax for connecting the signals to their respective slots used in the Qt library for C++, since it is the most prominent library for C++ using this mechanism, but we will keep using the `snake_case` syntax to keep uniformity of the code examples.

```
button *exit_button;
button *get_cefp_button;

connect(exit_button, SIGNAL(clicked()),
        main_window, SLOT(quit()));
connect(get_cefp_button, SIGNAL(clicked()),
        main_window,     SLOT(get_cefp())
```

When the `exit_button` is clicked, the connection will invoke the `quit` method of the `main_window` object. In the same way, clicking on the `get_cefp_button` will invoke the `get_cefp` method.

Compared to callbacks, signals and slots allow easier decoupling of components. The button does not know (nor it needs to) whether anybody is listening for its events – the signal is sent anyway. On the other hand, a called asynchronous function needs to know exactly which callback to call.

While this mechanism is most useful for handling the user interface events, it can have other applications as well. In the following example, we will implement a similar example to the one in the previous section.

```
void init() {
    connect(page, SIGNAL(page_retrieved(response)),
            this, SLOT(on_page_retrieved(response)));
}

void get_cefp() {
    page.get("http://people.inf.elte.hu/cefp/");
}

void on_page_retrieved(const response &result) {
    std::cout << "CEFP front page retrieved";

    if (result.is_valid()) {
        std::cout << "Success: " << result.body();
    } else {
```

```
        std::cout << "Error retrieving the page\n";
    }
}
```

In this implementation, the get_cefp method only needs to know which page to request, while it does not need to care which method will process the result.

2.3 Actor Systems

The third popular approach, albeit not that much in the C++ community, are the actor systems [8]. They were popularised by the Erlang [1] programming language, and a few of the more modern languages are adopting the idea (Scala's Akka library [12], the C++ Actor Framework [5] and the Distributed Haskell [7] to name a few).

Similar to the signals and slots, the system is broken into small components that are able to exchange messages. In these systems, it is common for the sender to decide who will be the recipient for each message, and not the other way round. For example, an actor A can choose that it will send the message to the actor B. The actor B is not able to request that it wants to listen to all messages from A – it will receive all messages sent to it no matter who sent them.

The previous example becomes something like this (notation is as used in the C++ Actor Framework).

```
void get_cefp(event_based_actor *self,
              const actor &page_actor)
{
    self->async_send(page_actor,
                     get("http://people.inf.elte.hu/cefp/"));
}

behaviour receive(event_based_actor *self) {
    return {
        [=] (const response_t &result) {
            if (result.is_valid()) {
                ...
            }
        }
    };
}
```

The async_send method is used to send messages. In this case, we are sending a single get message to the actor identified by page_actor. When the request is processed, that actor will send us back a message of type response_t which is handled in the behaviour defined by the receive function.

2.4 Problems with These Approaches

All previous approaches are valid, but have readability and maintainability issues.

The task we have is quite simple: request a page, and process it when it is retrieved. Something like this should be easy to implement. As easy as simply writing:

```
result = get_page("http://people.inf.elte.hu/cefp/");
if (result.is_valid()) {
    ...
}
```

The only reason we can not write this is that the `get_page` method has to be asynchronous, not to block the execution of the other parts of the system.

All the previous solutions require the program logic to be split into a part that handles the part of the logic before the asynchronous call, and the second part that comes after the asynchronous call has completed.

In the real-world problems, the program logic is rarely limited to only one asynchronous call. Systems like those tend to be broken into overly small subroutines that are difficult to write, understand and maintain. We need better abstractions than these.

3 Futures

The lowest level of abstraction we want to create are the *futures*. A future represents a handler for a value that is not yet known. While this may sound confusing, the concept is quite simple.

Just imagine the following conversation between Alice and Bob:

```
Alice: What is the time?
(Bob looks at his watch)
Bob:   It is 12:30.
```

When Alice asks the question, she only knows the type of the answer – that it will be a type that defines (at least) hours and minutes. We will call that type `time_t`. Her request for the current time can be written as follows:

```
Bob.get_time();
```

This way, she is asking Bob for the time, but the problem is that she is not saving the result anywhere – she will never learn what is the current time. Can we fix this by assigning it to a variable of type `time_t`?

```
time_t time = Bob.get_time();
```

If we want to be able to save the response like this, we first need to wait for Bob's reply. This means that Alice can not do anything until Bob answers the question. This would be a bad idea since we can not know how much time it will take Bob to reply, and even whether he will reply at all. The data flow for this case can be seen in the Fig. 2, where the caller is Alice, function is `Bob.get_time()`, and the resulting value is represented as a circle.

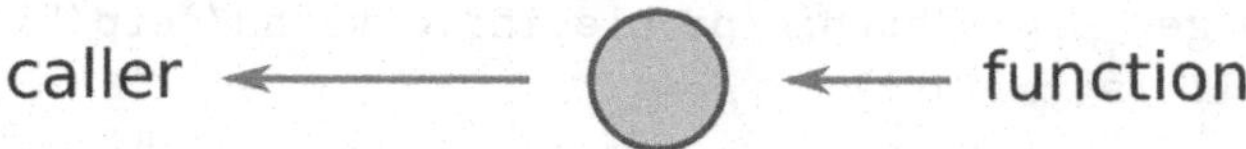

Fig. 2. Returning a proper value from a function

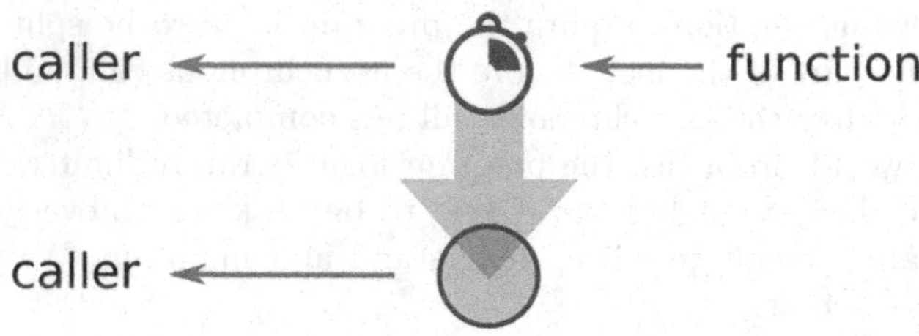

Fig. 3. Returning a future from function

Instead, we will do the following:

```
future<time_t> time = bob.get_time();
```

What does this do? It creates an empty container that can contain an instance of the `time_t` class. When Bob prepares the answer, he can just put it into the box, and Alice will be able to get it by calling `time.get()`. This will allow Alice to continue working on other things, and still get Bob's answer when it arrives. The data flow in the Fig. 3 shows that when the caller invokes the function, it will not receive the resulting value, but an object that can later be used to get it, when it becomes available.

3.1 Futures in C++

There are a few different classes for C++ that implement futures with slightly different features and semantics. The most notable ones are `std::future<T>` present in the standard library since C++11; `boost::future<T>` which is a drop-in replacement for the former, and has features that are planned for inclusion in the future revisions of C++ standard; `QFuture<T>` from the Qt library which has similar features to the previous ones, but with a different syntax; and the `folly::Future<T>` from the Facebook's Folly library which has special semantics inspired by the Future class as implemented in the Scala programming language.

All of these classes have a method `.get()` which returns a value contained in the future class. The difference is in the method's behaviour when the value is not yet available.

All but the `folly::Future<T>` block the execution of the caller until the result becomes available (Fig. 4). This is only useful if the caller creates a few asynchronous requests that should be executed in parallel. But in our example in which we call only `Bob.get_time()` it makes the asynchronous execution of the function useless and equivalent to not using the futures at all (Fig. 2). In the case of calling `.get()` on an unfinished future, the `folly::Future<T>` class will throw an exception, which is in accordance to the idea that asynchronous functions should never block the caller, and forces the caller to implement the logic of asynchronous execution in a proper way.

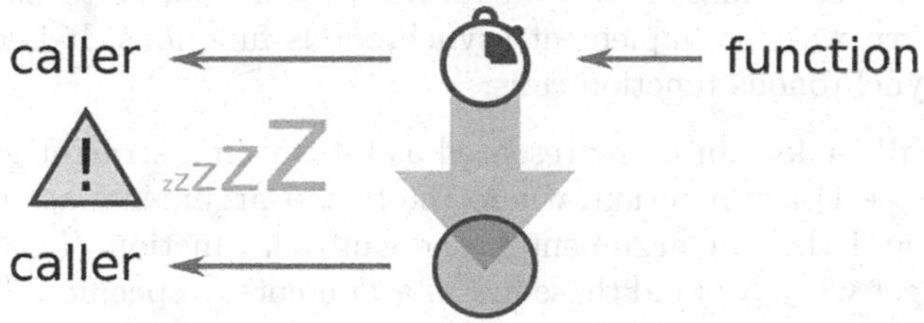

Fig. 4. Calling `.get()` on a future

3.2 Proper Way of Handling Futures

Having the caller blocked while it is waiting for the result defeats the purpose of the asynchronous API. The main reason why we wanted the time-consuming operations done asynchronously in the first place is to allow the main program to continue working (processing user input, accepting new network connections, creating new asynchronous requests, etc.) while it waits for the result. This means that designing the system around the `.get()` method of a future is a bad idea.

Instead of relying on the caller to get the value manually, we only need to provide it a way to define a continuation for a specific asynchronous operation. The continuation is a function that will be invoked when the result becomes available [6]. This way, we will never try to get the value from an unfinished future, we will just define what should be done with the value once it becomes available. In the following example, instead of Alice getting the result of the asynchronous computation, she is just scheduling a continuation (`print_time`) function which will print the result when Bob produces it (Fig. 5).

```
Bob.get_time().then(print_time);
```

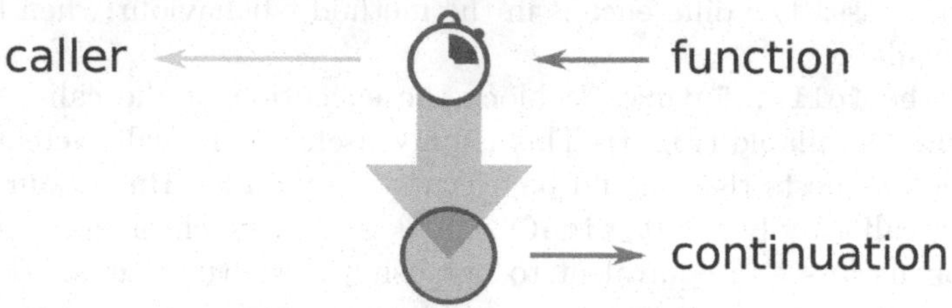

Fig. 5. Passing the continuation

The minimal interface a future should have consists of a constructor and a way to chain a continuation to said future. It will be able to handle all the previously shown ways to implement asynchronous functions. It is also be able to cover the synchronous function calls.

Calls with callbacks can be represented as futures in a straight-forward way. Let f be an $(n+1)$-ary function, where the first n arguments are used for the computation, and the last argument is the callback function. Then the unary function g we get when we bind those first n arguments to specific values behaves like the future (note that the `std::bind` function has nothing to do with monadic bind, it just implements partial application in C++).

```
auto g = std::bind(f, arg1, arg2, ..., argn, _1);
```

This successfully separates the definition of an asynchronous operation with its arguments (the constructor for this type of future), from the continuation specification.

Signals and slots can also be represented in a simple manner. The signal sender object, along with the signal provide the constructor for the future, while the slot represents the continuation.

Message passing in actor systems needs a bit more effort to in order to represent it as a future. An asynchronous operation that has a result (a returning value) in these systems consists of one message that is sent from the caller to the callee, and then the result is returned via another message sent back to the caller. The caller will need to be able to create a unique identifier for every call it makes, and the callee will need to return that identifier along with the calculated result. We will show how to represent this in the call-callback approach which we have shown is easy to represent using futures.

```
void f(arg1, arg2, ..., argn, callback) {
    auto request_id = generate_id();
    global_callbacks[request_id] = callback;
```

```
        callee.send_message(arg1, ..., argn, request_id);
    }

    void receive_message(value, request_id) {
        global_callbacks[request_id](value);
        global_callbacks.remove(request_id);
    }
```

The function f gets the arguments that will be passed to the actor that performs the asynchronous computation (callee) and the callback function that should be called when the result becomes available. The callback is saved to a structure that maps identifiers to callbacks. The callee will send beck the result, which will invoke receive_message function. This will, in turn, invoke the callback associated with the specified identifier.

Synchronous function calls can also be modelled with futures. If the n-ary function f is a synchronous one, we can easily create a callback-based function from it.

```
    void g(arg1, arg2, ..., argn, callback) {
        callback(f(arg1, arg2, ..., argn));
    }
```

The fact that we have created an abstraction that works for both synchronous and asynchronous computations will be quite useful later.

3.3 Continuation Monad

The structure future<T> that we have described in the previous section can be seen as a monad [14]. We just need to specify it more precisely.

We have seen the different constructors that the structure can have. We are only left with the constructor that creates future<T> from the value of T. It just needs to create a future which stores the value passed to it. As soon as the continuation is defined, it needs to call it and pass the saved value. If we use the interface of std::future, the implementation could be as follows:

```
    template <typename T>
    class future {
    public:
        future(T value)
            : _value(value)
        {
        }

        template <typename Continuation>
        void then(Continuation cont)
        {
```

```
        cont(_value);
    }

private:
    T _value;
};
```

The second thing we need to add is the monadic `bind` operation. The `.then` method looks like a perfect candidate, it just needs to have a proper signature. It needs to take a function from `T` to `future<U>`, and return the `future<U>`:

```
template <typename Continuation>
auto then(Continuation cont) -> future<decltype(cont(_value))>;
```

We will leave the implementation of this method as an exercise for the reader, since it is not important for the rest of the paper.

With these methods, it is easy to show that `future<T>` is a monad. In literature, it is commonly known as the *continuation monad.*

3.4 std::future and Similar Types

Now that we have seen what kind of structure we want to use as our minimal abstraction, we need yet to see whether the library-provided classes we have at our disposal match the requirements.

`std::future` does not have a `.then` method in C++11/14. The only way to get the value is through the `.get` method. It will be extended to support adding continuations in C++17. Until then, we can use `boost::future<T>` since it already contains the things that the standard one will have.

The `make_ready_future` function is the constructor – it takes a value of type, and creates a future that contains that value.

```
template <typename T>
    future<T> make_ready_future(T value);
```

Its `.then` method has the following signature and usage:

```
auto future<T>::then(Continuation &&cont);

future<int> f1 = answer_ultimate_question_of_life();
future<string> f2 = f1.then(
    [] (future<int> f) {
        return f.get().to_string(); // here .get() won't block
    }
);
```

The monadic bind requires the continuation to accept the value of type `T`, but here we have it receive `future<T>`. The rationale for this is that the `future<T>` can contain an exception instead of the value. While this breaks our definition, a proper version of this method can easily be implemented:

```
template <typename T, typename Continuation>
auto monadic_bind(future<T> f, Continuation cont) {
    return f.then([=] (future<T> f) { cont(f.get()); });
}
```

We have defined both the proper constructor and a monadic bind for the `boost::future<T>` (and `std::future<T>` from C++17). It it easy to implement for `QFuture<T>` and `folly::Future<T>` as well.

We can now write code like this:

```
get_page("http://people.inf.elte.hu/cefp/")
.then(
    [] (auto &&result) {
        std::cout << "CEFP front page retrieved";

        if (result.is_valid()) {
            std::cout << "Success: " << result.body();
        } else {
            std::cout << "Error retrieving the page\n";
        }
    }
)
```

or even something more complex like:

```
get_page("http://people.inf.elte.hu/cefp/")
.then(
    [] (auto &&result) {
        cout << result.headers();

        for (image: result.image_tags) {
            image.get().then(
                [] (auto &&image_result) {
                    // do something
                    // with image_result
                }
            );
        }
    }
)
```

4 Iterators and Algorithms

Before we proceed to our main abstraction for asynchronous system modelling, we need to explain the notion of algorithms, iterators, and ranges in C++.

The standard library in C++ (STL – Standard Template Library) provides a set of useful algorithms that can be applied to any structure that we can iterate over. We are going to demonstrate how a few of them are used – `std::accumulate`, `std::transform` and `std::sort`.

4.1 Accumulate (fold)

Say we have a task to sum all numbers in a list. We can implement this easily using a `for` loop:

```
list<int> xs = {1, 2, 3, 4, 5};
int result = 0;
for (auto x: xs) {
    result = result + x;
}
return result;
```

This works, but is unnecessarily verbose. The pattern of iterating through a collection of elements, and accumulating them using some function is a common one and it is to be expected that the programming language provides facilities to do it without manually implementing it. In C++, the algorithm used for this is `std::accumulate` and behaves similarly to Haskell's `foldl`. The signature is as follows:

```
T accumulate(InputIt first, InputIt last, T init,
             BinaryOperation op );
```

It receives a pair of iterators which define which elements should be iterated on, initial value and a binary operation that will be used for accumulation. If the operation is not specified, it defaults to summing the values.

With `std::accumulate`, we can implement the previous example like this:

```
result = std::accumulate(xs.cbegin(), xs.cend(), 0);
```

If we want to calculate the product of all items instead of the sum, we can do the following:

```
result = std::accumulate(xs.cbegin(), xs.cend(), 1,
            [] (int acc, int x) { return acc * x; });
```

4.2 Transform (map)

Next, lets try to square all numbers in a list. The code for it could be implemented like this:

```
list<int> xs = {1, 2, 3, 4, 5};
for (auto &x: xs) {
    x = x * x;
}
// xs = {1, 4, 9, 16, 25}
```

This modifies the original collection to contain the squares of the values stored in the original list. Again, this is a common pattern – to apply a function to each element of a collection and get a collection holding the results. The standard library provides an algorithm called `std::transform` that behaves similar to Haskell's map.

```
OutputIt transform(InputIt first1, InputIt last1, OutputIt d_first,
                   UnaryOperation unary_op);
```

The first two iterators define the collection whose items we want to transform, the third is the iterator that points to the destination collection in which we want to store the results. The last argument is the function that will be used to transform the elements. We can use it to implement the previous example in a more concise way:

```
std::transform(xs.begin(), xs.end(),
               xs.begin(), [] (int x) { return x * x; });
```

Note that we have passed the beginning of the same list that we are transforming (`xs`) as the third argument. This means that we will overwrite the old data, just like in the example above. If we want to preserve the old list, we can do it like this:

```
list<int> xs = {1, 2, 3, 4, 5};
vector<int> results;

std::transform(xs.cbegin(), xs.cend(),
               std::back_inserter(results),
               [] (int x) { return x * x; });

//      xs = {1, 2, 3,  4,  5};
// results = {1, 4, 9, 16, 25};
```

If we wanted to get the three largest squares, we could sort the results (this is inefficient, used only for the demonstration purposes), and create a new collection that will contain only the first three elements.

```
std::sort(results.begin(), results.end(), std::greater<>());

vector<int> top_three(results.cbegin(), results.cbegin() + 3);
```

4.3 Iterator Types

Those who are paying attention have probably noticed that `xs` was a list of integers, whereas the `results` is a vector. The reason for that is that the `std::sort` requires a special type of iterators that the list does not support. Sorting is usually implemented using the quick sort algorithm which requires random-access to items.

- **Input iterator** is the basic type of iterator. It only needs to support incrementing (move to the next element in collection) and equality comparisons (are the two iterators pointing to the same element).
- **Forward iterators** are a subset of Input iterators that allow multiple passes through the collection.
- **Bidirectional iterator** is a Forward iterator that also supports decrementing (move the iterator to point to the previous element).
- **Random-access iterator** is an iterator that allows non-sequential access to collection elements, more precisely, random-access.

Since `std::vector` stores its elements in a contiguous block of memory, it can efficiently provide access to any random element stored in it. On the other hand, `std::list` is implemented like a doubly linked list, so it only provides efficient sequential access. For that reason, `std::sort` does not work on lists.

Other algorithms we shown work on the lists without any problems – both `std::transform` and `std::accumulate` only require a single pass through the collection.

4.4 Composition

The problem with the standard algorithms is that they are not easily composed. Lets combine previous examples, and try to calculate a sum of squares of elements in a list.

In Haskell, it is a one-liner:

```
sum $ map (\ x -> x * x) xs
```

If we were to combine the previous C++ examples, we would get a code like this:

```
list<int> xs = {1, 2, 3, 4, 5};
list<int> squares;

std::transform(xs.cbegin(), xs.cend(),
               std::back_inserter(squares),
               [] (int x) { return x * x; });

int result = std::accumulate(squares.cbegin(),
                             squares.cend(), 0);
```

It is not as concise, and not even as efficient as the Haskell version. This code needs to allocate new memory in order to store the squares, when we do not really need to store them.

The main problem regarding composability is the fact that all algorithms accept iterator pairs separately instead of whole collections. And they do not return iterators, so their results can not be passed to other algorithms.

4.5 Easier Functional Objects Creation

While lambdas provide a nice in-line way of creating function objects like we saw before, the syntax is not as terse as it could be for some special cases.

Libraries like `boost.phoenix` and `boost.lambda` [9] provide more concise solutions for some of the special cases. Namely, they employ the idea of placeholders and leverage C++ operator overloading to achieve easier functional object creation that is usable in older C++ compilers (unlike lambdas which were introduced in C++11).

With these libraries, the following are equivalent:

```
// C++11 lambda
std::transform(xs.cbegin(), xs.cend(), xs.begin(),
               [] (int x) { return x * x; });

// Boost.lambda
std::transform(xs.cbegin(), xs.cend(), xs.begin(),
               _1 * _1);

// boost.phoenix
std::transform(xs.cbegin(), xs.cend(), xs.begin(),
               arg1 * arg1);
```

They also allow more complex statements which can bind regular variables as well as the placeholders:

```
std::for_each(xs.begin(), xs.end(),
              std::cout<< _1 << ' ');
```

It is also possible to create custom functions that support placeholders using these libraries, but we are going to skip that and demonstrate how to create your own predicates from scratch.

We want to create a predicate that will be able to test whether the value passed to it has an error or not. We want it to be possible to use it like this:

```
auto number_of_errors = std::count_if(
                    responses.cbegin(), responses.cend(),
                    error == true);
```

We can not achieve this with the aforementioned libraries because the dot (.) can not be overloaded in C++. If it was, we would be able to write `_1.error` and use it as a predicate.

We need to create an object called `error` that has the equality operator defined (`operator==`) and calling that operator should return a predicate. We can do it in the following manner:

```
class error_test_t {
public:
    error_test_t(bool error = true)
        : m_error(error)
    {}

    error_test_t operator==(bool error) const
    {
        return error_test_t(!!m_error ^ !!error));
    }

    template<typename T>
    bool operator() (T &&value) const
    {
        return value.error == m_error;
    }

private:
    bool m_error;
};

error_test_t error(true);
error_test_t not_error(false);
```

The `error` and `not_error` objects is already predicates, so we can have even more possible ways to use it, depending on the user preference:

```
auto number_of_errors = std::count_if(
                    responses.cbegin(), responses.cend(),
                    error);
// or
```

```
auto number_of_errors = std::count_if(
                        responses.cbegin(), responses.cend(),
                        error == true);

auto number_of_valid_responses = std::count_if(
                        responses.cbegin(), responses.cend(),
                        not_error);
// or
auto number_of_errors = std::count_if(
                        responses.cbegin(), responses.cend(),
                        error == false);
```

While the need to manually write predicates like this is unfortunate, they can be written only once, and used for any type. It makes the main program code much easier to read and write.

5 Ranges

One of the common things we saw in the previous examples was that all algorithms accepted iterator pairs – one that points to the beginning, and another that points to the end (more precisely, it points to the element immediately after the last element in the collection).

If it is a common pattern, we might want to abstract over it. This abstraction is called *ranges*. For the time being, lets think of them as just being pairs of iterators.

5.1 Convenience

The first benefit we are getting from replacing single iterators with ranges is convenience. Using the standard algorithms becomes more terse. It is easier to write just:

```
std::sort(xs);
std::accumulate(xs, 0);
```

than writing it with iterators:

```
std::sort(xs.begin(), xs.end());
std::accumulate(xs.cbegin(), xs.cend(), 0);
```

5.2 Composability

It also allows algorithms to return ranges as values which makes them composable. If the sorting function was defined to return a sored range, it would be easy to write a statement that gets 5 smallest elements in an array like this:

```
take(5, std::sort(xs));
```

So, the operations and transformations can be properly chained like in other functional programming languages.

5.3 Views

There are two types of ranges in C++, views and actions.

Views are just thin wrappers that represent a custom interpretation of underlying sequence of elements without changing the original sequence nor copying it. They are cheap to create and copy around.

If we want to get the first 5 elements in a collection, we can just write:

```
xs | view::take(5)
```

This will create a view that points to those elements, without copying them to a separate collection. With iterators, this could be implemented like this:

```
auto begin5 = xs.cbegin();
// Take first 5 if there are more than 5 elements,
// take everything otherwise
auto end5 = xs.length() > 5 ? xs.cbegin() + 5
                            : xs.cend();
```

We can also do something more complex like extracting only letters from a string and then converting them to uppercase.

```
auto xs = "Hello world!";
xs | view::filter(isaplha)
   | view::transform(toupper);
// xs = "HELLOWORLD";
```

5.4 Infinite Views

Since views do not actually contain any data, accessing an element in a view is a lazy operation – it is calculated when it is needed. This allows us to have infinite views, and apply transformations to them.

The following example calculates a sum of squares of first ten integers.

```
int sum = accumulate(
    view::ints(1) |
    view::transform([](int i){ return i*i; }) |
    view::take(10),
    0);
```

The view containing all integers is infinite, and so is the view we get when applying the square function to it. Since we can not sum all integers, we had to make this list finite to be able to pass it to **accumulate**. We did that by taking only the first ten elements using the take transformation.

5.5 Actions

When you need to mutate a container, or forward it through a chain of mutating operations, you can use actions. Actions own the data they contain and are eager, so they can not work on infinite collections.

We can use actions to sort a vector, and eliminate the duplicates like so:

```
xs = std::move(xs) | action::sort | action::unique;
// or shorter
xs |= action::sort | action::unique;
// or using the function call syntax:
action::unique(action::sort(xs));
```

5.6 Combining Views and Actions

While fundamentally different, views and actions can be used together. For example, we might want to get a list of 5 elements with biggest squares:

```
xs | view::transform(square)
   | action::sort
   | view::take(5);
```

The call to `transform` will create a simple view, no data will be changed. When the user requests the items to be sorted, the algorithm needs to evaluate all the elements of the view passed to it, so it saves them internally. The last step, again, just creates a view containing the first five elements.

5.7 Range Types

Like it was with iterators, ranges can have different features, and belong to different types. The types are the same ones iterators had (everything from input ranges to random-access ranges). A small difference here is that applying a transformation to a range can also change its type.

For example, if we call `action::sort` on a input range, sort will internally collect all the elements, and make them random-accessible so that it can perform sorting. After that, the resulting range is also a random-access one.

6 Reactive Streams

Now that we know what ranges are, we can continue with creating abstractions for asynchronous program execution.

We have created the continuation monad (or `future<T>`). It is interesting to note that all the transformations defined on ranges can also be applied to futures. You might want to have a square of the value that the future returns and write something like this:

```
future<int> f = answer_ultimate_question_of_life()
                                        | transform(square);
```

Instead of `f` being a future that will return 42, it will be a future that returns 1764 (42^2). While, theoretically, we can also apply `sort`, `filter`, etc. to a future, it does not make much sense, since it contains at most one element.

But what happens if we remove the limitation that the future can return only one value? Many processes in computing do not generate only one value, but series of values. Not a series in the sense that we get a collection of items at some point in the future, but in the sense that we get a new value from time to time (Fig. 6).

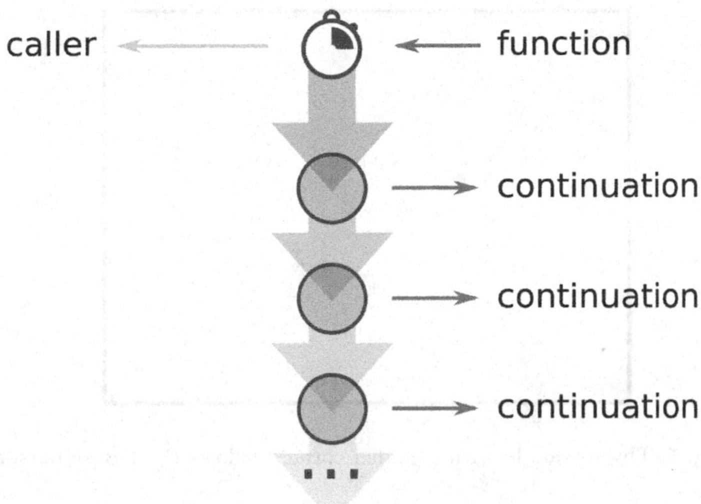

Fig. 6. Stream of values

Examples of this include mouse movement where we get a screen coordinate (with some additional data) every time the user moves the mouse cursor, keyboard events where we get which key is pressed, client connections on a web service where we get some information about a client whenever a new one connects to our service, and similar.

This can not be modelled by futures, but is quite similar in nature. Just think of it as a future that returns a value and another future of the same type.

In order for our previously defined structures to support this idea, the only thing that needs changing is to add the support for calling the continuation function (the function passed to `.then`) multiple times. We are not going to redefine the structures, but we are going to refer to them as reactive streams [15], and write `stream<T>` to mean a stream that contains elements of type `T`.

In order to explain the streams in a visual way, we are going to use the example of transforming the mouse coordinates that get generated while the user is moving the mouse cursor.

Our source stream will be called `mouse_position`, which we will connect to different objects which will show these coordinates after we apply transformations to them.

Initially, we can just connect the mouse position directly to a marker that will show the current position at all times like this:

```
mouse_position >>= mouse_cursor->move_to
```

Whenever the user moves the mouse, the new coordinates will be passed to the `move_to` method of the `mouse_cursor` object. The window will look like in the Fig. 7.

Streams look suspiciously like ranges. They are a collection of elements of the same type. The only difference is that we do not control when a specific element is going to be known. This also means that we do not know whether the stream has an end. We can also only move from beginning one element at a time.

Fig. 7. The rectangle with rounded corners follows the mouse cursor

Considering all this, we can say that reactive streams are similar to the lazy, infinite, input ranges. This limits us on which transformations we can apply to them.

Since they are infinite, all the actions on ranges are inapplicable to streams (unless we convert them to finite ones first). We are left only with views.

6.1 Map, or Transform

Lets try creating the `map` transformation. What does it do? When the stream gets a new value, it will send it to `map` which will perform a user-defined function and pass on the result.

First, we need a structure that will be able to store the transformation function, and the continuation to which to send the result.

```
template <typename Func, typename Cont>
struct map_cont {
    map_cont(Func t, Cont c)
        : transformation(f)
        , continuation(c)
    {
    }

    template <typename InType>
    void operator () (const InType &in) {
        continuation(transformation(in));
    }

    Func transformation;
    Cont continuation;
};
```

The only thing that the constructor does is to save the transformation and continuation functions. When we connect it to a stream, the stream will invoke the call operator (`operator()`) of the `map_cont` structure whenever a new value appears. The call operator will just apply the specified transformation to the value, and invoke the continuation with the result.

Now, in order to have a nice syntax for using this class, we need to define a few more things. We want to be able to write something like this (note that `a >>= b` is just a syntactic sugar for `a.then(b)`):

```
stream >>= map(some_transformation) >>= receiver;
```

This means the following:

- `map` needs to be a unary function, even if `map_cont` structure requires two arguments;
- `map(f)` needs to create a dummy structure that has a `.then` method, so that we can register a continuation for it.
- When a continuation is defined for the result of `map(f)` it needs to return the final `map_cont` object.

The following code manages all these requirements. The `map_impl` structure is the dummy structure that `map` returns, and it is used only as a way to implement currying and allow us to construct `map_cont` in two steps – the first step is the call to `map` and the second is binding it to a continuation. It is mostly boilerplate that only concerns the developers of libraries that wish to implement new DSLs like this one.

```
template <typename Func>
struct map_impl {
    map_impl(Func f)
        : f(f)
    {
    }

    template <typename Cont>
    auto then(Cont &&continuation)
    {
        return map_cont<Func, Cont>(
            transformation,
            std::forward<Cont>(continuation)
        );
    }

    Func transformation;
};

template <typename Func>
auto map(Func &&f)
{
    return map_impl<Func>(std::forward<Func>(f));
}
```

Now that we have a way to transform the mouse stream, we can create something more useful than an object that follows the mouse. For example, we can set the y coordinate to be a fixed number, and pass the events to a marker we will call `top_ruler`.

```
auto flatline_x = [](const point_t &point) {
    return point_t(point.x(), 10);
}

mouse_position >>= map(flatline_x) >>= top_ruler->move_to;
```

Now, we get a new object – a solid dot whose position is a projection of the mouse coordinate on the top of the window like in the Fig. 8.

Fig. 8. Top ruler projection

6.2 Forking a Stream

But now we have a problem. The rounded rectangle does not follow the mouse anymore. In order to be able to split a stream into two identical ones, we need to implement some kind of forking mechanism.

The syntax that we want to achieve is the following:

```
mouse_position >>= fork(
    mouse_cursor->move_to,
    map(flatline_x) >>= top_ruler->move_to,
    map(flatline_y) >>= left_ruler->move_to
)
```

For this, we will need the `fork` method which can accept an arbitrary number of continuation functions. We will need a structure that can accept n different functions, and call them all when its call operator is invoked. For that, we will need to use variadic templates.

First, we define what we want to create – a struct template that has an arbitrary number of template parameters.

```
template <typename ... Conts>
struct fork_impl;
```

Then we write the special case when we are only given one continuation function. It behaves just like `map_cont` except that it does not transaction on the value it received, it just passes it on – like a `map_cont` with identity function.

```
template <typename Cont>
struct fork_impl<Cont>
{
    fork_impl(Cont continuation)
        : continuation(continuation)
    {
    }

    template <typename InType>
    void operator() (const InType &in) {
        // passing the value to the continuation
        continuation(in);
    }

    Cont continuation;
};
```

Now onto the general case. We will use something similar to recursion. The structure that has n continuations defined will inherit one that has $n-1$. This will allow us to process just one of the continuations, and rely that the class we inherited knows how to implement the same behaviour for the rest.

```
template <typename Cont, typename ... Conts>
struct fork_impl<Cont, Conts...>: fork_impl<Conts...>
{
    using parent_type = fork_impl<Conts...>;

    fork_impl(Cont continuation, Conts... cs)
        : parent_type(cs...)
        , continuation(continuation)
    {
    }

    template <typename InType>
    void operator() (const InType &in) {
        // passing the value to the first continuation
        continuation(in);
        // passing the value to the other n-1 continuations
        parent_type::operator()(in);
    }

    Cont continuation;
};
```

With the `fork_impl` structure defined, creating the actual `fork` function is trivial:

```
template <typename ... Conts>
auto fork(Conts ... cs) {
    return fork_impl<Conts...>(std::forward<Conts>(cs)...);
}
```

We can now write the code we wanted, and we will get both the mouse cursor and the ruler items working properly (Fig. 9).

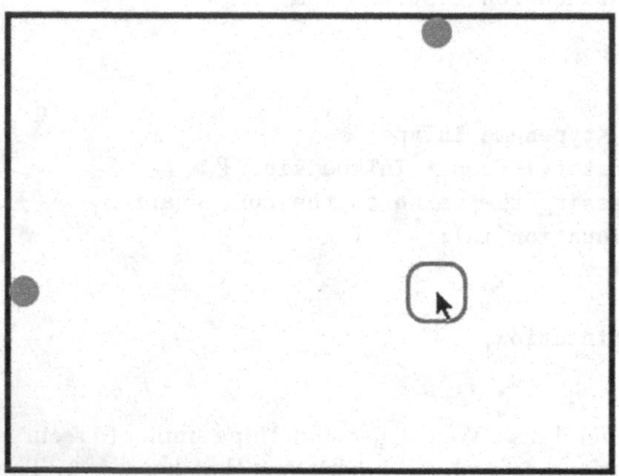

Fig. 9. Both rulers projection, and the cursor

6.3 Stateful Function Objects

Now a question arises. Are we allowed to pass anything that looks like a function to `map`? There are more than a few things in C++ that *look like* functions. From function pointers to proper classes that implement the call operator.

If we are allowed to pass anything we want, we can also pass functional objects that have mutable state. Say, an object that will try to move towards the mouse cursor, but slowly, without jumping (Fig. 10). For this, it will need to store its previous position and use it when calculating the new one.

```
class gravity_object {
public:
    gravity_object()
    {
    }

    point_t operator() (const point_t &mouse_position) {
        current_position.x = current_position.x * .99
                           + mouse_position.x * .01;
        current_position.y = current_position.y * .99
                           + mouse_position.y * .01;
```

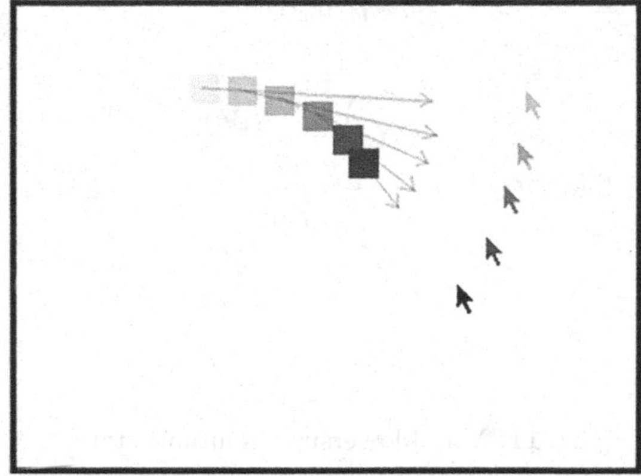

Fig. 10. Rectangle moves slowly towards the mouse

```
        return current_position;
    }

private:
    point_t current_position;
};
```

Would the following code be safe?

```
mouse_position >>=
    map(gravity_object()) >>= gravity_marker->move_to;
```

Usually, having mutable state in a concurrent system is ill-advised. It is one of the reasons why pure functional programming languages like Haskell are getting traction. There can be no data races if all data is constant.

Here, we have implemented an object that has mutable state, without mutexes or any synchronization at all.

It is obvious that immutable state can not lead to concurrency problems. But the question we are left with is whether all mutable state is bad. If we own the data, and we do not share it with anybody, and do not allow anyone else to change it, why would it be bad? We are in full control. Mutable state becomes a problem only when shared (Fig. 11).

It is worth noting that by passing `gravity_object()` to the `map` transformation, we are creating a new instance of that object. If we were to define a local variable of that type, and pass it to multiple different transformations, we would produce an error:

```
gravity_object gravity;

mouse_position >>= fork (
    map(gravity) >>= gravity_marker_1->move_to,
    map(gravity) >>= gravity_marker_2->move_to
);
```

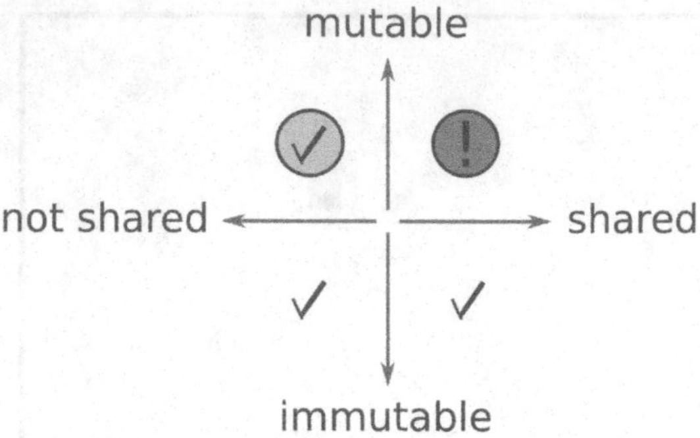

Fig. 11. Mutable versus immutable state

We are creating a single object with mutable state that is used to transform two separate reactive streams. We are sharing mutable state which can lead to bugs. In this case, the bug is very subtle – the gravity markers rectangle will move twice as fast (we will leave explanation of this statement to the reader).

6.4 Stream Filtering

Another useful stream transformation is filtering. Sometimes we want to ignore some type of events. For example, a button in the UI usually does not care about mouse movements outside of its area.

Like `map`, defining the `filter` transformation requires some boilerplate code to implement currying, which we will skip this time. The essence of filtering is in the following structure:

```
template <typename Pred, typename Cont>
struct filter_cont {
    filter_cont(Pred predicate, Cont continuation)
        : predicate(predicate)
        , continuation(continuation)
    {
    }

    template <typename InType>
    void operator () (const InType &in) {
        if (predicate(in)) {
            continuation(in);
        }
    }

    Pred predicate;
    Cont continuation;
};
```

The call operator gets a value from a stream connected to it, and it calls the continuation function only if the predicate function returns `true` for that value.

For example, we might want to filter out all the coordinates where y is not divisible by 100 like this:

```
mouse_position >>=
    filter([] (point_t point) { return point.y % 100 == 0; }) >>=
        snapping_marker;
```

This has the effect of snapping to guide-lines. In this case, the guide-lines are fixed to every 100 pixels, and are horizontal only (Fig. 12). If we wanted to snap to a grid, we could just check the x coordinate in the same way we are checking y.

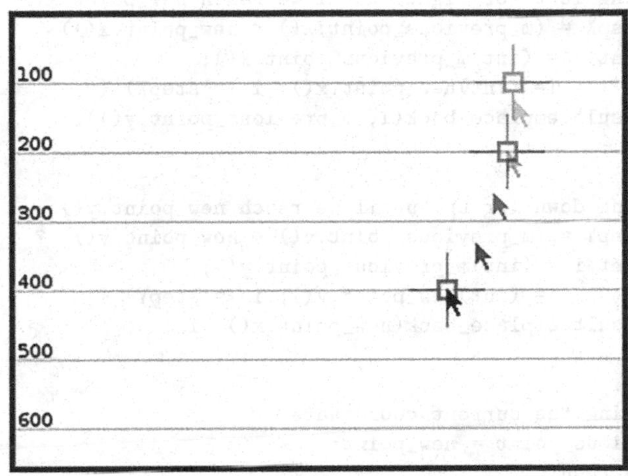

Fig. 12. The cross-hair is snapping to guide-lines

6.5 Generating New Stream Events

There is a bug in the previous example. As can be seen in the Fig. 12, one guide-line (at 300 pixels) has been skipped. This can happen because the mouse movement is not continuous, an there is a chance that while the mouse moves across the line, that the mouse event for the exact $y = 300$ will not be emitted. The faster the mouse cursor moves, the greater probability that it will skip the guide-line.

In order to remedy this, we need to make the stream of coordinates continuous. In this case, since the coordinates are integers, continuous means that we want to create a stream in which the difference in coordinates for two consecutive events is not greater than 1 pixel per axis. The simplest way to achieve this is to remember the previous mouse coordinate, and generate the Manhattan path to the new one.

```
class more_precision {
public:
    more_precision()
    {
```

```
    }

    template <typename Cont>
    void then(Cont &&c)
    {
        continuation = std::forward<Cont>(c);
    }

    std::vector<point_t> operator() (const point_t &new_point) {
        std::vector<point_t> result;

        // Going left (or right) until we reach new_point.x()
        int stepX = (m_previous_point.x() < new_point.x()) ? 1 : -1;
        for (int i = (int)m_previous_point.x();
                 i != (int)new_point.x(); i += stepX) {
            result.emplace_back(i, m_previous_point.y());
        }

        // Going down (or up) until we reach new_point.y()
        int stepY = (m_previous_point.y() < new_point.y()) ? 1 : -1;
        for (int i = (int)m_previous_point.y();
                i != (int)new_point.y(); i += stepY) {
            result.emplace_back(new_point.x(), i);
        }

        // Saving the current coordinate
        m_previous_point = new_point;
        return result;
    }

private:
    std::function<void(point_t)> continuation;
    point_t m_previous_point;

};
```

This will generate an array of coordinates for every new coordinate provided to the object. In order to use it to transform our stream, we can not use the `map` function because we would get a stream of coordinate arrays (`stream<vector<point_t>>`) instead of a stream of coordinates like we need. For this, we need to create a map-like function which flattens its result. We will call it `flat_map`.

```
    template <typename Func, typename Cont>
    struct flatmap_cont {
        flatmap_cont(Func transformation, Cont continuation)
            : transformation(transformation)
            , continuation(continuation)
        {
        }
```

```
    template <typename InType>
    void operator () (const InType &in) {
        auto results = transformation(in);

        // Call the continuation for all items in the
        // resulting array
        std::for_each(
            results.cbegin(), results.cend(),
            continuation);
    }

    Func transformation;
    Cont continuation;
};
```

Now, in order to fix the previous program, we only need to add a single stream transformation (Fig. 13):

```
mouse_position >>= flatmap(more_precision()) >>=
    filter([] (point_t point) { return point.y % 100 == 0; }) >>=
        snapping_marker;
```

7 Data-Flow Design

In order to write reactive systems, one must start to think about them as data-flows [2]. More specifically, to analyze what is the input to the system, what is the input and output of different system components, and how the data should be transformed between them (Fig. 14).

The input streams represent the data that is coming into the system from the outside world, while receivers represent either internal system components that react to the requests, or the data that is emitted back to the outside world.

The transformations that happen in-between, can be either simple ones described in the previous sections, or complete system components that receive some message types, and react to them by emitting different ones.

For example, lets consider a simple authentication component. The client sends a request for a resource to the service, along with its credentials. The authentication component processes the credentials, and if they are valid, modifies the request by removing the credentials, and adding the internal user identifier (Fig. 15).

The code corresponding to (using the functional object we have defined in the Sect. 4.5) this would look like this:

```
clients_stream          // stream<request_t>
    | authenticate()    // stream<authenticated_request_t>
    | fork(
        filter(error == true)  | report_error(),
        filter(error == false) | resource_service()
    )
```

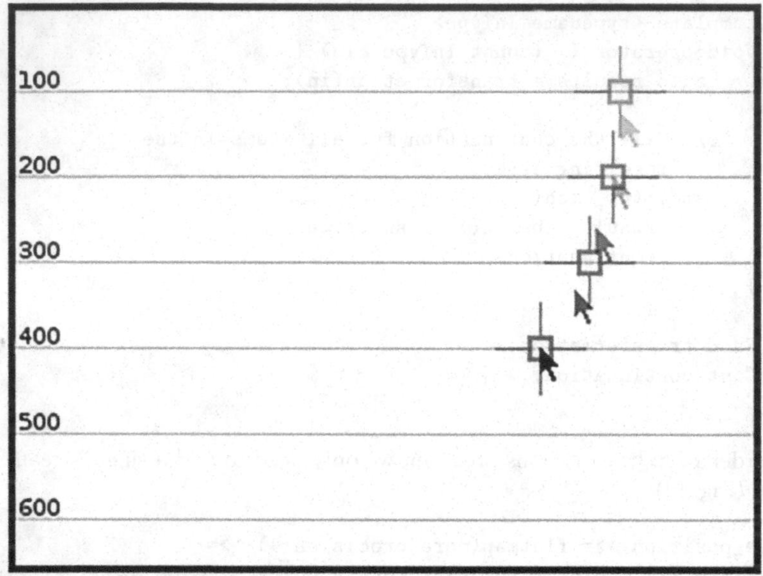

Fig. 13. The cross-hair is snapping to guide-lines, fixed

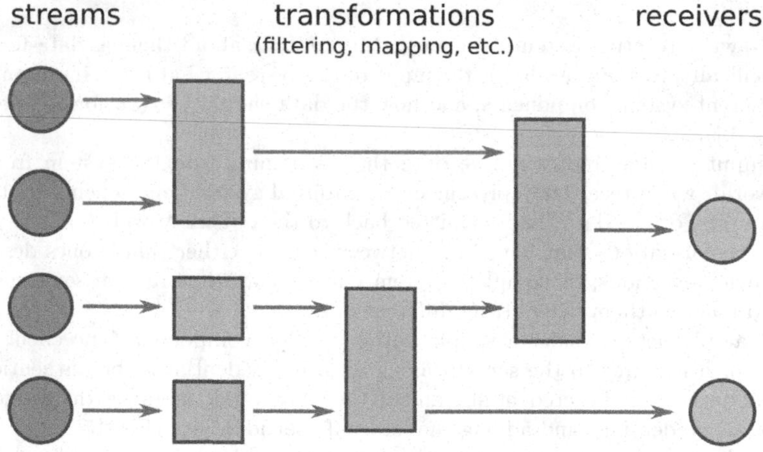

Fig. 14. Data flow through the system

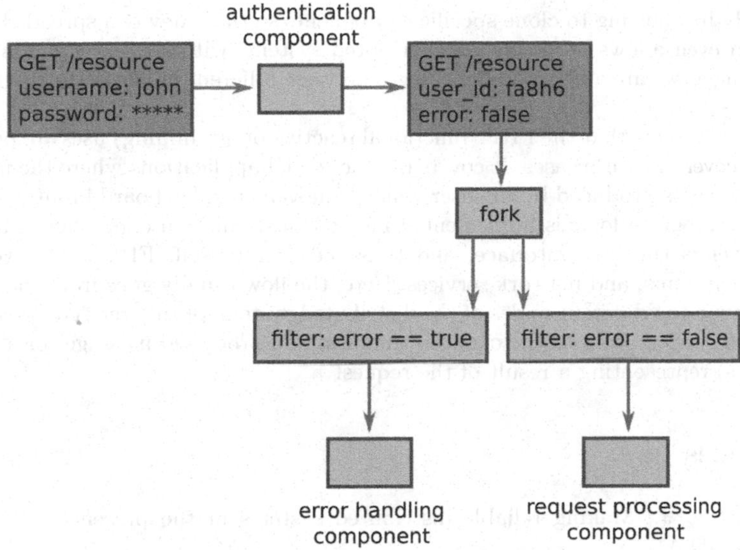

Fig. 15. Data flow for the client authentication service

8 Conclusion

Reactive programming is based on the idea of propagation of changes – reacting to events, as an alternative to the usual approach of scheduling an asynchronous operation, and waiting for its result. This idea allows software decomposition into independent components that communicate with each other only through messages (or events) without any shared data and the need for synchronization primitives like mutexes or transactional memory.

We can collect messages of the same type coming from a component into an abstraction called reactive stream. Reactive streams satisfy all the monad rules. They behave mostly like infinite lazy lists, with the exception that we should never ask for an element directly, but should only apply the monadic transformations on them. We can use all the usual transformations like `map`, `filter` and `fold`.

This abstraction allows us to look at the system design as a data flow. We have the data sources – the components that send the messages, data receivers – the components that receive the messages and process them, and we have the data transformations – either simple functions like `filter`, `map`, `fold` and alike, or more complex stateful components that receive messages, do something to them, and send new messages as the output. Composing these smaller components allow us to create complex software systems. This allows for easier reasoning about the system logic since it uses the building blocks that are already known to functional programmers, just brings them to a new level. It makes writing asynchronous programs to be almost as simple as writing synchronous ones.

Because there is no explicit synchronization involved, and the whole design revolves around creating independent and isolated components that have no shared data, our systems become easily scalable both vertically – adding new components requires just connecting them to an existing reactive stream, either as sources, or as receivers; and horizontally by allowing to clone specific components so that they can spread the load. The design even allows us to create distributed systems without any changes to the code, as long as we are able to send messages between different nodes in the distributed system.

The abstractions that the FRP (functional reactive programming) uses are powerful enough to cover most use cases. It covers interactive UI applications where the message sources are events produced by the user – mouse movements, keyboard input and alike; the internal program logic is implemented in the transformation components, and the final receiver is the user interface, and thus the user herself. FRP also covers the distributed systems, and network services. Here, the flow usually goes from the system client, through the different nodes of the distributed system, or different components of the network service, back to the client in the form of a processed message (or a stream of messages) representing a result of the request.

References

1. Armstrong, J.: Making reliable distributed systems in the presence of software errors (2003)
2. Bainomugisha, E., Carreton, A.L., van Cutsem, T., Mostinckx, S., de Meuter, W.: A survey on reactive programming. ACM Comput. Surv. **45**(4), 52:1–52:34 (2013)
3. Butenhof, D.: Recursive mutexes (2005)
4. Carmack, J.: In-depth: functional programming in C++ (2012)
5. Charousset, D., Hiesgen, R., Schmidt, T.C.: CAF-the C++ actor framework for scalable and resource-efficient applications. In: Proceedings of the 4th International Workshop on Programming based on Actors Agents and Decentralized Control, pp. 15–28. ACM (2014)
6. Claessen, K.: Functional pearls: a poor man's concurrency monad (1999)
7. Epstein, J., Black, A.P., Peyton-Jones, S.: Towards Haskell in the cloud. SIGPLAN Not. **46**(12), 118–129 (2011)
8. Hewitt, C., Bishop, P., Steiger, R.: A universal modular actor formalism for artificial intelligence. In: Proceedings of the 3rd International Joint Conference on Artificial Intelligence, IJCAI 1973, pp. 235–245. Morgan Kaufmann Publishers Inc., San Francisco (1973)
9. Järvi, J.: C++ function object binders made easy. In: Czarnecki, K., Eisenecker, U.W. (eds.) GCSE 1999. LNCS, vol. 1799, pp. 165–177. Springer, Heidelberg (2000). https://doi.org/10.1007/3-540-40048-6_13
10. Kohlhoff, C.: Boost.asio, 48(0), 2003–2013 (2003). http://www.boost.org/doc/libs/
11. Lee, E.A.: The problem with threads. Computer **39**(5), 33–42 (2006)
12. Maier, I., Rompf, T., Odersky, M.: Deprecating the observer pattern. Technical report (2010)
13. Rodgers, D.P.: Improvements in multiprocessor system design. SIGARCH Comput. Archit. News **13**(3), 225–231 (1985)
14. Steele, G.L., Sussman, G.J.: Lambda: the ultimate imperative. Technical report (1976)
15. Wan, Z., Hudak, P.: Functional reactive programming from first principles. In: ACM SIGPLAN Notices, vol. 35, pp. 242–252. ACM (2000)

Immutables in C++: Language Foundation for Functional Programming

Zoltán Porkoláb(✉)

Faculty of Informatics, Department of Programming Languages and Compilers, Eötvös Loránd University,
Pázmány Péter sétány 1/C, Budapest 1117, Hungary
gsd@elte.hu
http://gsd.web.elte.hu

Abstract. The C++ programming language is a multiparadigm language, with a rich set of procedural, object-oriented, generative and, since C++11, functional language elements. The language is also well-known for its capability to map certain semantic features into the language syntax; therefore, the compiler can reason about them at compile time. Supporting functional programming with immutables is one of such aspects: the programmer can mark immutable components and the compiler checks potential violation scenarios and also optimizes the code according to the constant expectations.

The paper targets the non-C++ programmer audience less familiar with the technical details of C++ immutables and functional elements, as well as those C++ programmers who are interested in the development of the newest standard. We will survey the functional programming features of modern C++. The various types of constants and immutable memory storage will be discussed as well as the rules of const correctness to enable the static type system to catch const violations. Const and static const members of classes represent support for immutables in object-oriented programming. Specific programming tools, like mutable and const_cast enable the programmer changing constness for exceptional cases. Constexpr and relaxed constexpr (since C++14) objects and functions as well as lambda expressions have recently been added to C++ to extend the language support for functional programming. We also discuss the fundamentals of C++ template metaprogramming, a pure functional paradigm operating at compile time working with immutable objects.

Understanding the immutable elements and the rich set of functional language features with their interactions can help programmers to implement safe, efficient and expressive C++ programs in functional style.

Keywords: C++ · Functional programming · Immutable · Const · Constexpr · Template metaprogramming

V. Zsók et al. (Eds.): CEFP 2015, LNCS 10094, pp. 75–110, 2019.
https://doi.org/10.1007/978-3-030-28346-9_3

1 Introduction

The C++ programming language is a strongly typed, compiled, multiparadigm programming language supporting procedural, object-oriented, generative and (partially) functional programming styles. Its root goes back to the procedural C programming language [17] extending it with essential object-oriented features, like classes, inheritance and runtime polymorphism inherited from Simula67 [38]. Soon generic programming, implemented via templates became fundamental part of the language [8]. The Standard Template Library (STL), part of the standard C++ library, is still the prime example for the generic paradigm [37].

Functional programming features [11] were barely represented in the earlier versions of the C++ language. One of the existing elements was the pointer to function originated in the C language. A pointer to a function allows the programmers to represent algorithms as data; store them in variables, pass them as parameters or returning them from functions. The applications using pointers to functions are restricted in both semantical power and syntactical ease.

Pointers to member functions also exist in C++. As member functions are bound to classes, the type of such a pointer includes information about the class itself. However, the implementation is tricky as the same pointer can point either to a non-virtual member function (represented as an "ordinary" function pointer) or to a virtual function (effectively an offset in the virtual table).

Besides pointers to functions C++ programmers can use *functors* as functional programming elements as predicates, comparisons or other kind of executable code to pass to standard algorithms as parameters. Functors are classes with function call (parenthesis) operator defined, and they behave like higher order functions: they can be instantiated (with constructor parameters if necessary), and can be called via the function call operator. Although functors are not necessarily *pure* as they may have state (separate for each instantiations), they are fundamental tools for implementing functional elements, like currying, binding, etc.

In many cases functors are syntactically interchangeable with pointers to functions, e.g. when passing them as template parameters to STL algorithms.

Despite all the restrictions, syntactical and semantical issues, early attempts were made to implement complex libraries to achieve functional programming in the C++ language [7,18]. Most notable, FC++ [20,21] has implemented lazy lists, Currying and function composition among other functional features. The following works on functional features in C++ also targeted template metaprogramming [32,33].

As functional programming becomes more and more popular – not only as powerful programming languages, but also as formalism to specify semantics [19,47] – further language elements supporting functional style have come into prominence [25]. The *lambda expressions* have been added to C++ first as a library for more direct support for functional programming [15,16]. Lambda expressions provide an easy-to-use definition of unnamed function objects – closures [14]. To eliminate the shortcomings of a library-based implementation, the C++11 standard introduced native lambda support. Lambda functions are directly translated to C++ functors, where the function call operator is defined as const member function. C++14 further enhanced the usability of lambda captures with *generalized* lambdas, and with the possibility of using initialization expressions in the capture [13].

Despite all these achievements towards programming in functional style, C++ is not and never will be a (pure) functional programming language. As it is neither a pure object-oriented nor a procedural language. C++ is essentially a *multiparadigm* programming language: it does not prefer a single programming style over the others. One can write (a part of) a C++ program using the set of features from one or more paradigms according the problem to solve [5]. Moreover, these paradigms are necessary collaborating to each other. STL containers and algorithms with iterators form a generic library. In the same time, containers are implemented as (templated) classes with features of object-oriented programming, e.g. separation of interface and implementation, public methods and operators, etc. (Virtual functions, however, are mostly avoided for efficiency reasons except in some i/o related details.) On the lower end of the abstraction hierarchy, member functions are implemented in a procedural way.

Functional programming interweaves this hierarchy. STL algorithms are often parameterized with lambdas or functors representing predicates and comparators. Although no language rule forbids them having states, most experts suggest to implement predicates and comparators as pure functions since algorithms may copy them.

The STL itself suggests a functional approach: instead of writing loops and conditional statements, the programmer is encouraged to use algorithms, like `std::for_each` and `std::remove_if`. When the highly composable *ranges* will be incorporated to C++17 or later [28] they will add an additional support to this style. As explained in [26], the range comprehensions are in fact, monads.

The design goals of C++ according to Stroustrup include type safety, resource safety, performance, predictability, readability and the ease of learning the language [40]. These goals were achieved in different language versions to different extents.

Resource safety can be achieved only by the thoughtful process of the programmer using the appropriate language elements. C++ is not automatically garbage collected. (Although the standard allows using garbage collection, everyday C++ implementations usually avoid it). The programmer, however, can use smart pointers, like `std::unique_ptr` or `std::shared_ptr` (part of the standard since C++11) to control heap allocated memory. What is different in C++ from other usual object-oriented languages is that the notion of *resource* is far more general than just memory: every user defined feature can be handled as resource and controlled by the *Resource Acquisition Is Initialization* (RAII) method: resources can be allocated by constructors and will be (and usually shall be) disposed by a destructor. Special care should be paid to copying objects (either by copy over existing objects or initializing newly created ones) using assignment operators and copy contructors.

One of the major distinctive feature of C++ is the ability to map large variety of semantic concepts to compiler checked syntactical notations. Let us investigate the code snippet written in ANSI C on Listing 1. The program crashes for obvious reasons: we opened `input.txt` for read-only, but later we try to write into it. In the C language, the concept whether a file has been opened for read-only, write-only or read-write is not mapped to the language syntax at all; therefore, the compiler is unable to check the correctness of the usage (and it does not even attempt to do it). If we fail to use the files properly, we won't get diagnostic messages (like warnings) about it, our program compiles and (likely) crashes at runtime.

```
#include <stdio.h>

int main()  // wrong C program
{
   FILE *fp = fopen( "input.txt", "r");
   // ...
   fprintf( fp, "%s\n", "Hello input!");
   // ...
   fclose(fp);
}

$ gcc -std=c99 -pedantic -Wall -W wrong.c
$ ./a.out
Segmentation violation
```

Listing 1: Erroneous usage of C style input/output

In the C++ standard library, however, there are separate (abstract) types for read-only and write-only streams. Read-write streams in fact are inherited from both bases. Real resources (e.g. files and *stringstreams*, i.e. streams working over in-memory character strings) are represented by objects belonging to derived classes inherited from either the input or the output base classes.

As input and output operations are defined in the respective base classes, improper usage of streams cause compile time errors, as seen on Listing 2. Although, the diagnostic message caused by the improper usage is a bit diffuse, the first lines point to the exact problem. Again, the essence of the solution was that the library mapped the concepts of opening a stream either for reading or writing into the appropriate C++ types and, thus, the compiler is able to detect the mismatch as type error.

The concept of *immutability* is handled in a very similar way. The type of a (mutable) variable of type `X` is different from the type of an immutable variable of the same type `X`. Although, such distinction is not unusual in other programming languages, the generality and completeness of the mapping are what makes C++ solution special. We are speaking about a language, where multiple aliases of the same memory area (in form of *pointers*, *references*) are usual, and where objects of user defined classes are expected to behave the very same way as built-in types do.

```
#include <fstream>

int main()
{
    std::ifstream f;
    // ...
    f << "Hello input!" << std::endl;
}

$ g++ -std=c++11 -pedantic -Wall -W w.cpp

w.cpp: In function ‘int main()’:
w.cpp:10:8: error: no match for ‘operator<<’ in ‘f << "Hello input!"’

w.cpp:10:8: note: candidates are:
/usr/include/c++/4.6/ostream:581:5: note: template<class _CharT,
  class _Traits, class _Tp> std::basic_ostream<_CharT, _Traits>&
  std::operator<<(std::basic_ostream<_CharT,_Traits>&&,const _Tp&)
/usr/include/c++/4.6/ostream:528:5: note: template<class _Traits>
  std::basic_ostream<char, _Traits>& std::operator<<(
    std::basic_ostream<char, _Traits>&, const unsigned char*)
...
```

Listing 2: C++ can detect erroneous input/output usage at compile time

This paper is organized as follows. In Sect. 2 we survey the various ways we can define immutable objects in C++. We analyse *const correctness*, the set of complex rules allowing C++ to catch constant violations at compile time in Sect. 3. Here we will also discuss how constness works in STL and how the programmer can make exceptions of constness via const_cast or mutables. The constexpr objects and functions became official part of C++ since version C++11, and were substantially extended in C++14. We overview their possibilities in Sect. 4. Lambdas, their usage and whether and how they are pure functions are explained in Sect. 5. Template metaprograms discussed in Sect. 6 are pure functional language elements forming a compile time Turing complete sublanguage of C++. All such elements are immutable of necessity. The paper concludes in Sect. 7.

2 Immutable Elements in C++

In this section we first survey the elementary immutable objects in C++. Then we will see how we can express immutability for more complex constructs.

2.1 Preprocessor Macros

The C++ preprocessor runs as the first step of the compiler. The preprocessor executes trigraph replacement, line splicing, tokenization, comment replacement, and finally: macro expansion and directive handling. In this last step, identifiers defined as macros are replaced by their defined values. Naturally, many of such macros are defined as literals, and; therefore, they are immutable as we will see in the next subsection.

2.2 String Literals

String literals are sequences of characters surrounded by double quotes (and optionally prefixed since C++11). By the C++11 standard [12], a string literal is an *lvalue*, a notion which are usually connected to modifiable memory location. String literals however are strictly *read-only* character arrays with static lifetime. In many environments, the compiler may place such literals to read-only storage. Any attempt to modify such string literals results in *undefined behaviour*. Moreover, compilers are allowed to re-use the storage of string literals for other equal or overlapping literals. Most of the modern compilers do this, but remember: this is not mandatory, actual compilers may choose different implementations.

```
#include <iostream>

int main()
{
    char *hello1 = "Hello"; // hello1 points to 'H' and hello2
    char *hello2 = "Hello"; // likely points to the same place

    std::cout << static_cast<void*>(hello1) << "\t"
              << static_cast<void*>(hello2) << std::endl;

    *hello1[1] = 'a';   // could cause runtime error
}

$ g++ -std=c++14 -pedantic -Wall -W string1.cpp
In function 'int main()':
 warning: deprecated conversion from string constant to 'char*'
 [-Wwrite-strings]
     char *hello1 = "Hello"; // hello1 points to 'H' and hello2
                    ^

 warning: deprecated conversion from string constant to 'char*'
 [-Wwrite-strings]
     char *hello2 = "Hello"; // likely points to the same place
                    ^

$ ./a.out
0x4009f5    0x4009f5
Segmentation fault (core dumped)
```

Listing 3: String literals are immutable objects

Both string literals in the code example in Listing 3 have type `const char[6]` (one extra character is allocated for the terminating zero character of the string) which is converted to a *pointer to const* – `const char *`. We will see in Sect. 3.1 that normally pointers to const are not converted to pointers to non-consts. Here the exceptional rule is explained by the reverse compatibility requirement with millions of lines of legacy C code, where such assignments were legal and frequent [9]. At least the compiler warns us that this usage is deprecated in modern C++.

String literals must not be confused with named character arrays, which can be initialized by string literals and all their elements are mutable (unless they are declared as constant arrays). In Listing 4 `arr1` and `arr2` are two separate mutable character arrays of type `char[6]` placed strictly into different memory areas. The arrays are initialized by the same sequence of characters. The second notion is just a simplification to denote character array initialization list.

```
#include <iostream>

int main()
{
    char arr1[] = {'H','e','l','l','o','\0'};
    char arr2[] = "Hello";
    const char arr3[] = "Hello forever";
    arr1[1] = 'a';    // ok, arr1 is mutable
}
```

Listing 4: Character arrays are mutable by default

Naturally both `arr1` and `arr2` are mutable, so we can modify any of the array elements (although setting/removing the zero character may confuse some string-related standard library functions). The `arr3` is declared as `const`, therefore, that array is immutable.

2.3 Named Constants

A *const object* is an object of type `const T` or a non-mutable subobject of such an object. Such named const objects have some less known properties. They may appear, for example, as `case` labels in `switch` statements, and they may serve as the size of static arrays.

In Listing 5, `c1` and `c2` are initialized with *constant expressions* (constants whose values can be computed by the compiler at compile time). Such constant objects can serve as case labels or as the size in an array declaration. (Since C++11 *variable sized arrays* are allowed, but only for objects with automatic life time, like non-static local variables.) Object `c3`, however, must not be used, as it is initialized with a runtime value coming from a non-constexpr function `f` as a return value. In all other aspects `c1`, `c2`, and `c3` have the same behaviour. Similar situations with *constexpr* function will be discussed in Sect. 4.

```
int f(int i) { return i; } // not constexpr

int main()
{
    const int c1 = 1;    // initialized at compile time, optimized out
    const int c2 = 2;    // initialized at compile time, but needs memory
    const int *p = &c2;  // ...since a pointer points to it
    const int c3 = f(3); // f() is initialized at runtime, needs memory

    static int t1[c1];
    static int t2[c2];

    int i;
    // read i
    switch(i)
    {
    case c1: std::cout << "c1"; break;
    case c2: std::cout << "c2"; break;
    // case label c3 does not reduce to an integer constant
    // case c3: std::cout << "c1"; break;
    }
}
```

Listing 5: Named constants

The compiler tries to optimize the const objects. Here the compiler may decide not to allocate memory for object `c1`, but should allocate memory for `c2` and `c3`. The reason, why `c3` requires memory is obvious: it is initialized at runtime, therefore the compiler cannot replace all of its occurrences with its value. The situation with object `c2` is a bit more interesting: its address is used to initialize a pointer (a pointer to const). Since pointers must point to legal memory locations by the C++ standard, the compiler must store `c2` in such a location.

2.4 Static Const Members

In object-oriented programming, we try to organize our code in classes. Objects are instantiations of such classes. The names of types, methods and data belonging to a certain class are expressed as members of that class. For immutables this is the same.

Immutable values, which are the same for all objects of a given class, are declared as **`static const`** in the class declaration. We may think of them as global constants nested into the namespace of the class. Static members of a class have a *static* lifetime, i.e. they are initialized before the start of the `main` function and destructed after the `main` function successfully finished. For elementary types this means that the initialization is done by the compiler. For those types having non-trivial constructor functions (like most of the standard containers) the constructor is called before starting the `main` function.

Static members are not subobjects of their class. Similar to other static members, static constants should also be defined to tell the compiler which source is responsible to store the static member. In this definition, static consts should be initialized either implicitly, having a default constructor or explicitly with an initializer expression. For *integral* and *enumeration* types (like `bool`, `char`, or `long` the initialization can be placed inside class definition. According the *One Definition Rule* (ODR) initialization should happen in exactly one of the places as seen on Listing 6.

```
class X
{
    static const int  c1 = 7; // ok, but remember definition
    // static const int  c2 = f(2); // error: not const expression
    static const double c3; // not integral, don't initialize here
};
void f()
{
  const int X::c1;                // must not re-initialized
  const double X::c3 = 3.14; // not integral, must initialized here
}
```

Listing 6: Static const members allocated outside of objects

Static consts are immutables with the same value for all objects of the class. There are situations where a member should be immutable for the lifetime of the object but having a different value for different objects.

(Non-static) const members represent such subobjects. Unlike their static counterparts, such constant members are *subobjects*, i.e. they are part of the object. In Listing 7, each object of class Y has its own (possibly different) immutable value, initialized by the constructor.

```
class Y
{
    Y() : id1( gen_id1() ) { }
    const int id1;
    const int id2 = gen_id2();// since C++11 same as Y():id2(gen_id()) { }
    int gen_id1() { ... }
    int gen_id2() { ... }
};
```

Listing 7: Non-static const members are allocated inside every instance

Object-level constants are immutable, but their values can be different in different objects. Hence, they must be stored in every object. Since C++11 we can initialize non-static data members – the meaning is the same as the use of the initializer list in the constructor as seen in Listing 7.

3 Const Correctness

In the previous chapter we had a survey of the immutable C++ objects. However, in C++ objects may be accessed via aliases: pointers, references. To catch possible violations of constness at compile time C++ provides a complex set of *const-correctness* rules. In the following we enumerate these rules.

3.1 Non-class Types

While C++ objects are mutable by default (with the exceptions we discussed in the previous section), const qualified objects are immutable. Any attempt to write to them causes compile time error. The const qualifier is part of the object's type: hence on Listing 8 the type of `ci` is `const int`.

```
          int  i = 4;  // not const
               i = 5;  // i is mutable
    const int ci = 6;  // const
              ci = 7;  // error: ci is immutable
```

Listing 8: Mutable and immutable variables

In C++ we use the *address-of* (`&`) operator to create a pointer value pointing to an object. We can access and modify mutable objects via pointers. The problem is that in most cases it is impossible to determine at compile time where a pointer points to at runtime. If ordinary pointers to type `T` could point to objects of type `const T`, then it would introduce a Trojan horse to modify immutable objects as we see on Listing 9.

```
int   i = 4;    // non const
int *ip = &i;
    *ip = 5;    // ok
const int ci = 6;   // const

if ( runtime_value )
{
    ip = &ci; // ???
}
*ip = 7;   // where does ip point now?
```

Listing 9: Const-correctness

In order to avoid this issue, C++ forbids the assignment of pointers to const-qualified objects to ordinary pointers. We can say that the type of `const T*` is not convertible to `T*`, as we see on Listing 10.

```
int     i = 4;
int   *ip = i;
const int ci = 6;  // const

if ( runtime_value )
{
    // this would be compile error:
    // ip = &ci;
}
*ip = 7;   // ok, ip points to mutable object
```

Listing 10: Constness must not be lost in assignment

Since pointers are fundamental in various situations in C++ including many use cases of the standard library, the language provides a way to set pointers to immutable objects. An object with type of pointer to `const T` can store a pointer value to an immutable object of type `T`, it can be dereferenced, but the dereferenced value is immutable. To keep const correctness, pointers to const values cannot be assigned to pointers to mutable objects. We must not "lose" constness.

This rule is not symmetric: we can still assign addresses of mutable objects to pointers to const variables. In that case, the pointed (originally mutable) object is handled as immutable when accessed via the pointer to const, see Listing 11.

```
int  i = 4;          // mutable
const int ci = 6;    // const

int *ip = &i;              // ok
const int *cip = &ci;      // ok

 ip  = cip;          // compile error: T* <- const T*
 cip = ip;           // ok:      const T* <- T*
*cip = 7;            // compile error: *cip is immutable
```

Listing 11: Conversion rules between pointers

There are different conventions to define a pointer to const. Some programmers prefer to use the `const T *` order, while others emphasize the immutability of the pointed location to move the `const` keyword between the type name and the * declarator in form of `T const *`. Both versions are supported by the literature and have the same meaning as long as we use the `const` keyword on the left side of the * declarator as on Listing 12.

```
const int *cip1;        // pointer to immutable
int const *cip2;        // cip2 has the same type as cip1's
int *const ptr1 = &i; // ptr1 is immutable
const int *ptr2;        // ptr2 points to immutable
const int *const ptr3 = &i;
```

Listing 12: Immutable pointers and pointers to immutables

To declare a pointer itself as immutable (pointing either to a mutable or an immutable object) we use the `const` keyword on the right side of the * declarator. In this way, in the next example we declare `ptr1`, `ptr2` and `ptr3` as a const pointer to mutable object, a non-const pointer to immutable object and a const pointer to immutable object, respectively.

Note, that const (immutable) objects (like `ptr1` and `ptr3`) must be initialized when defined.

3.2 Constness of Class Types

The rules discussed in the previous Subsect. 3.1 create a set of compile time guidelines to ensure that objects defined as consts won't be modified during runtime. However, these rules are not yet complete when we consider class types.

Consider the `Date` class on Listing 13 which encapsulates three `int` data members and provides related access methods representing a (very simplified) data class.

```
class Date
{
public:
    Date( int year, int month = 1, int day = 1);
    // ...
    int getYear();
    int getMonth();
    int getDay();

    void set(int y, int m, int d);
    // ...
private:
    int year;
    int month;
    int day;
};
```

Listing 13: The original Date class

The rules discussed in Subsect. 3.1 stand here too. Any attempt to modify a const object causes a compile error on Listing 14. The major difference between elementary types and classes is that elementary objects can be modified only by assignment (via the objects themselves, or via references or pointers denoting them), classes, however, can be also modified by member functions. How should the compiler handle the method calls?

```
void f()
{
  const Date my_birthday(1963,11,11);
        Date curr_date(2015,7,10);
  // my_birthday =  curr_date;    // compile error: my_birthday is const
  cout << myBirthday.getYear(); // read const
  myBirthday.set(2015,7,10);    // modify const?
  cout << currDate.getYear();   // read non-const
  currDate.set(2015,7,11);      // modify non-const
}
```

Listing 14: Access const and non-const objects via member functions

It is obvious, that `myBirthday.set(2015,7,10)` violates the seemingly complete set of const correctness rules. But how can the compiler make difference between methods allowed and forbidden for immutable objects?

The naïve approach to check the body of the methods fails for various reasons; the definition of the method can be in a different source file, the method can call other methods, etc. C++ has chosen a more syntax-driven approach: we should explicitly mark methods callable on immutable objects as **const** methods as part of their signature. Non-const methods cannot be applied to const objects regardless whether they attempt to modify their objects or not.

In the code snippet on Listing 15, the compiler allows the call of `getYear` on the immutable object `myBirthday`, since it is declared as a const method, but emits diagnostics for the call of `set`.

The `this` parameter, passed as the hidden first argument for all non-static methods is used to check the call. The `this` parameter of a const method is declared as pointer to const, whereas in a non-const method it is a pure pointer to the class. As the address of an immutable object is obviously a *pointer to const*, such an address can be passed to const methods. Otherwise, const methods can not be applied to non-const objects based on the required const to non-const conversion. On the other hand, since a non-const `this` argument can be converted to pointer to const, const methods are callable on non-immutable objects.

On the other hand, the compiler must not "trust" on whether the programmer denoted the constness in the correct way for the const methods. Here the situation is also covered by the rules we learned in Subsect. 3.1. Data members

```
class Date
{
public:
    Date( int year, int month = 1, int day = 1);
    // ...
    int getYear() const;
    int getMonth() const;
    int getDay() const;

    void set(int y, int m, int d);
    // ...
private:
    int year;
    int month;
    int day;
};
void f()
{
  const Date my_birthday(1963,11,11);  // immutable
        Date curr_date(2015,7,10);     // mutable
  // my_birthday =  curr_date;     // compile error: my_birthday is const
  cout << myBirthday.getYear();    // fine: const member on const
  // myBirthday.set(2015,7,10);    // error: non-const member on const
  cout << currDate.getYear();      // fine: const member on mutable
  currDate.set(2015,7,11);         // fine: non-const member on mutable
}
```

Listing 15: Const and non-const member functions

in member functions are accessed via the `this` pointer. As the `this` parameter for such methods is implicitly declared as pointer to const, all modifications via `this` are marked as errors by the compiler. Similarly, the calls of non-const methods from const methods yield errors.

The invisible `this` parameter can also be used for overloading. This pattern on Listing 16 is frequently used for access operators, which should be used both for reading const objects and for modifying mutables.

```
      T& operator[](size_t idx);
const T& operator[](size_t idx) const;
```

Listing 16: Overloading on constness

Only non-static member functions can be declared as const methods. Static member functions and namespace functions should be declared as `constexpr` to express their "pure" behaviour. We will discuss constexpr in Sect. 4.

3.3 Mutable

There are certain situations where we want to modify subobjects inside const objects. Consider the `Point` class on Listing 17 with objects accessed concurrently from multiple threads. To read consistent x and y pairs of coordinates, the method `getXY(int &x, int &y)` locks the object. For this purpose, we place a `mutex` object as a class member. Naturally, `getXY` is declared as a `const` method as it is just reading the object.

```
struct Point
{
    void getXY(int& x, int& y) const;

    double xCoord;
    double yCoord;
    std::mutex  m;
};
void Point::getXY(int& x, int& y) const    // does not compile
{
    std::lock_guard<std::mutex>  guard(m); // constructor locks m
    x = xCoord;
    y = yCoord;
}                                          // destructor unlocks m
```

Listing 17: Reading x and y coordinates is protected by a mutex

Unfortunately, the code above does not compile. Locking and unlocking obviously are changing the state of the mutex object, i.e. they are non-const methods. As we learned in Sect. 3.2, we normally cannot alter an object's (or its particular subobject's) state (like the mutex `m` in our example) using a const member function.

To make an exception from the rule, we can declare the mutex `m` as `mutable`. Mutable means that the (sub)object can be altered even when it is part of a const object or when accessed from a const member function.

```
struct Point
{
    void getXY(int& x, int& y) const;

    double xCoord;
    double yCoord;
    mutable std::mutex  m;
};
```

Listing 18: A class with a member declared as mutable

Mutables are exceptional objects, and we should use them only in exceptional cases. Such situations include among others managing internal states, like a cache or counters, and also managing mutexes, like in our example on Listing 18.

3.4 Constant Correctness in STL

The Standard Template Library (STL) is an essential part of the C++ language. The success of the STL is based on its flexibility and extensibility. Programmers can re-use standard containers and algorithms connecting them by iterators instead of writing specific code for each individual problem [4,27]. STL makes the programmer's work faster, safer and more predictable [29]. Naturally, the STL should support the const correct programming [22].

Consider the usual implementation of the `find` STL algorithm on Listing 19.

```
template <typename It, typename T>
It find( It begin, It end, const T& t)
{
    while (begin != end)
    {
        if ( *begin == t )
        {
            return begin;
        }
        ++begin;
    }
    return end;
}
```

Listing 19: Canonical implementation of the STL find algorithm

When we apply the algorithm to an immutable array, e.g. to a const array of integers on Listing 20, the iterator will be deduced to the same type as the first two parameters, i.e. to a pointer to const. Thus, const correctness stands.

For STL containers, the situation is a bit different as instead of pointers *iterators* and *const_iterators* are used to walk through container elements and to refer to them. Dereferencing (applying the star operator for) an `iterator` results in a left value reference to the `value_type` of the container. Dereferencing a `const_iterator` results in a non-writable *const reference*. The type `const_iterator` is not a `const iterator` which would mean an immutable iterator. However, a `const_iterator`, is a mutable object, e.g. one can modify it and can walk through the container, but the referred objects are handled as immutables as seen on Listing 21.

The `iterator` and `const_iterator` values are generated by the `begin` and `end` methods of the containers. Since C++11 the `std` namespace `begin` and `end` functions are also available. Namespace functions provide the iterators in a

```
const int t[] = { 1, 2, 3, 4, 5 };
auto len = sizeof(t)/sizeof(t[0]);
auto *p = std::find( t, t+len, 3)  // const int *p

if ( p != t+len )
{
    std::cout << *p; // ok to read
    // *p = 6;       // error to write
}
```

Listing 20: Const correctness in STL

```
void f(const std::vector<int> &v)
{
    auto i = std::find( v.begin(), v.end(), 3); // const_iterator
    if ( v.end() != i )
    {
        std::cout << *i; // ok to read
        // error: *i = 6;
    }
}
```

Listing 21: Const containers provide read only access to elements

unique and non-intrusive way for STL containers and classical C-style arrays. The trick here is the overloading on constness: const variations of the `begin` and `end` methods are the methods callable on constant containers and they return `const_iterator`.

C++11 provides more advanced type deduction with the `auto` keyword. Its motivation was mainly to shorten iterator and const_iterator declarations. However, it is a frequent situation when we want to apply a `const_iterator` to an originally non constant container. This will not work with `auto` and `begin` or `end` methods, as the auto declaration deduces the type from the initializer expression, which is the return value of the `begin` and `end` methods, i.e. an `iterator` in case of a non-const container [23].

```
void f(std::vector<int> &v, const std::vector<int> &cv)
{
    auto i = std::find(  v.begin() , v.end(), 3); //iterator
    auto i = std::find( cv.begin(), cv.end(), 4); //const_iterator
    auto i = std::find( v.cbegin(), v.cend(), 5); //const_iterator
}
```

Listing 22: Using `cbegin` and `cend` to return `const_iterator`

To enforce the return of const_iterator type even for non-const containers, new methods cbegin and cend were introduced in the C++11 standard, see Listing 22. Similar namespace methods exist as cbegin, cend, and crbegin, and crend for iterators and reverse iterators. For some mysterious reason, namespace functions returning const_reverse_iterator were missing in C++11, and the issue has been fixed only in C++14.

3.5 Casting Const Away

Based on the C/C++ philosophy that the ultimate control belongs to the programmer, there is an explicit cast to converting const objects to non-const ones. However, as all other cast operations, it should be used with extra care to avoid *undefined behaviour*. The basic rule is that we can cast away constness of pointers to objects and lvalues.

Even when the compiler allows us to cast constness away, the result may be surprising. In the example on Listing 23, we declare a variable const, then we modify it via const_cast and a non-const pointer.

```
#include <iostream>

int main()
{
  const int ci = 10;

  int *ip = const_cast<int *>(&ci);
  ++*ip;
  std::cout << ci << " " << *ip << std::endl;
}
$ g++ -std=c++11 -pedantic -Wall -W const.cpp
$ ./a.out
10 11
```

Listing 23: Const cast may lead to undefined behaviour

There are a few cases when we cannot avoid the use of const_cast. One example is when a member function modifying the object's state should be defined as a constant member function. Suppose, we have a tree data structure to store elements ordered by some key values. We might provide a member function to balance the tree. Calling such balance member function from insert, which is a non-const member function itself, is fine. However, when we want balance to be available as a standalone API method, we should decide about its constness. Strictly by C++ terms, balance is not a constant method as it is modifying the object's data. However, from the viewpoint of the user, the method behaves like a const: no new element has been inserted, the order of the elements remains the same. It is tempting to declare balance as const member function and simply cast the constness of the this pointer away to make class members modifiable.

Although, the scenario above is possible in technical terms, there are strong arguments against it. Using `const_cast` is extremely dangerous for objects that were originally declared as `const` (see Listing 23). Whenever it is possible, use `mutable` objects instead. Declaring a member function as `const` tells the user that this function can be used in a multithreaded environment in a safe way. That is not true in the example above (except that we use some very aggressive locking inside `balance`, which may ruin the performance).

4 Constexpr

Compile-time expressions, i.e. expressions that can be evaluated at translation time, always had a specific role in the C++ language. Such expressions can be used to define an array size, a `case` label or a non-type template argument. On the other hand, the compiler environment is enforced to compute these expressions; C++ template metaprogramming is largely based on this fact. The phrase *translation time* usually means compile time but may include link time activity as well [36].

Interesting enough, by the C++ standard, the value of an expression computed at translation time is not necessary equal to the value of the same expression computed at runtime [50]. Let us see the example on Listing 24 quoted from the standard. The size of the character array must be compiled at translation time, but the value of the integer variable *size* can be evaluated at runtime. In such cases their values may differ.

```
bool f()
{
    // Must be evaluated at translation time
    char array[1 + int(1 + 0.2 - 0.1 - 0.1)];

    // May be evaluated at run-time
    int size = 1 + int(1 + 0.2 - 0.1 - 0.1);

    return sizeof(array) == size; // unspecified: true or false
}
```

Listing 24: Compile-time expressions and run-time expressions

In classical C++03 constant expressions are restricted to the use of literals, built-in operators, and macros. They must not contain functions or operators of any kind, even when their return value could be trivially computed from the compile-time given arguments as we see on Listing 25.

C++11 makes constant expressions more manageable introducing `constexpr` functions and expressions. The idea is to make translation time constant computation more expressive and thus partially replacing unmanageable macro and template metaprogramming elements.

```
#define AVERAGE(X,Y)  (((x)+(y))/2)
double average(double x, double y) { return (x+y)/2; }

size_t s1 = sizeof(long);
size_t s2 = sizeof(short);

// constant expressions in C++03
const int a = (sizeof(long)+sizeof(short))/2;
const int b = AVERAGE(sizeof(long),sizeof(short));

// not constant expressions in C++03
const int c = AVERAGE(s1,s2);
const int d = average(sizeof(long),sizeof(short));
```

Listing 25: Constant and non-constant expressions in C++03

4.1 Constexpr Functions

C++11 introduced constexpr functions, functions that can be computed at translation time when all their parameters are known. As initially this feature was planned as a minor feature to replace hard to maintain macros and small template metaprograms, it had a minimalist design. The body of a constexpr function was restricted to a single *return* statement. Constexpr member functions also were implicitly constant member functions.

As the new feature was a success, constexpr rules have been relaxed. Constexpr functions since C++14 may contain declarations, sequences, and control statements similar to "normal" functions as demonstrated on Listing 26. The rules also have been changed in the way that non-static constexpr member functions are not const member functions any more.

```
// in C++11
constexpr int pow( int base, int exp) noexcept
{
    return  exp == 0 ? 1 : base * pow(base, exp-1) ;
}

// in C++14
constexpr int pow( int base, int exp) noexcept
{
    auto result = 1;
    for (int i = 0; i < exp; ++i) result *= base;
    return result;
}
```

Listing 26: Constexpr in C++11 and in C++14

Even in C++14 there are serious restrictions on constexpr functions. They must not contain `asm` definitions, `goto` statements, `try` blocks, and must not declare static or thread local variables. Member constexpr functions must not be virtual. These rules ensure compile time computability. Other C++ rules, e.g overloading, work as usual.

Rules for constexpr functions are also designed to avoid side effects as we experience on Listing 27. The safe rule is to access only variables which have life time started inside the `constexpr` expression.

```
constexpr int f(int n)
{
    static int value = n;  // error, cause side effect
    int i = 1;
    int j = n;             // ok, j is not constexpr
    constexpr int x = n;   // error
    constexpr int y = i;   // ok, life of i starts in f
    return y;
}
```

Listing 27: Constexpr rules are to avoid side effects

Sometimes there is a thin line between what can be constexpr and what can not. On the Listing 28 a ternary operator defines the value of member `m`. When the constructor parameter is true, the value of `m` can be computed at translation time. Otherwise, the initialization depends on a run-time value, so the compiler flags an error.

```
int x;                              // not constant
struct A
{
    constexpr A(bool b) : m( b ? 42 : x) { }
    int m;
};
constexpr int v = A(true).m;    // OK: constructor initializes m with 42
constexpr int w = A(false).m;   // error: initializer of m is x
                                // which is not known at translation time
```

Listing 28: Expression computed at translation time or flags an error depending on the value of `b`

One of the advantages of constexpr functions over template metaprograms is that template metaprograms can only emulate floating point numbers, usually with a pair of integer, while constexpr functions can work with native floating point types.

4.2 Constexpr Objects

Constexpr objects are constant objects having values that are known (or computable) at translation time. We can apply the `constexpr` keyword both for variables and for variable templates as seen on Listing 29.

```
constexpr size_t sizeof_long  = sizeof(long);
constexpr size_t sizeof_short = sizeof(short);
template <typename T>
T PI()
{
  constexpr T Pi = T(3.1415926535897932385);
  return Pi;
}
```

Listing 29: Constexpr objects

Not only objects of built-in types can be specified as constexpr objects, but also objects from those class types which can be safely constructed at translation time. Such types are called *literal types*. Literal types must not include any component which would indicate runtime activity, e.g. a virtual base. Scalar types, reference types, the `void`, and arrays of literal types are considered as literal types. Also classes with non-static members of (non-volatile) literal types, `constexpr` member functions, `constexpr` constructor and with trivial destructor are literal types [49].

On the Listing 30 we created a literal type representing a circle with a given radius set by the constructor, inspired by [3]. Member functions are defined to compute the perimeter and the area of the object as well as a non-const member function `magnify` to change the radius by a ratio. The namespace function `create` returns a new circle created by the first argument applying the second argument as magnifying ratio.

In the example we created a literal type `Circle` with a single attribute `radius` initialized by the only constructor. The constexpr getter methods `perim` and `area` are declared `const` since in C++14 non-static constexpr member functions are no longer implicit const member functions.

The `magnify` function is a constexpr but non-const member, as it changes the object's attribute value. Obviously, such a member cannot be applied to a constexpr object, but can be used for non-const objects, like the local `c2` object inside the `create` namespace function. Declaring `magnify` as `constexpr` guarantees, that all the constexpr restrictions are hold, therefore, the function can be safely called from the constexpr function `create`.

The local variable `c2` of `Circle` type is not defined constexpr inside the `create` function – we will modify it in the next line. We are allowed to create non-const local variables in constexpr functions. The important aspect here is that the lifetime of `c2` starts inside the constexpr function.

```
constexpr double sqr(double d) { return d*d; }
constexpr double Pi = 3.1415926535897932385;

class Circle // literal type
{
public:
    constexpr Circle( double r) noexcept : radius(r) { }
    constexpr double perim() const noexcept { return 2*radius*Pi; }
    constexpr double area() const noexcept { return sqr(radius)*Pi; }
    constexpr void magnify(double ratio) noexcept { radius *= ratio; }
private:
    double radius;
};
constexpr Circle create( const Circle &c, double ratio) noexcept
{
    Circle c2 = c;
    c2.magnify(ratio);
    return c2;
}
int main()
{
    constexpr Circle c(2.5);
    constexpr double p = c.perim();
    constexpr double a = c.area();
    constexpr Circle c2 = create(c,1.5);
}
```

Listing 30: A Circle class implemented as a literal type

In the main function all objects can be defined as constexpr. Such objects can be placed into ROM if the environment supports that. The constructors of these objects will run at translation time.

Constexpr functions and methods can be called with non-constexpr arguments. In such situations, they will be executed at run-time. Allowing to call constexpr functions at run-time avoid code duplication. However, the restrictions for these functions as described in this section still hold.

Constexpr functions are "running" at translation time, therefore, their inspection is extremely hard. The usual method is to inject a runtime argument, and debug the function at runtime. Proper constexpr debuggers are yet to be implemented.

5 Lambda Expressions

The Standard Template Library (STL) is a major component of the standard C++ library. In STL *containers* implement various data structures, and *algorithms* present numerous activities over them in form of namespace functions.

To provide a smooth, generic connection between these two components, algorithms access the containers via *iterators* [4,27].

STL supports functional style programming as it replaces the necessity of the iteration over containers with the use of predefined algorithms, like `remove_if` or `for_each`. Such algorithms are frequently parameterized by some *callable* objects. The predicate in `remove_if` and the repeated activity for `for_each` are provided as a callable parameter for these algorithms. In its most primitive form, such a callable object is a pointer to function.

However, these functions often require access to the local variables in the scope of the algorithms, e.g. the predicate for the `remove_if` may depend on the values of local variables in the call site. Ordinary C++ functions have no access to the context of the call site. To bridge the problem, a *functor* – a class with function call operator – can be defined and used instead of the function pointer. Function objects (instances of functor classes) can be created and the mentioned local variables are either copied into or referenced by its attributes. These objects are passed to the STL algorithms as parameters and can be called inside the algorithms. The procedure, however, requires a significant amount of boiler-plate code as we see on Listing 31.

```
struct BetweenFunctor
{
public:
    BetweenFunctor(int a, int b) : m_a(a), m_b(b) { }
    bool operator()(int n) const { return m_a < n && n < m_b; }
private:
    int m_a;
    int m_b;
};
void filter(vector<int>& v, int x, int y)
{
    v.erase( remove_if(v.begin(),v.end(),BetweenFunctor(x,y)),
             v.end());
}
```

Listing 31: Removing elements from a container using a functor

The idea to provide an easy-to-use definition of unnamed function objects – so called *closures* – which are capable of accessing (capturing) the variables in the call context led to the notion of *lambda expressions*. Lambdas have been introduced to C++ first as a user library in Boost.Lambda [16,48]. From C++11 they are part of the core language. Since then, lambdas are widely used as parameters in the Standard Template Library algorithms, functions executed by `std::thread`, and various other places.

Lambda expressions in C++ can be associated with equivalent functor classes and function objects. The runtime object created from the lambda expression is called *closure* and is assignable and callable. Its type, the *closure class* is unnamed. Nevertheless, we can refer to it by using the C++11 `decltype` expression. On Listing 32 we see the equivalent program snippet to Listing 31. Here we are using lambda expression to remove elements from the vector. The expressive power of the lambda solution over the functor is well worth observing.

```
void filter(vector<int> &v, int x, int y)
{
    v.erase( remove_if(v.begin(),v.end(),
                       [x,y](int n) { return x < n && n < y; }),
             v.end());
}
```

Listing 32: Removing elements from a container using lambda expression

We can understand the lambda construction by comparing it to the equivalent functor on Listing 31. The lambda expression starts with the `[ ]` *lambda introducer*. The optional *captured variables* `x` and `y` represent the data members of the functor class initialized by the `x` and `y` variables of the calling context respectively. The parameter and the function body of the lambda expression form the function call operator of the functor defined as a constant member. It can contain multiple statements. The return type is automatically deduced by the corresponding C++ language rules. When that type is not suitable, the required return type can be denoted explicitly [15].

5.1 Capture

The major advantage of a lambda over a functor is that the lambda can access the calling context using captured variables. These variables can be captured either by value or by reference. Default capture is by value: that is, the captured variables are copied into the closure object when it is created. As a consequence, further changes of the original variables captured by value are invisible in the lambda expression. We can imagine it as the capture by value creates a "snapshot" of the calling context.

When variables are captured by reference, the closure initializes references to the original storage. The lambda expression thus always sees the actual value of the captured variables. Capturing variables by reference is denoted by the `&` symbol.

On Listing 33, the `filter` function removes all elements from vector `v` which have a value between `x` and `y`. The parameters `x` and `y` of the function are captured by value, while the local variable `cnt` is captured by reference. Therefore, this latter variable can be modified from the lambda expression, and at the end of the function `cnt` contains the number of the elements removed.

```
void filter(vector<int> &v, int x, int y)
{
    int cnt = 0;
    v.erase( remove_if(v.begin(),v.end(),
                       [x,y,&cnt](int n) { if ( x < n && n < y )
                                             { ++cnt; return true; }
                                           else
                                             return false;      }),
             v.end());
}
```

Listing 33: Variables captured by value and by reference

Lambda expressions are equivalent with *constant* function call operators on the closure type. Any attempt from the lambda expression to modify the captured `x` and `y` will result in an error. Interesting enough, the lambda expression is allowed to modify the variables captured by reference. This has the same behaviour as we can experience with traditional classes: constant member functions can make modifications via reference members.

We can allow the modification of the *copies* of the variables captured by value. We indicate non-constness of the lambda function with the `mutable` keyword before the body of the lambda expression. However, the modifications affect only the copies, the original variables remain unchanged.

We can capture multiple values without enlisting them individually. The `[=]` sign means capturing *all* variables by value and `[&]` means capturing all by reference. We can mix values and reference captures, like `[=,&cnt]`. Naturally, when using the `=` or `&` notion, only the variables actually used in the lambda expression will be stored/referred. Global variables or static members are not captured, but can be used as usual.

5.2 Capturing this Pointer

The `this` pointer is not captured by default, it should be captured explicitly by value or by using the `[=]` notation. Capturing `this` is a necessary and sufficient requirement to access members of a class. In Listing 34 the lambda inside the `print` member function should capture `this` to access the data member `s`.

```
struct X
{
    int s;
    vector<int> v;
    void print() const {
        for_each(v.begin(), v.end(), [=](int n) { cout << n*s << " "; });
    }
};
```

Listing 34: Capturing `this` pointer

Capturing pointers and particularly capturing **this** can be dangerous. If the pointed memory area is destroyed but the pointer to it still holds in the closure object, calling the lambda can be fatal. In the example on Listing 35 the closure captures the **this** pointer and then it is stored in a **std::function** object. Later it is activated twice: once when the pointed object is still alive, and the second time after the object is destroyed. That second call will likely cause runtime error.

```
std::function<void (int)> f;

struct X
{
    X(int i) : ii(i) {}
    int ii;
    void addLambda()    {
        f = [=](int n) { if (n == ii) cout << n; else cout << ii; };
    }
};
int main()
{
    {
        std::unique_ptr<X> up = std::make_unique<X>(4);
        up->addLambda();
        f(4);  // calls lambda: ok
    } // destroys the X object

    f(4);  // calls lambda: likely aborts!
}
```

Listing 35: Wrong usage of lambda with captured **this** pointer

In C++17, there will be possible to capture the enclosing object by value, instead of capturing the **this** pointer.

5.3 Constant Initialization by Lambda

One of the special use cases of the lambda expressions are the initializations of constant objects. Constants must be initialized and later they must not be assigned to. In some cases, the initialization value heavily depends on the calling context and should be computed by complex calculations. The usual way to do this is to execute the necessary computations in a separate function and to initialize the constant object by the return value of that function. However, this solution has a number of drawbacks. The code of the function will be separated from the object to be initialized. Using the actual environment of the initialization requires to pass a possible large number of parameters to the function.

It would be somehow useful to handle the variable as non-const for a while, and make it immutable only after we calculated its "final" value. Although, this is not possible literally, we can simulate it by lambda.

```
void f()
{
    bool some_variable_in_context = ...;
    const int ci = [&]{
    int ci;  // non-const shadow variable
    ci = some_default_value;
    if ( some_variable_in_context )   // using the context
    {
        // and do some operations and calculate the value of ci
        ci = some_calculated_value;
    }
    return ci;
    } (); // note: () invokes the lambda!
    // using the const ci
    // ...
}
```

Listing 36: Initialization of a constant using lambda

On Listing 36 we are going to initialize the constant `ci` variable. Instead of initializing it by a function, we define a lambda expression right in the place of initialization capturing the whole context. In this lambda first we define a non-const variable with the same name as the const to be initialized. This "shadow" variable will be used to calculate the initializer value. The body of the lambda expression looks like and acts like the continuation of the original function. Once we calculated the required value, we close the lambda expression and immediately call it, thus, initializing the constant by its return value.

This method is usually more readable and manageable than the alternatives.

5.4 Generic Lambdas

Lambda expressions in C++11 were not generic: i.e. we had to apply various tricks to handle lambdas in templated environment. In C++14, however, we can write *generic* lambda expression, which works in a *polymorphic* way, similarly to a template functor [43]. To express generality we use the `auto` keyword at parameter declaration. Advanced C++14 return type deduction is also applied on the example on the Listing 37.

```
// in C++11
for_each( begin(v), end(v),
              [](const decltype(*begin(v))& x) { cout << x; } );
// in C++14
for_each( begin(v), end(v), [](const auto& x) { cout << x; } );
```

Listing 37: Generic (polymorphic) lambda expressions in C++14

5.5 Generalized Lambda Capture

As we have seen earlier, lambdas can capture variables in the environment either by value or by reference. The first will copy them into the closure object, the second will initialize a reference inside the closure object to the captured variable outside. Capture by reference can be dangerous, especially when the closure object lives longer than the captured variable. In the same time, not all variables can be captured by value. Since C++11 *move-only* types exist: types that cannot be copied only just moved. Objects from such types like `std::unique_ptr`, `std::thread` and many `iostream`-related types cannot be copied, thus we cannot capture them by value as it would apply the copy semantics.

To handle these types in a safe way from lambda expressions we should *move* them into the closure object. For old-style functors, the solution would be trivial, we could *move* the objects into the closure using the initializer list of the constructor. (However, you must not forget to use the `std::move` right-value cast operator.) To provide the same functionality for lambda expressions, C++14 presents generalized lambda capture, or *init capture*. An init capture behaves as if it declares and explicitly captures a variable declared as `auto` and initialized by the initialization expression. However, no real new variable is constructed: e.g. no additional copy and destruction operations will be executed.

```
// since C++14
#include <iostream>
#include <memory>
int main()
{
    int x = 10;
    std::unique_ptr<int> up = make_unique<int>(42);
    [&x = x, up = std::move(up), n = 1] { x = *up+n; } ();
    std::cout << x << std::endl;
}
$ ./a.out
43
```

Listing 38: Init (generic) capture in C++14

In Listing 38 variable `x` is captured by reference, the `unique_ptr` `up` is *moved* into the data member of the closure object and an `int` type data member is created and initialized to 1. The program prints 43. It is also important to notice, that the heap area allocated by `make_unique` and initialized to 42 is already destroyed when we reach the output calls, as its *ownership was moved* from the `up` pointer to the closure's data member which has been destructed at the end of the execution of the lambda expression.

6 C++ Template Metaprogramming

In [30] we explored C++ template metaprogramming as functional programming in a great detail. Thus, in this section we just briefly recap the generic idea and discuss immutability.

Templates are key language elements of C++ enabling algorithms and data structures to be parametrized by types or constants without performance penalties at runtime [39]. This abstraction is essential when using general algorithms, such as finding an element in a data structure, sorting, or defining data structures like vector or set. The generic features of these templates (like the behaviour of the algorithms or the layout of the data structures) are the same, only the actual type parameter is different. The abstraction over the type parameter – often called parametric polymorphism [6] – emphasizes that this variability is supported by compile-type template parameters. Reusable components – containers and algorithms – are implemented in C++ mostly using templates. The Standard Template Library (STL), an essential part of the C++ standard, is the most notable example [22,27].

Templates are code skeletons with placeholders for one or more type parameters. In order to use a template it has to be instantiated. This can be initiated either implicitly, when a template is referred with actual type parameters or explicitly. During instantiation the template parameters are substituted with the actual arguments and new code is generated. Thus, a different code segment is generated when a template is instantiated with different type parameters.

There are certain cases when a template with a specific type parameter requires a special behaviour, that is different from the generic one. Such "exceptions" can be specified using template specializations. During the instantiation of a template the compiler uses the most specialized version of that template.

Templates can refer to other templates (even recursively) thus complex chains of template instantiations can be created. This mechanism enables us to write smart template codes affecting the compilation process. To demonstrate this capability of C++ templates Erwin Unruh wrote a sample program [42]. The program, when compiled, emitted a list of prime numbers as part of the error messages. This way Unruh demonstrated that with cleverly designed templates it is possible to execute a desired algorithm at compile time. This compile-time programming is called *C++ Template Metaprogramming* (TMP) [1].

The classical example on Listing 39 demonstrates how to compute the value of factorial at compile time. We can see that the implementation uses recursion at compile-time. The static constant value, `Factorial<5>::value` is referred to inside the `main` function, thus the compiler is enforced to compute it. The instantiation process of the class `Factorial<5>` begins. Inside the `Factorial` template, `Factorial<N-1>::value` is referred. The compiler now is forced to instantiate `Factorial<4>`, then to instantiate `Factorial<3>`, etc. The `Factorial` template class is instantiated several times recursively. The recursion stops when `Factorial<1>` is referred to, since there is a *specialization* for that argument. At the end, the compiler generates five classes and `Factorial<5>::value` is calculated at compile time.

```
template <int N>
struct Factorial
{
    static const int value = N * Factorial<N-1>::value;
}
template<>
struct Factorial<1>  // specialization
{
    static const int value = 1;
};
int main()
{
    int r = Factorial<5>::value;  // known compile time
    cout << r << endl;
}
```

Listing 39: Simple factorial C++ template metaprogram

Similarly, one can use control branches using template specialization. In the example on Listing 40 example we declare the variable `i` to be of type `int` or `long` depending on whether the size of the `long` type is greater then the size of `int`.

```
template <bool condition, class Then, class Else>
struct if_
{
    typedef Then type;
};
template <class Then, class Else>
struct if_<false, Then, Else>
{
    typedef Else type;
};
int main()
{
    if_< sizeof(int)<sizeof(long), long, int>::type i;
    cout << sizeof(i) << endl;
    return 0;
}
```

Listing 40: (Runtime) conditional choice in template metaprograms

As template metaprograms are "executed" by the compiler, they fundamentally differ from usual runtime programs. Compilers among other actions evaluate constant values, deduce types and declare variables – all of these are immutable actions. Once a constant value has been computed, a type has been decided, a variable has been declared then they remain the same. There is no such thing as assignment in template metaprograms. In this way C++ template metaprograms are similar to the pure functional programming languages with referential transparency [30]. However, one can still write control-structures, using specializations. Loops are implemented using recursive templates, terminated by specializations. Control branches are based on partial or full specializations.

Having recursion and branching with pattern matching we have a complete programming language – executing programs at compile time. C++ templates have been proven to form a Turing complete sublanguage of C++ at compile time [44]. Template metaprograms are used intensively to implement active libraries [45], expression templates [46], DSL integrations [34], parser generation [41], target of translation of functional programming systems [35] or even for type safe hosting of SQL queries [10].

We can use data structures at compile time. For example the list structure used by most functional programming languages can be implemented by a class, `NullType`, representing the empty list and a template class, `Typelist`, representing the list constructor [2]. One can represent any list by using the constructor recursively. These classes can be implemented and used in Listing 41:

```
class NullType {};
template <class Head, class Tail>
struct Typelist {};

typedef Typelist< char,
                  Typelist<signed char,
                           Typelist<unsigned char, NullType>
                          >
                > Charlist;
```

Listing 41: Representing data in metaprograms

Preprocessor macros make the use of typelists more handy (on Listing 42):

```
#define TYPELIST_1(x) Typelist< x, NullType>
#define TYPELIST_2(x, y) Typelist< x, TYPELIST_1(y)>
#define TYPELIST_3(x, y, z) Typelist< x, TYPELIST_2(y,z)>
#define TYPELIST_4(x, y, z, w) Typelist< x, TYPELIST_3(y,z,w)>
// ...
typedef TYPELIST_3(char, signed char, unsigned char) Charlist;
```

Listing 42: Representing data with typelist at template metaprogramming

The most commonly used data types are implemented by the Boost.MPL library in an efficient way and with an easy to use syntax, without having to use the preprocessor for creating lists. The above list can be created using `boost::mpl::list` as shown in Listing 43.

```
typedef boost::mpl::list<char, signed char, unsigned char> Charlist;
```

Listing 43: Using typelist in boost metaprogramming library

The similarities between template metaprogramming and the functional paradigm are obvious. Static constants have the same role in template metaprograms as ordinary values have in the runtime ones. Template metaprogramming uses symbolic names (typenames, typedefs) instead of variables. Specific classes are used to replace runtime functions.

To bring C++ metaprogramming from an ad-hoc approach to a more structured form, Czarnecki and Eisenecker defined the term template metafunction as a special template class [6]. The template metafunction is the unit to encapsulate compile time computations in a standard way. The arguments of the metafunction are the template parameters of the class, the value of the function is a nested type of the template. The name of this nested type has been standardised by Boost.MPL, and it is called `type`. To evaluate a metafunction we provide actual parameters for the arguments, and we refer to the nested type as the value.

The possibility of writing compile-time metaprograms in C++ was not intentionally designed. Therefore, C++ compilers are not focused on template metaprograms as primary targets. The syntax of the metaprograms is far from trivial, and in most cases it is hard to understand. Debugging and profiling template metaprograms, although now supported by various tools [24, 31], are still challenging.

7 Summary

More than 35 years after it has been created, the C++ programming language has still among the most important and frequently used mainstream programming languages. One of the reasons of its vitality is that C++ has successfully addressed challenges that have emerged from time to time. The RAII idiom and its consequences, like smart pointers, handled resource safety issues, generative programming and the STL created a complex, fully comprehensive, still effective and easy to use standard library. Lately, the new memory model and the multithreading library addressed the emerging request for supporting concurrent programming.

Not independently from concurrent programming, we experience a growing enthusiasm for functional programming and its toolset. Historically C++ was not rich in language elements directly supporting the functional paradigm. In this paper we attempted the summarize those classical and new language elements that provide support for one of the major characteristics of functional paradigm: immutable programming. Immutability or referential transparency requires that objects must not change their value during runtime.

Although there is no direct support for immutable data types in C++, various existing language features can be used to achieve immutability. Constants, and const-correctness rules have been used in C++ from the beginning. STL supports and always supported constant correctness. Lambda functions, introduced to C++11, have a pure behaviour by default. Constant expressions, especially their extended form since C++14, provide a feasible way to implement immutable objects and pure functions. Template metaprograms are referentially transparent by nature, and compile time data structures, like typelists, are immutable. In the upcoming C++17 version constexpr lambdas, folding expressions will enhance the functional toolset of C++.

With this rich set of available language features, one can safely implement in modern C++ immutable data structures, pure functions and all the other means of functional programming.

References

1. Abrahams, D., Gurtovoy, A.: C++ Template Metaprogramming, Concepts, Tools, and Techniques from Boost and Beyond, p. 400. Addison-Wesley, Boston (2004). ISBN 0321-22725-6
2. Alexandrescu, A.: Modern C++ Design: Generic Programming and Design Patterns Applied. Addison-Wesley, Boston (2001)
3. Allain, A.: Constexpr - Generalized Constant Expressions in C++11. http://www.cprogramming.com/c++11/c++11-compile-time-processing-with-constexpr.html
4. Austern, M.H.: Generic Programming and the STL: Using and Extending the C++ Standard Template Library. Addison-Wesley, Boston (1998)
5. Coplien, J.O.: Multi-Paradigm Design for C++. Addison-Wesley Longman Publishing Co., Inc., Boston (1998)
6. Czarnecki, K., Eisenecker, U.W.: Generative Programming: Methods, Tools and Applications. Addison-Wesley, Boston (2000)
7. Dami, L.: More functional reusability in C/C++/ Objective-C with curried functions. Object Composition, pp. 85–98. Centre Universitaire d'Informatique, University of Geneva, June 1991
8. Ellis, M., Stroustrup, B.: The Annotated C++ Reference Manual. Addison-Wesley, Boston (1990)
9. Fejerčák, V., Szabó, Cs., Bollin, A.: A software reverse engineering experience with the AMEISE legacy system. In: Electrical Engineering and Informatics 6: Proceedings of the Faculty of Electrical Engineering and Informatics of the Technical University of Košice, pp. 357–362. FEI TU, Košice (2015). ISBN 978-80-553-2178-3
10. Gil, Y., Lenz, K.: Simple and safe SQL queries with C++ templates. In: Consela, C., Lawall, J.L. (eds.) 6th International Conference on Generative Programming and Component Engineering, GPCE 2007, Salzburg, Austria, 1–3 October, pp. 13–24 (2007)
11. Hudak, P.: Conception, evolution, and application of functional programming languages. ACM Comput. Surv. **21**(3), 359–411 (1989). https://doi.org/10.1145/72551.72554

12. The C++11 Standard: ISO International Standard, ISO/IEC 14882:2011(E) - Information technology - Programming languages - C++ (2011)
13. The C++14 Standard: ISO International Standard, ISO/IEC 14882:2014(E) - Programming Language C++ (2014)
14. Järvi, J., Powell, G., Lumsdaine, A.: The Lambda library: unnamed functions in C++. Softw. Pract. Exper. **33**(3), 259–291 (2003). https://doi.org/10.1002/spe.504
15. Järvi, J., Freeman, J.: C++ lambda expressions and closures. Sci. Comput. Program. **75**(9), 762–772 (2010)
16. Karlsson, B.: Beyond the C++ Standard Library, An Introduction to Boost. Addison-Wesley, Boston (2005)
17. Kernighan, B.W., Ritche, D.M.: The C Programming Language, vol. 2. Prentice-Hall, Englewood Cliffs (1988)
18. Kiselyov, O.: Functional style in C++: closures, late binding, and Lambda abstractions. In: Proceedings of the Third ACM SIGPLAN International Conference on Functional Programming, (ICFP 1998), p. 337. ACM, New York (1998). https://doi.org/10.1145/289423.289464
19. Koopman, P., Plasmeijer, R., Achten, P.: An executable and testable semantics for iTasks. In: Scholz, S.-B., Chitil, O. (eds.) IFL 2008. LNCS, vol. 5836, pp. 212–232. Springer, Heidelberg (2011). https://doi.org/10.1007/978-3-642-24452-0_12
20. McNamara, B., Smaragdakis, Y.: Functional programming in C++. In: Proceedings of the Fifth ACM SIGPLAN International Conference on Functional Programming, pp. 118–129 (2000)
21. McNamara, B., Smaragdakis, Y.: Functional programming in C++ using the FC++ library. SIGPLAN Not. **36**(4), 25–30 (2001)
22. Meyers, S.: Effective STL – 50 Specific Ways to Improve Your Use of the Standard Template Library. Addison-Wesley, Boston (2001)
23. Meyers, S.: Effective Modern C++. O'Reilly Media, Sebastopol (2014). ISBN 978-1-4919-0399-5, ISBN 10 1-4919-0399-6
24. Mihalicza, J., Pataki, N., Porkoláb, Z.: Compiler support for profiling C++ template metaprograms. In: Proceedings of the 12th Symposium on Programming Languages and Software Tools (SPLST 2011), pp. 32–43, October 2011
25. Milewski, B.: Functional Data Structures in C++. C++Now, Aspen (2015). https://www.youtube.com/watch?v=OsB09djvfl4
26. Milewski, B.: C++ Ranges are Pure Monadic Goodness. B. Milewski's blog. https://bartoszmilewski.com/2014/10/17/c-ranges-are-pure-monadic-goodness/
27. Musser, D.R., Stepanov, A.A.: Algorithm-oriented generic libraries. Softw.-Pract. Exper. **27**(7), 623–642 (1994)
28. Niebler, E.: Ranges for the Standard Library proposal, Rev. 1, N4128, 10 October 2014. http://www.open-std.org/jtc1/sc22/wg21/docs/papers/2014/n4128.html
29. Pataki, N., Szűgyi, Z., Dévai, G.: C++ standard template library in a safer way. In: Proceedings of Workshop on Generative Technologies (WGT 2010), pp. 46–55 (2010)
30. Porkoláb, Z.: Functional programming with C++ template metaprograms. In: Horváth, Z., Plasmeijer, R., Zsók, V. (eds.) CEFP 2009. LNCS, vol. 6299, pp. 306–353. Springer, Heidelberg (2010). https://doi.org/10.1007/978-3-642-17685-2_9
31. Sinkovics, Á.: Interactive metaprogramming shell based on clang. In: Lecture at C++Now Conference. Aspen, Co., US (2015). https://www.youtube.com/watch?v=oCbeXpJKzlM

32. Sinkovics, Á., Porkoláb, Z.: Expressing C++ template metaprograms as lambda expressions. In: Horváth, Z., Zsók, V., Achten, P., Koopman, P. (eds.) Proceedings of Tenth Symposium on Trends in Functional Programming, Komárno, Slovakia, 2–4 June 2009, pp. 97–111 (2009)
33. Sinkovics, Á., Porkoláb, Z.: Implementing monads for C++ template metaprograms. In: Science of Computer Programming. https://doi.org/10.1016/j.scico.2013.01.002, http://www.sciencedirect.com/science/article/pii/S0167642313000051. ISSN 0167-6423. Accessed 23 Jan 2013
34. Sinkovics, Á, Porkoláb, Z.: Domain-specific language integration with C++ template metaprogramming. In: Formal and Practical Aspects of Domain-Specific Languages: Recent Developments, pp. 32–55. IGI Global (2013). https://doi.org/10.4018/978-1-4666-2092-6.ch002. Accessed 30 Apr 2014
35. Sipos, Á., Zsók, V.: EClean – an embedded functional language. Electron. Not. Theoret. Comput. Sci. **238**(2), 47–58 (2009)
36. Sommerlad, P.: C++14 Compile-time computation (ACCU 2015). http://wiki.hsr.ch/PeterSommerlad/files/ACCU2015VariadicVariableTemplates.pdf
37. Stepanov, A.: From Mathematics to Generic Programming, 1st edn. Addison-Wesley, Boston (2014). ISBN-10: 0321942043, http://www.open-std.org/jtc1/sc22/wg21/docs/papers/2013/n3649.html
38. Stroustrup, B.: A history of C++: 1979–1991. In: The Second ACM SIGPLAN Conference on History of Programming Languages (HOPL-II), pp. 271–297. ACM, New York (1996). https://doi.org/10.1145/154766.155375
39. Stroustrup, B.: The C++ Programming Language, 4th edn. Addison-Wesley Professional, Boston (2013). ISBN-10 0321563840
40. Stroustrup, B.: The Design and Evolution of C++. Addison-Wesley, Boston (1994)
41. Szűgyi, Z., Sinkovics, Á., Pataki, N., Porkoláb, Z.: C++ metastring library and its applications. In: Fernandes, J.M., Lämmel, R., Visser, J., Saraiva, J. (eds.) GTTSE 2009. LNCS, vol. 6491, pp. 461–480. Springer, Heidelberg (2011). https://doi.org/10.1007/978-3-642-18023-1_15
42. Unruh, E.: Prime number computation. ANSI X3J16-94-0075/ISO WG21-462
43. Vali, F., Sutter, H., Abrahams, D.: N3649 Generic (Polymorphic) Lambda Expressions (Revision 3). http://www.open-std.org/jtc1/sc22/wg21/docs/papers/2013/n3649.html
44. Veldhuizen, T.: C++ Templates are Turing Complete. Technical report, Indiana University Computer Science (2003). http://citeseerx.ist.psu.edu/viewdoc/summary?doi=10.1.1.14.3670
45. Veldhuizen, T., Gannon, D.: Active libraries: rethinking the roles of compilers and libraries. In: Proceedings of the SIAM Workshop on Object Oriented Methods for Inter-operable Scientific and Engineering Computing, OO 1998 (1998)
46. Veldhuizen, T.: Expression Templates. C++ Report, vol. 7, pp. 26–31 (1995)
47. Zsók, V., Koopman, P., Plasmeijer, R.: Generic executable semantics for d-clean. Electron. Not. Theoret. Comput. Sci. **279**(3), 85–95 (2011)
48. Järvi, J.: The Boost Lambda library. http://www.boost.org/doc/libs/1_60_0/doc/html/lambda.html
49. Literal types in Draft C++14 standard. Working Draft, Standard for Programming Language C++. ANSI C++ N4290, 19 November 2014. 3.9. [10]. http://www.open-std.org/jtc1/sc22/wg21/docs/papers/2014/n4296.pdf
50. Constant expressions in Draft C++14 standard. Working Draft, Standard for Programming Language C++. ANSI C++ N4290, 19 November 2014. 5.20. [4]

Programming in a Functional Style in C++

Rainer Grimm(✉)

Rottenburg, Germany
rainer@grimm-jaud.de

Abstract. C++ is a multiparadigm programming language. So the programmer may choose and combine between structural, procedural, object oriented, generic or functional features of C++ to solve his problem. Especially the functional aspect of C++ lambda functions with, type inference and the function std::bind and std::function has grown in modern C++ and is quietly evolving with the next C++ standard.

1 Introduction

This lecture gives an overview of the functional capabilities of modern C++, compares them with Haskell features and shows, how you can use them. In addition, the lecture tries to peek into the future and gives you an idea of what to come in the near future. So this paper is divided in two parts. At first I describe the functional capabilities of classical C++, then I will peek into the future.

2 Functional Programming in C++

C++ is not a functional programming language. But C++ allows to program in a functional way. Examples? Automatic type derivation, typical for functional programming languages, is one of the most used features in C++11:

Listing 1.1: Automatic type derivation with auto

```
std::vector <int> myVec;
auto itVec = myVec.begin();
for (auto v: myVec) std::cout << v << "";
```

So in the simple example itVec is of type iterator and v a integer in the range-based for loop. With C++ 11 C++ knows lambda functions. These are functions without names that are often used as parameters for functions.

Listing 1.2: Lambda functions

```
int a = 2000;
int b = 11;
auto sum = std::async ([=] {return a + b;});
std::cout << sum.get () << std::endl;
```


V. Zsók et al. (Eds.): CEFP 2015, LNCS 10094, pp. 111–136, 2019.
https://doi.org/10.1007/978-3-030-28346-9_4

3 Functional Programming: The Definition

Functional programming is easy to define. Functional programming is programming with mathematical functions. You guessed it probably. The key point in this definition is the term mathematical functions. These are functions that always return the same result, if they are called with the same arguments. Therefore, they behave like infinite large lookup tables. This feature, which always produces the same result when given the same arguments, is also called referential transparency and has far-reaching consequences:

- Functions may not have any side effects, i.e. state outside the function body change.
- The function call can be replaced by its result, resorted or automatically moved to another thread.
- The program flow is controlled by the data dependencies and not by the order of the instructions.
- Mathematical functions can be significantly easier refactored or tested, because the functions can be considered in isolation.

4 Characteristics of Functional Programming

The definition of functional programming is short and crisp, but does not really help further. More helpful is it already, to describe the characteristics of functional programming and its implementation in C++. The Fig. 1 sets out the strategy for the next section.

4.1 First-Class Functions

Functional programming languages are distinguished by first-class functions. First-class functions behave as data and are often used in C++ in the Standard Template Library (STL). Thus, first-class functions can

- Be used as an argument of a function:

```
std::accumulate(vec.begin(),vec.end(),
        []{int a,int b}{return a+b;})
```

- Be returned by a function:

```
std::function<int(int, int)> makeAdd(){
  return [](int a, int b) {return a + b;};
}
std::function <int(int, int)> myAdd= makeAdd();
myAdd(2000,11); // 2011
```

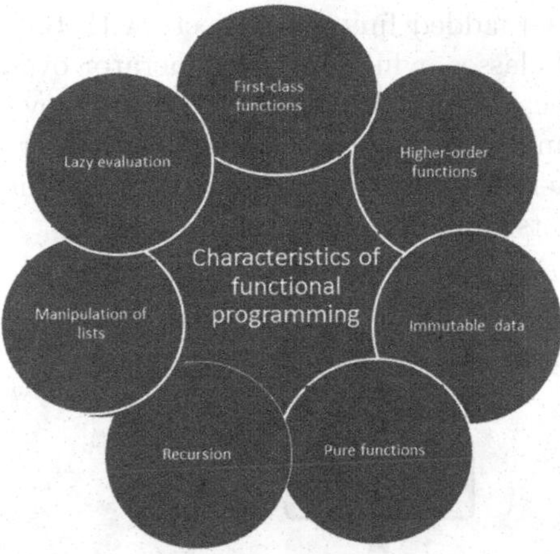

Fig. 1. Characteristics of functional programming

The `makeAdd` function returns the lambda function `[](int a, int b) {return ab;}` back. The function requires two int arguments and returns an int value: `std::function<int(int,int)>`. The return type of the function `makeAdd` can be bound to the generic function wrapper `myAdd` and can be executed. In particular, the expressiveness of first-class features beautifully shows the C++ implementation of the dispatch table in Listing 1.3.

Listing 1.3: Dispatch table

```
std::map <const char, function <double (double, double)>> tab;

tab.insert({'+',[](double a, double b){return a + b;}});
tab.insert({'-',[](double a, double b){return a - b;}});
tab.insert({'*',[](double a, double b){return a * b;}});
tab.insert({'/',[](double a, double b){return a / b;}});

std::cout<< "3.5+4.5=" << tab['+'](3.5,4.5) << std::endl; // 8
std::cout<< "3.5*4.5=" << tab['*'](3.5,4.5) << std::endl; // 15.75
tab.insert({'^',[](double a, double b) {return std::pow(a, b);}});
std::cout<< "3.5^4.5=" << tab['^'](3.5,4.5) << std::endl;// 280 741
```

The `std::map` maps a `const char` to a function that takes two double values and returns double value. It is this signature corresponding to the four functions in the following lines. They represent the basic arithmetic operations. Now, if the std::map is called with the key `'+':tab['+'](3.5,4.5)`, the lambda function is used as a value for the key '+'. The result is that it evaluates the lambda function with the values of (3.5, 4.5). Even subsequently allows the dispatch table to be extended by the power function.

The Extension of the Function Concept. In the development of C++, the extension of the function concept can be very nicely observed (Fig. 2). C has only functions. C++ added function objects with the first standard 1998. These are instances of classes, which the call operator overloaded so that their instantiated objects behave like a function. As objects they can hold state. With C++ 11 C++ is expanded to include lambda functions; with C++ 14 generic lambda functions. Generic lambda functions are lambda functions that have type parameters as arguments similar to templates.

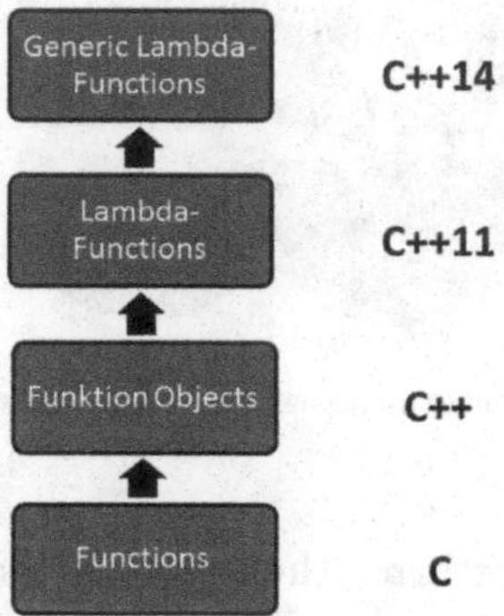

Fig. 2. The evolution of the function concept

4.2 First-Class Functions

Higher-order functions are the counterparts of first-class functions. Higher-order functions accept as an argument or return as a result a function. Any programming language that permits programming in functional style supports at least the three functions map, filter and fold. map applies a function to each element of a list, filter removes items from the list that do not satisfy a predicate. fold is the most powerful of the three functions. fold applies a binary operation successively on all pairs of a list until the list is reduced to one element. The easiest way to get a feeling for the three functions in to use them. I use a list including natural number and strings as input data. In the case of C++, the list is a std::vector:

Listing 1.4: Input data for Haskell and C++

```
// Haskell
vec = [1..9]
str = ["Programming","in","a","functional","style."]
// C++
std::vector<int> vec{1,2,3,4,5,6,7,8,9}
std::vector<string> str{"Programming","in","a",
                        "functional","style."}
```

The result will be shown for the sake of simplicity in the syntax of Haskell.

map applies a callable unit to each element of a list. A callable unit is anything that behaves like a function. This can be a function, a function object or a lambda function. The ideal candidate for higher-order functions is a lambda function. This is for two reasons. Firstly, the functionality is expressed compact and thus easy to understand. On the other hand defines lambda their functionality exactly at the spot where it is needed. Through this code, the compiler receives locality maximum insight into the source code and can therefore optimize very well.

Listing 1.5: Comparison of map and std::transform

```
// Haskell
map (\a -> a * a) vec
map (\a -> length a) str

// C++
std::transform(vec.begin(),vec.end(),vec.begin(),
               [](int i){return i*i;});

std::transform(str.begin(),str.end(),std::back_inserter(vec2),
     [](std::string s){return s.length ();});

// [1,4,9,16,25,36,49,64,81]
// [11,2,1,10,6]
```

Of course there is a different syntax for lambda functions in Haskell and C++. So a lambda function in Haskell is introduced by a slash `\a -> a * a`, however, in C++ by square brackets: `[](int i){return i * i;}`. But, these differences are just of syntactic nature.

filter only leaves the items in the list that satisfy the predicate. Here, a predicate is a callable unit. A predicate has to return true or false for each argument.

Listing 1.6: Comparison of filter and std::remove_if

```
// Haskell
filter (\x-> x <3 || x> 8) vec
filter (\x -> isupper (head x)) st

// C++
auto it = std::remove_if(vec.begin(),vec.end (),
     [](int i){return ((i <3) or (i> 8))!});
auto it2 = std::remove_if(str.begin(), str.end (),
     [](std::string s) {return !(std::isupper (s[0]));});

// [1,2,9]
// ["Programming"]
```

The function composition `isupper (head x)` checks for each word if the first letter `(head x)` is a capital letter. Because std::remove_if removes the arguments, that satisfy the predicate, the logical expression must be inverted.

fold is the most powerful of the three higher-order functions. fold can implement map and filter. Listing 1.7 shows in Haskell and C++ the calculation of the factorial of 9 and string concatenation by using foldl or std::accumulate.

Listing 1.7: Comparison of foldl and std::accumulate

```
// Haskell
foldl (\a b -> a * b) 1 vec
foldl (\a b -> a ++ ":" ++ b) "" str

// C++
std::accumulate(vec.begin(),vec.end (), 1,
      [](int a, int b) {return a * b; });
std::accumulate(str.begin(),str.end(), std::string(""),
      [](std::string a, std::string b){return a + ":" + b; });

// 362 800
// ":Programming:in:a:functional:style."
```

foldl needs like its C++ counterpart std::accumulate a starting value. This is the case of the calculation of the faculty the 1, this is in the case of string concatenation, the empty string "". While Haskell uses two plus signs in the lambda function `(\a b  a ++ ":" ++ b)` to add the strings together, the simple plus sign is sufficient in C++: `a + ":" + b`.

4.3 Immutable Data

Pure functional programming languages like Haskell are distinguished primarily by the fact that their data are immutable. Thus assignments of the form x = x + 1 and accordingly ++x are not possible. The consequence is that Haskell has no loops. These are based on the modification of a loop variable. Haskell does not modify any existing data but creates new ones when needed. Immutable data has a beautiful property. They are implicit thread-safe, because they lack a necessary condition for a critical area. A critical area is characterized by the access of two or more threads simultaneously on the same data. At least one thread tries to change this data.

The immutability of data in Haskell can be seen in the Quicksort algorithm.

Listing 1.8: Haskells Quicksort algorithm

```
qsort [] = []
qsort (x:xs)= qsort[y|y <- xs,y < x] ++ [x] ++
              qsort[y|y <- xs,y >= x]
```

The Quicksort algorithm `qsort` consists of two function definitions. The first line is quicksort, applied to the empty list. This is the empty list. The second line depicts the general case in which the list has at least one element of: `x: xs`.

x is the beginning and xs the rest of the list by convention. The strategy of the Quicksort algorithm can be expressed almost directly in Haskell. Use the first element of the list x, the so-called pivot element and build a one element list out of it [x]. Then add all elements of the list before the list [x], that are smaller than x `(qsort [y | y <- xs, y <x ])` and add all element after the list [x], that are at least as large as x `(qsort [y | y <- xs, y> = x])`. The recursion terminates when quicksort is applied to the empty list. The key point of the algorithm is that in each recursion, a new list is generated.

The use of fixed data is based in C++ on the discipline of the programmer. With constant data template metaprogramming and constant expressions C++ provides three options. The options one and two are presented with few words, however constant expressions deserve much more attention. By the instruction `const int value = 1; value` will be constant. Template metaprogramming takes place at compile time. At compile time, there is no modification. Therefore, all values at compile time are constant.

Now to constant expressions. This supports C++ in three forms: as a variable, user-defined types and functions. The special feature of constant expressions is that they can be evaluated at compile time.

pi becomes by the term `constexpr double pi = 3.14` a constant expression. pi is thus implicitly const and must be initialized by a constant expression 3.14.

To create an object of a user-defined, which is a `constexpr`, the user-defined type has a few limitations. So its constructor must be a constant expression itself. Thus the object can only use methods, that are constant expressions themselves. At compile time, no calls to virtual methods are of course possible. Meets the custom type all restrictions, its objects can be created and used at compile time.

For functions as constant expressions there are limitations, so that they can be performed at compile time. Firstly, all arguments must be constant expressions. Secondly, they cannot contain static and thread-local data. Which expressiveness constant expressions have, can be seen in Listing 1.9. In this user defined Literals are used to calculate distances at compiletime.

Listing 1.9: Constant expressions to calculate distances

```
#include <iostream>
#include <ostream>

class Dist{
public:
  constexpr Dist(long double i):m(i){}

  friend constexpr Dist operator+(const Dist& a, const Dist& b){
    return Dist(a.m + b.m);
  }
  friend constexpr Dist operator-(const Dist& a,const Dist& b){
    return Dist(a.m - b.m);
  }
  friend constexpr Dist operator*(double m, const Dist& a){
    return Dist(m*a.m);
```

```
  }
  friend constexpr Dist operator/(const Dist& a, int n){
    return Dist(a.m/n);
  }
  friend std::ostream& operator<<(std::ostream& out,
                                   const Dist& myDist){
    out << myDist.m << " m";
    return out;
  }
private:
  long double m;
};

namespace Unit{
  Dist constexpr operator "" _km(long double d){
    return Dist(1000*d);
  }
  Dist constexpr operator "" _m(long double m){
    return Dist(m);
  }
  Dist constexpr operator "" _dm(long double d){
    return Dist(d/10);
  }
  Dist constexpr operator "" _cm(long double c){
    return Dist(c/100);
  }
}

Dist constexpr getAverageDist(std::initializer_list<Dist> inList){
  auto sum= Dist(0.0);
  for ( auto i: inList) sum = sum + i;
  return sum/inList.size();
}

using namespace Unit;

int main(){
  constexpr Dist work= 63.0_km;
  constexpr Dist workPerDay= 2 * work;
  constexpr Dist abbreToWork= 5400.0_m; // abbrevation to work
  constexpr Dist workout= 2 * 1600.0_m;
  constexpr Dist shop= 2 * 1200.0_m;     // shopping

  constexpr Dist distPerWeek1= 4*workPerDay - 3*abbreToWork
                               + workout + shop;
  constexpr Dist distPerWeek2=4*workPerDay -3*abbreToWork
                              + 2*workout;
  constexpr Dist distPerWeek3= 4*workout + 2*shop;
  constexpr Dist distPerWeek4= 5*workout + shop;
  constexpr Dist averagePerWeek=
          getAverageDist({distPerWeek1,distPerWeek2,
                          distPerWeek3,distPerWeek4});

  std::cout << "Average per week: " << averagePerWeek
```

```
        << std::endl;
}
```

User defined literals are built-in literals, which are complemented with their own suffixes. This is possible for strings, characters, integers and floating point numbers. This can be seen in Listing 1.9.

Now to the analyses of the program. As a frequent traveler, it is always interesting for me to know how many meters I drive per week on average by car. Thanks to user defined literals, I can express all distances in a natural way. So the direct route to work is `63_km`. An abbreviation that is present from time to time is `5400.0_m`. A trip to the remote `1600.0_m` gym and `1200.0_m` remote wholesalers is also occasionally on the plan. Now it is time to add all distances per week and calculate the average over the weeks. Figure 3 shows the execution of the program in the unit meters.

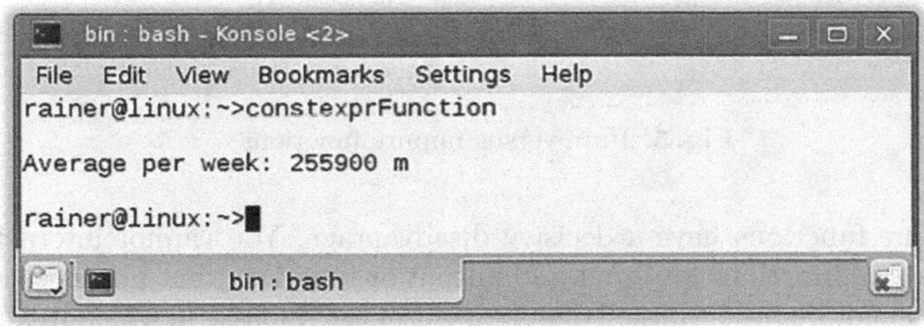

Fig. 3. User defined literals

How does the magic work? The compiler maps the user defined Literals to the literal operators. In these operators, the corresponding literal Dist objects are created and normalized to meters. Figure 4 provides all the steps as examples, which are necessary to add two user defined literals. The blue arrows are done by the compiler, for the red steps, the programmer has to implement the code.

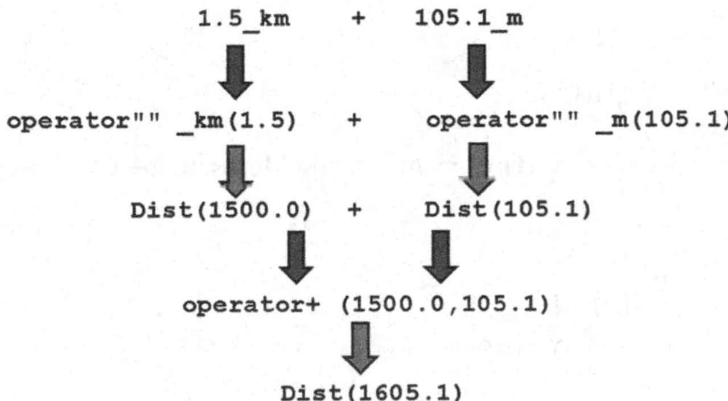

Fig. 4. Processing of user defined literals

But what is special about the program? Except for calling the output function std::cout all objects and functions are defined as constant expressions. Special is, the whole program can be evaluated at compile time. So of course all properties are constant.

4.4 Pure Functions

Pure functions are very similar to mathematical functions. They are the reason why Haskell is called a pure functional programming language. Figure 5 compares pure and impure functions.

Pure functions	Impure functions
Always produce the same result when given the same arguments.	May produce different results for the same arguments.
Never have side effects.	May have side effects.
Never alter state.	May alter the global state of the program, system, or the world.

Fig. 5. Pure versus impure functions

But pure functions have a decisive disadvantage. You cannot interact with the world. The functions for input and output or functions that produce random numbers cannot be pure. Haskell dissolves out of the impasse in which it embedds a impure, imperative subsystems in the programming language. What is the story about the purity of C++? This is based like dealing with fixed data on the discipline of the programmer. Listing 1.10 presents three pure functions.

Listing 1.10: A function, a metafunction and a constexpr function as pure function

```
int powFunc(int m, int n){
  if (n == 0) return 1;
  return m * powFunc(m, n-1);
}

template<int m, int n>
struct PowMeta{
  static int const value = m * PowMeta<m,n-1>::value;
};

template<int m>
struct PowMeta<m,0>{
  static int const value = 1;
};

constexpr int powConst(int m, int n){
```

```
  int r = 1;
  for(int k=1; k<=n; ++k) r*= m;
  return r;
}

int main(){
  std::cout << powFunc(2,10) << std::endl;              // 1024
  std::cout << PowMeta<2,10>::value << std::endl;       // 1024
  std::cout << powConst(2,10) << std::endl;             // 1024
}
```

Even if the three functions return the same result, they arc very different. `powFunc` is a classic function. It is running during the runtime of the program and can also handle non-constant expressions. In contrast `PowMeta` is a meta-function that is performed at compile time of the program. Therefore, it requires constant expressions as arguments. The constexpr function `powConst` can be performed at compile time and at runtime of the program. To be executed at compile time, it requires constant expressions as arguments.

Pure functional languages have no mutable data. Instead of loops they use recursion.

4.5 Recursion

The metafunction in Listing 1.10 has already shown it. Recursions occur at compile time instead of loops. This allows the Factorial function in Listing 1.11 to be written much more compact in Haskell.

Listing 1.11: Recursion in Haskell

```
fac 0 = 1
fac n = n * fac (n-1)
```

A fine difference however between the recursive factorial function in Haskell and the recursive factorial function in C++ exists. Strictly speaking the C++ - variant is not recursive. In fact each iteration the general class template with the template argument N creates a new template with the template argument $N-1$. The recursion will end with the full template specialization for N equal to 0.

Listing 1.12: Factorial <N>::value instantiate Factorial <N-1>::value

```
template <int N>
struct Factorial{
  static int const value = N * Factorial <N-1>::value;
};

template <>
struct Factorial<0>{
```

```
  static int const value= 1;
};
```

If recursion is used along with lists and pattern matching, compact functions can be implemented in Haskell. This is only partly true in C++.

4.6 Processing of Lists

LISt Processing (LISP) is characteristic of functional programming languages. Since lists are the universal data structure, they are the ideal basis for functional composition.

Processing of lists follows the functional model:

- Process the first element of the list.
- Recursively process the rest of the list, which is reduced by the first element.

Since the processing of lists is idiomatic for functional programming, there have been names established for the first element of the list and the rest of the list: (x, xs), (head, tail) or (car, cdr).

The functional model for the processing of lists can be implemented directly in Haskell and C++:

Listing 1.13: Summation of a list in Haskell

```
mySum [] = 0
mySum (x: xs) = x + xs mySum
mySum [1,2,3,4,5]      -- 15
```

Listing 1.14: A variable number of template arguments in C++

```
template<int ...>
struct mySum;

template<>
struct mySum<>{
  static const int value = 0;
};

template<int head, int ... tail>
struct mySum<head, tail ...>{
  static const int value = head + mySum<tail ...>::value;
};

int sum = mySum<1,2,3,4,5>::value; // 15
```

While the Haskell program is easy to consume, the C++ program is difficult to digest. Even with the imperative eye of a C++ developer. The C++ syntax requires that the primary or general template has to be defined at first. The fully specialized class template follows (meta-function). This class template is applied to the empty argument list. If the template argument list containts one or more elements, the partially specialized class template comes in use. A few more words about the three points, called ellipse. Through this, the class template (last line) can accept any number of template arguments.

Both Haskell and C++ use pattern matching to apply the correct function. There is a subtle difference between both. Haskell follows the first-match strategy, C++ the best-match strategy.

4.7 Lazy Evaluation

Lazy evaluation means, that an expression is only evaluated, when it is needed. This strategy has two major advantages. On the one hand, time and memory can be saved. Algorithms on the other hand, can be formulated for infinite data structures. Of course it is only possible at runtime to request finite number of elements.

Listing 1.15 shows three impressive examples in Haskell. The complexity increases.

Listing 1.15: Lazy evaluation in Haskell

```
length [2 + 1, 3 * 2, 1/0, 5-4] -- 4

successor i = i: (successor (i + 1))
take 5 (1 successor) -- [1,2,3,4,5]

odds = takeWhile (<1000). filter odd.map(^ 2)
[1 ..] = [1,2,3,4,5,6,7,8,9,10,11,12,13,14,15 ... control-C
odds [1 ..]                            -- [1,9,25, ..., 841.961]
```

In the first line Haskell calculates the length of the list, although the argument is not a valid expression 1/0. Successor i defines the infinite number sequence of natural numbers. With take 5 only the first five are required, the term is well defined. But well-defined is not the expression [1 ..] for requesting all natural numbers. Therefore, the program execution should be interrupted with control-C. Of course it is possible to use [1 ..] when only finitely many elements are requested. Exactly that takes place in `odds[1 ..]`. `odds` introduces the power of the functional composition in Haskell. 6 The dot (.) is the symbol of the function composition. The phrase can be read directly with a bit of practice from right to left: first turn of the square function, then filter out all straight elements and continue as long as the numbers are less than one thousand.

C++ uses eager evaluation by default. That is figuratively speaking, that, in contrast to C++ Haskell evaluates the expressions from the inside to the outside. With the short circuit evaluation in logical expressions C++ is only a bit lazy. If in a logical expression, the result of the overall expression prematurely is known, the rest of the expression has not be fully evaluated. Therefore, the following code fragment is executable although 1/0 is undefined:

```
if (true or (1/0)) std::cout<<"Short Circuit evaluation" << std::endl;
```

5 Functional Programming in C++17 and C++20

C++ will receive many new features with the upcoming C++-Standards that do not have much in common at first glance. So the algorithms of the Standard Template Library will act with the range library directly on the containers. With Concepts Lite C++ 20 you can make demands on template parameters, using std::optional. C++17 has a data type that can have a value or not. The composition of asynchronous function calls will be allowed by C++20 and thus fix the shortcomings of std::future in C++11. This new features are based on powerful, functional concepts like function composition, type classes and monads. Functional concepts will be put on significantly more formal basis with the C++17 and C++20.

5.1 Fold Expressions

C++11 knows variadic templates. Variadic templates are templates which may have any number of template parameters. This arbitrary number is held in the parameters Pack. New is in C++17, that a parameter pack can be directly reduced by a binary operator. So functions from Haskell like foldl, foldr, foldl1 and foldr1 [7] can be directly translated to C++ (Listing 1.16).

Listing 1.16: Calculating the truth value with variadic templates and fold expressions

```
#include <iostream>
bool allVar(){
  return true;
}

template<typename T, typename ...Ts>
 bool allVar(T t, Ts ... ts){
return t && allVar(ts...);
}

template<typename... Args>
bool all(Args... args) { return (... && args); }

int main(){
  std::cout << std::boolalpha;
  std::cout << "allVar(): " << allVar() << std::endl;
  std::cout << "all(): " << all() << std::endl;
  std::cout << "allVar(true): " << allVar(true) << std::endl;
  std::cout << "all(true): " << all(true) << std::endl;
  std::cout << "allVar(true, true, true, false): "
            << allVar(true,true, true, false) << std::endl;
  std::cout << "all(true, true, true, false): "
            << all(true, true, true, false) << std::endl;
}
```

The two function templates **allvar** and **all** provide at compile time if and only true if all arguments are true. **allvar** applys variadic templates, all variadic templates in combination with fold expressions. First to **allvar**. Variadic templates use recursion to their arguments to evaluate. The boundary condition is, that the parameter pack has to be empty. The actual recursion takes place in the function template **allvar** in the line. The three dots – called ellipse – define the parameter pack. Parameter Packs allow two operations. They can be packed and unpacked. Everything is packed in the parameters Pack `template<typename T, typename ...Ts>`, unpacked in the following lines. The line `return t && allVar(ts...);` requires special attention. In it the head t of the parameter pack will be linked with the rest of the parameters packs via `&&`. The call `allvar (TS ...)` leads here to the recursion. This call includes a parameter pack that is successively reduced to its first element. This is much easier with C++17. In C++17, the parameter pack can be reduced directly via a binary operator. Figure 6 shows the two algorithms in use.

Output:

```
allVar(): true
all(): true
allVar(true): true
all(true): true
allVar(true, true, true, false): false
all(true, true, true, false): false
```

Fig. 6. Comparison of variadic templates and fold expressions

Now to the two variations of the fold expression, leading to the four different forms of expression fold. On the one hand fold expression depends on the binary operator having a default value or not, on the other hand they can process the pack parameters starting from left or right. The difference you can see between the two algorithms **allvar** and **all**. **all** already has the default value true for the empty parameters Pack.

C++17 supports 32 binary operators in fold expression [8]:

+ − ∗ / % ^ & | = < > << >> += −= ∗= /= %= ^= &= |=
<<= >>= == != <= >= && || , .∗ −>∗

Some binary operators already have a default value:

∗(1), +(0), &(−1), |(0), &&(true), ||(false), (void())

For binary operators, for which no default value is defined, a default value must be specified. For binary operations, for which a default value is defined, a start value can be specified.

Whether a parameter pack is processed from the left or right depends on whether the ellipse left or right of the parameter pack. The same rule applies to fold expression with starting value.

5.2 Ranges Library

With the range library [11] of Eric Niebler working with the containers is clearly more comfortable and powerful. Comfortable because the algorithms of the Standard Template Library (STL) can act on the containers directly and don't need a start and end iterator. Powerful because with the ranges library C++20 gets lazy evaluation, significantly improved function composition and range comprehension.

Lazy Evaluation. Haskell is thoroughly lazy. Lazy evaluation allows Haskell to define algorithms for infinite data structures that only ask a finite number of elements. It is thus possible in a very elegant way to separate the algorithm for calculating an infinite data structure from its application.

The range library allows the uncommented line Haskell code to be directly translated to C++.

Listing 1.17: Lazy evaluation with the ranges library

```
#include <range/v3/all.hpp>
#include <iostream>
#include <tuple>

using namespace ranges;

int main(){
  std::cout << std::endl;

  // take 5 [1..] -- [1,2,3,4,5]

  auto num = view::take(view::ints(1),5);
  ranges::for_each(num, [](int i){std::cout << i << " ";});

  std::cout << "\n\n";


  auto pairs= view::zip_with([](int i, char c){ return
            std::make_pair(i,c);},view::ints(0),"ranges");

  ranges::for_each(pairs, [](std::pair<int,char> p){
        std::cout << "(" << p.first << ":" << p.second << ")";
  });

  std::cout << "\n\n";
}
```

The term `view::ints(1)` produces an infinite sequence of natural numbers, starting with the 1. However only 5 natural numbers are needed. In the ensuing `ranges::for_each` loop the five natural numbers are issued using the lambda function. Admittedly this is beautiful. On the other hand it allows the algorithm function composition to be more elegant:

`auto num = view::ints(1) | view::take(5)`. More on that point later. Secondly the future C++20 standard will support the direct output of the range by the Range-Based for loop:
`for (n:num) std::cout << num << "".`

The `view::zip_with` function known from functional programming assumes multiple lists and a lambda function and zips this with the help of the lambda function to a new list. So in line 20 the lambda function zips the infinite series of natural numbers, starting with 0 with the finite string `"ranges"`. The result (Fig. 7 is a finite tuple whose pairs can be addressed with first or second.

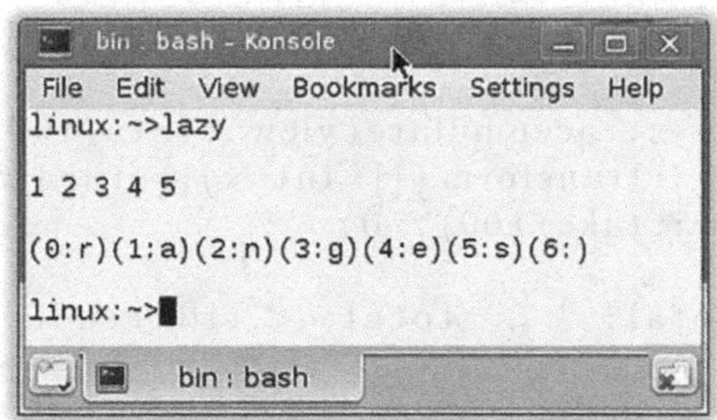

Fig. 7. Lazy evaluation with the ranges library

Function Composition. Function composition in Haskell has a great similarity with Lego blocks. The newly composed functions express their functionality very compact and can be read for the trained eye as prose. The power of the functional composition in Haskell is based on three components. First Haskell functions do exactly one task, second they act on the central data structure list and third they use the period (.) for the composition of functions. The situation is similar with the new range library. It has a rich set of functions, which is inspired by Haskell, act on the central data structure range and use the from the Unix shell or Windows PowerShell known pipe symbol (|) for composition of functions.

Listing 1.18 juxtaposes the commented Haskell code to the new C++ code.

Listing 1.18: Function composition with the ranges library

```
#include <range/v3/all.hpp>
#include <numeric>
#include <iostream>

using namespace ranges;

int main(){
  std::cout << std::endl;
  // odds= takeWhile (< 1000) . filter odd . map(^2)
  // odds [1..] — [1,9,25, ... , 841,961]
```

```
auto odds= view::transform([](int i){return i*i;}) |
      view::remove_if([](int i){return i % 2 == 0; }) |
      view::take_while([](int i){return i < 1000;});
auto oddNumbers= view::ints(1) | odds;

ranges::for_each(oddNumbers,
          [](int i){ std::cout << i << " "; });

std::cout << "\n\n";

// total= sum $ take 100
                 $ map(\x -> x*x)[100..1000] -- 2318350

auto total= ranges::accumulate(view::ints(100,1000) |
                view::transform([](int x){return x*x;}) |
                view::take(100), 0);

std::cout << "total: " << total << std::endl;

std::cout << std::endl;
}
```

The C++ expression is challenging to read. Figure 8 shows the program in action.

Fig. 8. Function composition with the ranges library

Range Comprehension. List comprehension is Syntactic Sugar [6] of the sweetest kind for functional algorithms map and filter and makes it possible to directly generate a new list at runtime. The list comprehension is very reminiscent of the mathematical notation of course. That is not an accident, because the functional programming languages Haskell is based on mathematical concepts.

With the range library C++20 supports range comprehension. This is not as easy to digest as list comprehension (Listing 1.19).

Listing 1.19: List versus range comprehension

```
#include <range/v3/all.hpp>
#include <iostream>

using namespace ranges;

int main(){
  std::cout << std::endl;
  // odds= [ x*x | x <-[1..] , odd x ]
  // takeWhile (<1000) odds  -- [1,9,25, ... , 841,961]

  auto odds= view::ints(1)
    | view::for_each([](int i){return yield_if(i%2 == 1,i*i);});

  ranges::for_each(odds
      | view::take_while([](int i){ return i <1000;}) ,
      [](int i){ std::cout << i << " "; });

  std::cout << "\n\n";
}
```

The uncommented list comprehension brings its functionality directly to the point. Ask for the natural numbers (`x <- [1 ..]`), keep the elements that are odd (`odd x`) and create the square of it (`x*x`). This corresponds to odd x as the filter, `x*x` as the map function. Subsequently, the list will be evaluated, as long as the elements are smaller than 1000 (`take while (<100)`).

The same algorithm is used in C++. Here is the result of the program: Fig. 9.

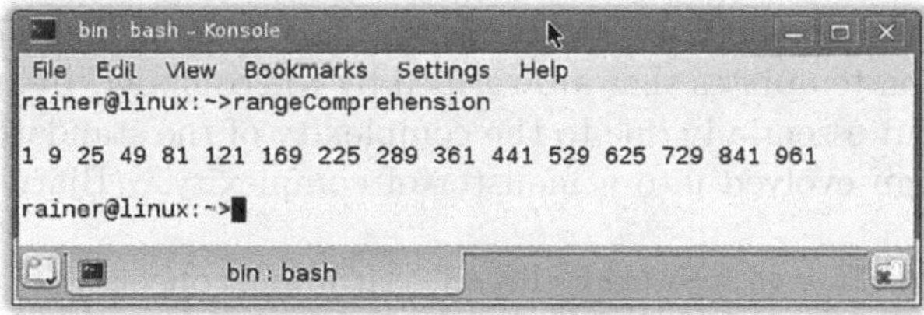

Fig. 9. List versus range comprehension

If you use in range comprehension several producers of natural numbers or filter functions, it will become very understanding resistant. Listing 1.20 introduces the Pythagorean triple in Haskell and C++. The Pythagorean triple consists of the natural numbers, which can occur as the length of a rectangular triangle.

Listing 1.20: Pythagorean triple with list comprehension and range comprehension

```
triples=[(x, y, z)|z <-[1..], x <-[1..z],y <-[x..z]
```

```
                    ,x^2 + y^2 == z^2]

auto triples =
  view::for_each(view::ints(1), [](int z){
    return view::for_each(view::ints(1, z), [=](int x){
      return view::for_each(view::ints(x, z), [=](int y){
        return yield_if(x*x + y*y == z*z,
                        std::make_tuple(x, y, z));
      });
    });
  });
```

The views algorithms (`view::for_each`) of the range library are distinguished in that way, that they are lightweight wrapper over the underlying range. They apply their arguments only on request and cannot change them. With Actions (`action::remove_if`) the range library contains an additional set of algorithms that can change their arguments and produce new range. In contrast to the views they evaluate their arguments immediately.

Thus, in order for the range library to be type safe, Eric Niebler used the type traits library [1]. This is no longer necessary with C++20.

5.3 Concepts Lite

The central idea of generic programming with templates in C++ is to define functions and classes that can be used with different types. It often happens, however, that a template with an inappropriate type is instantiated. The results are often pages of cryptic error messages at compile time, for which templates have gained notoriety. Therefore Concepts were planned as one of the most important feature for the C++11 standard. They should make it possible to make demands on templates that are verified by the compiler. In July 2009 they were removed but essentially due to the complexity of the standard. "The C++ 0x concept design evolved into a monster of complexity." (Bjarne Stroustrup) [12].

With C++20 C++ gets concepts lite [3]. Although concepts lite are simplified concepts in the first implementation, they have a lot to offer.

- Allow programmers to directly formulate the requirements for the templates as part of the interface
- Support the function overloading and the specialization of class templates based on the requirements on the templates.
- Generate significantly improved error messages by comparing the requirements of the template parameter with the current template arguments.

The additional value of concepts lite doesn't influences the compile time of the program. Concepts lite are inspired by Haskell's type classes. But concepts lite describes semantic categories and not syntactic constraints. There will be available type categories such as DefaultConstructible, MoveConstructible, CopyConstructible, AssignableMove, CopyAssignable or Destructible. For the container categories such as ReversibleContainer, AllocatorAwareContainer, SequenceContainer, ContinousContainer, AssociativeContainer or UnorderedAssociativeContainer.

Concepts Lite for Class Templates and Member of Classes. Concepts Lite is part of the template declaration. The function template sort requires, that

```
template <Sortable Cont>
void sort (Cont & container) {...}
```

the container must be sortable.

This can also be written explicitly as a requirement for the template parameter:

```
template <typename Cont>
  requires Sortable <Cont> ()
void sort (Cont & container) {...}
```

`Sortable` itself must be a constant expression of the kind predicate. This means `Sortable` can be evaluated at compile time and returns true or false.

The sort algorithm is now used by a container `lst`, which is not sortable. The compiler complained with an error message.

```
std::list <int> lst = {1998,2014,2003,2011};
sort(lst); // ERROR: lst is no random-access container with <
```

Concepts lite can be used in all kind of templates. This allows defining a class template `MyVector` (Listing 1.21), who can have only objects as elements:

Listing 1.21: My vector only for objects

```
template <Object T>
MyVector class {};

MyVector <int> v1; // OK
MyVector <int&> v2; // ERROR: int& is no object
```

In this case, the compiler complains, that the pointer object is not an object. `MyClass` can be further refined.

```
template <Object T>
class MyVector {
  ...
  requires copyable<T>()
  void push_back (const T& e);
  ...
};
```

Now the member function `push_back` of `MyVector` requires that the elements must be `copyable`.

Extended Functionality. A template can have multiple requirements for template parameters.

```
template<SequenceContainer S, EqualityComparable<value_type<S >> T>
Iterator_type<S> find (S && seq, const T & val) {...}
```

Function overloading is also supported by concepts lite (Listing 1.22).

Listing 1.22: Function overloading

```
template <InputIterator I>
void advance (I & iter, int n) {...}

template <BidirectionalIterator I>
void advance (I & iter, int n) {...}

template <RandomAccessIterator I>
void advance (I & iter, int n) {...}

std::list <int> lst {1,2,3,4,5,6,7,8,9};
std::list <int>::iterator i = lst.begin ();
std::advance (i, 2); // BidirectionalIterator
```

The function template `std::advance` places its iterator n position further. Depending on whether the iterator can only go forward, positioned in both directions or on arbitrary positions, different function templates are used. In the specific case of the list BidirectionalIterator is used.

Concepts Lite support the specialization of class templates (Listing 1.23).

Listing 1.23: Specialization of class templates

```
template <typename T>
MyVector class {};

template <Object T>
MyVector class {};

MyVector <int> v1;  // Object T
MyVector <int&> v2; // typename T
```

Thus the compiler used for `MyVector<int&> v2` the template without requirements, for `MyVector<int> v1` the partial specialization.

C++17 gets monads. Monads in the first approximation are a strategy to encapsulate side effects in C++. C++20 has a monad with the range library. As well the new data type `std::optional` in C++17 and the extensions of the futures, which were introduced in C++11, are monads.

5.4 std::optional

`std::optional` [4] is inspired by Haskell's Maybe monad [5]. `std::optional`, which should be originally available already in the small C++14-Standard, is a calculation that can contain a value. So the find algorithm or the query of a hash table has to deal with the fact that the request cannot be answered. Usually special values are used for the non-existents of a value. Examples are null pointers, empty strings or special integer values. This technique is time- consuming and error-prone, as these non-results must be treated specially and they are syntactically indistinguishable from a regular result. Listing 1.24 provides `std::optional` in more detail.

Listing 1.24: Asking for the result with std::optional

```
#include <experimental/optional>
#include<iostream>
#include<vector>

optional<int> getFirst(const std::vector<int>& vec){
  if ( !vec.empty() ) return optional<int>(vec[0]);
  else return optional<int>();
}

int main(){

  std::vector<int> myVec{1,2,3};
  std::vector<int> myEmptyVec;

  auto myInt= getFirst(myVec);

  if (myInt){
    std::cout << "*myInt: " << *myInt << std::endl;
    std::cout << "myInt.value(): " << myInt.value() << std::endl;
    std::cout << "myInt.value_or(2017):" << myInt.value_or(2017)
              << std::endl;
  }

  std::cout << std::endl;

  auto myEmptyInt= getFirst(myEmptyVec);

  if (!myEmptyInt){
    std::cout << "myEmptyInt.value_or(2017):"
              << myEmptyInt.value_or(2017)
              << std::endl;
  }

}
```

`std::optional` is the current time in the namespace `std::experimental`. That will change with C++17. Figure 10 shows the output of the program with the help of the online compiler on cpprefence.com [2].

Possible output:

```
*myInt: 1
myInt.value(): 1
myInt.value_or(2017):1

myEmptyInt.value_or(2017):2017
```

Fig. 10. std::optional

5.5 std::future Extensions

Modern C++ supports tasks. Tasks are pairs of **`std::promise`** and **`std::future`** objects that are connected via a channel. This channel can also communicate above thread boundaries. The **`std::promise`** (sender) pushes a value into the channel for which the **`std::future`** (receiver) waits. The sender can use his channel to the receiver not only for a value, but also for a notification or an exception.

The easiest way to create a promise is the function template **`std::async`** (Listing 1.25). This behaves like an asynchronous function call.

Listing 1.25: Creation of a future with std::async

```
int a = 2000
int b = 11;
std::future<int> sum = std::async ([=] {return a + b;});
std::cout<< sum.get () << std::endl;
```

The call **`std::async`** performs several actions. On the one hand it produces the two communication endpoints promise and future; secondly, it combines them with a channel. The promise use the lambda function **`[=]{return a + b;}`** as a work package. The lambda function get their arguments a and b from the calling context. C++ - runtime decides whether the promise will be executed in the same or a separate thread. Decision criteria can be the size of the work package, the utilization of the system or the number of cores.

By the **`sum.get()`** call the future ask the result from the channel. This can be done only once. If the promise has not yet produced its value, the get-call of the future is blocked.

Tasks allow significantly easier and safer handling of threads, they have no common state. Therefore a deadlock happens significantly less often. Nevertheless their C++11-implementation has one major drawback. The composition of **`std::future`** objects is not possible. This will change with C++20. Listing 1.26 present some examples from the official proposal n3721 [10].

Listing 1.26: Extensions of std::future

```
future<int> f1= async([]() {return 123;});
future<string> f2 = f1.then([](future<int> f) {
  return f.get().to_string();
});
```

```
future<int> futures[] = {async([](){return intResult(125);}),
                         async([](){return intResult(456);})};

future<vector<future<int>>> any_f = when_any(begin(futures),
                                              end(futures));

future<int> futures[] = {async([](){return intResult(125);}),
                         async([](){return intResult(456);})};

future<vector<future<int>>> all_f = when_all(begin(futures),
                                              end(futures));
```

The future `f2` will be executed when the future `f1` is done. Chaining can of course significantly expand: `f1.then(...)then(...)then(...)....` The future `any_f` is executed when one of his futures finished. Unlike the future `all_f`. It runs if all of its futures are done.

Of course, a question still remains. What have futures in common with functional programming? A lot! The extended futures are a Monad. For this purpose, a function for a monad is required that lifts the simple type in the complex type. Secondly, it requires a feature that allows the composition of the complex type. `make_ready_future` transformed a simple type in a complex type, a so called monadic value. The two functions `then` and `future<future <T>>` are equivalent to the bind operator in Haskell. The bind operator ensures that a monadic value can be transformed in another monadic value. bind provides the function composition in the Monad.

5.6 Conclusion

This question will probably make many readers of this article. C++17 [9] and C++20 take - as the other popular programming languages Java, Scala, Python or C# - very many ideas of functional programming in order to master the challenges of a modern programming language. These are generally the challenges of multicore architectures and the challenges of generic programming. Haskell expressiveness and type safety is based on mathematical concepts. The mathematical concepts are not only for Haskell the key for mastering the upcoming challenges.

References

1. Type traits, 13 February 2016. http://en.cppreference.com/w/cpp/header/type_traits
2. Webpage, 13 February 2016. http://en.cppreference.com/w/
3. Proposal n3701, 2 July 2013. https://isocpp.org/blog/2013/07/new-paper-n3701-concepts-lite-a.-sutton-b.-stroustrup-g.-dos-reis
4. std::optional, 13 May 2016. http://en.cppreference.com/w/cpp/experimental/optional
5. Maybe monad, 18 June 2016. https://en.wikipedia.org/wiki/Monad_
6. Syntactic sugar, 26 February 2016. https://en.wikipedia.org/wiki/Syntactic_sugar

7. Fold variations in haskell, 3 April 2016. https://en.wikibooks.org/wiki/Haskell/Lists_III#Folds
8. Fold variations in haskell, 3 April 2016. http://en.cppreference.com/w/cpp/language/fold
9. C++17, 3 June 2016. https://en.wikipedia.org/wiki/C
10. Proposal n3721, 3 June 2016. http://www.open-std.org/jtc1/sc22/wg21/docs/papers/2013/n3721.pdf
11. Eric Niebler: Ranges library, 3 March 2016. https://ericniebler.github.io/std/wg21/D4128.html
12. Bjarne Stroustrup: Concepts, 13 March 2016. https://isocpp.org/blog/2013/02/concepts-lite-constraining-templates-with-predicates-andrew-sutton-bjarne-s

Functional, Reactive Web Programming in F#

Adam Granicz(✉) and Loic Denuziere

IntelliFactory, Budapest, Hungary
{granicz.adam,loic.denuziere}@intellifactory.com
http://intellifactory.com

Abstract. In these lecture notes, we present the basics of functional and reactive web programming through WebSharper, a mature web development framework for F# [7], and its UI.Next [9] library for constructing reactive markup with two-way data binding. You will learn the theory behind similar technologies, discover its advantages, and develop simple applications using the concepts learned.

Keywords: Functional programming · Reactive programming · F# · WebSharper

1 Introduction

Reactive programming is a useful paradigm for specifying applications depending on data that changes throughout the course of the application's execution. Instead of specifying callbacks to be executed when a piece of data changes, reactive programming approaches allow the construction of a *dataflow graph*, wherein changes to data sources are propagated through the graph. Elements in the display layer may then be written declaratively as a function of nodes in the dataflow graph, reducing the need for callbacks.

2 WebSharper

WebSharper is a mature, open source reactive web framework for F#. It offers a uniform, single-language programming model; a host of web development abstractions such as formlets, flowlets, and piglets; and an ecosystem of dozens of extensions to popular JavaScript libraries, enabling programmers to developer robust client-server, HTML, and single-page applications (SPAs) in F#.

The reader is encouraged to browse through the documentation [1] for an in-depth treatment of various WebSharper topics, including installation, getting started, project templates, the main F# to JavaScript compiler, working with JavaScript libraries, extending .NET compilation coverage via proxying, pagelets, sitelets, formlets, flowlets, and piglets, among others.

In this tutorial, we are primarily interested in WebSharper's reactive foundation `UI.Next` [9] and its associated web abstractions for reactive formlets, piglets, and sitelets [8].

V. Zsók et al. (Eds.): CEFP 2015, LNCS 10094, pp. 137–160, 2019.
https://doi.org/10.1007/978-3-030-28346-9_5

3 WebSharper UI.Next

UI.Next is a client-side WebSharper library providing a novel, pragmatic and convenient approach to UI reactivity. It includes:

- A *dataflow layer* for expressing user inputs and values computed from them as time-varying values. This approach is related to Functional Reactive Programming (FRP), but differs from it in significant ways discussed later.
- A *reactive DOM* library for displaying these time-varying values in a functional way. Instead of explicitly inserting, modifying and removing DOM nodes, we work with values that represent a virtual DOM tree based on inputs. These inputs are nodes of the dataflow layer, rather than a single state value associated with the component.

3.1 Dynamic Dataflow

In UI.Next, the flow of time-varying values is represented as a dataflow graph. This graph consists of two primitives: Vars, which are observable mutable reference cells, and Views, which are projections of Vars in the dataflow graph, and can be manipulated via standard functional combinators such as Map and Bind.

When the value of an input node (a Var) is set, it is propagated through the internal nodes (Views) down to the output node (Sink).

Reactive Variables. A value of type Var<'T> is an input node in the dataflow graph. Its value can be imperatively read or set using the Value property, the functions Var.Get and Var.Set, or the := operator. In the following example, v is a Var<string>.

```
let v = Var.Create "initial value"
// Update the value of v
v := "another value"    // Var.Set v "another value"
// Read the value of v
v.Value                 // Var.Get v
```

Reactive variables can also be associated with an element in the DOM layer, either through various DOM combinators that create input controls bound to reactive variables, or through observing them through reactive Views.

Reactive Views. A value of type View<'T> is an internal node in the dataflow graph. It is not possible to explicitly get or set the value of a View<'T>. Instead, at any time its value is determined by the value of the nodes that precede it in the dataflow graph, and can be observed by other Views. For instance, the following snippet defines a reactive view vUpper, which reflects the uppercased value of its corresponding variable v.

```
let v = Var.Create ""
let vUpper = View.Map (fun t -> t.ToUpper()) v.View
```

Operations on Reactive Views. The following list summarizes the core reactive view constructors and combinators. An up to date description of these operators is found in the project documentation [1].

– The simplest way to create a `View<'T>` is by using the `View` property of a reactive variable, which creates a view whose value is always the current value of the variable.
– `View.Const :'T -> View<'T>` creates a view whose value never changes.

```
let v = View.Const 1 // v's value will always be 1
```

– `View.FromVar : v:Var<'T> -> View<'T>` creates a view whose value is always the current value of v. It is equivalent to `v.View`.
– `View.Map : f:('A ->'B) -> v:View<'A> -> View<'B>` creates a view whose value is always the result of calling `f` on the current value of `v`.

```
let v = Var.Create "initial"
let vw = View.Map (fun t -> t.ToUpper()) v.View
// vw's current value is now "INITIAL"
```

– `View.MapAsync : f:('A -> Async<'B>) -> v:View<'A> -> View<'B>` creates a view whose value is always the result of calling `f` on the current value of `v`. Note that if `v` is updated before the previous asynchronous call returns, then this previous call is discarded.
– `View.Map2 : f:('A ->'B ->'C) -> va:View<'A> -> vb:View<'B> -> View<'C>` creates a view whose value is always the result of calling `f` on the current values of `va` and `vb`.

```
type Person = { Name: string; Age: int }

let name = Var.Create "John Doe"
let age = Var.Create 42
let person = View.Map2 (fun n a -> { Name=n; Age=a }) name age
// person's current value is now { Name="John Doe"; Age=42 }
name <- "Jane Doe"
// person's current value is now { Name="Jane Doe"; Age=42 }
```

– `View.Apply : vf:View<'A ->'B> -> va:View<'A> -> View<'B>` creates a view whose value is always the result of calling the current value of `vf` on the current value of `va`. It is particularly useful in combination with `View.Const` to do the same as `View.Map2` but with more than two views:

```
type Person = { FirstName: string; LastName: string; Age: int }

let first = Var.Create "John"
let last = Var.Create "Doe"
let age = Var.Create 42
let (<*>) f x = View.Apply f x
```

```
let vPerson =
    View.Const (fun f l a -> { FirstName=f; LastName=l; Age=a })
        <*> first.View
        <*> last.View
        <*> age.View
```

- `View.Bind : f:('A -> View<'B>) -> View<'A> -> View<'B>` is an important combinator as it allows a subgraph to change depending on its inputs. For example, in the following code, when `isEmail`'s value is `true`, the graph contains `email` as a node, and when it is `false`, it contains `username` as a node instead.

```
type UserId =
    | Username of string
    | Email of string

let isEmail = Var.Create false
let username = Var.Create ""
let email = Var.Create ""
let userId =
    isEmail |> View.Bind (fun isEmail ->
        if isEmail then
            View.Map Email email.View
        else
            View.Map Username username.View
    )
```

- `View.Join : View<View<'A>> -> View<'A>` "flattens" a view of a view. It can be used equivalently to `Bind`, as the following equalities hold:

```
View.Bind f x = View.Join (View.Map f x)
View.Join x = View.Bind id x
```

Dynamic composition via `View.Bind` and `View.Join` should be used with some care. Whenever static composition (such as `View.Map2`) can do the trick, it should be preferred. One concern here is efficiency, and another is state, identity and sharing.

- `View.SnapshotOn : init:'B -> va:View<'A> -> vb:View<'B> -> View<'B>` produces a snapshot of `vb`: a `View` that has the same value as `vb`, except that it is only updated when `va` is updated. Before `va` is first updated, the result `View` has the value `init`.
`SnapshotOn` is typically used to bring events such as submit buttons into the dataflow graph. In the example below, `loginData` is initialized with `None`, and is updated with the current login data wrapped in `Some` whenever `submit` is updated. It is then possible to map a `View` or a `Sink` on `loginData` that performs the actual login.

```
type LoginData = { Username: string; Password: string }
```

```
let submit = Var.Create ()
let username = Var.Create ""
let password = Var.Create ""
let loginData =
    View.Const (fun u p -> Some { Username = u; Password = p })
    <*> username.View
    <*> password.View
    |> View.SnapshotOn None submit.View
```

- `View.Convert : f:('A ->'B) -> v:View<seq<'A>> -> View<seq<'B>>` maps views on sequences with "shallow" memoization. The process remembers inputs from the previous step, and reuses outputs from the previous step when possible instead of calling the converter function. Memory use is proportional to the longest sequence taken by v. Since only one step of history is retained, there is no memory leak. Requires equality on `'A`.
- `View.ConvertBy : key:('A ->'K) -> f:('A ->'B) -> v:View<seq<'A>> -> View<seq<'B>>` is a variant on `Convert` that uses a key function to determine identity on inputs, rather than an equality constraint on the type `'A` itself.
- `View.ConvertSeq : f:(View<'A> ->'B) -> v:View<seq<'A>> -> View<seq<'B>>` is an extended form of `Convert` where the conversion function accepts a reactive view. At every step, changes to inputs identified as being the same object are propagated via that view. Requires equality on `'A`.
- `View.ConvertSeqBy : key:('A ->'K) -> f:(View<'A> ->'B) -> v: View<seq<'A>> -> View<seq<'B>>` is a variant on `ConvertSeq` that uses a key function to determine identity on inputs, rather than an equality constraint on the type `'A` itself.

Sinks. Once a graph is built out of `Vars` and `Views`, it needs to be run to react to changes. The function `View.Sink : f:('T -> unit) -> v:View <'T> -> unit` is the output node of the dataflow graph. This function calls `f` with the current value of `v` whenever it is updated. It is highly recommended to have a single `Sink` running per dataflow graph; memory leaks may happen if the application repeatedly spawns `Sink` processes that never get collected.

Using `loginData` from the previous section, the following code extracts the username-password pair from the underlying reactive variables when the state of `submit` is updated:

```
do
   loginData
   |> View.Sink (function
       | None -> ()
       | Some loginData ->
          Rpc.LoginUser loginData // A user-defined function
          |> Async.Start)
```

It is relatively rare to call View.Sink directly. Instead, reactive views are generally bound to the DOM layer, which calls Sink when inserted into the document.

3.2 Reactive DOM

In UI.Next, sequences of reactive HTML or SVG elements are represented by the Doc monoid type. Unlike in previous WebSharper DOM representations, the Doc API is mostly generative: it is not advised to imperatively insert nodes or change their contents. Instead, dynamic nodes are generated based on a dataflow graph.

Creating Doc Values. The following list contains the core Doc operations. Most of these functions are located in the namespace WebSharper.UI.Next. Dynamic functions that involve Vars, Views or Dom.Elements are under WebSharper.UI.Next.Client.

- Doc.TextNode | text : string -> Doc creates a Doc composed of a single text node with the given content.

  ```
  let node = Doc.TextNode "WebSharper"
  ```

- Doc.TextView : View<string> -> Doc creates a Doc composed of a single text node whose contents is always equal to the value of the given reactive view. Also aliased as textView.

  ```
  let text = Var.Create "WebSharper"
  let doc = Doc.TextView text.View
  // doc HTML equivalent is now: WebSharper
  text.Value <- "UI.Next"
  // doc HTML equivalent is now: UI.Next
  ```

- Doc.Static : Dom.Element -> Doc creates a Doc from an existing DOM element.
- Doc.Element|SvgElement : string -> seq<Attr> -> seq<Doc> -> Doc creates a Doc composed of a single HTML/SVG element with the given tag name, attributes and child nodes.
- Doc.EmbedView : View<Doc> -> Doc creates a time-varying Doc from a view on a Doc.
- Doc.BindView : ('T -> Doc) -> View<'T> -> Doc creates a time-varying Doc from a view and its rendered Doc. Also available as a method .Doc(f) on View<'T>.

HTML Attributes. Each HTML attribute has suffixed variants to cater to different usage scenarios. For each HTML5 attribute x, these are:

- attr.x : value:string -> Attr: creates an attribute x with the specified value. Equivalent to Attr.Create"x" value.

- `attr.xDyn : value:View<string> -> Attr`: creates an attribute `x` whose value varies with the given view. Equivalent to `Attr.Dynamic "x" value`.
- `attr.xDynPred : value:View<string> -> pred:View<bool> -> Attr`: creates an attribute `x` with a time-varying value, which is set or unset based on the given time-varying predicate. Equivalent to `Attr.DynamicPred "x" value pred`
- `attr.fooAnim : value:View<'T> -> convert:('T -> string) -> trans:Trans<'T> -> Attr`: creates an animated attribute `x` with the given time-varying value and transition. Equivalent to `Attr.Animated "foo" trans view convert`.

Next to ordinary attributes, additional syntax is available for dealing with event handlers. For every HTML event `x`, the following are available:

- `on.x : (Dom.Element -> #Dom.Event -> unit) -> Attr`: creates an event handler for `x`. The exact subtype of `Dom.Event` passed depends on the actual event; for example, `on.click` passes a `Dom.MouseEvent`.
- `on.xView : View<'T> -> (Dom.Element -> #Dom.Event -> 'T ->unit) -> Attr`: creates an event handler for `x`, which also passes the current value of the given view.

HTML Combinators. HTML constructors are defined in the `WebSharper.UI.Next.Html` namespace. For each HTML5 element `x`, two functions are available:

- `x: children:seq<Doc> -> Doc`: constructs an HTML node `x` with the given subnodes. Equivalent to

  `Doc.Element "x" [] children`
- `xAttr: attrs:seq<Attr> -> children:seq<Doc> -> Doc`: constructs an HTML node `x` with the given attributes and subnodes. Equivalent to

  `Doc.Element "x" attrs children`

The following snippet gives an actual example:

```
div [
    buttonAttr [
        attr.''class'' "my-button"
        on.click (fun e arg -> JS.Alert "clicked!")
    ] [
        text "Click me"
    ]
]
```

SVG elements are similarly available in the `SvgElements` module.

Combining Reactive Markup. Docs are modeled as a monoid type. The following operations are available for combining them:

- `Doc.Append : Doc -> Doc -> Doc` appends two node sequences.
- `Doc.Concat : seq<Doc> -> Doc` concatenates a sequence of node sequences.
- `Doc.Empty : Doc` creates an empty document.

Input Forms. And finally, reflecting user input into variables and providing two-way data binding is accomplished via a series of functions that take reactive variables along with additional arguments and construct various forms of input controls.

These include:

- `Doc.Input : seq<Attr> -> Var<string> -> Doc` creates a textbox from a sequence of attributes and a reactive variable.
- `Doc.InputArea : seq<Attr> -> Var<string> -> Doc` creates a textarea.
- `Doc.PasswordBox : seq<Attr> -> Var<string> -> Doc` creates a textbox for password input.
- `Doc.CheckBox : ('T -> string) -> list<'T> -> Var<list<'T>> -> Doc` creates a set of check boxes from the given list. Requires a function to show each item, and a list variable which is updated with the currently-selected items.
- `Doc.Select : seq<Attr> -> ('T -> string) -> list<'T> -> Var<'T> -> Doc` creates a selection box from the given list. Requires a function to show each item, and a variable which is updated with the currently-selected item.
- `Doc.Button : caption: string -> seq<Attr> -> (unit -> unit) -> Doc` creates a button with the given caption and attributes. Takes a callback which is executed when the button is clicked.
- `Doc.Link : caption: string -> seq<Attr> -> (unit -> unit) -> Doc` creates a link with the given caption and attributes which does not change the page, but instead executes the given callback.

3.3 List Models

`Vars` are the observable equivalent of mutable reference cells, and store a single value. However, a common need for web applications is to use a reactive *collection* of values. For this purpose, `UI.Next` provides `ListModels` [8], which are observable ordered key-value collections. A value of type `ListModel<'K, 'T>` is a collection of items of type `'T` identified by a key of type `'K`.

The general API of `ListModels` is listed below, providing members to insert, delete, and update individual items in the collection wrapped by it.

```
type ListModel<'k,'t when 'k:equality> =
    member View : View<seq<'t>>
    member Add : 't -> unit
```

```
    member RemoveByKey : 'k -> unit
    member UpdateBy : ('t -> option<'t>) -> 'k -> unit
    member Key : ('t -> 'k)
module ListModel =
    val Create : ('t -> 'k) -> seq<'t> -> ListModel<'k, 't>
```

Just like a `Var<'T>` is observable as a `View<'T>` using the function `View.FromVar`, a `ListModel<'K, 'T>` is observable as a `View<seq<'T>>` using the function `ListModel.View`. These `View` values can be integrated into the dataflow graph by a variety of combinators, including `Doc.BindSeqCached` that maps elements of the underlying collection to reactive DOM and uses shallow memoization to process incremental changes only, thus providing rendering updates only where needed.

In their basic form, `ListModels` only manage client-side state with no persistence. Simple client-only persistence can be added by using a `Store` implementation or using the built-in alternative to store list models in HTML5 local storage. For instance, a simple data list model for storing names and ages can be defined as:

```
type Person = { Name: string; Age: int }
with
    static member Create name age =
        { Name = name; Age = age }

let MyPeopleRegister =
    ListModel.CreateWithStorage
        (fun p -> p.Name)
        (Storage.LocalStorage "people" Serializer.Default)
```

Using such a store avoids losing client-side data on page refreshes, and can be a good aid in simple client-side scenarios.

3.4 Reactive Templates

The programmatic use of reactive variables and their views to generate reactive markup, while straightforward, has the obvious disadvantage that it requires embedding markup into code. `UI.Next` employs an innovative use of F# type providers [2] to automate this chore. This involves reading a markup document passed as an argument to the type provider, and scanning for various placeholders with reactive semantics within inner templates declared via special `data` attributes.

String Variables. The simplest form of a placeholder holds a string value. This is defined using the syntax `{v}`, and generate a string member `v`.

Reactive Variables and Views. The following markup snippet defines a reactive variable for an input box using a special data attribute `data-var`, and uses its view (referred to with `$!{...}`) to show what was typed in it:

```
<input data-var="Username" />
<p>You typed: $!{Username}</p>
```

The type of a reactive variable defined with `data-var` is determined as follows:

- An `<input type="text">`, an `<input>` with no or unrecognized `type` attribute, or a `<textarea>`, yields a `Var<string>`.
- An `<input type="number">` yields a `Var<float>`.
- An `<input type="checkbox">` yields a `Var<bool>`.
- A `<select>` yields a `Var<string>`, corresponding to the values of its `<option>` subnodes.

Event Handlers. Event handlers are defined using `data-event-xxx`, where `xxx` is the name of the HTML event being bound. The following snippet binds a click event handler to a button, added as a new member `Add` with type `Dom.Element -> Dom.Event -> unit`.

```
<button data-event-click="Add">Add</button>
```

Attributes. Attributes, pairs of attribute names and values, can be dynamically added or removed using `data-attr`, which defines a new member of type `Attr`. Attribute values can be embedded via string variables directly.

Reactive Markup. `Doc` content placeholders can be added using `data-hole` and `data-replace`. The former retains the containing node, the latter doesn't, both defining a new member of type `seq<Doc>`. Placeholders named `scripts`, `meta` and `styles`, ignoring case, that are otherwise used in server-side templating, are ignored.

Nested Templates. Nested templates are defined using `data-template="Name"`. The HTML element on which this attribute is placed will not be inserted into the final document. If this is required, an alternate form `data-children-template="Name"` can be used.

This and the previous placeholders trigger the `UI.Next` templating type provider to generate a type for each template, with appropriately typed members to correspond to each placeholder.

For instance, assuming a parent template node with `data-template="NewUserDialog"` in an external designer file `main.html`, the above placeholders will enable the following F# code:

```
open WebSharper.UI.Next.Templating
type App = Template<"main.html">

...
div [
    App.NewUserDialog.Doc(
        Username = ...
        Add = (fun e args -> ...)
    )
]
```

Here, `Username`, of type `Var<string>`, can be used to assign values programmatically, or retrieving the value currently typed into the corresponding input box, and `Add` can be used to set up a click event handler for its associated button.

Dealing with list models follows a similar construction, typically involving a pair of nested templates. The following template snippet gives an example:

```
<div data-children-template="Messages">
  <ul data-hole="Container">
    <li data-template="Message">
      $!{Title}
    </li>
  </ul>
</div>
```

4 Examples

The examples in this section are `UI.Next` Single-Page Applications (SPAs). These are the simplest form of WebSharper applications, and are based on a single HTML markup file and a corresponding F# code base that generates included JavaScript content. The F# code typically interacts with the markup by dynamically inserting and updating DOM nodes. The former is accomplished by utility functions such as `Doc.RunById`, which takes a `Doc` value and renders it into the DOM node with the specified `id`.

The reader is encouraged to try the examples in this section. The easiest way to do so is to start from a Single-Page Application template, shipped with WebSharper for various popular IDE integrations such as Visual Studio or Xamarin Studio. These can be obtained from the project website [1]. The code for the main F# file and/or the master markup document to apply within the SPA application template is given below.

Using the SPA template, a simple application setup looks like the following:

```
namespace YourApplication

open WebSharper.UI.Next
open WebSharper.UI.Next.Html
```

```
open WebSharper.UI.Next.Client

[<JavaScript>]
module Client =
    let Main =
    // Generate DOM content
    ...
```

4.1 Reactive Views

This example, shown in Fig. 1, demonstrates how to react to user input. A simple textbox, bound to a reactive variable, is used for taking an input value, which is then transformed into a list of various mapped views and embedded into reactive DOM.

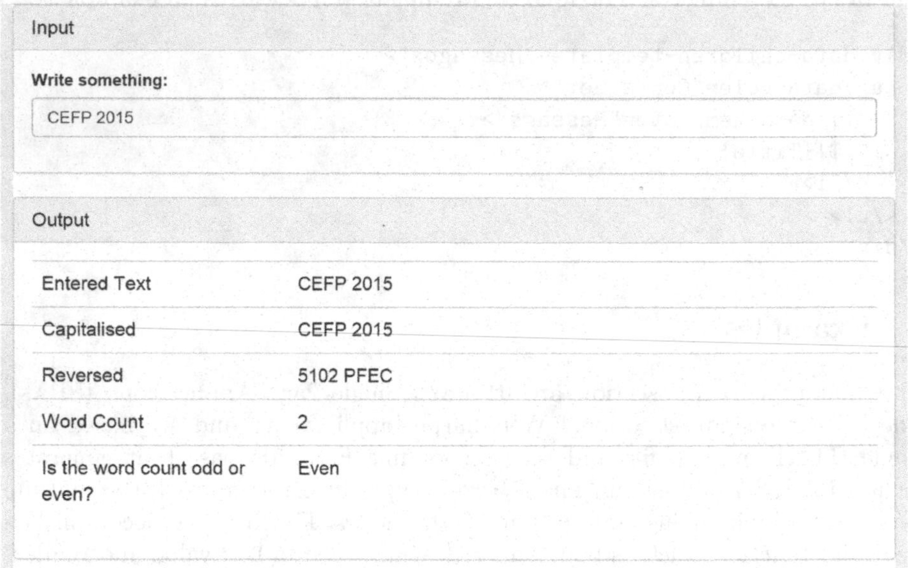

Input

Write something:

CEFP 2015

Output

Entered Text	CEFP 2015
Capitalised	CEFP 2015
Reversed	5102 PFEC
Word Count	2
Is the word count odd or even?	Even

Fig. 1. Reactive views of a simple input

To construct markup, we use a module B (short for Bootstrap, a popular JavaScript/CSS library that we assume is linked from the master HTML document) with various helpers that yield annotated DOM nodes.

```
[<JavaScript>]
module B =
    let cls s = attr.``class`` s
    let panel els = divAttr [cls "panel panel-default"] els
    let panelHeading els = divAttr [cls "panel-heading"] els
```

```
let panelTitle els = h3Attr [cls "panel-title"] els
let panelBody els = divAttr [cls "panel-body"] els
let form els =
    formAttr
        [cls "form-horizontal"; Attr.Create "role" "form"]
        els
let formGroup els = divAttr [cls "form-group"] els
let labelFor id els =
    labelAttr
        [cls "col-sm-2 control-label"; attr.``for`` id] els
let formControl id v =
    divAttr [cls "col-sm-10"] [
        Doc.Input [cls "form-control"; attr.id id] v
    ]
let table els = tableAttr [cls "table"] els
```

With these DOM shorthands, we can implement the entire application as follows. First, we create a reactive variable input, and bind that to a textbox via Doc.Input.

```
let Main =
    let input = Var.Create ""
    let inputField =
        B.panel [
            B.panelHeading [
              B.panelTitle [text "Input"]
            ]
            B.panelBody [
              B.form [
                B.formGroup [
                  B.labelFor "inputBox" [text "Write something:"]
                  B.formControl "inputBox" input
                ]
              ]
            ]
        ]
```

Next, we map the view of input to the desired forms. Changes to the user input are automatically propagated to these views.

```
    let view = input.View
    let viewCaps =
        View.Map (fun s -> s.ToUpper()) view
    let viewReverse =
        View.Map (fun s ->
            new string(Array.rev(s.ToCharArray()))) view
    let viewWordCount =
```

```
        View.Map (fun s -> s.Split([| ' ' |]).Length) view
    let viewWordCountStr =
        View.Map string viewWordCount
    let viewWordOddEven =
        View.Map (fun i ->
            if i % 2 = 0 then "Even" else "Odd") viewWordCount
```

These are then rendered into a table, where each row contains the various mapped views.

```
    let views =
        [
            ("Entered Text", view)
            ("Capitalised", viewCaps)
            ("Reversed", viewReverse)
            ("Word Count", viewWordCountStr)
            ("Is the word count odd or even?", viewWordOddEven)
        ]

    let tableRow (lbl, view) =
        tr [
            td [text lbl]
            tdAttr [attr.style "width:70%"] [textView view]
        ] :> Doc

    let tbl =
        B.panel [
            B.panelHeading [
                B.panelTitle [text "Output"]
            ]
            B.panelBody [
                B.table [
                    tbody [
                        Doc.Concat (List.map tableRow views)
                    ]
                ]
            ]
        ]
```

And last, we wrap the input and table content into a DIV node and insert it into a "main" placeholder.

```
    div [
        inputField
        tbl
    ]
    |> Doc.RunById "main"
```

4.2 Reactive Formlets

Formlets [3,4] are one of the fundamental web abstractions available in the WebSharper ecosystem and its reactive foundations [8]. They provide a type-safe, composable encoding of web forms using a highly declarative syntax, making them a perfect tool for quick prototyping of user interfaces that need to collect user input.

Consider the following example. It implements a simple web form for inputting a string/int pair, along with basic client-side validation, and a submit button that echos the input on success.

```
namespace Samples

open WebSharper
open WebSharper.JavaScript
open WebSharper.UI.Next
open WebSharper.UI.Next.Html
open WebSharper.UI.Next.Client
open WebSharper.UI.Next.Formlets

[<JavaScript>]
module Client =
    type Person = { FirstName: string; Age: int }

    let Main =
        Formlet.Return (fun fn age -> { FirstName=fn; Age=age })
        <*> Controls.Input "First name"
        <*> (Controls.Input "20"
            |> Validation.IsMatch "^[1-9][0-9]*$" "Need an integer"
            |> Formlet.Map int)
        |> Formlet.WithSubmit "Submit"
        |> Formlet.Run (fun person ->
            JS.Alert (person.FirstName + "/" + string person.Age)
        )
        |> Doc.RunById "main"
```

This formlet code would look exactly the same using ordinary WebSharper formlets, e.g. those found in the `WebSharper.Formlets` namespace. However, as implemented here, `UI.Next` formlets offer a fundamentally more powerful feature: data binding.

The code below implements the same age/name formlet, but uses reactive variables bound to the two input controls.

```
...
open WebSharper.UI.Next.Notation

[<JavaScript>]
```

```
module Client =
    type Person = { FirstName: string; Age: int }

    let Main =
        let first = Var.Create "First name"
        let age = Var.Create "20"
        Formlet.Return (fun fn age -> { FirstName=fn; Age=age })
        <*> Controls.InputVar first
        <*> (Controls.InputVar age
            |> Validation.IsMatch "^[1-9][0-9]*$" "Need an integer"
            |> Formlet.Map int)
        ...
```

In particular, note the use of `Controls.InputVar` along with the newly created reactive variables. The two-way binding created between the user control and the reactive variables ensure that changes to one are propagated to the other. For instance, upon submitting a given name/age pair, we can set the contents of the input controls freely by assigning the reactive variables as shown below.

```
        ...
        |> Formlet.Run (fun person ->
            JS.Alert (person.FirstName + "/" + string person.Age)
            first := "Enter another name"
            age := "20"
        )
```

4.3 Reactive Piglets

Piglets [5] improve on formlets by retaining the same concise, declarative construction and type-safe, composable build-up, and adding the extra flexibility of decoupling the presentation layer from a piglet's definition. By doing so, developers are free to customize the presentation of a piglet in any way they prefer, as opposed to the inherent look and feel that formlets come hardcoded with. Piglets also enable reusing piglet definitions and retargeting their presentation to different execution platforms or content delivery channels, making them an excellent choice for modern web applications.

Ordinary WebSharper piglets are defined in the `WebSharper.Piglets` namespace, and their reactive counterparts are implemented in `WebSharper.Forms`, now the primary means of constructing reactive user interfaces in WebSharper.

The following example demonstrates using reactive piglets for a simple login dialog.

```
namespace LoginWithReactivePiglets

open WebSharper
open WebSharper.UI.Next
```

```
[<JavaScript>]
module Client =
  open WebSharper.JavaScript
  open WebSharper.UI.Next.Html
  open WebSharper.UI.Next.Client
  open WebSharper.UI.Next.Notation
  open WebSharper.Forms

  let loginForm =
    let user, password = Var.Create "", Var.Create ""
    Form.Return (fun user pass -> user, pass)
    <*> (Form.YieldVar user
        |> Validation.IsNotEmpty "Must enter a username")
    <*> (Form.YieldVar password
        |> Validation.IsNotEmpty "Must enter a password")
    |> Form.WithSubmit
    |> Form.Run (fun (u, p) ->
      user := ""; password := "" // Reset input controls
      JS.Alert("Welcome, " + u + "!")
    )
    |> Form.Render (fun user pass submit ->
      div [
        div [label [text "Username: "]; Doc.Input [] user]
        div [label [text "Password: "]; Doc.PasswordBox [] pass]
        Doc.Button "Log in" [] submit.Trigger
        div [
           Doc.ShowErrors submit.View (fun errors ->
             errors
               |> Seq.map (fun m -> p [text m.Text])
               |> Seq.cast
               |> Doc.Concat)
        ]
      ]
  )
  |> fun s -> s.RunById "main"
```

In this application, note the use of `Form.YieldVar`, a variant of `Form.Yield`, that binds a reactive variable to a piglet for its input. These piglets are in turn composed into larger piglets using the piglet `<*>` bind operator, whose return value is composed as a tuple. Similar to formlets, a piglet can be acted upon, e.g. taking its return values and producing a side-effect. In addition to `Form.Run`, the equivalent of `Formlet.Run` for reactive piglets, we make use of `Form.Render` to give a render implementation to our piglet.

The presentation uses `UI.Next` HTML combinators and various `Doc` functions, such as `Doc.Input`, `Doc.PasswordBox`, `Doc.Button`, and `Doc.ShowErrors` to produce reactive markup. This latter function takes the view of the submitter and renders any validation and other error messages into a `Doc`.

Alternate Rendering. Piglets enable different rendering functions for the same piglet definition. In the example below, we extend the login piglet with a checkbox and provide a Bootstrap-based rendering using `WebSharper.Forms.Bootstrap`, an additional library which essentially wraps the common reactive input controls in Bootstrap-specific markup.

Username

this_user

Password

Must enter a password

Keep me logged in

Log in

Must enter a password

Fig. 2. A reactive login piglet using Bootstrap rendering

```
namespace LoginWithBootstrap

open WebSharper
open WebSharper.UI.Next
open WebSharper.UI.Next.Html

[<JavaScript>]
module Client =
  open WebSharper.JavaScript
  open WebSharper.UI.Next.Client
  open WebSharper.UI.Next.Notation
  open WebSharper.Forms
  module B = WebSharper.Forms.Bootstrap.Controls

  let cls = Attr.Class

  let loginForm =
    let user, password = Var.Create "", Var.Create ""
    Form.Return (fun user pass check -> user, pass, check)
```

```
<*> (Form.YieldVar user
    |> Validation.IsNotEmpty "Must enter a username")
<*> (Form.YieldVar password
    |> Validation.IsNotEmpty "Must enter a password")
<*> Form.Yield false
|> Form.WithSubmit
|> Form.Run (fun (u, p, check) ->
  JS.Alert("Welcome, " + u + "!")
  user := ""; password := ""
)
|> Form.Render (fun user pass check submit ->
  form [
    B.Simple.InputWithError "Username" user submit.View
    B.Simple.InputPasswordWithError "Password" pass submit.View
    B.Simple.Checkbox "Keep me logged in" check
    B.Button "Log in" [cls "btn btn-primary"] submit.Trigger
    B.ShowErrors [attr.style "margin-top:1em;"] submit.View
  ]
)
|> fun s -> s.RunById "main"
```

`WebSharper.Forms.Bootstrap` provides standard Bootstrap rendering, and eliminates much of the notational overhead for constructing input controls. For instance, `Controls.ShowErrors` no longer needs to specify how to convert error messages into reactive markup, it's performed automatically using a default rendering strategy as shown in Fig. 2.

4.4 Reactive Templates

Our final example is a simple TODO task register shown in Fig. 3. The application can input and manage simple tasks to be performed. It involves a designer template `index.html` that contains the core look and feel, and `UI.Next` reactive placeholders for the dynamic content. It defines a `Main` template that has a `ListContainers` master placeholder and a nested template `ListItem`. Both the `Main` and the `ListItem` templates contain various reactive placeholders defined via `data-xxx` attributes and `!{...}`.

```
<!DOCTYPE html>
<html lang="en">
<head>
  <meta chartset="utf-8" />
  <meta name="viewport"
        content="width=device-width,initial-scale=1.0" />
  <title>My TODO list</title>
  <link rel="stylesheet" href="//.../bootstrap.min.css" />
  <style> ...  </style>
```

```
</head>
<body>
  <div style="width: 400px">
    <h1>My TODO list</h1>
    <div id="tasks"></div>
    <div style="display: none" data-children-template="Main">
      <ul class="list-unstyled" data-hole="ListContainer">
        <li data-template="ListItem">
          <div class="checkbox">
            <label data-attr="ShowDone">
              <input type="checkbox" data-var="Done" />
              ${Task}
              <button class="btn btn-danger btn-xs pull-right"
                      type="button"
                      data-event-click="Clear">X</button>
            </label>
          </div>
        </li>
      </ul>
      <form onsubmit="return false">
        <div class="form-group">
          <label>New task</label>
          <div class="input-group">
            <input class="form-control" data-var="NewTaskName" />
            <span class="input-group-btn">
              <button class="btn btn-primary"
                      type="button"
                      data-event-click="Add">Add</button>
            </span>
          </div>
          <p class="help-block">
            You are going to add: $!{NewTaskName}<span></span></p>
        </div>
        <button class="btn btn-default"
                type="button"
                data-event-click="ClearCompleted">
          Clear selected tasks</button>
      </form>
    </div>
  </div>
</body>
</html>
```

The corresponding F# application is a stunningly concise 40-line application. It starts by invoking the templating type provider passing the designer template `index.html`. This causes the runtime to parse this file, identify the reactive placeholders, and generate the corresponding code and type space.

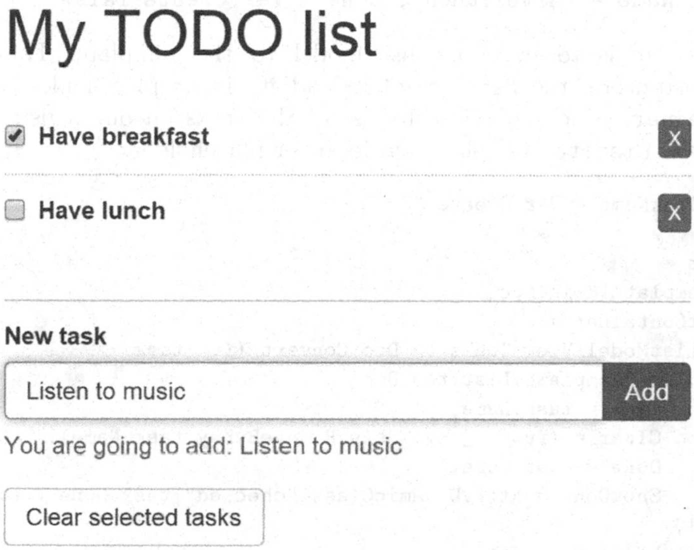

Fig. 3. A simple reactive TODO application

```
namespace TODOList

open WebSharper
open WebSharper.JavaScript
open WebSharper.JQuery
open WebSharper.UI.Next
open WebSharper.UI.Next.Client

[<JavaScript>]
module Code =
  type MainTemplate = Templating.Template<"index.html">
```

We represent tasks using a record that stores the task's name and its completion status in a reactive variable. A task will be identified by its name, so trying to add the same task twice will result in the same task. This is specified in the list model constructor, along with a couple initial tasks on the list.

```
  [<NoComparison>]
  type Task = { Name: string; Done: Var<bool> }
```

```
let Tasks =
  ListModel.Create (fun task -> task.Name)
    [ { Name = "Have breakfast"; Done = Var.Create true }
      { Name = "Have lunch"; Done = Var.Create false } ]
```

What's left is to bind our list model to the template. This requires that we instantiate the Main template and its inner placeholders, including ListContainer, which contains the list of the tasks on our register. This in turn uses the ListItem template and its inner placeholders.

```
let NewTaskName = Var.Create ""

let Main =
  MainTemplate.Main.Doc(
    ListContainer =
      [ListModel.View Tasks |> Doc.Convert (fun task ->
        IndexTemplate.ListItem.Doc(
          Task = task.Name,
          Clear = (fun _ _ -> Tasks.RemoveByKey task.Name),
          Done = task.Done,
          ShowDone = Attr.DynamicClass "checked" task.Done.View id)
      )],
    NewTaskName = NewTaskName,
    Add = (fun _ _ ->
      Tasks.Add { Name=NewTaskName.Value; Done=Var.Create false }
      Var.Set NewTaskName ""),
    ClearCompleted = (fun _ _ ->
      Tasks.RemoveBy (fun task -> task.Done.Value))
  )
  |> Doc.RunById "tasks"
```

Note the use of event handlers to remove a given task, to clear completed ones, or to add a new task. These all operate on the main list model, and the necessary UI changes are automatically propagated.

We should also note that changes to the design template require recompilation, however, the strongly-typed nature of templating eliminates a large class of possible errors, including inconsistencies around event handling and identity.

5 Related Work

Functional Reactive Programming (FRP) [12] is a paradigm relying on values, called *Signals* or *Behaviours* which are a function of time, and *Events*, which are discrete occurrences which change the value of Behaviours.

FRP has spawned a large body of research, in particular concentrating on efficient implementations: naïvely implemented, purely-monadic FRP is prone to space leaks. One technique, arrowised FRP [13], provides a set of primitive behaviours and forbids behaviours from being treated as first-class, instead allowing the primitive behaviours to be manipulated using the arrow abstraction.

Elm [14] is a functional reactive programming language for web applications, which has attracted a large user community. Elm implements arrowised FRP, using the type system to disallow leak-prone higher-order signals.

While `UI.Next` draws inspiration from FRP, it does not attempt to implement FRP semantics. Instead, `UI.Next` consists of observable mutable values which are propagated through the dataflow graph, providing a monadic interface with imperative observers. Consequently, presentation layers such as the reactive DOM layer can be easily integrated with the dataflow layer. Such an approach simplifies the implementation of reactive web abstractions such as Flowlets and Piglets.

The Reactive Extensions (Rx) [11] library is designed to allow the creation of event-driven programs. The technology is heavily based on the observer pattern, which is an instance of the publish/subscribe paradigm. Rx models event occurrences, for example key presses, as observable event streams, and has a somewhat more imperative design style as a result. The dataflow layer in `UI.Next` models time-varying values, as opposed to event occurrences.

Facebook React[1] is a library which, in a similar way to our approach, allows developers to construct reactive DOM nodes programmatically. This process is enabled through JSX, an HTML-like markup language with facilities for property-based data binding. The key concept behind React is the use of an automated "diff" algorithm, driven by a global notion of time instead of a dataflow system: as a result, DOM updates are batched for efficiency. Our use of a dataflow system enables more control over DOM node identity, and is better able to work with various persistence approaches [10].

Flapjax [6] is a dataflow-backed programming language providing full FRP functionality which can also be used as a JavaScript library. Flapjax provides similar functionality to UI.Next, but integrates with the DOM layer differently: signals are instead inserted using a library function. This results in a distinctly different development style for applications in the two systems.

6 Conclusions

In this tutorial, we highlighted the foundations in `UI.Next`, WebSharper's dynamic dataflow library, and discussed the main machinery for its support for two-way data binding via reactive variables and their views embedded into reactive markup. We demonstrated the applicability of these concepts through numerous examples that can serve as a ground for further exploration.

Acknowledgements. `UI.Next` and the larger WebSharper ecosystem is the work of many individuals. The authors would like thank their past IntelliFactory colleagues Simon Fowler and Anton Tayanovskyy for their work on the initial version of `UI.Next`, and Andras Janko for his work on WebSharper and its templating support.

[1] https://facebook.github.io/react/.

References

1. Granicz, A., Denuziere, L., et al.: The WebSharper website. http://websharper.com. Accessed 10 Dec 2015
2. Syme, D., Battocchi, K., Takeda, K., Malayeri, D., Petricek, T.: Themes in information-rich functional programming for internet-scale data sources. In: Proceedings of the Workshop on Data-Driven Functional Programming (DDFP), Rome, Italy (2013)
3. Bjornson, J., Tayanovskyy, A., Granicz, A.: Composing reactive GUIs in F# using WebSharper. In: Hage, J., Morazán, M.T. (eds.) IFL 2010. LNCS, vol. 6647, pp. 203–216. Springer, Heidelberg (2011). https://doi.org/10.1007/978-3-642-24276-2_13
4. Cooper, E., Lindley, S., Wadler, P., Yallop, J.: An idioms guide to formlets. Technical report, University of Edinburg (2008)
5. Denuziere, L., Rodriguez, E., Granicz, A.: Piglets to the rescue. In: 25th Symposium on Implementation and Application of Functional Languages, IFL 2013, Nijmegen, The Netherlands (2013)
6. Meyerovich, L.A., et al.: Flapjax: a programming language for Ajax applications. In: ACM SIGPLAN Notices, vol. 44 (2009)
7. Syme, D., Granicz, A., Cisternino, A.: Expert F# 3.0. Springer, Berkeley (2012). https://doi.org/10.1007/978-1-4302-4651-0
8. Denuziere, L., Granicz, A., Fowler, S.: Reactive abstractions for functional web applications. In: Implementation and Application of Functional Languages (IFL) (2015)
9. Fowler, S., Denuzière, L., Granicz, A.: Reactive single-page applications with dynamic dataflow. In: Pontelli, E., Son, T.C. (eds.) PADL 2015. LNCS, vol. 9131, pp. 58–73. Springer, Cham (2015). https://doi.org/10.1007/978-3-319-19686-2_5
10. Denuziere, L., Granicz, A.: Enabling modular persistence for reactive data models in F# client-server web applications. In: Constrained and Reactive Objects Workshop (CROW) (2016)
11. Meijer, E.: Reactive extensions (Rx): curing your asynchronous programming blues. In: ACM SIGPLAN Commercial Users of Functional Programming (CUFP), Baltimore, Maryland (2010)
12. Elliott, C., Hudak, P.: Functional reactive animation. In: ICFP 1997, vol. 32, no. 8, pp. 263–273. ACM. New York (1997)
13. Hudak, P., Courtney, A., Nilsson, H., Peterson, J.: Arrows, robots, and functional reactive programming. In: Jeuring, J., Jones, S.L.P. (eds.) AFP 2002. LNCS, vol. 2638, pp. 159–187. Springer, Heidelberg (2003). https://doi.org/10.1007/978-3-540-44833-4_6
14. Czaplicki, E., Chong, S.: Asynchronous functional reactive programming for GUIs. In: Proceedings of the 34th ACM SIGPLAN Conference on Programming Language Design and Implementation, PLDI 2013, New York, NY, USA, pp. 411–422 (2013)

Functional Languages in Design of Coloured Petri Nets Models

Štefan Korečko(✉)

Department of Computers and Informatics,
Faculty of Electrical Engineering and Informatics,
Technical University of Košice, Letná 9, 041 20 Košice, Slovakia
stefan.korecko@tuke.sk

Abstract. Coloured Petri nets are a formal method that allows to create sophisticated event-driven models. In addition, there exists a software tool, called CPN Tools, which provides a support for creation, simulation and state space-based verification of CPN models. An interesting feature of CPN Tools is that it uses CPN ML, a slightly modified version of the SML functional language, for data manipulation. In this chapter we describe basic concepts of Coloured Petri nets (CPN), SML and CPN ML and by means of an example illustrate how CPN ML can be used to build a concrete, timed CPN model from an abstract, low-level Petri net model in such a way that the structure of the abstract model is preserved. We also explore possibilities of already existing SML code utilization in CPN models.

1 Introduction

Petri nets (PN) [1] can be regarded as a family of modelling languages that originates from a formalism introduced[1] by Carl Adam Petri in his dissertation "Kommunikation mit Automaten" (Communication with Automata) in 1962. Nowadays, dozens of Petri net types exist. They vary in modelling and expressive power, notation, typical areas of use and other properties but have the same basic features. First, they are able to express the behaviour of non-deterministic, parallel and concurrent systems. Second, they have a form of bipartite oriented graphs. In these graphs, the first type of vertices is place. Places have a round shape and hold objects called tokens. The vertices of the second type are transitions and are rectangular. Another common feature is that their semantics, or behaviour, is defined as a so called token game: a state of a Petri net is expressed by tokens that are held in its places and this state can change only by a firing of a transition of the net. The firing consumes some of the existing tokens and creates new ones. The nature of the tokens and the exact form of the transition firing are examples of properties in which Petri net types differ one from each

[1] In fact, Petri invented the formalism more than 20 years earlier, in August 1939, when he used it to describe chemical processes [12].

V. Zsók et al. (Eds.): CEFP 2015, LNCS 10094, pp. 161–206, 2019.
https://doi.org/10.1007/978-3-030-28346-9_6

other. In the most of the types the effect of the firing is local; it only affects places directly connected with the fired transition.

In this chapter we deal with one particular type of Petri nets, the Coloured Petri nets (CPN) [6,8]. This choice has several reasons. The first one is that CPN are one of those PN types that offer great modelling power while being compatible with basic types of Petri nets, such as Place/Transition nets (PT nets). This means that the formal analysis techniques developed for PT nets can be used for CPN as well. The second one is the availability of a sophisticated software tool, called CPN Tools [15], which allows to create, simulate and analyse CPN models. And, finally, the most important reason is that in CPN Tools the functional language CPN ML, a slightly modified version of Standard ML (SML), is used to define types of tokens and expressions that manipulate with tokens or collect data. The full power of SML is at the modeller's disposal and we show how it can be utilized. No previous experience with SML or Petri nets is needed, however we assume that the reader has at least basic programming skills and is aware of the principles of functional programming. We also encourage the reader to get familiar with CPN Tools in the course of reading Sects. 5 and 6. The web page [15] provides enough material to accomplish this.

The rest of the chapter is organized as follows. In Sect. 2 we deal with the basic concepts of Petri nets and in Sects. 3 and 4 briefly describe the functional languages SML and CPN ML. Armed with this knowledge we go back to Petri nets and introduce Coloured Petri nets, including their timed version, in Sect. 5. The ways in which SML can be used in CPN models are shown in Sect. 6, where a timed CPN model of a simple manufacturing process is built step by step. This model also uses some of the functions and modules defined in Sect. 3. The chapter concludes with a summary of what was achieved and some tips for further reading.

To emphasize important terms we render them in *italic typeface*. A `monospace font` is used for names of places and transitions and for code in SML and CPN ML.

2 Basic Concepts of Petri Nets

With respect to the nature of the tokens in places we distinguish two basic classes of Petri nets:

Low-level Petri nets have tokens that are all the same, it is impossible to distinguish between them. The nets from C.A. Petri's dissertation and PT nets belong to this class. The tokens are usually rendered as black dots inside a place they occupy or only their amount is shown next to or inside the place.

High-level Petri nets have tokens with different values. Usually, types of these tokens are defined, too, and one place may hold only tokens of one type. This is the case of CPN, which are a member of this class. The word "coloured" in their name emphasizes the fact that tokens are "coloured" by various values ("colours") and are not just undistinguishable black dots.

In this section we use low-level PT nets to explain basic concepts of Petri nets, i.e. markings and transition firing, and how PN can express properties like non-determinism and parallelism. Features specific to Coloured PN and their timed version will be presented later, in Sect. 5. All PN shown in this and the following sections have been created in the CPN Tools software.

2.1 Markings and Transition Firing

The amount and values of tokens in some place p of a Petri net is called *marking of* p and is denoted $M(p)$. If we fix ordering of places of the net, for example to $p_1, p_2 \dots, p_n$, we can write the marking of the whole net in a vector form as

$$M = (M(p_1), M(p_2) \dots, M(p_n)).$$

Markings represent states of PN. To distinguish between different markings we use lower and upper indices, for example M', M_1', M_2. M_0 is usually reserved for the *initial marking*, that is the marking in which the net is when it begins its computation. A *computation of PN* is a sequence of firings (executions) of its transitions.

A transition t can be *fired* (*executed*) if and only if there are enough tokens of required values in all pre-places of t in the corresponding marking M. We say that t is *enabled* in M. *Pre-places of* t are places from which there are directed arcs to t and *post-places of* t are places to which there are directed arcs from t. When t fires, it removes tokens from its pre-places and adds tokens to its post-places. This means that the *net reaches a new marking.* Amount and values[2] of tokens that are required for a firing of t and are removed and added by the firing are defined by *arc inscriptions*, associated with the arcs from and to t. Computations of PN can be written in the form of *occurrence sequences* (*trajectories*), which consist of transitions fired and markings reached.

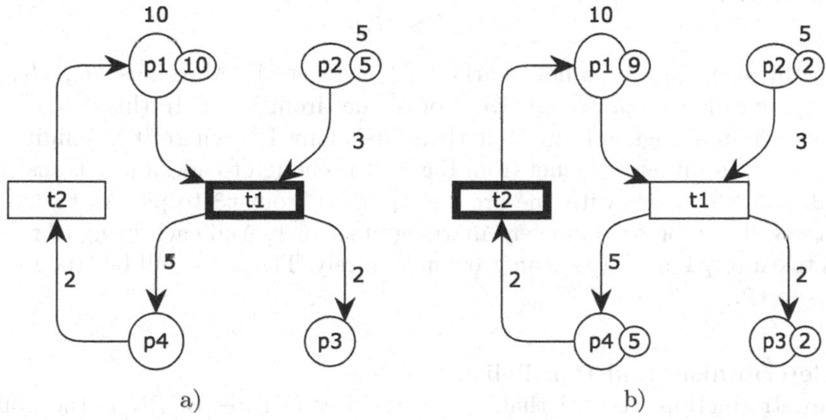

Fig. 1. PT net in its initial marking M_0 (a) and subsequent marking M_1 (b)

[2] In high-level PN.

In PT nets the firing process is fairly simple as the tokens are undistinguishable, markings are only amounts of tokens and arc inscriptions are natural numbers. A transition firing example can be seen in Fig. 1. Figure 1(a) shows a small PT net in its initial marking M_0,

$$M_0 = (M_0(\mathtt{p1}), M_0(\mathtt{p2}), M_0(\mathtt{p3}), M_0(\mathtt{p4})) = (10, 5, 0, 0).$$

The amount of tokens in given place is shown right to it in a small circle or ellipse. The number above the place (e.g. `10` for `p1`) is an *initial marking inscription* that defines its initial marking and the number next to an arc (e.g. `2` for the arc from `p4` to `t2`) is the corresponding *arc inscription*. The arcs with no inscriptions shown have arc inscriptions equal to `1`. Similarly, each place p without the initial marking inscription has $M_0(p) = 0$ (e.g. `p3` and `p4` in Fig. 1).

The arc inscriptions define the amount of tokens removed from or added to corresponding places when a transition is fired. In M_0 the transition `t1` is *enabled*[3], because there is at least one token in its pre-place `p1` and at least `3` tokens in its pre-place `p2`. The result of `t1` firing in M_0 is a new marking M_1,

$$M_1 = (9, 2, 2, 5).$$

The net in M_1 can be seen in Fig. 1(b). In M_1 the transition t_2 can be fired and its firing leads to $M_2 = (10, 2, 2, 3)$. Here, again, only t_2 can fire and the firing results in $M_3 = (11, 2, 2, 1)$. M_3 is a *dead marking*, because no transition can fire in M_3: there is one token missing in `p2` to fire `t1` and one token missing in `p4` to fire `t2`. So, only one occurrence sequence (excluding its parts) is possible in the net from Fig. 1 and this can be written as

$$(10, 5, 0, 0)\ [\mathtt{t1}{>}\ (9, 2, 2, 5)\ [\mathtt{t2}{>}\ (10, 2, 2, 3)\ [\mathtt{t2}{>}\ (11, 2, 2, 1).$$

The inscription

$$M_0\ [t{>}\ M_1$$

means "by firing t in M_0 a new marking M_1 is reached". Markings M_0, M_1, M_2 and M_3 are called *reachable markings* of the net from Fig. 1. In this case the set of reachable markings is finite, but there are many PN where it is infinite. To make the set infinite for the net from Fig. 1, it is enough to add a new transition, say `t3`, and a new arc with the arc inscription `1` from `t3` to `p4`. As `t3` has no pre-places, it can be fired in every marking of the net. And each firing of `t3` will add a token to `p4`, so $M(\mathtt{p4})$ can grow indefinitely. The same will be true for `p1`, thanks to `t2`.

Nondeterminism and Parallelism

In the introduction we said that one of the key features of PN is the ability to describe non-deterministic and parallel behaviour. How this can be done we

[3] This is indicated by the thick frame around the transition in Fig. 1.

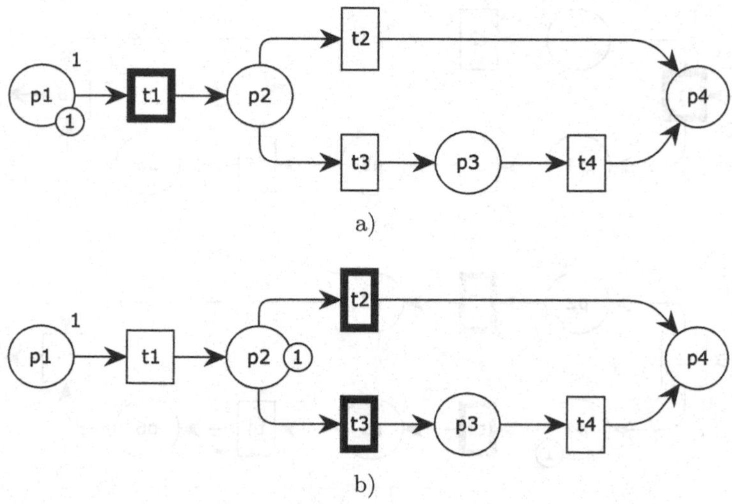

Fig. 2. PT net of a non-deterministic process in M_0 (a) and M_1 (b)

demonstrate on the following two examples, shown in Figs. 2 and 3. Both these nets are *1-bounded*, i.e. for each place p in them and each reachable marking M it holds that $M(p) \leq 1$. Places of such nets can be interpreted as (local) states: The net (or its part) is in the state represented by the place p if and only if $M(p) = 1$. Their transitions are usually interpreted as events, which cause state changes.

There is only one token present in each reachable marking of the net from Fig. 2. After the firing of `t1` in M_0 the net reaches M_1 (Fig. 2b), where two alternative paths are possible. The first one consists of `t2` and the second one of `t3`, `p3` and `t4`. In M_1 both `t2` and `t3` are enabled, but only one of them can fire. This is because they have one common pre-place `p2` with only one token in M_1 (M_1(`p2`)=1). There are only two possible occurrence sequences from M_0 to a dead marking, the sequence

$$(1,0,0,0)\ [\texttt{t1}\!>\ (0,1,0,0)\ [\texttt{t2}\!>\ (0,0,0,1)$$

and

$$(1,0,0,0)\ [\texttt{t1}\!>\ (0,1,0,0)\ [\texttt{t3}\!>\ (0,0,1,0)\ [\texttt{t4}\!>\ (0,0,0,1).$$

The net in Fig. 3 doesn't look very different from the previous one: Instead of the part with two transitions and their common pre-place (`p2`, `t2`, `t3` in Fig. 2) we have one transition with two post-places (`t1`, `p2`, `p4`). Similar difference is in the right part of the net (`t2`, `t4`, `p4` vs. `p3`, `p6`, `t5`). Consequence of these changes is that we still have two paths for the process execution (`t2` and `t3`, `t4`), but now both of them are executed in parallel. This is because `t2` and `t3` have separate pre-places and both of them have a token in M_1 (Fig. 3b). We have

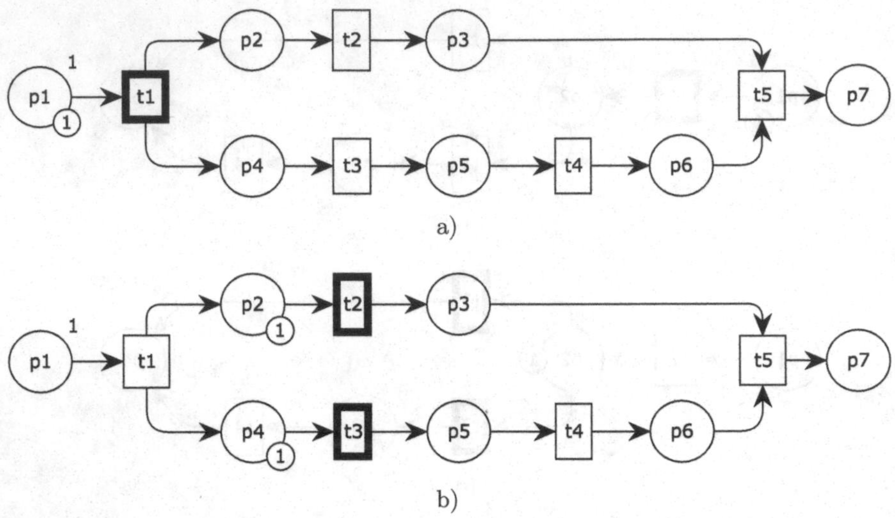

Fig. 3. PT net of a process with two parallel sub-processes in M_0 (a) and M_1 (b)

three possible occurrence sequences from M_0 to a dead marking:

$$M_0\ [\texttt{t1}\textgreater\ M_1\ [\texttt{t2}\textgreater\ M_2\ [\texttt{t3}\textgreater\ M_3\ [\texttt{t4}\textgreater\ M_4\ [\texttt{t5}\textgreater\ M_5$$
$$M_0\ [\texttt{t1}\textgreater\ M_1\ [\texttt{t3}\textgreater\ M_6\ [\texttt{t2}\textgreater\ M_3\ [\texttt{t4}\textgreater\ M_4\ [\texttt{t5}\textgreater\ M_5$$
$$M_0\ [\texttt{t1}\textgreater\ M_1\ [\texttt{t3}\textgreater\ M_6\ [\texttt{t4}\textgreater\ M_7\ [\texttt{t2}\textgreater\ M_4\ [\texttt{t5}\textgreater\ M_5$$

where

$$M_0 = (1,0,0,0,0,0,0), M_1 = (0,1,0,1,0,0,0), M_2 = (0,0,1,1,0,0,0),$$
$$M_3 = (0,0,1,0,1,0,0), M_4 = (0,0,1,0,0,1,0), M_5 = (0,0,0,0,0,0,1),$$
$$M_6 = (0,1,0,0,1,0,0), M_7 = (0,1,0,0,0,1,0)$$

The transition `t2` represents a fork event and `t3` a join event, so the process modelled by the net has two parallel sub-processes. The first one consists of `p2`, `t2` and `p3` and the second one of `p4`, `t3`, `p5`, `t4` and `p6`. We can also see that all markings of the net, except of M_0 and M_5, have exactly two tokens in two separate places. The first token is in `p2` or `p3` and represents the local state of the first sub-process. The second token is in `p4`, `p5` or `p6` and represents the local state of the second sub-process. And together these two local states form one global state of the net.

3 Standard ML

Standard ML or *SML* is a general-purpose functional programming language, a descendant of Robin Milner's ML language. This means that it belongs to the same family of functional languages like Calm, OCalm or F#. SML is a type-safe statically typed language with an extensible type system. SML implements the

Hindley–Milner type inference algorithm, so it is not necessary to define types of values in most cases. In addition, a programmer doesn't need to care about allocating and freeing the memory as SML provides an efficient automatic storage management for data structures and functions [3]. The most recent version of SML is from 1997 and its formal specification can be found in [11], where the language is defined by means of typing rules and the natural (operational) semantics. The language itself consists of a core language for small-scale programming and a module system for large-scale programming [2]. In SML these modules are called *structures*.

A distinctive feature of SML is that it is not a pure functional language. It supports the typical features of functional languages, such as pattern-matching, currying and higher-order functions but it also allows us to write expressions with side effects, loops or sequences of commands. By means of references it is also possible to define variables, similar to those in imperative programming languages. We can say that SML is both functional and imperative language, but the preferred way is to use it as a functional one.

All the code samples presented in this chapter can be evaluated ("run") using available SML compilers, such as MLton [16], Poly/ML [17] or Standard ML of New Jersey (SML/NJ) [19].

3.1 Expressions and Primitive Types

As it is typical for functional languages, computation in SML is based on the evaluation of expressions. The expressions consist of values, operators, identifiers, reserved words and other elements, as defined in [11]. Each valid expression evaluates to a value of given type. SML offers a few *primitive types* and an opportunity to create an infinite number of user-defined types using *type constructors* such as products, records and lists. The primitive types used in this chapter are integers, strings, booleans and an empty type called `unit`.

Integers. The basic *integer type* is `int` and values of this type can be written in decimal (e.g. `15`) or hexadecimal (e.g. `0xf`) form. The unary operator `~` is used for negative numbers, so `~5` is minus five. Infix operators `+`, `-`, `*`, `div` and `mod` are provided for addition, subtraction, multiplication, integer division and the remainder after division. An example of integer expression is `(0xff+45) div 2 mod 7-5`, which evaluates to `~2`.

Character Strings are defined in the `string` type. Strings have to be enclosed in double quotes (i.e. `"Hi!"`). All the comparison operators are available here, too, and they compare strings lexicographically. The infix operator `^` provides string concatenation, for example `"Hi "^"there!"` evaluates to `"Hi there!"`.

Booleans. The type `bool` stores the boolean values `true` and `false`. The boolean operators are `andalso` for logical conjunction, `orelse` for disjunction and `not` for negation. An example of an expression that evaluates to `true` is `(25.2<3.0 orelse not(13=4)) andalso ("a"<"ab")`.

Unit. SML also includes a type that is an equivalent of the *void type*, which we can find in many programming languages. This type is called `unit` and contains only one value, `()`.

Type Conversion. SML doesn't convert values of one type to another automatically, so the expressions like `"The value is "^5` or `3+5.0` will cause an error. Fortunately, conversion functions for this job are provided. Some of them are listed in Table 1, where the symbol "≡" is used as a shortcut for "evaluates to".

Table 1. Selected conversion functions

From	To	Function	Examples
`int`	`real`	`real`	`real 3` ≡ `3.0`
`int`	`string`	`Int.toString`	`Int.toString 123` ≡ `"123"`
`real`	`int`	`round`	`round 3.49` ≡ `3`
			`round 3.51` ≡ `4`
`real`	`int`	`floor`	`floor 3.49` ≡ `3`
			`floor 3.51` ≡ `3`
`real`	`string`	`Real.toString`	`Real.toString 1.2E2` ≡ `"120.0"`

Conditional Expressions and Pattern Matching. For a conditional expression various ways of evaluation exist and which one is chosen depends on a condition that is its part. SML offers two kinds of these, the *if-than-else* and *case expressions.*

The *if-then-else* is the simpler one and has the syntax

`if` *cnd* `then` exp_1 `else` exp_2

where *cnd* is a boolean expression and exp_1 and exp_2 are expressions, which must have the same type. If *cnd* = `true`, it evaluates to exp_1, otherwise to exp_2. An example of *if-than-else* is

```
if 12<20 then "ordering works" else "something's wrong"
```

which evaluates to `"ordering works"`.

The *case expression* with *n rules* has the form

```
case cexp of
    cpat1 => exp1
  | cpat2 => exp2
    ...
  | cpatn => expn
```

Each rule consists of a pattern ($cpat_i$) and an expression (exp_i). All patterns have to be of the same type as *cexp*. The expressions exp_1 to exp_n must have the same type, too. The evaluation of the case expression starts with matching *cexp* against the pattern $cpat_1$. If *cexp* fits $cpat_1$ then it evaluates to exp_1. Otherwise the evaluation continues with matching *cexp* against $cpat_2$. If the evaluation goes through all the patterns and *cexp* doesn't fit any of them then it ends with an error (nonexhaustive match failure). To prevent the error it is a good practice to make $cpat_n$ cover all the cases not included in $cpat_1$ to $cpat_{n-1}$. This can be done using the *wildcard pattern*, which is represented by the underscore character (_) in SML and means "any value". For example, the expression

```
case 1 of
  1 =>"red"
| 2 =>"orange"
| 3 =>"green"
| _ =>"unknown"
```

evaluates to `"red"` but if we replace `1` by `7` then it evaluates to `"unknown"`.

It should be also noted that *if-than-else* is just a special case of the case expression, namely

```
case cnd of
    true  => exp1
  | false => exp2
```

3.2 Variables and Functions

In SML we can also create *named values* (*variables*). This can de done using a *variable definition* of the form

```
val vname = exp
```

where *vname* is the name of the variable and *exp* is an SML expression, which specifies its value. It is not necessary to specify the type of the value, but it can be done using the extended form

```
val vname = exp : type
```

Here, *type* is the name of the type. These named values are usually called *variables* (e.g. [2,3]), but they are different from those in languages such as Java or C++. SML variables don't vary. Once a value is assigned to a variable by the `val` construct, it will not change. If we use `val` with the same *vname* again, the SML environment will destroy the original variable and create a new one, with the same name and possibly different type. For example, consider the following SML construct consisting of two variable definitions:

```
val a = 2*3
val a = case a of
          0 => false
        | _ => true
```

During its processing a variable a is created first. Then its value (6) is used in the second definition and the result of the whole processing is

```
val a = true : bool
```

The first a and the second a are different variables. The first one is of type int, the second one of type bool.

Functions. The case expression we used in the assignment above is in fact a conversion from int to bool and may come handy in many situations. So, it will be nice to have it available in a form of function, say int2bool, which takes an integer as the argument and returns the corresponding boolean value. Functions are defined using the form

fun *fname arg* = *bexp*

where *fname* is the name, *arg* the argument (arguments) and *bexp* an expression, which forms the body of the function. Then the function int2bool can be defined as

```
fun  int2bool a = case a of
                     0 => false
                   | _ => true
```

However, functions that use pattern matching can be written in a more elegant form by replacing the argument by individual patterns. If this form is used, the name of the function appears before each pattern and = replaces =>:

```
fun int2bool 0 = false
  | int2bool _ = true
```

Both definitions result in

```
val int2bool = fn : int -> bool
```

This tells us that in SML functions are in fact variables that are mappings from one type to another (here from int to bool). Alternatively, we can define functions using the keywords val and fn:

```
val int2bool = fn a => case a of 0 => false | _ => true
```

and we can also specify types in the definition:

```
val int2bool: int->bool = fn a: int => case a of 0 => false
                                                | _ => true
```

In SML each function has *exactly one argument* and returns *exactly one value*. This may be seen as too restrictive, because in the real life we often use functions of two or more arguments. The need for more arguments can be satisfied in two ways. The first one is to replace n arguments with one argument, which is an n-tuple. How to do this we show in Sect. 3.3. The second way is to define them as so-called *curried functions.*

Curried functions are functions that return functions. In SML we create a curried function using the same form as for the previous ones, but instead of one argument we write more arguments, separated by the space character. From this, one may get an impression that a multi-argument function is created, but it is not true. Let us, for example, assume that we need to define a function `linVal`, which computes the value of the expression

$$a * x + b,$$

where a, b and x are arguments. In SML we define it as

```
fun linVal a b x = a * x + b
```

and it is a function of the type

```
int -> int -> int -> int
```

This means that `linVal` takes an integer and returns a function of the type `int -> int -> int` (again a curried function), which returns a function of the type `int -> int` and, finally, this function returns the resulting value of the type `int`. So, the evaluation of expression

```
linVal 5 6 7
```

first returns a function with the body

```
5 * x + b
```

this takes 6 for `b` and returns a function with the body

```
5 * x + 6
```

which takes 7 for `x` and returns `41`. Curried functions allow us to define functions that are special cases of the more general ones. For example, if we would like to have a function that computes

$$5x + 6,$$

we can define it as

```
fun linVal_a5b6 x = linVal 5 6 x
```

which is of the type `int -> int`. Of course, `linVal_a5b6 7` evaluates to `41`.

The pattern matching can be used with curried functions, too. This comes handy when we need to deal with special cases of argument values in a function definition. Such cases can also be found in our `linVal` function, the most prominent of them is that if $\mathtt{a} = 0$ ($\mathtt{x} = 0$) then the expression is reduced to `b` and the value of `x` (`a`) doesn't matter. To define `linVal` with these cases treated separately we write

```
fun linVal 0 b _ = b
  | linVal _ b 0 = b
  | linVal a b x = a * x + b
```

The wildcard pattern is used for arguments that are not considered in given case.

Recursive functions , i.e. functions that call themselves, can be written in SML, too. For example, the factorial function can be defined as

```
fun fact 0 = 1
  | fact n = n * fact(n-1)
```

or as

```
val rec fact =  fn 0 => 1
                 | n => n * fact(n - 1)
```

Notice that the keyword `rec` must be added to indicate the recursive nature of the function if the `val ... fn` form is used.

Some functions are *mutually recursive*, i.e. they call each other and cannot be defined separately. In this case we write their definitions one after each other and use the keyword `and` instead of `fun` for all but the first of them. The functions `max` and `isPrioritized` of the functor `Heap` in Sect. 3.6 are mutually recursive.

Limiting the Scope. Sometimes it is necessary to limit the scope of defined objects, such as variables (including functions), types or structures, to certain expression or definition. In SML there are two constructs for this task,

$$\texttt{let}\ \mathit{def}\ \texttt{in}\ \mathit{exp}\ \texttt{end}$$

and

$$\texttt{local}\ \mathit{def}\ \texttt{in}\ \mathit{def}_1\ \texttt{end}$$

where def and def_1 are definitions of one or more objects and exp is an expression. If we, for example, wish to define a function that multiplies its argument by the π constant and where π is given as a local variable, then we can define it as

```
local
 val pi=3.14159265359
in
 fun mulByPi x = pi*x
end
```

or

```
fun mulByPi x = let
                  val pi=3.14159265359
                 in
                  pi*x
                 end
```

Notice that the positions of `local` and `let` are different. This is because the let construct limits the scope to an expression that evaluates to a certain value and the local construct to expressions that are definitions. It is also impossible to define types or structures using the `let` construct. Because of this the functions `iHeapSortDsc` and `iHeapSortAsc` in Sect. 3.6 use `local`.

3.3 Tuples, Records and Lists

So far we used only values of primitive types like `int` or `bool`. SML also provides means to construct and handle values of more complex, *structured types*. In this section we deal with three most frequently used ones.

Tuples are value sequences of fixed length where each value (field) may be of a different type. To create an n-tuple the following construct is used:

$$(exp_1,\ \ldots exp_n)$$

Here, n is the number of fields and exp_1 to exp_n are expressions that evaluate to certain values. For example,

```
(2<3,2+3,Int.toString(2)^"3")
```

evaluates to a triple `(true,5,"23")` of the type `bool * int * string`. The symbol `*` stands for the Cartesian product. Tuples can be members of other tuples, e.g.

```
(true,(2,3,(3.0,"a")))
```

which is of the type `bool * (int * int * (real * string))`.

Tuples can also be used to define a function of n arguments, $n \geq 2$ as a function of one argument that is an n-tuple. So, `linVal` from Sect. 3.2 can be redefined as

```
fun linVal (a, b, x) = a * x + b
```

This time the type of `linVal` will be `int * int * int -> int`, instead of `int -> int -> int -> int` and the call with arguments 5, 6 and 7 will be `linVal(5,6,7)`. Patterns in function definition work in the same way as for curried functions, e.g.

```
fun linVal (0, b, _) = b
  | linVal (_, b, 0) = b
  | linVal (a, b, x) = a * x + b
```

To access individual fields of tuples we can use pattern matching, as in the definition of `linVal` above, or indices of the fields in the tuple. As an example, lets us consider a variable `tp`,

```
val tp = ((1,2),((3,4),5))
```

and that we would like to extract the value 2 to a variable `a` and 4 to a variable `b`. Using pattern matching, this can be done easily by the definition

```
val ((_,a),((_,b),_))  = tp
```

Here the structure of the tuple on the left hand side resembles that of `tp` and wildcards are used on the positions from which we do not need to read any data. To access the fields via indices the notation

`#`*i tpl*

is used. The symbol *i* is the index, defining the position of the accessed field within the tuple and *tpl* is the tuple. The first value in a tuple has the index 1. For example, to extract 2 and 4 from `tp` to `a` and `b` we write:

```
val a  = #2 (#1 tp)
val b  = #2 (#1 (#2 tp))
```

Each of these definitions contains more than one index, because `tp` has nested tuples. The first index is for the innermost tuple and the last index for the outermost one.

Records are like tuples but with named fields. They are also written in a similar manner, in the form

$$\{name_1 = exp_1, \ldots name_n = exp_n\}$$

where n is the number of fields, $name_1$ to $name_n$ are names of the fields and exp_1 to exp_n are expressions as in the case of tuples. An example of a record value is in the following definition, which assigns a record about an assembled product to a variable `prd`:

```
val prd = { id                 = 35,
            ptype              = "left joint",
            assemblyDuration = 175,
            prdQuality         = 64          }
```

Then the type of `prd` is

```
{assemblyDuration:int, id:int, prdQuality:int, ptype:string}
```

Field names are a part of the type, so a record with the same number and types of fields but different names will be of a different type. Values in the individual fields can be accessed using the pattern matching or field names. So, if we need to copy the value `"left joint"` to a variable `a` and `175` to `b`, we can do it by writing

```
val {id = _, ptype = a,assemblyDuration = b, prdQuality = _} = prd
```

or

```
val a  = #ptype            prd
val b  = #assemblyDuration prd
```

When creating a record or specifying a record pattern the order of the fields doesn't matter, e.g. `{a=5,b=4}` is equal to `{b=4,a=5}`.

We introduced records as tuples with field names but the relation between these type constructors is quite opposite. Actually, in SML tuples are records with field names `1`, `2`, `3` and so on.

Lists are sequences of values, too, but all elements of a list are of the same type and list size is not fixed. They are defined in the form

$$[exp_1, \ \ldots exp_n]$$

where n is the number of elements, $n \geq 0$, and exp_1 to exp_n are expressions that evaluate to values of the same type. For example, a variable holding a list of 5 integers can be defined as

```
val lst = [1,2,3,4,5]
```

and is of the type `int list`, i.e. a list of elements of the type `int`. The first element of a list (`1` for `lst`) is called the *head* of the list and the rest (`[2,3,4,5]` for `lst`) is called the *tail*. An empty list can be created using the expression `[]` or `nil`. To manipulate lists two basic operators exist in SML.

The first operator is `::` and its purpose is to enable adding an element to the beginning of a list. For example,

```
0::lst
```

evaluates to the list

```
[1,2,3,4,5]
```

The operator can be also used to store the head and tail in separate variables, e.g. the evaluation of

```
val h::t = lst
```

results in the creation of two variables

```
val h = 1 : int
val t = [2,3,4,5] : int list
```

The second operator[4] is `@` and implements the list concatenation. This means that the evaluation of

```
lst@[6, 7, 8]
```

results in the list `[1,2,3,4,5,6,7,8]`.

3.4 User-Defined Types

The type constructors, such as those in Sect. 3.3, can be combined in infinitely many ways to create values of new types. But not only that; we can also give names to these types and introduce new type constructors. To do this, SML provides constructs `type` and `datatype`.

Type Abbreviations. The construct `type` allows us to give names (abbreviations) to types that can be created using already existing type constructors. One of the syntactical forms of the construct is

$$\texttt{type}\ \mathit{tname}\ \texttt{=}\ \mathit{texp}$$

where *tname* is the name of the type and *texp* is an expression that defines the type. The form of *texp* depends on what kind of type we wish to define. If our goal is just to rename an existing type then *texp* is its name, e.g.

```
type str =string
```

For record types *texp* looks like

$$\{\mathit{name}_1\ :\ \mathit{texp}_1 \ldots,\ \mathit{name}_n\ :\ \mathit{texp}_n\}$$

where name_1 to name_n are names of the fields and texp_1 to texp_n are type expressions defining types of the fields. Then the assembled product record `prd` from Sect. 3.3 can be of the type `PRD`,

[4] In CPN ML the `@` operator is replaced by `^^`, because `@` is reserved for so-called delay expressions.

```
type PRD = {id:int, ptype:string, assemblyDuration:int,
            prdQuality:int}
```

For n-tuples the type definition uses the Cartesian product symbol * and *texp* has the form

$$(texp_1 \ldots \ * \ texp_n)$$

and for lists *texp* is

$$texp_e \texttt{ list}$$

where $texp_e$ defines the type of the list elements. Of course, we can combine these expressions and create more complex types. For example, a type PRDlst, which is a list of records about assembled products, can be defined as

```
type PRDlst = {id:int, ptype:string, assemblyDuration:int,
prdQuality:int} list
```

or, after the type PRD is defined, as

```
type PRDlst = PRD list
```

Now we can use the abbreviation when defining variables:

```
val prods:PRDlst = [
       {id=1, ptype="lArm", assemblyDuration=29, prdQuality=70},
       {id=2, ptype="rArm", assemblyDuration=49, prdQuality=61}]
```

or functions:

```
fun getFisrtPrdType [] = "list empty"
  | getFisrtPrdType ((h::t):PRDlst) = #ptype (h)
```

The fact that these types are just abbreviations can be observed when we define prods without the ":PRDlst" part. Then the type inference mechanism of SML will not identify it as the type PRDlst but as the general type {assemblyDuration:int, id:int, prdQuality:int, ptype:string} list.

New Types. To define a brand new type, a type that cannot be constructed from the existing ones, the keyword datatype is used. One of the forms of a new type definition is

$$\texttt{datatype } tname \texttt{ = } tcexp_1 \texttt{ | } \ldots tcexp_n$$

where *tname* is the name of the new type and $tcexp_1$ to $tcexp_n$ are expressions that define *constructors* by which the individual values of the type are created.

The simplest constructors are *nullary constructors*, which just name values that belong to the type. A datatype defined exclusively by them is in fact an enumerated set, for example

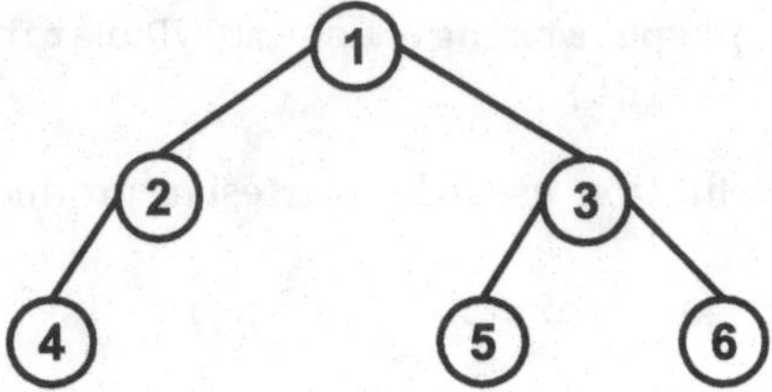

Fig. 4. Binary tree of integers example

```
datatype DevStatus = on | off | broken
```

with exactly three values, `on`, `off` and `broken`. After a datatype is created, we can use its values when defining variables, e.g.

```
val stat1 = off
```

or for pattern matching, e.g.

```
fun devOk broken = false
  | devOk _      = true
```

The type of `stat1` will be correctly inferred to `DevStatus` and `devOk stat1` evaluates to `true`.

More sophisticated constructors can be found in definitions of *recursive types*. A recursive type is a type where values can be composed of other values of the same type. The syntax of their definition in SML follows the inductive way in which they are usually described. As an example, let us consider the binary tree of integers type, which can be described as follows:

1. An empty tree is a binary tree of integers (`iTree`).
2. If r is an integer and T_1, T_2 are `iTree`s, then a structure where r is the root, T_1 is the left sub-tree and T_2 is the right sub-tree is also an `iTree`.

One form of `iTree` definition in SML is

```
datatype iTree = empty | tNode of iTree * int *  iTree
```

The definition has two constructors, corresponding exactly to the first and the second case in the description above. The nullary constructor `empty` represents an empty tree and `tNode` is for the general case, where a tree is a triple consisting of its left sub-tree, a root storing an integer value and its right sub-tree. The keyword `of` separates the name of the constructor from its definition. Concrete values are then defined exclusively by means of these two constructors. For example, a variable `tr` holding the tree from Fig. 4 is defined as

```
val tr = tNode(tNode(tNode(empty,4,empty),2,empty),1,
tNode(tNode(empty,5,empty),3,tNode(empty,6,empty)))
```

In a similar fashion we can define types for trees holding values of other types than `int`. However, one may wonder whether it is possible to define a tree without specifying exactly what is the type of its elements. It is, using so-called *parametrised datatypes*. An example of such datatype is `list`, which is defined as

```
datatype 'a list = nil | :: of 'a * 'a list
```

in SML. Notice that instead of exactly specifying the type of list elements the type parameter `'a` is used. The name of each type parameter has to start with `'`. The type constructors of `list` are `nil` and `::` and the variable `lst` from Sect. 3.3 can be alternatively defined as

```
val lst = 1::2::3::4::5::nil
```

A general, parametrised, definition of binary trees can be found under the name `tree` inside the structure `Tree` in Sect. 3.6. This structure also contains examples of functions working with parametrised types. The type abbreviations can be parametrised, too.

3.5 Higher-Order Functions

SML treats functions as values, so it's not a problem to create a function that takes functions as arguments. Such functions are called *higher-order functions* and can be used to break complex functions over recursive types into simpler ones with common functionality defined only once.

For example, suppose that we need functions `isPrdLstAsc` and `isPrdLstDsc` of the type `PRD list -> bool`. The first one returns `true` if the elements of its argument (a list of product records) are in ascending order, `false` otherwise. The second one does the same but for descending order. The `PRD` type is as specified in Sect. 3.4 and the ordering is defined by its `assemblyDuration` field. Both functions share certain functionality, namely they apply a logical operation (i.e. a function returning boolean) to each pair of adjacent values in the list and return a boolean value. We define the common functionality in a higher-order function `isOrdered`:

```
fun isOrdered ([], ordRel)     = true
  | isOrdered ([a], ordRel)    = true
  | isOrdered ((a::b::t), ordRel) = if ordRel(a,b) then
                                      isOrdered(b::t, ordRel)
                                    else false
```

Its first argument is a list to be examined and the second one is a function `ordRel`, which returns `true` if its two arguments are in the correct order and `false` otherwise. In `isOrdered` we have two special cases, an empty list and a list of one element. In both of them the function returns `true`. In the third case the `ordRel` is subsequently applied to adjacent elements of the list, starting from the beginning. The function `isOrdered` doesn't always traverse the whole list.

It stops and returns `false` as soon as it finds two adjacent elements that are not in order.

As `ordRel` we use two functions, `geqPrd` and `leqPrd`. The code of `geqPrd` is

```
fun geqPrd(x:PRD,y:PRD) =
    if (#assemblyDuration x) >= (#assemblyDuration y)
    then true else false
```

and `leqPrd` differs only in the use of operator `<=` instead of `>=`. Finally, we can define the desired functions as

```
fun isPrdLstDsc l = isOrdered(l, geqPrd)
fun isPrdLstAsc l = isOrdered(l, leqPrd)
```

3.6 Structures, Signatures and Functors

One of the key features of Standard ML is that it is a modular language. It means that definitions of variables, functions, exceptions, types and other objects can be organized into named units, called *structures*. There is also another type of unit, which exists for each structure and that is called *signature*. While a structure contains definitions of variables (and functions), i.e. their full code, a signature only declare them; it specifies their types. We can see signatures as types of structures or as interfaces that corresponding structures implement. The third type of unit is *functor*, a parametrised structure. Functors map their parameters, which include functions, types and structures, to structures.

Instead of describing these three types of units in general, we present here an example, which uses all of them. It is an implementation of the heapsort algorithm for sorting lists of records of the `PRD` type[5]. The implementation is based on an unstructured implementation of heapsort, available at [13].

Heapsort is a comparison-based sorting algorithm, which uses a binary heap to sort a sequence of items of the same ordered type. The *binary heap* is a complete binary tree, where so-called heap property holds. In a *complete binary tree* every level, except the last one, has to be full and if the last level is not full then all nodes in it have to be as far left as possible. For example, if we remove the node 6 from the tree in Fig. 4 and insert it as the right son of the node 2 then the tree will be complete. The *heap property* assumes an existence of some ordering function $ord(x, y)$, which returns *true* if x and y are ordered, *false* otherwise (e.g. $\leq$ or $\geq$). The values x, y are of the type of elements stored in the heap. Then the heap property holds if for each node r of the tree $ord(r, n) = true$ for all nodes n from the left and right sub-trees of r. The heap property implies that the greatest element with respect to *ord* will be the root of the heap. The heapsort algorithm for sorting a non-empty sequence *seq* can proceed as follows:

1. Create a heap h from all the elements of *seq*.

---
[5] As defined in Sect. 3.4.

2. Create a new empty sequence *oseq*.
3. Let r be the root of h and l and r its left and right sub-trees. Take r and append it to the end of *oseq*.
4. If both l and r are empty, go to step 6. Otherwise go to step 5.
5. Merge l and r to a new heap and name it h. Go to step 3.
6. Return *oseq*.

We split the implementation of the algorithm into one structure and one functor and define signatures for them. The structure, named `Tree`, implements the signature `TREE` and contains everything needed to define and manipulate binary trees. The code of the signature `TREE` is as follows:

```
signature TREE = sig
 datatype 'a tree = empty | tNode of 'a tree * 'a *  'a tree
 val inorder : 'a tree -> 'a list -> 'a list
 val height : 'a tree -> int
 val isFull : 'a tree -> bool
 val isComplete : 'a tree -> bool
 val cbtInsert : 'a -> 'a tree -> 'a tree
 val list2cbt : 'a list -> 'a tree -> 'a tree
end
```

The type `tree` defined in the signature is a generalisation of `iTree` from Sect. 3.4 and can hold elements of any type. The signature also declares functions to work with trees. The first one, `inorder` should convert a binary tree into a list using the inorder tree traversal, `height` should return the number of levels of a tree, `isFull` should return `true` if all levels of a tree are full, `isComplete` should return `true` if a tree is complete, `cbtInsert` should insert a new element into a tree in such a way that it remains complete and `list2cbt` should add all elements of a list to a complete binary tree. All these functions are implemented in the `Tree` structure, which is a good example of utilisation of the pattern matching for recursive types:

```
structure Tree:TREE = struct

 datatype 'a tree = empty | tNode of 'a tree * 'a *  'a tree

 fun inorder empty s = s
   |  inorder (tNode(l,n,r)) s = inorder l (n :: (inorder r s))

 local
   fun maxN (x:int) y = if x > y then x else y
 in
   fun height empty = 0
     |  height (tNode(l,_,r)) = 1 + maxN (height l) (height r)
 end
```

```
fun isFull empty = true
  | isFull (tNode(l,_,r)) = height l = height r  andalso
                             isFull l andalso isFull r

fun isComplete empty = true
  | isComplete (t as tNode(l,_,r)) =
      isFull t orelse
       ((height l) = (height r) + 1 andalso isFull r
                                    andalso isComplete l)
      orelse
       ((height l) = (height r) andalso isFull l
                                andalso isComplete r)

fun cbtInsert item empty = tNode (empty,item,empty)
  | cbtInsert item (t as tNode(l,n,r)) =
      if isFull t orelse
         (height l = height r + 1 andalso isFull r andalso
          isComplete l andalso not (isFull l))
      then tNode (cbtInsert item l,n,r)
      else tNode (l,n,cbtInsert item r)

fun list2cbt [] t = t
  | list2cbt (x::xs) t = list2cbt xs (cbtInsert x t)

end
```

The fact that the structure `Tree` implements or, in other words, *ascribes to* the signature `TREE` is expressed by the part "`Tree:TREE`" at the beginning of the structure definition. There are two types of ascription in SML. We use here the *transparent ascription*, which means that the types defined in the structure are externally visible. The second one is the *opaque ascription* and makes the types from the structure invisible. The symbol `:>` is used instead of `:` for the opaque ascription. In functions `isComplete` and `cbtInsert` the keyword `as` is used to define abbreviations for too long arguments. Then these abbreviations are used inside the functions instead of the arguments. The type `tree` is declared in both `Tree` and `TREE`. This is because we need to use its type constructors in the `Heap` functor. Otherwise it will be enough to declare the type as `type'a tree` in `TREE`.

The heapsort algorithm, together with auxiliary functions to manipulate the heap are defined in the `Heap` functor, which ascribes to the `HEAP` signature. `HEAP` declares the type `Item` of elements in the heap and four functions. The first one, `buildFromList`, should create a heap from a list of type `Item`, `insert` should insert a new element to a heap, `isHeap` should check whether a tree is a heap and the last one, `toSortedList` should transform a heap into a sorted array using the heapsort algorithm.

```
signature HEAP = sig
 structure T:TREE
 type Item
 val buildFromList : Item list -> Item T.tree
 val insert : Item -> Item T.tree -> Item T.tree
 val isHeap : Item T.tree -> bool
 val toSortedList : Item T.tree -> Item list
end
```

Because we want our implementation to work with different types and ordering functions, we implement the signature as the functor `Heap`. The functor has two arguments. The first is a type `Itm` of elements in the list to be sorted and the second one is a function `ord` that defines the ordering to be established by the sorting.

```
functor Heap(type Itm val ord : Itm * Itm -> bool):HEAP = struct

 structure T = Tree
 type Item=Itm
 exception nonEmptyNode

 fun heapify T.empty = T.empty
   | heapify(t as T.tNode(T.empty,n,T.empty)) =  t
   | heapify(T.tNode(T.empty,n,r)) = raise  nonEmptyNode
   | heapify(t as T.tNode(T.tNode(T.empty,m,T.empty),n,T.empty)) =
      if ord(n,m) then t
      else T.tNode(T.tNode (T.empty,n,T.empty),m,T.empty)
   | heapify(T.tNode(T.tNode(l,m,r),n,T.empty)) =
      raise  nonEmptyNode
   | heapify(t as T.tNode(l as T.tNode(l1,m,r1),n,
                            r as T.tNode(l2,q,r2))) =
      if ord(n,m) andalso ord(n,q) then t
      else if ord(m,n) andalso ord(m,q) then
         T.tNode(heapify(T.tNode(l1,n,r1)),m,r)
      else T.tNode (l,q,heapify(T.tNode(l2,n,r2)))

 fun max n T.empty = true
   | max n (T.tNode (l,m,r)) = ord(n,m) andalso (isPrioritized l)
                                 andalso (isPrioritized r)
 and
     isPrioritized (T.empty) = true
   | isPrioritized (T.tNode (l,n,r)) = (max n l) andalso (max n r)

 fun cbt2heap T.empty = T.empty
   | cbt2heap (T.tNode(l,n,r)) =
        heapify (T.tNode (cbt2heap l, n, cbt2heap r))
```

```
fun buildFromList l = cbt2heap (T.list2cbt l T.empty)

fun insert item t = cbt2heap (T.cbtInsert item t)

fun merge t s = cbt2heap (T.list2cbt (T.inorder t []) s)

fun isHeap t = T.isComplete t andalso isPrioritized t

fun toSortedList T.empty = []
  | toSortedList (T.tNode(l,n,r)) = n :: toSortedList (merge l r)
end
```

In addition to the functions declared in HEAP the functor Heap contains other ones that help to implement the heapsort. The most complex one is heapify, which re-establish the heap property inside a heap. The function isPrioritized checks whether the heap property holds and is defined using the mutually recursive function max. The function cbt2heap transforms a complete binary tree to a heap by calling heapify and merge merges two trees into one heap.

If we take the functions geqPrd and leqPrd from Sect. 3.5 as ordering functions, we can define a function prdHeapSortDsc for sorting a list of PRD records in descending order as

```
local
  structure h = Heap(type Itm=PRD val ord= geqPrd)
in
  fun prdHeapSortDsc [] = []
  |   prdHeapSortDsc [a] = [a]
  |   prdHeapSortDsc l = h.toSortedList(h.buildFromList l)

end
```

A function prdHeapSortAsc for sorting in the opposite direction can be defined in a similar way, by using leqPrd instead of geqPrd.

Existing implementations of SML already come with a bunch of structures, signatures and functors, called the *Standard ML basis library*. They provide a lot of useful functionality and their description can be found at [18]. In Table 1 we already encountered two function from the library, Int.toString and Real.toString, which are defined in structures Int and Real.

4 CPN ML

CPN ML is a functional programming language that embeds the Standard ML and extends it with constructs for defining colour sets, variables [8] and for dealing with multisets. There are also other changes, like the replacement of the operator @ for the list concatenation by ^^ and use of @ for delay expressions. CPN ML also comes with its own library of functions that, for example, includes generators of random numbers and variates or the function `time()`, which returns the actual value of so-called simulated time[6]. On the other hand, as CPN Tools internally uses SML/NJ [8] for CPN ML evaluation, almost any valid piece of SML code, including the Standard ML basis library, can be used with CPN Tools. Specifics of CPN ML are exhaustively described at [15], here we just briefly describe the most significant differences.

4.1 Colour Sets and Variables

In CPN, *colour sets* are used as types of tokens, places, values, variables and expressions. They are defined by the `colset` keyword, which is an equivalent of the `type` keyword from SML. This means that we can (and also have to) name colour sets created as subsets of other colour sets or by type constructors available in CPN Tools but we cannot introduce new type constructors. Fortunately, the constructors in CPN ML cover some cases that can only be solved using the `datatype` construct in SML. There are two types of colour sets, *simple* and *compound.*

Simple colour sets are like primitive types in SML, but with some distinctive features. One of them is that it is possible to replace values in a colour set with alternative ones or define a colour set as an interval of values from another one. Both of these are achieved by using the keyword `with`. For example, a colour set containing integers from `0` to `127` can be defined as

```
colset ASCII = int with 0..127;
```

and a colour set, which is the `bool` type with the value[7] `disagree` instead of `false` and `agree` instead of `true` as

```
colset Agr = bool with (disagree, agree);
```

Types from SML cannot be directly used as colour sets, they have to be renamed, for example `colset INT = int;`. Simple colour sets include enumerated sets, so an alternative to the data type `DevStatus` from Sect. 3.4 can be defined as

```
colset DevStatus = with  on | off | broken;
```

Compound colour sets are those defined by other colour sets. For example, the record colour set `PRD` and the list colour set `PRDlst` from Sect. 6 belong here.

Variables are necessary for describing relations between values of tokens removed and created during transition firings. They were a part of CPN long before the decision to use SML for net inscriptions has been made, so there is no way of avoiding them. They are defined in the form

$$\texttt{var}\ vname_1 \ldots,\ vname_n\ :\ cset;$$

[6] See Sect. 5.3 for details.

[7] We can use any pair of values, the first one is always for *true* and the second one for *false*.

where $vname_1$ to $vname_n$ are names of variables and *cset* is the name of a colour set that is their type. Notice that all definitions of colour sets and variables end with the semicolon symbol. This is mandatory, a definition without it will cause error in CPN Tools.

4.2 Multisets

Multisets are like sets, but allow multiple occurrences of the same elements. They are also called *bags* and in CPN describe groups of tokens in markings and various kinds of expressions. Formally a *multiset* m over a non-empty set S is defined as a function $m : S \rightarrow \mathbb{N}$, represented as a formal sum:

$$\sum_{s \in S} m(s)'s.$$

$\mathbb{N}$ is the set of natural numbers and the values $\{m(s) | \ s \in S\}$ are the *coefficients* of the multiset. We say, that s belongs to m ($s \in m$) if and only if $m(s) \neq 0$. For example, a multiset holding two members of value 4, three members of value 5 and one member of value 9 can be written as the formal sum

$$2'4 + 3'5 + 1'9.$$

In CPN ML the syntax is a bit different, because the apostrophe and plus symbols are reserved for other purposes. Namely, the back-quote (grave accent) symbol "`" is used instead of "′" and the single plus is replaced by "++". So, in CPN ML our multiset will be written as

```
2`4++3`5++1`9
```

The back-quote operator is called *multiset constructor* and ++ is *multiset addition.* There are also other operators and functions for multisets. Some of them are listed in Table 2.

Table 2. Selected multiset operators and functions

Operator (function)	Name	Example
`empty`	empty multiset ($\emptyset$)	
`==`	equality	``1`2++3`1 == 3`1++1`2`` $\equiv$ `true`
`<><>`	inequality	``1`8++3`1 <><> 3`1++1`2`` $\equiv$ `true`
`<<`	less than	``2`1++1`2 << 3`1++1`2`` $\equiv$ `true`
`>>=`	greater than or equal	``3`1++8`2 >>= 3`1++1`2`` $\equiv$ `true`
`--`	subtraction	``3`1++8`2 -- (3`1++1`2)`` $\equiv$ ``7`2``
`**`	scalar multiplication	``4**(3`1++1`2)`` $\equiv$ ``12`1++4`2``
`size`	size	``size(3`1++1`2)`` $\equiv$ `4`
`cf`	number of appearances	``cf(1,3`1++1`2)`` $\equiv$ `3`

If a multiset contains only one element then the number of occurrences and the back-quote may be omitted, e.g. `1‘5` is the same as `5` and `1‘()` is the same as `()`. However, we should be careful when a multiset is specified as one non-negative integer value. For example, the expression `5` means `1‘5` if the multiset is over an integer colour set and `5‘()` if it is over a colour set defined as equal to the SML type `unit`. In the following section we use the term *multiset expression*, which denotes an expression that evaluates to a multiset.

5 Coloured Petri Nets

Coloured Petri Nets belong to the class of high-level Petri nets, so tokens held in their places can be of various values. There are still the same basic elements as in PT nets, i.e. places, transitions and arcs, but their definition and markings and the firing process of CPN are more complicated. In addition, each CPN contains a part called *declarations* with CPN ML code defining colour sets, variables, values and functions of the net. CPN ML code can be also loaded from text files. To do this a declaration of the form

```
use "fname";
```

where *fname* is the name of the file to be loaded, has to be added to the net declarations.

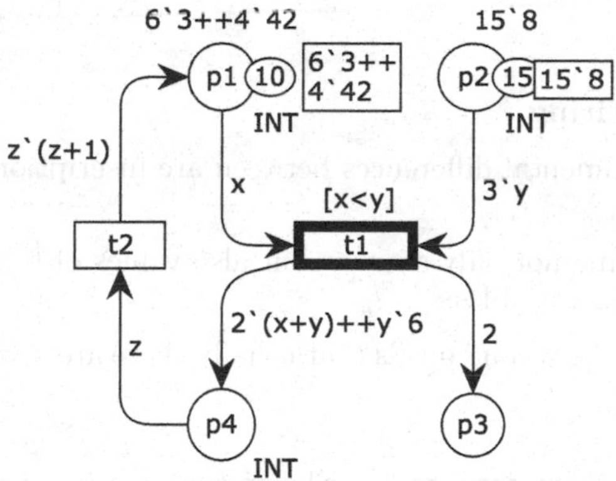

Fig. 5. A small CPN in its initial marking M_0

An example of a small CPN can be seen in Fig. 5. This net uses two colour sets, `INT` and `UNIT`, and three variables, `x`, `y` and `z`. All of them have to be defined in the declarations of the net, which can be written as follows:

```
colset UNIT = unit;
colset INT = int;
var x,y,z: INT;
```

All the PT nets presented in Sect. 5 are valid Coloured Petri nets with `UNIT` used as the colour set for all places.

5.1 Place, Transition and Arc Inscriptions

In PT nets we define a name and an initial marking for each place. In CPN we also specify a colour set for each place and all tokens in the place have to be from it. Markings are multisets of tokens, so initial markings are defined as multiset expressions. For example, the place in the top left corner of Fig. 5 has the name `p1`, the initial marking `6‘3++4‘42` and `INT` as its colour set. If the colour set of a place is `UNIT` then its name is not shown (even in the cases when it is not equal to the `unit` type). This is the case of the place (named) `p3` in Fig. 5. Places `p3` and `p4` have no initial marking inscriptions, so their initial markings are empty multisets.

For transitions we now have four different inscriptions: name, guard, time, and code segment inscriptions. The transitions in Fig. 5 have the names `t1` and `t2` and one of them, `t1`, also has a guard expression in the form `x<y`. Guard expressions are additional conditions for transition firings and their role is explained in Sect. 5.2. Time inscriptions are used in timed CPN and are treated in Sect. 5.3. A code segment inscription contains a CPN ML code that is executed when the corresponding transition is fired. An example of a code segment can be seen in Fig. 13 (transition `newSetOfParts`).

Arc inscriptions are multiset expressions, which define what tokens are removed or created when transitions fire. Their role is explained in the next section.

5.2 Transition Firing

There are two fundamental differences between arc inscriptions in PT nets and CPN:

1. In CPN they define not only amount but also values of tokens.
2. They may contain variables.

The consequence of the second one is that usually there are several ways in which a transition can fire.

Binding Element. If we want to describe an enabling or a firing of a transition t precisely, then we do not say that a transition is enabled (fires) but a binding element is enabled (fires). The *binding element* is a pair in the form

$$(t, < var_1 = val_1 \ldots, var_n = val_n >), \tag{1}$$

where t is the transition, var_1 to var_n are variables that occur in arc inscriptions of the arcs adjacent to t and val_1 to val_n are values assigned to these variables. Examples of binding elements for the transition `t1` from Fig. 5 are

$$(\texttt{t1}, < \mathtt{x} = 3, \mathtt{y} = 8 >) \text{ and} \tag{2}$$

$$(\texttt{t1}, < \mathtt{x} = 42, \mathtt{y} = 8 >). \tag{3}$$

If we say that a transition t is enabled (fires), we mean that some binding element containing t is enabled (fires).

Before defining enabling and firing we introduce two multisets, $ms(p,t,be)$ and $ms(t,p,be)$:

- $ms(p,t,be)$ is an empty multiset if there is no arc from p to t. If there is an arc a from p to t then $ms(p,t,be)$ is a multiset to which $eArc(p,t,be)$ evaluates. $eArc(p,t,be)$ is the inscription on the arc from p to t with var_1 to var_n replaced by val_1 to val_n according to a binding element be.
- $ms(t,p,be)$ is defined in the similar way but for an arc from t to p.

For the sake of simplicity we assume that there is always at most one[8] arc going from p to t or from t to p. The *occurrence sequences* for CPN are defined similarly to those in PT nets but they contain binding elements instead of transitions.

Enabling. A binding element be of the form (1) is *enabled* in a marking M if and only if

1. For each pre-place p of t it holds that the multiset $ms(p,t,be)$ is less than or equal to $M(p)$.
2. The expression obtained from the guard of t by replacing var_1 to var_n by val_1 to val_n according to be evaluates to `true`.

This means that in the initial marking M_0 of our net (Fig. 5), which can be written[9] as

$$M_0 = (\texttt{6`3++4`42}, \texttt{15`8}, \emptyset, \emptyset),$$

only the binding element (2) is enabled. The second one, (3), is not because the guard of `t2` (i.e. `42<8`) evaluates to `false`.

Firing. The result of the *firing* of be in M is a new marking M', $M\ [be\!>M'$, computed for each place p as

$$M'(p) = M(p) \ \texttt{--}\ ms(p,t,be)\ \texttt{++}\ ms(t,p,be),$$

where $ms(p,t,be)$ and $ms(t,p,be)$ are as defined above and `--` and `++` are multiset operators from Sect. 4.2. For example, if we fire the step (2) in the initial marking M_0 of our net (Fig. 5), it will result in a new marking M_1 (Fig. 6), computed as

$$\begin{aligned}
M_1(\texttt{p1}) &= \texttt{(6`3++4`42) -- 1`3 ++ } \emptyset &&= \texttt{5`3++4`42}\\
M_1(\texttt{p2}) &= \texttt{15`8 -- 3`8 ++ } \emptyset &&= \texttt{12`8}\\
M_1(\texttt{p3}) &= \emptyset \texttt{ -- } \emptyset \texttt{ ++ (8`6++2`11)} &&= \texttt{8`6++2`11}\\
M_1(\texttt{p4}) &= \emptyset \texttt{ -- } \emptyset \texttt{ ++ 2`()} &&= \texttt{2`()}
\end{aligned}$$

Notice that the inscription of the arc from `t1` to `p4` uses the values of consumed tokens not only to compute values of new tokens (`x+y`) but also to define the number of new tokens (`y`6`). In $M_1$ both `t1` and `t2` can be fired.

[8] In fact, if there are two or more arcs, they can be always replaced by one.

[9] Assuming the ordering `p1`, `p2`, `p3`, `p4` of places. The symbol $\emptyset$ denotes an empty multiset.

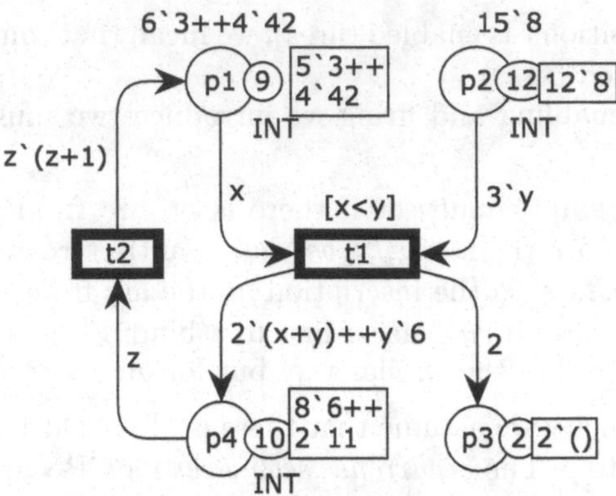

Fig. 6. CPN from Fig. 5 in marking M_1

5.3 Time in CPN

In Sect. 2 we said that transitions often represent events or actions, which occur or are executed when they fire. But in real life actions usually have a duration and some time needs to pass between two event occurrences. To capture time-related features in CPN models we need to use their timed version, called *timed CPN*. They differ from "ordinary" CPN is several ways:

- In a timed CPN a value called *timestamp* can be associated with tokens. A timestamp of a token is written after its ordinary value with the symbol `@` as a delimiter. For example, the expression `5@10` represents a token with the value `5` and timestamp `10`. The timestamp of a token is the time when the token was created.
- Colour sets can be timed. A *timed colour set* is a colour set, where each value includes a timestamp. So, a token with a timestamp has to be a member of a timed colour set. The keyword `timed` is used to declare that a colour set is timed. The aforementioned value `5@10` can be a member of a timed colour set, declared as `colset INTtm = int timed;`
- Arc inscriptions may include so-called *delay expressions*, which define timestamps of newly created tokens. These expression have the form `@+`*expr*, where *expr* is an arithmetic expression of the integer type.
- A delay expression can be also associated with a transition, as so-called *transition time inscription*. It has the same effect as if the expression is added to each outgoing arc of the transition.
- Delay expressions can also be a part of the initial marking inscriptions of places, whose types are timed colour sets. They define timestamps of tokens in M_0.

The time in CPN models is called *simulated time* and is represented as a non-negative integer. Its value is 0 when a computation (simulation) starts and

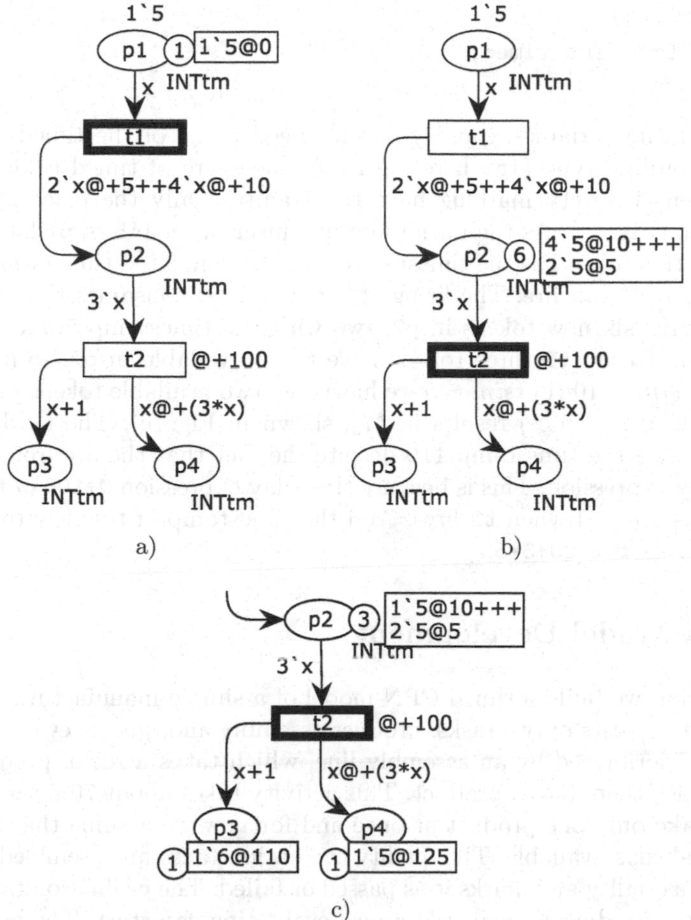

Fig. 7. Timed CPN in M_0, $tsim = 0$ (a) M_1, $tsim = 10$ (b) and M_2, $tsim = 10$ (c)

may only increase during the simulation. The actual value of the simulated time can be obtained by calling the CPN ML function `time()`.

The time aspect is incorporated into transition enabling and firing by introducing the notion of *token availability*: A token `v@s` is available at simulated time *tsim* if and only if $tsim \geq$ `s`. This means that all what was said in Sect. 5.2 remains valid, but only available tokens are taken into account. Tokens generated by firings have timestamps computed by corresponding delay expressions. All tokens without timestamps are regarded as tokens with timestamps equal to 0, so they are always available.

We explain how the computation of timed CPN proceeds on an example in Fig. 7. It shows a small timed CPN in three subsequent markings. The net has only three declarations, namely:

```
colset INT = int;
colset INTtm = int timed;
var x,y: INT;
```

Notice, that the variables `x` and `y` doesn't need to be of the timed version of the corresponding type (`int` here). All the places are of timed colour sets, so all the tokens in every marking have timestamps. Only the place `p1` holds a token in M_0 (Fig. 7a). As the initial marking inscription `1‘5` of `p1` has no delay expression, this token has the timestamp `0`. In the simulated time $tsim = 0$ only the transition `t1` can fire. The firing $(\mathtt{t1}, < \mathtt{x} = 5 >)$ consumes the token from `p1` and creates six new tokens in `p2`, two with the timestamp `5` and four with `10` (Fig. 7b). To fire `t2` three tokens have to be available in `p2`, so it becomes enabled in $tsim = 10$ (in $tsim = 5$ we have only two available tokens in `p2`). The firing of $(\mathtt{t2}, < \mathtt{x} = 5 >)$ results in M_2, shown in Fig. 7c). The newly created token in `p3` has the timestamp `110` despite the fact that the arc from `t2` to `p3` has no delay expression. This is because the delay expression `@+100` of `t2` applies to all tokens created when `t2` fires. And the timestamp of the new token in `p4` is computed as `10+100+3*5`.

6 CPN Model Development

In this section we build a timed CPN model of a simple manufacturing process. The process consists of two tasks: product assembly and quality evaluation. The assembly is performed by an assembly line, which takes a set of product parts and assembles them into a product. This activity takes about 70 s, the assembly line can make only one product at once and for now we assume that a new set of parts is always available. The quality evaluation takes an assembled product, evaluates its quality and marks it as passed or failed. The evaluation takes about 130 s. After a product is evaluated a new evaluation can start. The quality of a product depends on the quality of its parts and the assembly duration.

The model is built step by step, staring with a basic, low-level, one in Subsect. 6.1. Next, data to be stored in tokens and durations of individual activities are added in Subsects. 6.2 and 6.3. The quality evaluation process is implemented in Sect. 6.4 and in Sect. 6.5 randomness is introduced to the model. In Sect. 6.6 we abandon the assumption that a new set of parts is always available and implement an arrival process for the sets. Finally, in Sect. 6.7 we extend our model by a procedure, which records selected failed products to an XML file.

In addition to presenting a CPN model development process, this section highlights two interesting aspects of SML utilization in CPN Tools. First, two approaches to modelling are demonstrated in Subsects. 6.3 and 6.4: an approach that primarily uses CPN places, transitions and arcs and an approach that prefers SML code. Second, in Subsect. 6.7 it is shown how an already existing SML code can be embedded into CPN models. Contrary to the previous sections, in what follows we don't show enabled transitions and actual markings in CPN models.

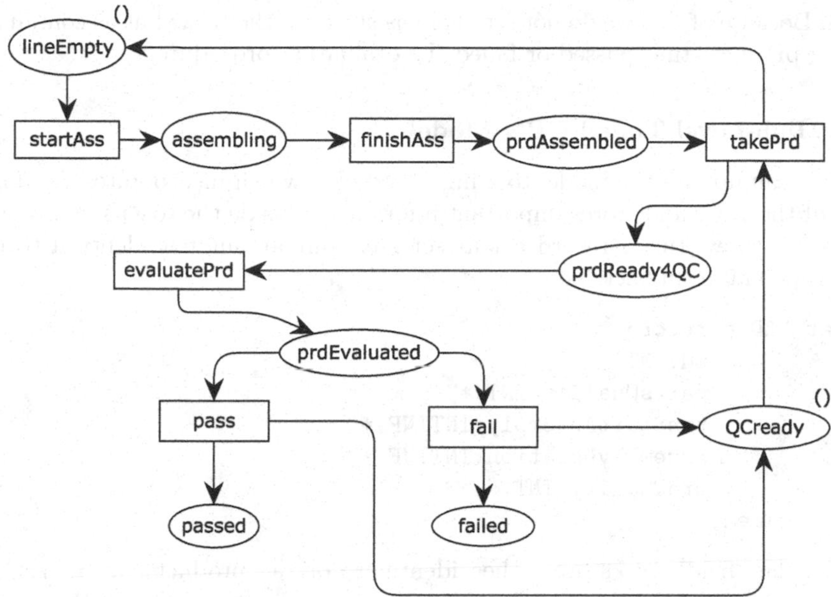

Fig. 8. Low-level PN representation of the manufacturing process

6.1 Low-Level PN Model

When creating a CPN model, it is good to start with a low-level one, which captures the "essence" of the system modelled. In our case it is the sequence of actions within the tasks and interaction between them. The low-level model can be seen in Fig. 8 and one of the goals we will try to accomplish by utilisation of CPN ML is to keep a resulting timed CPN as similar to this model as possible.

The assembly task is modelled by places `lineEmpty`, `assembling` and `prdAss- embled` and transitions `startAss` and `finishAss`. The places `prdReady4QC`, `prdEvaluated`, `passed`, `failed` and `QCready` and transitions `evaluatePrd`, `pass` and `fail` belong to the quality evaluation. The transition `takePrd` belongs to both tasks and represents an event on which both these concurrent tasks synchronize.

In the initial marking we have tokens in `lineEmpty` and `QCready`, which means that both tasks are ready to begin. However, only the assembly can start by a firing of `startAss`. A token in `assembling` means that a product is being assembled and a token in `prdAssembled` that the assembly is done (by a firing of `finishAss`). Now, `takePrd` can be fired, representing the removal of the product from the assembly line and the start of its evaluation (a token in `prdReady4QC`). In the meanwhile, a new assembly can start. A firing of `evaluatePrd` means that the product has been evaluated (a token in `prdEvaluated`) and can be marked as passed (by a firing of `pass`) or failed (by a firing of `fail`). After this an evaluation of a new product can start as we have a token in `QCready` again. The places `passed` and `failed` differ from others, they can hold more than one token. Because of this we do not see them as states of the tasks but as containers storing products that passed or failed the evaluation procedure.

6.2 High-Level Timed CPN Model

Now we can update the model to a high-level one, which incorporates the durations of the tasks and stores important information inside the tokens. For tokens we create a new timed record colour set `PRD`, similar but not identical to the SML type `PRD` from Sect. 3.4.

```
colset PRD = record
             id:INT *
             partsQuality:INT *
             tmsStartAssembly:INTINF *
             assemblyDuration:INTINF *
             prdQuality:INT
       timed;
```

where the field `id` stores the identifier of a product or a set of parts, `partsQuality` stores the value representing quality of the parts, `tmsStartAssembly` the value of the simulated time when the assembly of the product started, `assemblyDuration` is the time needed to assembly the product and `prdQuality` is the value on the basis of which it will be decided whether the product passes or fails. The overall structure of the net doesn't change, but all places except of `lineEmpty` and `QCready` are now of the colour set `PRD` (Fig. 9).

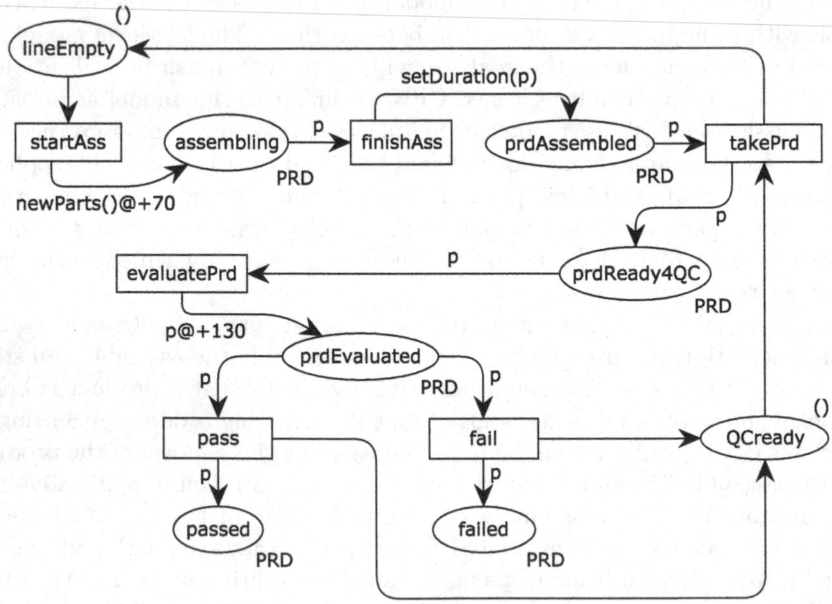

Fig. 9. Deterministically timed CPN model of the manufacturing process

This is because tokens in them are products or sets of parts in corresponding stage of the assembly or evaluation.

To be able to pass values from one token to another and update fields we define a variable p as

```
var p:PRD;
```

and functions

```
fun newParts():PRD={
  id=0,
  partsQuality=55,
  tmsStartAssembly=time(),
  assemblyDuration=0,
  prdQuality=0}
```

and

```
fun setDuration(p:PRD)={
  id= (#id p),
  partsQuality=(#partsQuality p),
  tmsStartAssembly=(#tmsStartAssembly p),
  assemblyDuration=time()-(#tmsStartAssembly p),
  prdQuality=(#prdQuality p)}
```

How they are used in arc inscriptions can be seen in Fig. 9. Of course, we can put the expressions from these functions directly to the corresponding arc inscriptions, but using functions increases readability of the net and makes future changes in data representation easier (i.e. only declarations will be modified, the net stays as it is).

The function `newParts` creates a record for a new token. For now, the fields `id` and `partsQuality` are set to constant values, but we will change this in Sects. 6.3 and 6.5. The field `tmsStartAssembly` holds an actual simulated time of the corresponding `startAss` firing. Finally, `assemblyDuration` and `prdQuality` are set to `0`, because their values will be computed later. The `assemblyDuration` is computed by the second function, `setDuration`. The net also contains delay expressions for the duration of assembly (`@+70`) and evaluation (`@+130`).

6.3 Adding Id Generator

There are some underdeveloped features in our model and the one we deal with first is the product identifier (id) generation. Each product should have a unique id. There are several ways how to implement the generator and here we show two of them. The first one we call a "PN way", because it extends the structure of the net and uses minimum of CPN ML code. The second one, an "ML way" leaves the net as it is and uses CPN ML code only. Going the PN way means adding a new place that stores the id of the next product to be assembled. This

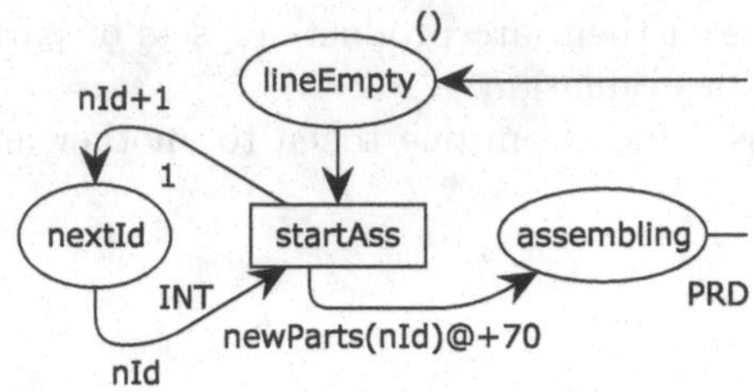

Fig. 10. Part of the CPN model with the place nextId added

place (`nextId`) is connected to the transition `startAss` (Fig. 10). Of course, we also need to add `var nId:INT;` to the declarations of the net and change the first two lines of the function `newParts` definition to

```
fun newParts(nid):PRD={
  id=nid,
```

The ML way is to use a global variable to store the id for a next product. In CPN ML global variables are implemented using one of the imperative features of SML, namely the possibility to implement variables as references. The global variable can be declared as

```
globref nextPrdId=0;
```

and to increase its value after an assembly of a new product starts we add the expression

```
action
inc nextPrdId
```

to the code segment inscription of the transition `startAss`. The first two lines of the `newParts` definition will now be

```
fun newParts():PRD={
  id=(!nextPrdId),
```

The symbol `!` is the dereferencing operator of SML. One difference between the two approaches is that when the PN way is used the id generation starts from 1 again when the net is reset to its initial marking. In ML way it continues from the last used value.

6.4 Quality Evaluation Process

Above we said that the quality evaluation of a product is based on the quality of its parts and the duration of its assembly. Let us assume that the quality of the parts can be measured and whether the product passes or fails depends on the following criteria, where $pq(p)$ is the quality of parts and $ad(p)$ is the assembly duration of a product p:

- If the $pq(p) \leq 50$ then p fails
- If $50 < pq(p) < 78$ then
  - if $ad(p) \leq 71$ then p passes
  - if $ad(p) > 71$ then p fails
- If $pq(p) \geq 78$ then
  - if $ad(p) \leq 80$ then p passes
  - if $ad(p) > 80$ then p fails.

This evaluation process can be implemented in several ways and we again show a PN and an ML way of doing it. Both implementations store the result of the evaluation in the field `prdQuality` of a token representing p added to the place `prdEvaluated` and this result is `1` if p passes and `0` if p fails. The value of `prdQuality` is then used in guards of the transitions `pass` and `fail`, which are the same in both implementations.

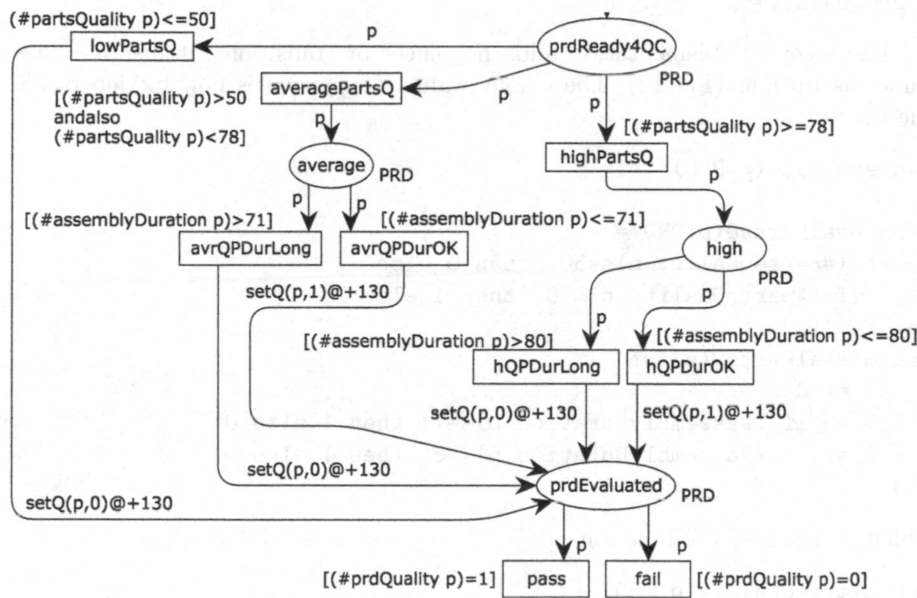

Fig. 11. Part of the model implementing the evaluation process in PN way

Using the PN way, i.e. putting as much of the process to places and transitions as possible, may result in a significant addition to the structure of the net. This can be seen in Fig. 11, where everything but the places `prdReady4QC` and `prdEvaluated` and transitions `pass` and `fail` is new. The rest of the net is not shown, because it remains the same as in Fig. 9. Except the inscriptions shown in Fig. 11, the only new piece of code the net uses is the function

```
fun setQ(p:PRD, q:INT)={
```

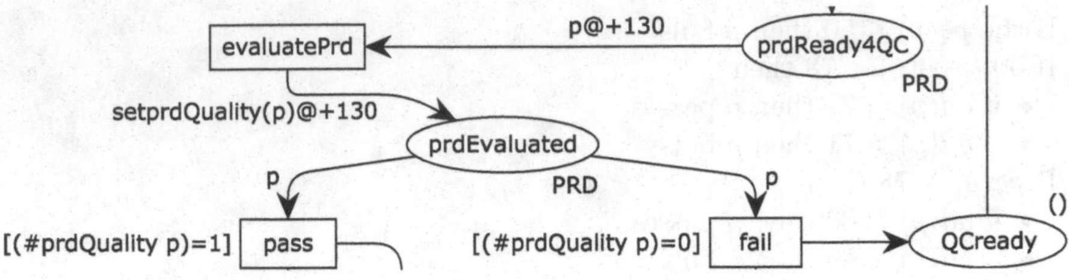

Fig. 12. Part of the model with modified inscriptions (ML way)

```
  id= (#id p),
  partsQuality= (#partsQuality p),
  tmsStartAssembly=(#tmsStartAssembly p),
  assemblyDuration=(#assemblyDuration p),
  prdQuality=q}
```

The second implementation adds no places or transitions; it just modifies some inscriptions (Fig. 12). The whole evaluation process is now hidden inside the function

```
fun evaluate(p:PRD):INT=
let
 fun evalPartsQ(p:PRD)=
   if (#partsQuality p)<=50  then 0 else
     if (#partsQuality p)<78  then 1 else 2;
in
 case evalPartsQ(p) of
    0 => 0
  | 1 => if (#assemblyDuration p)<=71 then 1 else 0
  | 2 => if (#assemblyDuration p)<=80 then 1 else 0
end
```

which is called by the function

```
fun setprdQuality(p:PRD)={
  id= (#id p),
  partsQuality=(#partsQuality p),
  tmsStartAssembly=(#tmsStartAssembly p),
  assemblyDuration=(# assemblyDuration p),
  prdQuality=evaluate(p)}
```

to update the `prdQuality` field.

6.5 From Deterministic to Stochastic Model

The evaluation process added in the previous section made our net completely deterministic. With the assembly duration set to 70 and the parts quality to 55 (as in Sect. 6.2) all the products will pass. Of course, this is not very realistic as processes like these are usually of stochastic nature. To capture such nature in a CPN model, CPN ML offers functions that generate random values from various random distributions. Now we will use some of them to make our model stochastic and thus more realistic. We will do this with the model that has both the id generator and the quality evaluation process implemented in the ML way. However, identical modifications can be applied to a model that implements both or one of these parts in the PN way. The same is true for the functionality implemented in Sects. 6.6 and 6.7.

Let us assume that on the basis of corresponding measurements we found out that

- the product assembly duration follows the normal distribution with mean $\mu = 69$ and variance $\sigma^2 = 13$,
- the quality evaluation duration follows the normal distribution with $\mu = 131$ and $\sigma^2 = 10$ and
- the parts quality can be characterized by an integer value *pq*, where $0 \leq pg \leq 100$, which follows the normal distribution with $\mu = 81$ and $\sigma^2 = 21$ but approximately 1 in 10 sets has only half of the quality.

To reflect this in our model we first prepare the function

```
fun normTm(mean: int, variance: int) =
  round(normal(real(mean),real(variance)))
```

which returns a value drawn from the normal distribution with given `mean` and `variance` and the function

```
fun getPartsQuality() = let
    val usualQ= normal(81.0,21.0)
    val dvd = if uniform(0.0,1000.0)<=100.0 then uniform (1.8,2.1)
                                                 else 1.0
  in ((floor (usualQ/dvd)) mod 101)
end
```

which computes the parts quality value according to what was said above. The functions `normal` and `uniform` are CPN ML functions for generating random values from normal and uniform distributions. They have real arguments and return a real value, so some of the SML conversion functions, presented in Table 1 are used to convert from and to integers. Then we replace the line

```
partsQuality=55,
```

in the function `newParts` (from Sect. 6.2) with

```
partsQuality=getPartsQuality(),
```

and modify the corresponding arc inscriptions. The new ones will be

- `newParts()@+normTm(69,13)` on the arc from `startAss` to `assembling` and
- `setprdQuality(p)@+ normTm(131,10)` on the arc from `evaluatePrd` to `prdEvaluated`.

This can also be seen in Fig. 13 in the next section.

6.6 Adding Input Queue

The next modification we make is an addition of a more realistic representation of the parts sets arrival. Until now, we assumed that there is always a new set of parts available when the assembly line is empty. Now we change this to the following arrival procedure:

- The sets of parts arrive in intervals characterized by the exponential distribution with mean = 143.
- When a new set arrives, it enters a queue, where it waits to be assembled.

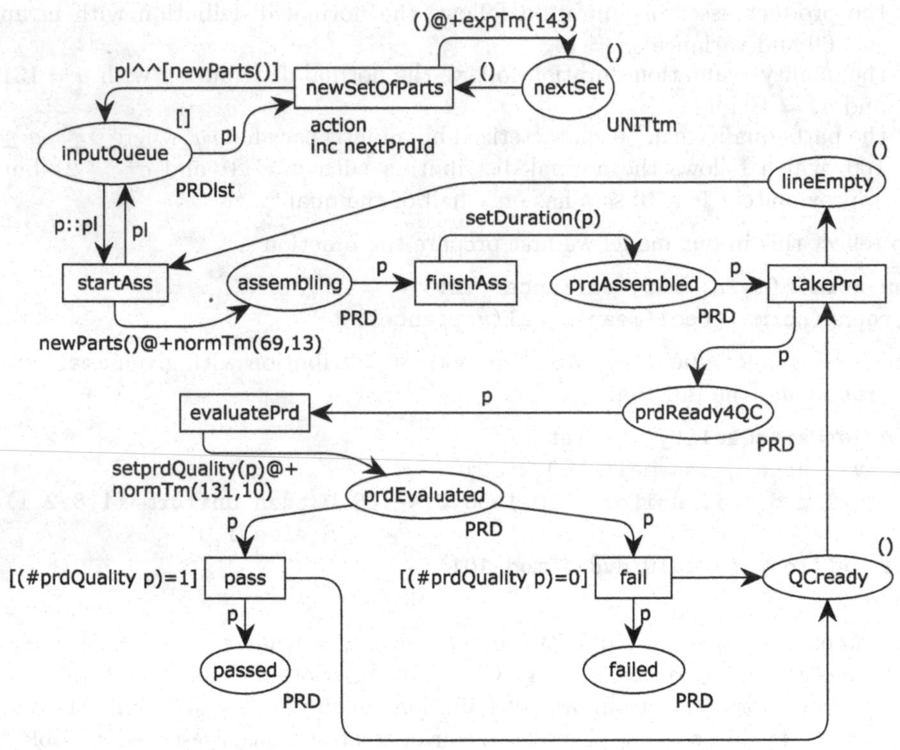

Fig. 13. Manufacturing process CPN model with input queue

In CPN we usually represent queues as lists and the enqueue and dequeue operations with operators `^^` and `::`. The head of the list will be the front of the queue. To draw an integer value from the exponential distribution we add a new function

```
fun expTm(mean: int) =
  round(exponential(1.0/real(mean)))
```

to the declarations of the net, where we also define two new colour sets and a variable:

```
colset UNITtm = UNIT timed;
colset PRDlst = list PRD;
var pl: PRDlst;
```

The function **exponential** is provided by CPN ML to get the corresponding random value. After this we implement the arrival procedure in our CPN model by adding new places **nextSet**, **inputQueue** and a transition **newSetOfParts** (Fig. 13). The time of a new set arrival is stored as the timestamp of the token in **nextSet** and the token in **inputQueue** represents the queue. The transition **newSetOfParts** implements the enqueue operation and **startAss** the dequeue operation.

6.7 Failed Products Recording

The CPN model we created is evidently suitable for simulation. We can easily perform a simulation run by firing corresponding sequence of binding elements, but the question is how to conveniently collect data during the run. Fortunately, CPN Tools offer a feature called *monitors*, designed especially for this task. A monitor is a collection of CPN ML functions, which are executed when certain events, such as firings of transitions associated with them, occur.

Now, let's assume that during the simulation runs of our model we need to record critical fails in descending order to an XML file for every work shift. One work shift is 4 h long and a critical fail is a failed product with the assembly duration longer than 70 s. The order is defined by the assembly duration, too. To accomplish this we

1. prepare functions for sorting lists of failed products and add them to the CPN model,
2. extend the structure of the net with places, transitions and arcs that collect failed products into a sorted list for each shift and
3. define a write-in-file monitor, which processes the sorted list and appends it to the XML file at the end of each shift.

The XML file is called `criticalFailsPerShift.xml` and for each shift it has to contain information about the time it ended (in seconds) and id, assembly duration and parts quality of every critical fail during the shift. For a simulation run lasting two shifts with one critical fail in the first shift has and two fails in the second one the file should look as follows:

```
<failedProducts>
 <shift endTime="14440">
  <prd id="83">
   <partsQuality>76</partsQuality>
   <assemblyDuration>76</assemblyDuration>
```

```
  </prd>
 </shift>
 <shift endTime="28880">
  <prd id="137">
   <partsQuality>72</partsQuality>
   <assemblyDuration>73</assemblyDuration>
  </prd>
  <prd id="154">
   <partsQuality>41</partsQuality>
   <assemblyDuration>73</assemblyDuration>
  </prd>
 </shift>
</failedProducts>
```

SML Functions for Sorting. The lists of failed products should be sorted and for this task we can use the already introduced SML code, namely

1. the functions `isOrdered`, `geqPrd` and `isPrdLstDsc` from Sect. 3.5,
2. the structure `Tree` from Sect. 3.6, but with the first line

   ```
   structure Tree:TREE = struct
   ```

   replaced with

   ```
   structure Tree = struct
   ```

3. the functor `Heap` from Sect. 3.6, but with the first line

   ```
   functor Heap(type Itm val ord: Itm*Itm -> bool):HEAP = struct
   ```

   replaced with

   ```
   functor Heap(type Itm val ord : Itm * Itm -> bool) = struct
   ```

4. the function `prdHeapSortDsc` from Sect. 3.6.

The signatures `TREE` and `HEAP` are not used, because CPN Tools doesn't allow them in declarations. Omission of the signatures is the reason why the first lines of `Tree` and `Heap` have to be modified. There are two ways of how to include the code into our CPN model:

1. Add the code directly to the declarations of the model. This will result in six new declarations, one for each function, structure and functor.
2. Put all the code to a text file and link it with the model by means of the SML command `use`. If we, for example, name the file `prdListUtils.sml` and place it in the same folder as the CPN model then the only declaration we need to add to the model is the `use` command, namely `use"prdListUtils.sml";`.

The code will work with our model despite the fact that it was designed for the `PRD` type from Sect. 3.4 while the model uses the slightly different colour set `PRD`, introduced in Sect. 6.2. This is thanks to the fact that both of them

- have the same name,
- are defined by the record type constructor and
- have the `assemblyDuration` field, the only field used in the code.

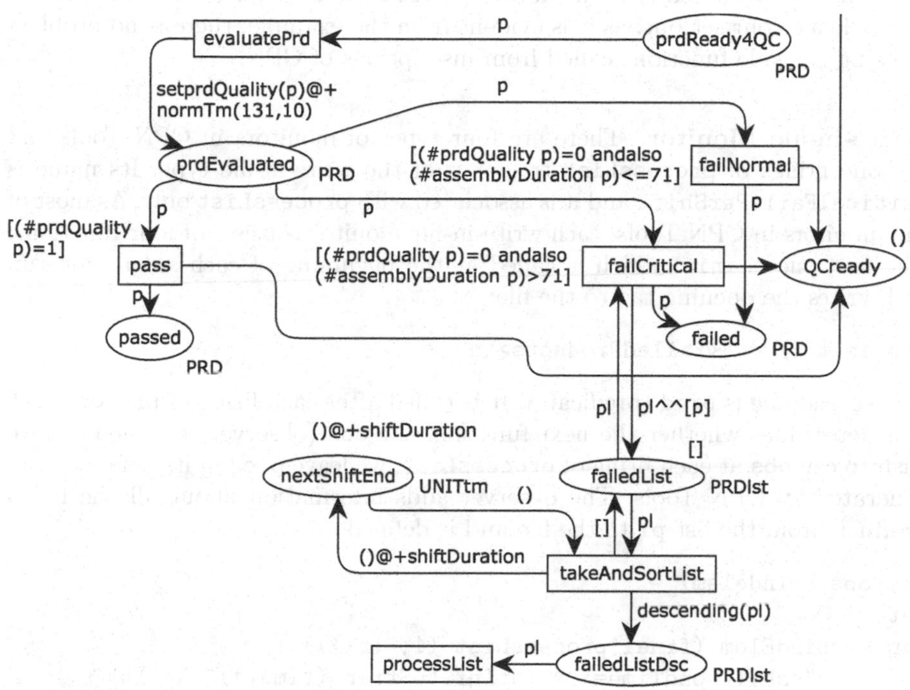

Fig. 14. Part of the CPN model from Fig. 13 modified for the failed products recording

Modified CPN Model. Now we are ready to modify the CPN model itself (Fig. 14). We split the transition `fail` into `failNormal`, which works as the original one, and `failCritical` for the critical fails. A firing of `failCritical` does the same as of `failNormal` plus it updates a list of critical fails, stored in a new place `failedList`, by corresponding failed product record. Another new transition is `takeAndSortList`, which fires at the end of each work shift. This is ensured by the place `nextShiftEnd` and adjacent arcs. The firing of `takeAndSortList` empties the list in `failedList` and adds its ordered version to `failedListDsc`. The `shiftDuration` is a value defined as

```
val shiftDuration =14440;
```

and `descending` is a function, which calls the functions added in step 1:

```
fun descending(pl)= if isPrdLstDsc(pl) then pl
                    else prdHeapSortDsc(pl)
```

The purpose of the transition `processList` is to empty `failedListDsc` and trigger a monitor, which saves the ordered list to `criticalFailsPerShift.xml`. It should be also noted that the data type `tree` from the structure `Tree` cannot be made a colour set but, as it is evident from the example, there is no problem in using it inside functions called from inscriptions of CPN.

Write-in-file Monitor. There are four types of monitors in CPN Tools and the one firings of `processList` trigger is of the write-in-file type. Its name is `criticalFailsPerShift` and it is associated with `processList` only. As most of the monitors in CPN Tools, each write-in-file monitor consists of four functions. The first one is `init`, which is called at the beginning of each simulation run and writes the opening tag to the file:

```
fun init () = "<failedProducts>\n"
```

The second one is `pred` (predicate). It is called after each firing of `processList` and determines whether the next function, the `obs` (observer) is called. As we wish to call `obs` at each firing of `processList`, we leave `pred` in its default form, generated by CPN Tools. The observer adds information about all the failed products from the list `pl` to the file and is defined as

```
fun obs (bindelem) =
let
fun obsBindElem (final'processList (1, {pl})) =
        "<shift endTime=\""^IntInf.toString(time())^"\">\n"^
        (foldr (op ^) "" (map prd2Xml pl))^"</shift>\n"
  | obsBindElem _ = ""
in
obsBindElem bindelem
end
```

provided that a page on which the model is created in CPN Tools is named `final`. The code of `obs` contains three functions we didn't encounter yet, `foldr`, `map` and `prd2Xml`. The first two are higher-order functions, defined in the `List` structure of the Standard ML basis library [18]. The function `map` is used to transform the list `pl` of product records to a list of product inscriptions in XML and `foldr` concatenates these inscriptions to one string. How a product record (of the colour set `PRD`) is transformed to XML is defined by the third function, which must be added to the declarations of the model and has the form

```
fun prd2Xml(p:PRD) =
     " <prd id=\""^Int.toString(#id p)^"\"><partsQuality>"^
     Int.toString(#partsQuality p)^
     "</partsQuality><assemblyDuration>"^
     IntInf.toString(#assemblyDuration p)^
     "</assemblyDuration></prd>\n"
```

The last function of the monitor is `stop`. It is called at the end of each simulation run and in our case it encloses the file:

```
fun stop () = "</failedProducts>"
```

7 Conclusion

In this chapter we provided an introduction to Coloured Petri nets and explored the possibilities that its pairing with the SML functional language offers. However, we barely scratched the surface and some features haven't been mentioned at all. These include polymorphism and some of the imperative aspects of SML and formal definition, properties and analytical methods on the side of Petri nets. To learn more about SML we recommend the tutorial [2] and books [14], [11] and [3]. A reader interested in Petri nets can find a general introduction to various types of Petri nets, including available formal analysis techniques, in [1]. Coloured Petri nets are comprehensively described in the three-volume book [4,5,7] and the more recent book [8]. The formal definition of Coloured Petri nets and its properties in a compact form can be found in [6].

The manufacturing process example from Sect. 6 promoted a design approach where a low-level model of a system, capturing its fundamental properties, is built first and CPN ML is used in such a way that only minimal modifications of the net structure are necessary on the way to the final model. One of the advantages of the approach is that formal analysis techniques such as place or transition invariants [1] can be applied to the low-level model to prove that it really preserves the fundamental properties. This approach was already successfully used during the development of simulation models for evaluation of a parallel ray-tracing implementation modifications [9,10] at the home institution of the author. However, the fact that the structure is preserved doesn't automatically mean that the fundamental properties are preserved, too. This can be also observed in our example, where firings of the transitions `pass` and `fail` change from nondeterministic in Figs. 8 and 9 to deterministic in Figs. 11 and 12 and back to nondeterministic in Fig. 13.

In Sect. 6.7 we shown how already existing SML code can be re-used in a CPN model. What we have done with the structure and functor for the heapsort algorithm can be adapted for other cases as well. However, the modeller should be aware of limitations (e.g. no support for signatures) and specific features (e.g. the operator `^^` for list concatenation instead of the SML operator `@`) of CPN ML. In addition, necessary level of similarity between the data types for which the re-used code has been originally designed and the colour sets used in the corresponding CPN model should be maintained and only values compatible with the colour sets of the model should be stored as tokens in places.

References

1. Desel, J., Reisig, W.: Place/transition Petri Nets. In: Reisig, W., Rozenberg, G. (eds.) ACPN 1996. LNCS, vol. 1491, pp. 122–173. Springer, Heidelberg (1998). https://doi.org/10.1007/3-540-65306-6_15
2. Gilmore, S.: Programming in standard Ml 1997: a tutorial introduction. Technical report, Laboratory for Foundations of Computer Science, The University of Edinburgh, January 2003. http://homepages.inf.ed.ac.uk/stg/NOTES/notes.pdf
3. Harper, R.: Programming in Standard ML. Carnegie Mellon University, Pittsburgh (2011). http://www.cs.cmu.edu/~rwh/smlbook/book.pdf
4. Jensen, K.: Coloured Petri Nets: Basic Concepts, Analysis Methods and Practical Use, vol. 1. Springer, Heidelberg (1997)
5. Jensen, K.: Coloured Petri Nets: Basic Concepts, Analysis Methods and Practical Use, vol. 2. Springer, Heidelberg (1997)
6. Jensen, K.: An introduction to the theoretical aspects of coloured Petri Nets. In: de Bakker, J.W., de Roever, W.-P., Rozenberg, G. (eds.) REX 1993. LNCS, vol. 803, pp. 230–272. Springer, Heidelberg (1994). https://doi.org/10.1007/3-540-58043-3_21
7. Jensen, K.: Coloured Petri Nets - Basic Concepts, Analysis Methods and Practical Use, vol. 3. Springer, Heidelberg (1997). https://doi.org/10.1007/978-3-642-60794-3
8. Jensen, K., Kristensen, L.M.: Coloured Petri Nets: Modelling and Validation of Concurrent Systems. Springer, Heidelberg (2009). https://doi.org/10.1007/b95112
9. Korečko, Š., Sobota, B.: Building parallel raytracing simulation model with Petri nets and B-method. In: Proceedings of Eurosim 2010, Praha, Česká republika (2010)
10. Korečko, Š., Sobota, B.: Using coloured petri nets for design of parallel raytracing environment. Acta Universitatis Sapientiae. Informatica **2**(1), 28–39 (2010)
11. Milner, R., Tofte, M., Macqueen, D.: The Definition of Standard ML. MIT Press, Cambridge (1997). http://sml-family.org/sml97-defn.pdf
12. Petri, C.A., Reisig, W.: Petri net. Scholarpedia **3**(4), 6477 (2008). http://www.scholarpedia.org/article/Petri_net
13. Stansifer, R.: The SML program: heap.sml (2015). http://cs.fit.edu/~ryan/sml/programs/heap-sml.html
14. Ullman, J.D.: Elements of ML Programming, ML97 Edition, 2nd edn. Prentice Hall, Upper Saddle River (1998)
15. CPN Tools (2015). http://cpntools.org/
16. MLton (2015). http://mlton.org/
17. Poly/ML (2015). http://www.polyml.org/
18. Standard ML Basis Library (2015). http://sml-family.org/Basis/
19. Standard ML of New Jersey (2015). http://www.smlnj.org/

Single Assignment C (SAC)

The Compilation Technology Perspective

Clemens Grelck(✉)

Institute of Informatics, University of Amsterdam,
Science Park 904, 1098XH Amsterdam, The Netherlands
c.grelck@uva.nl

Abstract. Single Assignment C (SAC) is a data parallel programming language that combines an imperative looking syntax, closely resembling that of C, with purely functional, state-free semantics. Again unlike the functional programming mainstream, that puts the emphasis on lists and trees, the focus of SAC as a data-parallel language is on (truly) multi-dimensional arrays. SAC arrays are not just loose collections of data cells or memory address ranges as in many imperative and object-oriented languages. Neither are they explicitly managed, stateful data objects as in some functional languages, may it be for language design or for performance considerations. SAC arrays are indeed purely functional, immutable, state-free, first-class values.

The array type system of SAC allows functions to abstract not only from the size of vectors or matrices but even from the number of array dimensions. Programs can and should be written in a mostly index-free style with functions consuming entire arrays as arguments and producing entire arrays as results. SAC supports a highly generic and compositional programming style that composes applications in layers of abstractions from universally applicable building blocks. The design of SAC aims at combining high productivity in software engineering of compute-intensive applications with high performance in program execution on today's multi- and many-core computing systems.

These CEFP lecture notes provide a balanced introduction to language design and programming methodology of SAC, but our main focus is on the in-depth description and illustration of the associated compilation technology. It is literally a long way down from state-free, functional program code involving multi-dimensional, truly state-free arrays to efficient execution on modern computing machines. Fully compiler-directed parallelisation for symmetric multi-socket, multi-core, hyper-threaded server systems, CUDA enabled graphics accelerators, workstation clusters or heterogeneous systems from a single architecture-agnostic source program adds a fair deal of complexity. Over the years, we have developed an intricate program transformation and optimisation machinery for this purpose. These lecture notes provide the first comprehensive presentation of our compilation technology as a whole.

V. Zsók et al. (Eds.): CEFP 2015, LNCS 10094, pp. 207–282, 2019.
https://doi.org/10.1007/978-3-030-28346-9_7

1 Introduction

The on-going multi-core/many-core revolution in processor architecture has arguably more radically changed the world's view on computing than any other innovation in microprocessor architecture before. For several decades the same program could be expected to run faster on the next generation of computers than on the previous. The trick that worked so well all the time was clock frequency scaling. The next generation of machines would simply run identical code at a higher clock frequency and, thus, in less time. Several times in the (short) history of computing the end of clock frequency scaling was predicted, but every time some technology breakthrough appeared right in time to continue, often even with a higher gradient than before.

About ten years ago the necessary technology breakthrough, however, failed to appear: the "free lunch" was finally over [1]. While sequential processing speed has still grown ever since, gains have been modest and often came at a high price. Instead parallel processing has moved from the niche of high performance computing into the mainstream. Today it is literally impossible to purchase a sequential computer. Multi-core processors rule the consumer market from desktops to laptops, tablets and smartphones [2,3]. Even TV sets are powered by multi-core processors these days, and safety- and time-critical cyber-physical systems will be next. Server systems are usually equipped with two or four processor sockets. Equipped with 8-core or even 16-core processors they reach levels of parallelism that were until recently only found in supercomputers.

As Oracle's Ultra SPARC T series [4,5] (code name Niagara) demonstrates, it is not uncommon to compromise sequential compute performance for the ability to fit more cores onto the same die space or into the same power budget. Taking this approach to the extreme, general-purpose graphics processing units (GPGPUs), the other big trend of our time, combine thousands of fairly restricted compute units in one device. They can compute workloads that match the architectural restrictions much faster than state-of-the-art general-purpose processors. And, increasingly relevant, they can do this with a fraction of the energy budget. With the fairly general-purpose CUDA programming model, particularly NVidia graphics cards have become integral parts of many high-performance computing installations [6].

These days even a fairly modest computer, consisting of a multi-core processor and a graphics card, is a veritable heterogeneous system. Heterogeneity in computing resources appears to be the direction for the foreseeable future. ARM's big.LITTLE single-ISA processor design with some powerful but energy-hungry cores and some less powerful energy-saving cores is likely to mark the begin of a new era [7,8].

Unlike ARM's big.LITTLE, the common combination of a multi-core processor and one, or possibly several, graphics accelerator(s) also forms a distributed system with multiple distinguishable memories. Another example of such a distributed memory accelerator design is Intel's Xeon Phi: 60 or more general-purpose x86 cores with extra-large vector registers and a high-speed interconnect [9–11].

The radical paradigm shift in computer architecture has a profound impact on the practice of software engineering:

All software must become ready for parallel execution!

Parallel programming per sé is hardly new, but it was largely confined to the niche of high performance computing. Programming methodologies and tools are geared towards squeezing the maximum possible performance out of an extremely expensive computing machinery through low-level machine-specific programming. Programming productivity concerns are widely ignored as running code is often more expensive than writing it.

What has changed with the multi-/many-core revolution is that any kind of software and likewise any programmer is affected, not only specialists in high performance computing centers with a PhD in computer science. Engineering parallel software is notoriously difficult because it adds a completely new design space: how to divide computational work into independent subparts, where and when to synchronise, how to balance the workload among cores and processors, etc, etc.

What has also changed is the variety of hardware. With existing programming technology this variety immediately affects software engineering. Programmers are confronted with a variety of programming models that even exceeds the variety of architectural models. Even a fairly modest computing system requires the combination and integration of several such models. Heterogeneous systems add a number of challenges to software engineering: where to compute what for highest performance or lowest power consumption or some combination thereof, where to store data, when to avoid copying data back and forth between memories, etc, etc.

All these developments make it technologically and economically challenging to write software that makes decent use of the variety and heterogeneity of today's computing systems. The quintessential goal of the SAC project lies in the co-design of programming language technology and the corresponding compiler technology that effectively and efficiently maps programs from a single source to a large variety of parallel computing architectures [12,13].

Our fundamental approach is *abstraction*. The guiding principle is to let the programmer define *what* to compute, not *how* exactly this is done. With respect to parallel program execution, we let the programmer express concurrency to be understood as an opportunity for parallel execution, but it is up to compiler and runtime system to decide where and when to exploit this opportunity. In any case it remains their responsibility to organise parallel program execution correctly and efficiently. Our goal is to put expert knowledge, once and for all, into compiler and runtime system, instead of again and again into low-level application programs.

Specifying *what* to compute, not exactly *how* to compute sounds very familiar to functional programmers. And indeed, SAC is a purely functional language. As the name Single Assignment C suggests, SAC combines an imperative looking syntax, closely resembling that of C, with purely functional, state-free semantics. Thus, despite the syntax, SAC programs deal with values, and program execution computes new values from existing values in a sequence of context-free substitution steps.

SAC is an *array programming language* in the best tradition of APL [14,15], J [16] or Nial [17]. Thus, the focus of SAC is on (truly) multi-dimensional arrays as purely functional, state-free, first-class values of the language. SAC arrays are characterised by their *rank*, i.e. a natural number describing the number of axes, or dimensions, by their *shape*, i.e. a rank-length vector of natural numbers that describe the extent of the array along each axis/dimension, and, last not least, by the contiguous row-major sequence of elements. As in C proper, indexing into arrays always starts at zero: legal index vectors are greater equal zero and less than the corresponding shape vector value in each element. The length of an index vector must be equal to the length of the shape vector to yield a scalar array element or less than the length of the shape vector to yield a subarray.

SAC functions consume array values and produce new array values as results. How array values are actually represented, how long they remain in memory and whether they actually become manifest in memory at all, is left to compiler and runtime system. Abstracting from all these low-level concerns allows SAC programs to expose the algorithmic aspects of some computation in much more clarity because they are not interspersed with the organisational aspects of program execution on some concrete target architecture.

The array type system of SAC allows functions to abstract not only from the size of vectors or matrices but likewise from the number of array dimensions. Programs can and should be written in a mostly index-free style with functions consuming entire arrays as arguments and producing entire arrays as results. SAC supports a highly generic programming style that composes applications in layers of abstractions from basic building blocks that again are not built-in to the language, but defined using SAC's versatile array comprehension construct WITH-loop.

The design of SAC aims at combining high productivity in software engineering of compute-intensive applications with high performance in program execution on the entire range of today's multi- and many-core computing systems. From literally the same source code the SAC compiler currently generates executable code for symmetric (potentially hyper-threaded) multi-core multi-processor systems with shared memory, general-purpose graphics processing units (GPGPUs) as well as the MicroGrid [18], an innovative general-purpose many-core processor architecture developed at the University of Amsterdam. Most recently we added clusters of workstations or more generally distributed memory systems to the list of supported architectures [19]. Likewise, we explored opportunities for heterogeneous computing using multiple accelerators or combing the computational power of accelerators with that of the CPU cores [20]. Figure 1 illustrates our compilation challenge.

Eventually, we aim at compiling a single SAC source program to the whole spectrum of relevant computing architectures. However, before looking into the challenges of parallel program execution or the intricacies of different target

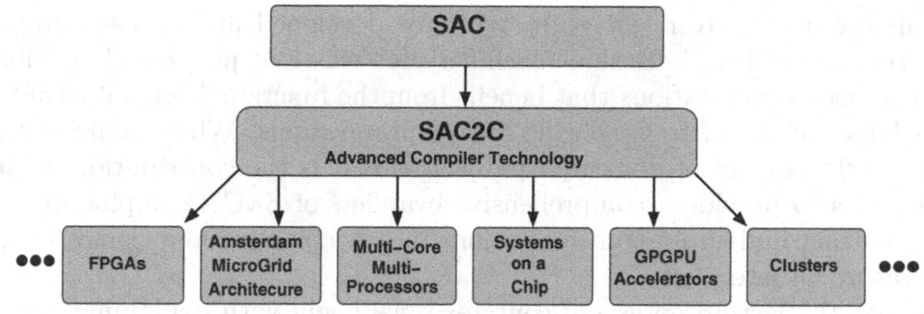

Fig. 1. The SAC compilation challenge: past, present and future work

architectures, we must be able to generate sequential code with competitive performance. After all, we cannot expect more than a linear performance increase from parallel execution. Sequential performance should be competitive not only with other high-level, declarative programming approaches, but also in relation to established imperative programming languages, such as C, C++ or Fortran. To this effect we have developed a great number of high-level and target-independent code transformations and optimisations. These code transformations systematically resolve the layers of abstractions introduced by the programming methodology advocated by SAC. They systematically transform code from a human-readable and -maintainable representation into one that allows for efficient execution by computing machines. Only after that we focus on code generation for the various computing architectures.

For any of the supported target architectures all decisions regarding parallel execution are taken by the compiler and the runtime system. To this effect we fully exploit the data-parallel semantics of SAC that merely expresses concurrency as the opportunity for parallel execution, but only compiler and runtime system effectively decide where, when and to what extent to actually harness this opportunity. The right choice depends on a variety of concerns including properties of the target architecture, characteristics of the code and attributes of the data being processed.

These CEFP lecture notes are not the first of their kind. In [21] we gave a thorough and fairly complete introduction to SAC as a programming language and the advocated programming methodology and design philosophy. At the same time we merely glanced over implementation and compilation aspects. Stringent co-design of programming language and compilation technology, however, is of paramount importance to achieve our overall goals. After all it is one story to define a programming language, but it is another (and much more time and effort consuming) story to actually develop the necessary compilation technology.

In these second CEFP lecture notes we tell this other story and focus on the compilation technology that is so critical for success. It is literally a long way down from state-free, functional program code involving multi-dimensional truly state-free multi-dimensional arrays to efficient compiler-directed parallel program execution. Over the years, we have developed an intricate program transformation and optimisation machinery for this sole purpose. It combines many textbook optimisations that benefit from the functional semantics of SAC with a large variety of SAC-specific array optimisations. While many of them have been the subject of dedicated publications, it is the contribution of these lecture notes to provide a comprehensive overview of SAC's compilation technology, putting individual transformations into perspective and demonstrating their non-trivial interplay.

To keep the lecture notes self-contained, we begin with explaining the language design of SAC in Sect. 2 and our programming methodology of abstraction and composition for rank-generic, index-free array programming in Sect. 3. We illustrate the SAC approach in Sect. 4 by a brief application case study, namely convolution with cyclic boundary conditions and convergence check. Turning to compilation technology, we first sketch out the overall compiler design and explain its frontend in Sect. 5. High-level, mostly target-independent code optimisation is the subject of Sect. 6. In Sect. 7 we outline several crucial lowering steps from a high-level functional intermediate representation amenable to far-reaching code transformations towards code generation for imperative machines. At last, in Sect. 8 we touch upon code generation: first for sequential execution and then on the various compilation targets supported by SAC at the time of writing. In Sect. 9 we illustrate the entire compilation process by going step-by-step through the compilation of the application case study introduced in Sect. 4. We complete the lecture notes with an annotated bibliography on the subject of performance evaluation on various architectures in Sect. 10 and a brief discussion of related work in Sect. 11 before we draw some conclusions in Sect. 12.

2 Language Design

In this section we describe the language design of SAC. First, we rather briefly sketch out the scalar language core and the relationship between imperative syntax and functional semantics. We continue with the array calculus underlying SAC and, in particular, SAC's versatile array comprehension construct: WITH-loop. We complete the section with a glimpse on SAC's type system.

2.1 The Scalar Language Core: A Functional Subset of C

The scalar core of SAC is the subset of ANSI/ISO C [22] for which functional semantics can be defined (surprisingly straightforwardly). In essence, SAC adopts from C the names of the built-in types, i.e. `int` for integer numbers, `char` for ASCI characters, `float` for single precision and `double` for double precision floating point numbers. Conceptually, SAC also supports all variants derived by type specifiers such as `short`, `long` or `unsigned`, but for the time being we merely implement the above mentioned standard types. SAC strictly distinguishes between numerical, character and Boolean values and features a built-in type `bool`.

As a truly functional language SAC uses type inference instead of C-style type declarations (the latter are optional). This requires a strict separation of values of different basic types. As expected, type `bool` is inferred for the Boolean constants `true` and `false` and type `char` for character constants like `'a'`. Any numerical constant without decimal point or exponent is of type `int`. Any floating point constant with decimal point or exponent specification by default is of type `double`. A trailing `f` character makes any numerical constant a single precision floating point constant, a trailing `d` character a double precision floating point constant. For example, `42` is of type `int`, `42.0` is of type `double`, `42.0f` and `42f` are of type `float` and `42d` again is of type `double`.

SAC requires explicit conversion between values of different basic types by means of the (overloaded) conversion functions `toi` (conversion to integer), `toc` (conversion to character), `tof` (conversion to single precision floating point), `tod` (conversion to double precision floating point) and `tob` (conversion to Boolean). To this end we decided to deliberately distinguish SAC from C: We use C-like type casts for casting values between types that are synonyms of each other, as introduced via C-like `typedef` declarations. However, we use more explicit conversion functions whenever the actual representation of a value needs to be changed. The motivation here is similar as with the explicit `bool` type for Boolean values: clean up the language design (a bit) in corners where even modern versions of C struggle due to the need for keeping backwards compatibility.

Despite these minor differences in details, SAC programs generally look intriguingly similar to C programs. SAC adopts the C syntax for function definitions and function applications. Function bodies are statement sequences with a mandatory `return`-statement at the end. In addition, SAC features assignment statements, branches with and without alternative (`else`), loops with leading (`while`) and with trailing (`do...while`) predicate and counted loops (`for`). All of these constructs have exactly the same syntax as C proper.

In addition to constants, expressions are made up of identifiers, function applications and operator applications. SAC supports most operators from C, among them all arithmetic, relational and logical operators. As usual, Boolean conjunction and disjunction only evaluate their right operand expression if necessary. SAC also supports C-style conditional expressions, operator assignments (e.g. `+=` and `*=`) as well as pre and post increment and decrement operators (i.e. `++` and `--`). For the time being, SAC does neither support the bitwise operations of C, nor the `switch`-statement.

Given the proper separation between Boolean and numerical values, predicates in branches, conditional expressions and loops must be expressions of type `bool`, not of type `int`. While C-style variable declarations are superfluous due to type inference, they are nonetheless permitted and may serve documentation purposes. If present, declared types are checked against inferred types.

The language kernel of SAC is enriched by a number of features not present in C, e.g. a proper module system and an I/O system that combines the simplicity of imperative I/O (e.g. simply adding a print statement where one is needed) with a save integration of state manipulation into the purely functional context of SAC "under the hood". In the absence of a general notion of tuples or records, SAC features functions with multiple return values: a comma-separated list of return types in the function header corresponds to a comma-separated list of expressions in the function's `return`-statement. For this sole purpose, SAC also supports simultaneous assignment to multiple identifiers if and only if the right hand side expression is the application of a function with multiple return values. As usual a function with the reserved name `main` defines the starting point of program execution.

Despite its imperative appearance, SAC is a purely functional programming language. This is achieved on the one hand side by the absence of global variables and pointers and on the other hand by a functional "interpretation" of imperative syntax as follows. Sequences of assignment statements with a trailing `return`-statement are semantically equivalent to nested `let`-expressions with the expression in the `return`-statement being the final goal expression. Imperative-style branching constructs are semantically equivalent with functional conditionals where the code following the branching construct is (conceptually) duplicated in both branches. Last not least, we consider the `for`-loop syntactic sugar for a `while`-loop, just as Kernighan and Ritchie [23], while both `while`-loops and `do-while`-loops are semantically equivalent to tail recursion. For a more in-depth explanation of the semantic equivalence between core SAC and OCaml we refer the interested reader to [21].

2.2 Multidimensional Stateless Arrays

On top of the scalar language core SAC provides genuine support for truly multidimensional stateless arrays based on a formal calculus. This calculus dates back to the programming language APL [14,24] and was later adopted by other array languages such as J [16,25,26] or NIAL [17,27] and also theoretically investigated under the name ψ-calculus [28,29].

In this array calculus any array is represented by a natural number (named *rank*), a vector of natural numbers (named *shape*) and a vector of whatever data type is stored in the array (named *data vector*). The *rank* of an array is the number of dimensions or axes. The elements of the shape vector determine the extent of the array along each of the array's dimensions or axes.

The rank of an array equals the length of that array's shape vector. The product of shape vector elements equals the length of the data vector and, thus, the number of elements of an array. The data vector contains the array's elements along ascending axes with respect to the shape vector (i.e. *row-major*). Figure 2 shows a number of example arrays and illustrates the relationships between rank, shape vector and data vector.

As shown in Fig. 2, the array calculus nicely extends to scalars. A scalar value has rank zero while the shape vector is the empty vector and the data vector contains a single element, which is the scalar value itself. All this is completely consistent with the rules and invariants sketched out before.

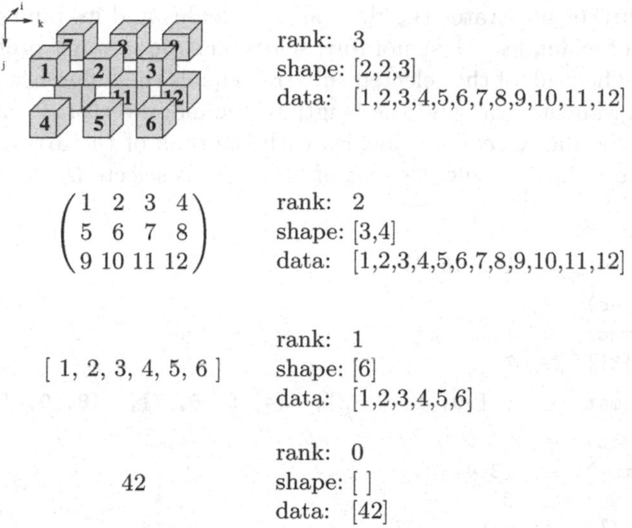

Fig. 2. Truly multidimensional arrays in SAC and their representation by data vector, shape vector and rank scalar

In sharp contrast to all other realisations of this array calculus, from APL to the ψ-calculus, SAC only defines a very small number of built-in operations on arrays that are directly related to the underlying calculus:

- `dim(a)`
  yields the rank scalar of array *a*;
- `shape(a)`
  yields the shape vector of array *a*;
- `sel(iv, a)`
  yields the element of array *a* at index location *iv*, provided that *iv* is a legal index vector into array *a*, i.e. *iv* is not longer than `shape(a)` and every element of *iv* is greater equal to zero and less than the corresponding element of `shape(a)`;
- `reshape(sv, a)`
  yields an array that has shape *sv* and the same data vector as array *a*, provided that *sv* and *a* are shape-compatible;
- `modarray(a, iv, val)`
  yields an array with the same rank and shape as array *a*, where all elements are the same as in array *a* except for index location *iv* where the element equals *val*.

For programming convenience SAC supports some syntactic sugar to express applications of the `sel` and `modarray` built-in functions:

```
        sel(iv, a)    ≡  a[iv]
a = modarray(a, iv, v); ≡  a[iv] = v;
```

Figure 3 further illustrates the SaC array calculus and its built-in functions by a number of examples. Most notably, selection supports any prefix of a legal index vector. The rank of the selected subarray equals the difference between the rank of the argument array and the length of the index vector. Consequently, if the length of the index vector coincides with the rank of the array, the rank of the result is zero, i.e. a single element of the array is selected.

```
             vec  ≡  [4,5,6,7]

       dim( vec)  ≡  1
     shape( vec)  ≡  [4]
        vec[[3]]  ≡  7

             mat  ≡  [ [ 0, 1, 2, 3],  [4, 5, 6, 7],  [8, 9, 10, 11] ]

       dim( mat)  ≡  2
     shape( mat)  ≡  [3,4]
      mat[[1,2]]  ≡  6
         mat[[]]  ≡  mat
        mat[[1]]  ≡  vec

             mat  ≡  reshape( [3,4], [0,1,2,3,4,5,6,7,8,9,10,11])
   [[4,5],[6,7]]  ≡  reshape( [2,2], vec)
```

Fig. 3. SaC built-in functions in the context of the array calculus

Using an index *vector* instead of a rank-specific sequence of individual indices for selecting elements (or subarrays) from an array is mainly motivated by our ambition for rank-invariant programming that we will discuss later in this chapter. For simple programs with constant index vectors, however, this choice sometimes leads to pairs of opening and closing square brackets that may appear unusual, as can be observed in Fig. 3. Here, the outer pair of brackets stems from the syntactic sugar for selection while the inner pair stems from constructing the index vector from a sequence of scalar constants or expressions. For a more common look and feel, the SaC standard library provides a number of overloaded selection functions for fixed array ranks. In the remainder of this paper we will deliberately not make use of this feature in order to rather expose the underlying concepts instead of hiding them.

2.3 With-Loop Array Comprehensions and Reductions

With only five built-in array operations (i.e. `dim`, `shape`, `sel`, `reshape` and `modarray`) SaC leaves the beaten track of array-oriented programming languages like APL and FORTRAN-90 and all their derivatives. Instead of providing dozens if not a hundred or more hard-wired array operations such as element-wise extensions of scalar operators and functions, structural operations like shift and rotate along one or multiple axes and reduction operations with eligible built-in and user-defined operations like sum and product, SAC features a single but versatile array comprehension construct: the WITH-loop.

We use WITH-loops to implement all the above array operations and many more in SAC itself. Rather than hard-wiring them into the language, we provide a comprehensive standard library of array operations. WITH-loops come in three variants, named `genarray`, `modarray` and `fold`. Since the WITH-loop is by far the most crucial syntactical deviation from C, we also provide a formal definition of the (simplified) syntax in Fig. 7.

```
A = with {
      ([1,1] <= iv < [4,4]) : e(iv);
    }: genarray( [5,4], default );
```

[0,0]	[0,1]	[0,2]	[0,3]
[1,0]	[1,1]	[1,2]	[1,3]
[2,0]	[2,1]	[2,2]	[2,3]
[3,0]	[3,1]	[3,2]	[3,3]
[4,0]	[4,1]	[4,2]	[4,3]

$\Longrightarrow$

⟦*default*⟧	⟦*default*⟧	⟦*default*⟧	⟦*default*⟧
⟦*default*⟧	⟦$e[iv \leftarrow [1,1]]$⟧	⟦$e[iv \leftarrow [1,2]]$⟧	⟦$e[iv \leftarrow [1,3]]$⟧
⟦*default*⟧	⟦$e[iv \leftarrow [2,1]]$⟧	⟦$e[iv \leftarrow [2,2]]$⟧	⟦$e[iv \leftarrow [2,3]]$⟧
⟦*default*⟧	⟦$e[iv \leftarrow [3,1]]$⟧	⟦$e[iv \leftarrow [3,2]]$⟧	⟦$e[iv \leftarrow [3,3]]$⟧
⟦*default*⟧	⟦*default*⟧	⟦*default*⟧	⟦*default*⟧

Fig. 4. The `genarray`-variant of the WITH-loop array comprehension

We begin with the `genarray`-variant in Fig. 4. Any WITH-loop array comprehension expression begins with the key word `with` (line 1) followed by a *partition* enclosed in curly brackets (line 2), a colon and an *operator* that defines the WITH-loop variant, here the key word `genarray`. The `genarray`-variant is an array comprehension that defines an array whose shape is determined by the first expression after the key word `genarray`. The *shape expression* must evaluate to a non-negative integer vector. The example WITH-loop in Fig. 4, hence, defines a matrix with 5 rows and 4 columns.

By default all element values of the new array are defined by the second expression, the so-called *default expression*. The middle part of the WITH-loop, the *partition* (line 2 in Fig. 4), defines a rectangular index subset of the defined array. A partition consists of a *generator* and an *associated expression*. The generator defines a set of index vectors along with an *index variable* representing elements of this set. Two expressions, which must evaluate to non-negative integer vectors of the same length as the value of the shape expression, define lower and upper bounds of a rectangular range of index vectors. For each element of this index vector set the associated expression is evaluated with the index variable instantiated according to the index position. In the case of the `genarray`-variant the resulting value defines the element value at the corresponding index location of the array.

The default expression itself is optional. An element type dependent default value (i.e. the matching variant of zero: `false`, `'\0'`, `0`, `0f`, `0d` for types `bool`, `char`, `int`, `float`, `double`, respectively) is inserted by the compiler where needed.

The default expression may likewise be obsolete if the generator covers the entire index set of the corresponding array.

```
B = with {
      ([1,1] <= iv < [4,4]) : e(iv);
    }: modarray( A);
```

[0,0]	[0,1]	[0,2]	[0,3]
[1,0]	[1,1]	[1,2]	[1,3]
[2,0]	[2,1]	[2,2]	[2,3]
[3,0]	[3,1]	[3,2]	[3,3]
[4,0]	[4,1]	[4,2]	[4,3]

$\Longrightarrow$

$[\![A[[0,0]]]\!]$	$[\![A[[0,1]]]\!]$	$[\![A[[0,2]]]\!]$	$[\![A[[0,3]]]\!]$
$[\![A[[1,0]]]\!]$	$[\![e[iv \leftarrow [1,1]]\!]$	$[\![e[iv \leftarrow [1,2]]\!]$	$[\![e[iv \leftarrow [1,3]]\!]$
$[\![A[[2,0]]]\!]$	$[\![e[iv \leftarrow [2,1]]\!]$	$[\![e[iv \leftarrow [2,2]]\!]$	$[\![e[iv \leftarrow [2,3]]\!]$
$[\![A[[3,0]]]\!]$	$[\![e[iv \leftarrow [3,1]]\!]$	$[\![e[iv \leftarrow [3,2]]\!]$	$[\![e[iv \leftarrow [3,3]]\!]$
$[\![A[[4,0]]]\!]$	$[\![A[[4,1]]]\!]$	$[\![A[[4,2]]]\!]$	$[\![A[[4,3]]]\!]$

Fig. 5. The `modarray`-variant of the WITH-loop array comprehension

The second WITH-loop-variant is the `modarray`-variant illustrated in Fig. 5. While the partition (line 2) is syntactically and semantically equivalent to the `genarray`-variant, the definition of the array's shape and the default rule for element values are different. The key word `modarray` is followed by a single expression. The newly defined array takes its shape from the value of that expression, i.e. we define an array that has the same shape as a previously defined array. Likewise, the element values at index positions not covered by the generator are obtained from the corresponding elements of that array. It is important to note that the `modarray`-WITH-loop does not destructively overwrite the element values of the existing array, but we indeed define a new array.

The third WITH-loop-variant, illustrated in Fig. 6, supports the definition of reduction operations. It is characterised by the key word `fold` followed by the name of an eligible reduction function or operator and the neutral element of that function or operator. For certain built-in functions and operators the compiler is aware of the neutral element, and an explicit specification can be left out. SAC requires fold functions or operators to expect two arguments of the same type and to yield one value of that type. Fold functions must be associative and commutative. These requirements are stronger than in other languages with explicit reductions (e.g. `foldl` and `foldr` in many mainstream functional languages). This is motivated by the absence of an order on the generator defined index subset and ultimately by the wish to facilitate parallel implementations of reductions.

Note that the SAC compiler cannot verify associativity and commutativity of user-defined functions. It is the programmer's responsibility to ensure these properties. Using a function or operator in a `fold`-WITH-loop implicitly asserts these properties. Of course, floating point arithmetic strictly speaking is not associative. It is up to the programmer to judge whether it is "sufficiently associative". This problem is not specific to SAC, but appears in all programming environments that

```
B = with {
      ([1,1] <= iv < [4,4]) : e(iv);
    }: fold( ⊕, neutr);
```

[1,1]	[1,2]	[1,3]
[2,1]	[2,2]	[2,3]
[3,1]	[3,2]	[3,3]

$$\Longrightarrow \quad [\![neutr]\!] \oplus [\![e[iv \leftarrow [1,1]]\!] \oplus [\![e[iv \leftarrow [1,2]]\!] \oplus [\![e[iv \leftarrow [1,3]]\!] \oplus [\![e[iv \leftarrow [2,1]]\!] \oplus [\![e[iv \leftarrow [2,2]]\!] \oplus [\![e[iv \leftarrow [2,3]]\!] \oplus [\![e[iv \leftarrow [3,1]]\!] \oplus [\![e[iv \leftarrow [3,2]]\!] \oplus [\![e[iv \leftarrow [3,3]]\!]$$

Fig. 6. The `fold`-variant of the WITH-loop array comprehension

support parallel reductions, e.g. the reduction clause in OPENMP [30,31] or the collective operations of MPI [32].

WithLoopExpr ⇒ **with** { *Partition* } : *Operator*

Partition ⇒ *Generator* : *Expr* ;

Generator ⇒ (*Range* [*Stride*])

Range ⇒ *Expr RelOp Identifier RelOp Expr*

RelOp ⇒ <= | <

Stride ⇒ **step** *Expr* [**width** *Expr*]

Operation ⇒ **genarray** (*Expr* [, *Expr*])
| **modarray** (*Expr*)
| **fold** (*FoldOp* [, *Expr*])

FoldOp ⇒ *Identifier* | *BinOp*

Fig. 7. Formal definition of the (simplified) syntax of WITH-loop expressions

As can be seen in the formal definition of the syntax of WITH-loop expressions in Fig. 7, generators are not restricted to defining dense, contiguous ranges of index vectors, but the key words `step` and `width` optionally allow the specification of strided index sets where the step expression defines the periodicity in each dimension and the width expression defines the number of indices taken in each step. Both expressions must evaluate to positive integer vectors of the same length as the lower and upper bounds of the index range specification.

We now illustrate the concept of WITH-loops and its use by a series of examples. For instance, the matrix

$$A = \begin{pmatrix} 0 & 1 & 2 & 3 & 4 & 5 & 6 & 7 & 8 & 9 \\ 10 & 11 & 12 & 13 & 14 & 15 & 16 & 17 & 18 & 19 \\ 20 & 21 & 22 & 23 & 24 & 25 & 26 & 27 & 28 & 29 \\ 30 & 31 & 32 & 33 & 34 & 35 & 36 & 37 & 38 & 39 \\ 40 & 41 & 42 & 43 & 44 & 45 & 46 & 47 & 48 & 49 \end{pmatrix}$$

can be defined by the following WITH-loop:

```
A = with {
      ([0,0] <= iv < [5,10]): iv[[0]] * 10 + iv[[1]];
    }: genarray([5,10]);
```

Note here that the generator variable iv denotes a 2-element integer vector. Hence, the scalar index values need to be extracted through selection prior to computing the new array's element values.

The following modarray-WITH-loop defines the new array B that like A is a 5×10 matrix where all inner elements equal the corresponding values of A incremented by 50 while the remaining boundary elements are obtained from A without modification:

```
B = with {
      ([1,1] <= iv < [4,9]): A[iv] + 50;
    }: modarray(A);
```

This example WITH-loop defines the following matrix:

$$B = \begin{pmatrix} 0 & 1 & 2 & 3 & 4 & 5 & 6 & 7 & 8 & 9 \\ 10 & 61 & 62 & 63 & 64 & 65 & 66 & 67 & 68 & 19 \\ 20 & 71 & 72 & 73 & 74 & 75 & 76 & 77 & 78 & 29 \\ 30 & 81 & 82 & 83 & 84 & 85 & 86 & 87 & 88 & 39 \\ 40 & 41 & 42 & 43 & 44 & 45 & 46 & 47 & 48 & 49 \end{pmatrix}$$

Last not least, the following fold-WITH-loop computes the sum of all elements of array B:

```
sum =  with {
         ([0,0] <= iv < [5,10]): B[iv];
       }: fold(+, 0);
```

which yields 2425.

All three types of WITH-loops can be combined with strided generators. As a simple illustration consider the following example:

```
B = with {
      ([0,0] <= iv < [5,10] step [2,4] width [1,2]): 99;
    }: modarray(A);
```

which yields the matrix

$$A = \begin{pmatrix} 99 & 99 & 2 & 3 & 99 & 99 & 6 & 7 & 99 & 99 \\ 10 & 11 & 12 & 13 & 14 & 15 & 16 & 17 & 18 & 19 \\ 99 & 99 & 22 & 23 & 99 & 99 & 26 & 27 & 99 & 99 \\ 30 & 31 & 32 & 33 & 34 & 35 & 36 & 37 & 38 & 39 \\ 99 & 99 & 42 & 43 & 99 & 99 & 46 & 47 & 99 & 99 \end{pmatrix}$$

As pointed out earlier, WITH-loops can be much more complex than presented here so far. For example, WITH-loops may feature multiple partitions defining different computations for disjoint index subsets or multiple operators simultaneously defining multiple array comprehensions or reductions.

2.4 Array Type System

In Sect. 2.1 we introduced the basic types `int`, `float`, `double`, `char` and `bool`, but when discussing arrays in Sect. 2.2, we carefully avoided any questions regarding array types. While SAC is monomorphic in scalar types including the base types of arrays, any scalar type immediately induces a hierarchy of array types with subtyping. Figure 8 illustrates this type hierarchy for the example of the base type `int`. The shapely type hierarchy has three levels characterised by different amounts of compile time knowledge about shape and rank.

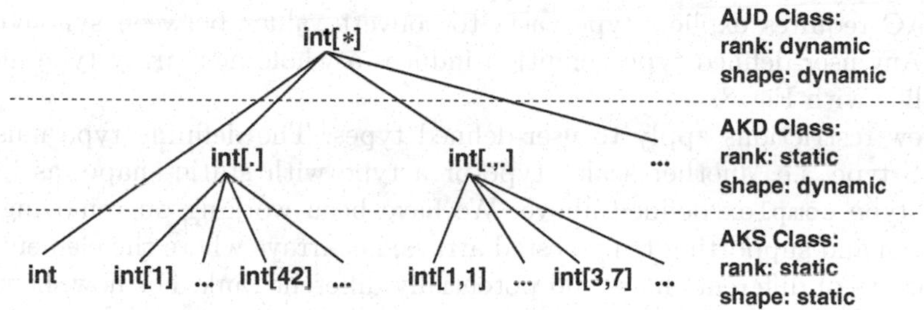

Fig. 8. The SAC array type system with the subtyping hierarchy

On the lowest level of the subtyping hierarchy (i.e. the most specific types) we have complete compile time information on the structure of an array: both rank and shape are fixed. We call this class *AKS* for *array of known shape*. On the intermediate level we still fix the rank of an array, but abstract from its concrete shape. We call this class *AKD* for *array of known dimension*. For example, a vector of unknown length or a matrix of unknown size fall into this category. The most common supertype neither prescribes shape nor rank at compile time. We call such types *AUD* for *array of unknown dimension*. Our syntax for AUD types is motivated by that of regular expressions: the Kleene star in the AUD type stands for any number of dots, including none.

Note the special case for arrays of rank zero (i.e. scalars). Since there is only one vector of length zero, the empty vector, the shape of a rank-zero array is automatically known and the type `int[]` is merely a synonym for `int`.

```
int[20,20] (-) (int[20,20] A, int[20,20] B) {...}
int[.,.]   (-) (int[.,.]   A, int[.,.]   B) {...}
int[*]     (-) (int[*]     A, int[*]     B) {...}
```

Fig. 9. Overloading with respect to the array type hierarchy

SAC supports overloading of functions and operators. The example in Fig. 9 shows three overloaded instances of the subtraction operator, one for 20×20-matrices, one for matrices of any shape and one for arrays of any rank. Applications are dispatched (possibly at runtime) to the most specific instance available. To keep dispatch decidable we require parameter monotony: For any two instances F_1 and F_2 of some function F with the same number of parameters and the same base types for each parameter either each parameter type of F_1 is a subtype of the corresponding parameter type of F_2 or vice versa. Static dispatch is a typical SAC compiler optimisation to be discussed in Sect. 6.

SAC supports user-defined types: any type can be abstracted by a name. Following our general design principle, we reuse the C `typedef` syntax. For example, a type `complex` can be defined as `typedef double[2] complex;`. Remember that SAC requires explicit type casts to convert values between synonymous types. Any user-defined type definition induces a whole new array type hierarchy in line with Fig. 8.

A few restrictions apply to user-defined types. The defining type must be an AKS type, i.e. another scalar type or a type with static shape, as in the case of type `complex` defined above. We have been working on removing this restriction and supporting truly nested arrays, i.e. arrays where the elements are again arrays of different shape and potentially different rank. For now, however, this is an experimental feature of SAC; details can be found in [33].

For the time being, SAC does syntactically support mixed array types such as `int[.,10]` or `float[100,.,100]` with the obvious meaning, but they do not extend the subtyping hierarchy. Instead, such types would be treated as `int[.,.]` and `float[.,.,.]` with an additional assertion.

3 Programming Methodology: Abstraction and Composition

So far, we have introduced the most relevant language features of SAC. Now, we explain the methodology of programming in SAC, or how the language features are supposed to be combined to actual programs. Our two over-arching software engineering principles are the *principle of abstraction* discussed in Sect. 3.1 and the *principle of composition* illustrated in Sect. 3.4.

3.1 The Principle of Abstraction

As pointed out in Sect. 2.2, SAC only features a very small set of built-in array operations. Commonly used aggregate array operations are defined in SAC itself and provided through a comprehensive standard library. Figure 10 demonstrates this by means of an overloading of the binary subtraction operator for 20×20-element integer matrices. Note that we leave out the default expression as the generator covers the entire index set.

```
int[20,20] (-) (int[20,20] A, int[20,20] B)
{
    return with {
               ([0,0] <= iv < [20,20]): A[iv] - B[iv];
           }: genarray( [20,20]);
}
```

Fig. 10. Overloaded subtraction operator for arrays of known shape (AKS), namely 20×20-element integer matrices

A single WITH-loop suffices to define element-wise subtraction: we define a new array C of size 20×20 and define each element to be the difference of the corresponding elements of argument arrays A and B. As the shape is statically known, we can easily use vector constants for result shape and generator bounds, and the code still very much resembles our introductory examples in Sect. 2.3.

Of course, it would be very inconvenient to provide numerous instances of the subtraction operator for all kinds of array shapes that may occur in a program and completely impossible to provide a library with all potentially needed overloaded instances. What we need is more abstraction. As defined in Fig. 7, all relevant syntactic positions of WITH-loops may host arbitrary expressions. Only in the examples so far we merely used constants for the purpose of illustration.

```
int[.,.] (-) (int[.,.] A, int[.,.] B)
{
  shp = min( shape(A), shape(B));
  return with {
             ([0,0] <= iv < shp): A[iv] - B[iv];
         }: genarray( shp);
}
```

Fig. 11. Overloaded subtraction operator for arrays of known dimension (AKD), namely integer matrices (2d-arrays) of any size

Figure 11 demonstrates the transition from a shape-specific implementation to a shape-generic implementation of element-wise subtraction. We stick to two dimensions, but abstract from the concrete size of argument matrices. Whereas the generator-associated expression remains unchanged, this generalisation immediately raises a crucial question: how to deal with argument arrays of different shape? There are various plausible answers to this question, and the solution adopted in our example is to compute the element-wise minimum of the shape vectors of the two argument arrays. With this solution we safely avoid out-of-bound indexing while at the same time restricting the function domain as little as possible. The vector `shp` is used both in the shape expression of the WITH-loop and as upper bound in the generator. With fixed rank a constant vector still suffices as lower bound.

One could argue that in practice, it is very rare to encounter problems that require more than 4 dimensions, and, thus, we could simply define all relevant operations for one, two, three and four dimensions. However, for a binary operator that alone would already require the definition of 16 instances. Hence, it is of practical relevance, and not just theoretical beauty, to also abstract from the rank of argument arrays, not only the shapes. Thus, SAC supports fully rank-generic programming, as illustrated in Fig. 12.

```
int[*] (-) (int[*] A, int[*] B)
{
  shp = min( shape(A), shape(B));
  return with {
           (0*shp <= iv < shp): A[iv] - B[iv];
         }: genarray( shp);
}
```

Fig. 12. Overloaded subtraction operator for arrays of unknown dimension (AUD), thus integer arrays of any rank and size

Apart from using the most general array type `int[*]`, the rank-generic instance is surprisingly similar to the rank-specific one. The main issue is an appropriate definition of the generator's lower bound, i.e. a vector of zeros whose length equals that of the shape expression. We achieve this by multiplying the shape vector by zero.

3.2 How It Really Works: Rank-Generic Subtraction

While increasing the level of abstraction we must be able to deal with increasingly differently shaped argument arrays. With fully rank-generic code we may easily end up subtracting a 3×3-element matrix from a 5-element vector. How does the *trick* with the minimum function work in practice? Let us explore this example in more detail beginning with the following expression:

```
                [[1,2,3],
[1,2,3,4,5] -    [4,5,6],
                 [7,8,9]]
```

Instantiating the rank-generic instance of the subtraction operator with these actual arguments yields

```
{
                                               [[1,2,3],
   shp = min(shape([1,2,3,4,5]), shape([4,5,6], ));
                                                [7,8,9]]
   return with {
           (0*shp <= iv < shp):
                                                       [[1,2,3],
             sel(iv, [1,2,3,4,5]) - sel(iv, [4,5,6] ) ;
                                                        [7,8,9]]
         }: genarray(shp);
}
```

Note that we use the `sel` operator to denote indexing into arrays for better readability here and from now onwards. In a first step we evaluate the shape queries in line 3 to

```
{
  shp = min([5], [3,3]);
  ...
}
```

Now, what's the minimum of `[5]` and `[3,3]`? For this we need to learn more about the `min` function. Following our general design principles, `min` is only built-in for scalar values, but not for vectors. In fact, we can expect to find an instance of `min` in the standard library that is defined in the same spirit as our rank-generic subtraction operator, i.e. as shown in Fig. 13. However, here we face our first problem: we again use `min` to define the minimum shape of the two argument arrays, which refers back to the rank-generic definition of `min`. To avoid this non-terminating recursion we need another instance of `min` specifically for 1-element vectors:

```
int[1] min (int[1] A, int[1] B)
{
  return min(A[[0]], B[[0]]);
}
```

```
1   int[*] min (int[*] A, int[*] B)
2   {
3     shp = min( shape(A), shape(B));
4     return with {
5               (0*shp <= iv < shp): min( A[iv], B[iv]);
6            }: genarray( shp);
7   }
```

Fig. 13. Rank-generic definition of minimum function

The trick here is that the shape of the shape of any array is guaranteed to be a 1-element vector. Hence, we may see at most one recursive application of the rank-generic instance of `min` before we are guaranteed to apply the above shape-specific instance, which in turn applies the built-in scalar instance of `min`. Let us illustrate this with our original subtraction example. Instantiation of the rank-generic instance of `min` and using some pseudo syntax that of course is not legal SAC code but otherwise pretty self-explaining we obtain:

```
{
  shp = {
          shp = min(shape([5]), shape([3,3]));
          res = with {
                  (0*shp <= iv < shp):
                    min(sel(iv, [5]), sel(iv, [3,3]));
                }: genarray(shp);
          return res;
        }

  return with {
           (0*shp <= iv < shp):
                                                   [[1,2,3],
             sel(iv,[1,2,3,4,5]) - sel(iv, [4,5,6] ) ;
                                                    [7,8,9]]
         }: genarray(shp);
}
```

Evaluating the (inner) shape queries in line 3 yields `shp = min([1], [2]);` and with the 1-element vector instance of `min`, as shown before, we end up with `[1]` as value for the inner instance of `shp`. With that we can now proceed to evaluate the (inner) WITH-loop. This yields a 1-element vector whose only element is the minimum of the first elements of the vectors `[5]` and `[3,3]`:

```
{
  shp = [min(sel([0], [5]), sel([0], [3,3]))];
  ...
}
```

With the result shape `[3]` at hand we obtain for the running example:

```
{
  return with {
           ([0] <= iv < [3]):
                                                   [[1,2,3],
             sel(iv,[1,2,3,4,5]) - sel(iv, [4,5,6] ) ;
                                                    [7,8,9]]
         }: genarray([3]);
}
```

which yields the following vector:

```
[1 - [1,2,3], 2 - [4,5,6], 3 - [7,8,9]]
```

At this stage we are guaranteed to end up with recursively applying subtraction to a scalar and an array or vice versa, depending on the rank difference of the original arguments. As of now, we would recursively apply the rank-generic instance of subtraction, but that would not work. We leave it as an exercise to the reader to figure out why. Instead, we provide two more instances of the subtraction operator, as shown in Fig. 14. With these at hand we obtain the following intermediate representation by instantiation and simplification:

```
[ with {
    ([0] <= iv < [3]): 1 - sel(iv, [1,2,3]);
  }: genarray([3]),
  with {
    ([0] <= iv < [3]): 2 - sel(iv, [4,5,6]);
  }: genarray([3]),
  with {
    ([0] <= iv < [3]): 3 - sel(iv, [7,8,9]);
  }: genarray([3]),
]
```

and, at last, the final result:

```
[[ 0,-1,-2],
 [-2,-3,-4],
 [-4,-5,-6]]
```

What we effectively do overall is to split the rank-generic operation into an outer operation and an inner operation. The index space of the outer operation has as rank the minimum of the two argument arrays' ranks and as shape the element-wise minima of their shape vectors. This outer shape is called the frame shape. The inner operation is guaranteed to be on scalar elements of at least one of the two argument arrays, i.e. the one with the lesser rank. Selecting with the index vector of the outer operation from the other argument array, that is the one with greater rank, yields an entire subarray. Hence, it is guaranteed that for the inner operation we use one of the function instances shown in Fig. 14. That yields an array of the same shape as the subarray argument.

3.3 Alternatives and Extensions

It is one of the strengths of SAC that the exact behaviour of array operations is not hard-wired into the language definition. This sets SAC apart from all other languages with dedicated array support. Alternative to our above solution with the minimum shape, one could argue that any attempt to subtract two argument arrays of different shape is a programming error. This would be the view of FORTRAN-90 or APL. The same could be achieved in SAC by comparing the two argument shapes and raising an exception should they differ. The important message here is that SAC does not impose a particular solution on its users: anyone can provide an alternative array module implementation with the desired behaviour.

```
int[*] (-) (int a, int[*] B)
{
  return with {
           (0*shape(B) <= iv < shape(B)): a - B[iv];
         }: modarray( B);
}

int[*] (-) (int[*] A, int b)
{
  return with {
           (0*shape(A) <= iv < shape(A)): A[iv] - b;
         }: modarray( A);
}
```

Fig. 14. Additional overloaded instances of the subtraction operator as they are found in the SAC standard library

A potential wish for future versions of SAC is support for a richer type system, in which shape relations like equality can be properly expressed in the array types. For example, matrix multiplication could be defined with a type signature along the lines of

```
double[a,c] matmul(double[a,b] X, double[b,c] Y)
```

This leads to a system of dependent array types that we have studied in the context of the dependently typed array language Qube [34,35]. However, how to carry these ideas over to SAC in the presence of overloading and dynamic dispatch requires a plethora of future research. A first step into this direction can be found in [36].

3.4 The Principle of Composition

The generic programming examples of the previous section pave the way to define a large collection of rank-generic array operations that is even more comprehensive than what other array languages offer built-in while retaining the same universal applicability to arrays of any shape and rank.

With-loops, however, should only be used to implement the most basic array operations. Anything beyond can be much more elegantly and concisely expressed following the other guiding software engineering principle in SAC: the *principle of composition*. For instance, Fig. 15 shows the definition of a generic convergence check. Two argument arrays `new` and `old` of any shape and rank are deemed to be convergent if for every element (reduction with logical conjunction) the absolute difference between the new and the old value is less than a given threshold `eps`.

The answer to the question what should and what would happen if the two argument arrays are of different shape or even of different rank is inherited from the definition of the element-wise subtraction operator, as demonstrated in-depth in Sect. 3.2. The compositional specification of the convergence check is entirely

```
bool is_convergent (double[*] A, double[*] B, double eps)
{
  return all( abs( A - B) < eps);
}
```

Fig. 15. Programming by composition: specification of a generic convergence check

based on applications of predefined array operations from the SAC standard library: element-wise subtraction, absolute value, element-wise comparison and reduction with Boolean conjunction. This example demonstrates how application code can be designed in an entirely index-, loop-, and comprehension-free style.

Ideally the use of WITH-loops as versatile but accordingly complex language construct would be confined to defining basic array operations like the ones used in the definition of the convergence check. And, ideally all application code would solely be composed out of these basic building blocks. This leads to a highly productive software engineering process, substantial code reuse, good readability of code and, last not least, high confidence into the correctness of programs. The case study on generic convolution developed in Sect. 4 further demonstrates how the principle of composition can be applied in practice.

4 Programming Case Study: Convolution

In this section we illustrate programming in SAC by means of a case study: convolution with cyclic boundary conditions. As an algorithmic principle convolution has countless applications in image processing, computational sciences, etc. Our particular focus is on the programming methodology outlined in the previous section: abstraction and composition.

4.1 Algorithmic Principle

Convolution follows a fairly simple algorithmic principle. Essentially, we deal with a regular multidimensional grid of data cells, as illustrated in Fig. 16. Convolution is an iterative process on this data grid: in each iteration the value at each grid point is recomputed as a function of the existing old value and the values of a certain neighbourhood of grid points. This neighbourhood is often referred to as *stencil*.

In Fig. 16 we show two common stencils. With a *five-point stencil* (left) only the four direct neighbours in the two-dimensional grid are relevant. By including the four diagonal neighbours we end up with a *nine-point stencil* (right). In the context of cellular automata these neighbourhoods are often referred to as *von Neumann neighbourhood* and *Moore neighbourhood*, respectively. With higher-dimensional grids, we obtain different neighbourhood sizes, but the principle can straightforwardly be carried over to any number of dimensions.

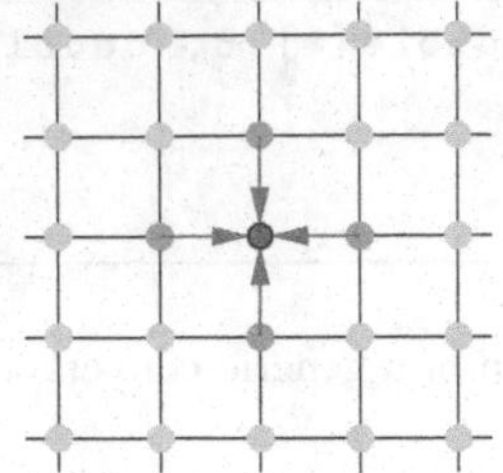 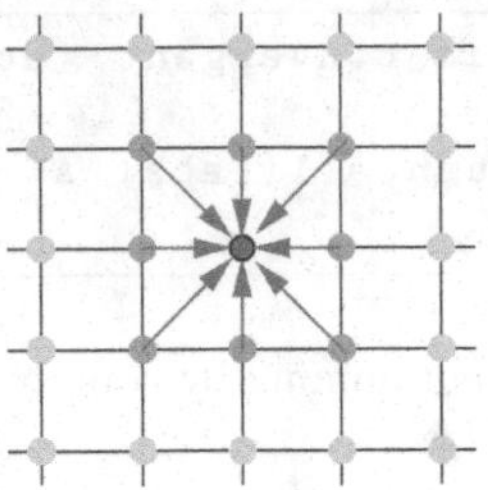

Fig. 16. Algorithmic principle of convolution, shown is the 2-dimensional case with a 5-point stencil (left) and a 9-point stencil (right)

Since any concrete grid is finite, boundary elements need to be taken care of in a different way. In our case study we opt for *cyclic boundary conditions*, i.e., the left neighbour of the leftmost element is the rightmost element and vice versa. In principle, any function from a set of neighbouring data points to a single new one is possible, but in practice variants of weighted sums prevail. Iteration on the grid is continued until a given level of convergence is reached, i.e., for any grid cell the change in value between the previous and the current iteration is less than a given threshold.

4.2 Iterative Process with Convergence Check

In our case study we take a top-down approach and first look at organising a sequence of convolution steps until the required convergence criterion is met, see Fig. 17. We make use of a `do-while`-loop because the number of convolution steps needed is a-priori unknown, but we need to make at least one step to check for convergence. We reuse the `is_convergent` function introduced in Sect. 3.4 as the loop predicate. Note that the code is entirely shape- and rank-generic.

```
double[*] convolution (double[*] A,
                       double[.] weights,
                       double eps)
{
  do {
    B = A;
    A = convolution_step( B, weights);
  }
  while (!is_convergent( A, B, eps));

  return A;
}
```

Fig. 17. Rank-generic convolution with convergence test

Looking at the code in Fig. 17 it is important to understand the functional semantics of SAC. The C-style *assignment statement* in line 6 merely creates a new λ-binding to the existing array value. By no means does it copy the array value itself. This behaviour clearly sets SAC apart from imperative array languages such as Fortran-90 or Chapel [37].

4.3 Convolution Step

For illustration purposes we start with an index-free and shape- but not rank-generic implementation of the convolution step. As shown in Fig. 18, the function `convolution_step` expects a vector of double precision floating point numbers and a vector of likewise weights; it yields a (once) convolved vector. The implementation is based on the `rotate` function from the SAC standard library, which rotates a given vector by a certain number of elements towards ascending or descending indices.

```
double[.] convolution_step (double[.] A,
                            double[3] weights)
{
  return    weights[[0]] * A
          + weights[[1]] * rotate(  1, A)
          + weights[[2]] * rotate( -1, A);
}
```

Fig. 18. 1-dimensional index-free convolution step

Rotation towards ascending indices means moving the rightmost element of the vector (the one with the greatest index) to the leftmost index position (the one with the least index). This implements cyclic boundary conditions almost for free. We multiply each of the three array values with the corresponding weight and sum up the results to yield the convolved vector. This implementation makes use of a total of seven data-parallel operations: two rotations, three scalar-array multiplications and two element-wise additions.

We now generalise the one-dimensional convolution to the rank-generic convolution shown in Fig. 19. We use the same approach with rotation towards ascending and descending indices, but now we are confronted with a variable number of axes along which to rotate the argument array.

We solve the problem by using a `for`-loop over the number of dimensions of the argument array `A`, which we obtain through the built-in function `dim`. In each dimension we rotate `A` by one element towards ascending indices and by one element towards descending indices. We use an overloaded, rank-generic version of the `rotate` function that takes the rotation axis as additional (first) argument. As in the 1-dimensional case, we multiply each rotated array value (as well as the original argument array) by the corresponding element of the weight vector and sum up all resulting array values using element-wise addition.

```
double[*] convolution_step (double[*] A,
                            double[.] weights)
{
  R = weights[[0]] * A;

  for (i=0; i<dim(A); i++) {
    R +=    weights[[2*i+1]] * rotate( i,  1, A)
          + weights[[2*i+2]] * rotate( i, -1, A);
  }

  return R;
}
```

Fig. 19. Rank-generic index-free convolution step definition

4.4 Rank-Generic Array Rotation

For completeness and as an example of possibly surprising implementation complexity we show the implementation of rotation in Fig. 20. We first check the arguments: should the rotation offset be zero or the rotation axis not a legal axis of the argument array, we simply return the latter. It might be interesting to note that this also covers the case of the argument array being a scalar as included in the type `double[*]`. In this case the rank of the argument array would be zero, thus turning any possible offset illegal. Of course, any rotation of a scalar yields the scalar again.

After normalising the offset to the range between zero and one less than the size of the array in the rotation axis we define the two vectors, `lower` and `upper` that exactly divide the index space of the argument array in the rotation axis at the desired offset. One final multi-generator WITH-loop defines the result array for all regular cases. Here, we make use of two features of WITH-loops that we haven't used so far: multiple generators and the dot notation. Multiple generators associate disjoint partitions of the index space with different expressions while dots as lower or as upper bounds in generators refer to the least and the greatest legal index vector in the relevant index space.

4.5 Further Variations of Convolution

Convolution allows for a plethora of further variations. As space limitations prevent us from investigating convolution any further, we refer the interested reader to [21]. There we show examples of convolution, among others, for fixed boundary conditions, red-black convolution, generalised stencils, etc. We, furthermore, recommend [21], but also the literature discussed in Sect. 10, for applications of SAC to domains other than convolution.

```
double[*] rotate (int axis, int offset, double[*] A)
{
  if (offset == 0  axis >= dim(A)  axis < 0) {
    R = A;
  }
  else {
    max_rotate = shape(A)[axis];

    if (max_rotate == 0) {
      R = A;
    }
    else {
      offset = offset % max_rotate;

      if (offset < 0) {
        offset = offset + max_rotate;
      }

      lower = 0 * shape(A);
      lower[axis] = offset;

      upper = shape(A);
      upper[axis] = offset;

      R = with {
          ( .     <= iv <  upper ): A[iv+shape(A)-upper];
          ( lower <= iv <=   .   ): A[iv-lower];
        }: modarray( A );
    }
  }

  return R;
}
```

Fig. 20. Rank-generic definition of array rotation from the SAC standard library

5 Compilation Technology: Overview and Frontend

In this section we discuss the fundamental challenges of compiling SAC source code into competitive executable code for a variety of parallel computing architectures and outline how compiler and runtime system address these issues. Following an overview of the compiler architecture in Sect. 5.1 we explain the compiler frontend in more detail in Sect. 5.2 before we elaborate on type inference and specialisation in Sect. 5.3.

Subsequently, Sects. 6, 7 and 8, focus on architecture-independent optimisation, a sequence of lowering steps and, at last, code generation for various parallel architectures, respectively.

5.1 SAC Compiler Organisation

Despite the intentional syntactic similarities, SAC is far from merely being a variant of C. SAC is a complete programming language, that only happens to resemble C in its look and feel. A fully-fledged compiler is needed to implement the functional semantics and to address a series of challenges when it comes to achieving high performance.

Figure 21 shows the overall internal organisation of the SAC compiler sac2c. It is a many-pass compiler built around a slowly morphing abstract intermediate code representation. We chose this design to facilitate concurrent compiler engineering across individuals and institutions. Today, we have around 200 compiler passes, and Fig. 21 only shows a macroscopic view of what is really going on behind the scenes. In particular, we leave out all compilation passes that are not directly related to our core business, such as the module system, the I/O system or the foreign code interfaces. As a research compiler sac2c is very verbose: compilation can be interrupted after any pass and the intermediate representation visualised in the form of annotated source code.

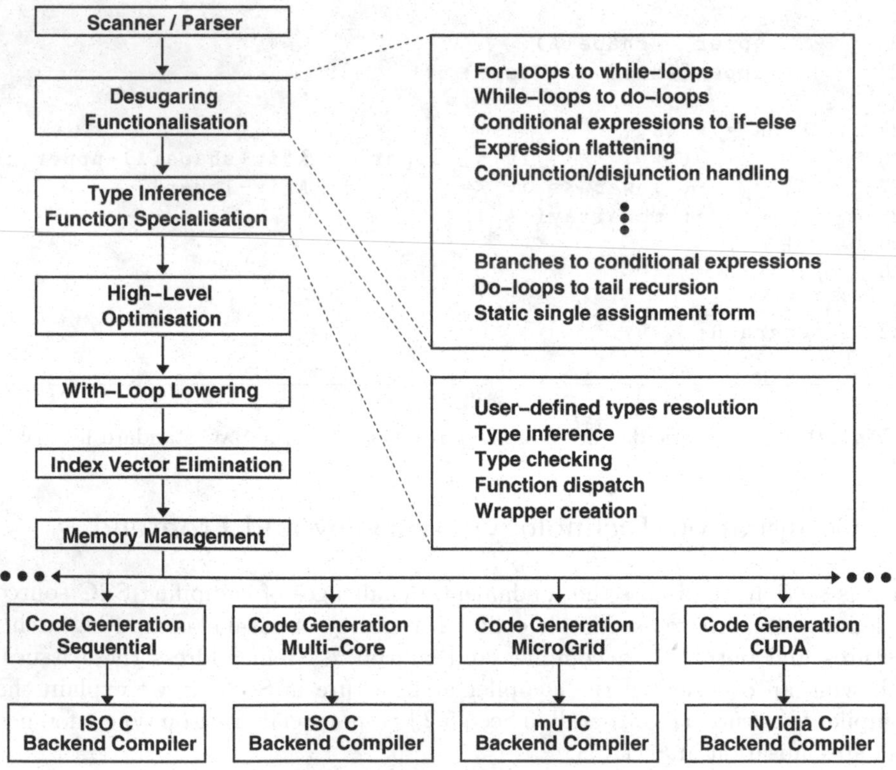

Fig. 21. Compilation process with focus on front end transformations

Over the years, we have developed a complete, language-independent compiler engineering framework, that has successfully been re-used in other compiler-related research projects [38]. Also the Compiler Construction courses (Bachelor/Master) at the University of Amsterdam are based on this framework. The framework automatically generates large amounts of boilerplate code for abstract syntax tree management as well as tree traversal and compiler driver code from abstract specifications. It is instrumental in keeping a compiler of this size and complexity manageable. In the following sections, however, we leave out such engineering concerns and take a more conceptual view on the SAC compilation process.

5.2 Compiler Front End

As in any compiler lexicographic and syntactic analyses transform program source code from a textual representation into an abstract syntax tree. All remaining compilation steps work on this internal intermediate representation, that is subject to a large number of lowering steps towards final target-specific code generation.

The first major code transformation shown in Fig. 21 is concerned with desugaring and *functionalisation*. Here, we turn the imperative(-looking) source code into a functional representation and considerably reduce the overall number of language features. Typical desugaring transformations are the concentration on a single sequential loop construct instead of the three loop constructs featured by the language: `while`, `do-while` and `for`, just as in C proper. Another important desugaring measure is the systematic elimination of nested expressions through the introduction of additional fresh local variables.

The functionalisation passes are more specific to the design of SAC: they actually implement the transformational semantics of branches and loops, as outlined in Sect. 2.1. Here, imperative-style `if-else` constructs are transformed into properly functional conditional expressions, and loops are transformed into tail-recursive functions.

5.3 Type Inference and Function Specialisation

This part of the compiler implements the array type system outlined in Sect. 2.4. It annotates types to local variables and checks all type declarations provided in the source code. Furthermore, the type inference system resolves function dispatch in the context of subtyping and overloading. Where possible, function applications are dispatched statically. Where necessary, wrapper functions are introduced that implement dynamic dispatch between multiple potential overloaded function instances. More information on the type system of SAC and its implementation can be found in [39].

The other important aspect handled by this part of the compiler is *function specialisation*. Shape- and rank-generic specifications are a key feature of SAC, and from a software engineering point of view, all code should be written in rank-generic (AUD) or at least in shape-generic (AKS) style. From a compiler perspective, however, shape- and rank-specific code offers much better optimisation opportunities, works with a much leaner runtime representation and generally shows considerably better performance. In other words, we are confronted with a classical trade-off between abstraction and performance.

A common trick to reconcile abstract programming with high runtime performance is specialisation. In fact, the SAC compiler aggressively specialises rank-generic code to rank-specific (shape-generic) code and again shape-generic code into shape-specific code.

Specialisation can only be effective to the extent that rank and shape information is somehow accessible by the compiler. While `sac2c` makes every effort to infer the shapes needed, there are scenarios in which the required information is simply not available in the code. For this scenario we still provide two ways out: the programmer could simply help the compiler through the use of specialisation directives. On the technology-wise more challenging side, we have been developing an adaptive compilation framework [40,41] that aims at generating specialisations at application runtime and so to step-by-step adapt binary code to the actually used array shapes.

6 Architecture-Independent Optimisation

High-level, target-independent code optimisation constitutes a major part of the SAC compiler; it alone accounts for a substantial fraction of overall compiler engineering. Only the most prominent and/or relevant transformations are actually included in Fig. 22. They can coarsely be classified into two groups: standard optimisations and array optimisations. In the following we first look into standard optimisations before we look deeper into the organisation of the optimisation process as a whole. Following that, we introduce SAC's three most relevant array optimisations: WITH-loop-folding, WITH-loop-fusion and WITH-loop-scalarisation. We end the section with a brief sketch of further array optimisations.

6.1 Standard Optimisations

Many of the standard optimisations are well-known textbook optimisations. In our context, they are also crucial as enabling transformations for the array optimisations discussed towards the second half of this section.

Function inlining replaces applications of statically dispatched functions by their properly instantiated definitions. Apart from avoiding function call overhead in binary code, function inlining results in larger code contexts for other optimisations and, thus, is an important enabler for both standard and array optimisations. As of now, however, we refrain from automatically inlining functions based on heuristics such as code size, call intensity or recursive nature and rely on program annotation using the keyword `inline` preceding the function definition.

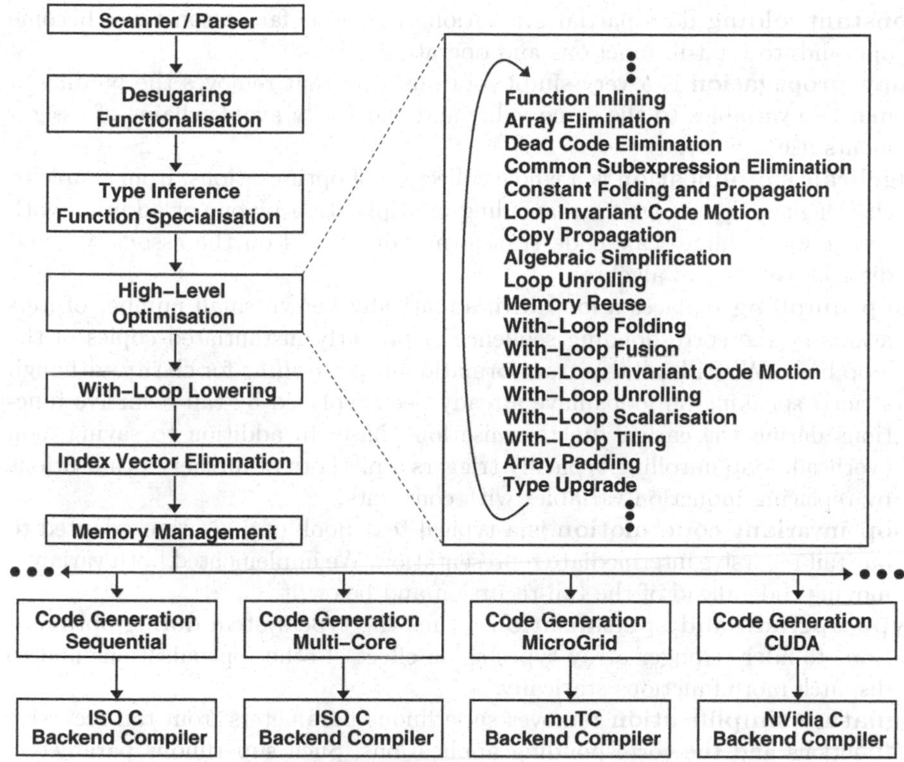

Fig. 22. Compilation process with focus on optimisation subsystem

Array elimination replaces (very) small arrays by the corresponding scalar values and adapts all code accordingly. Despite the name, we list array elimination here under standard optimisations due to its simplicity. It is, however, important to note that the purely functional semantics of SAC arrays is crucial for the effectiveness of array elimination.

Dead code elimination removes all code that does not contribute to the result of a computation. Again, the functional semantics allows us to do dead code elimination much more aggressively than what syntactically almost identical C code would support. In our highly optimising compiler scenario dead code elimination is also instrumental in relieving the intermediate code representation from parts that only became dead as a result of other optimisations.

Common subexpression elimination searches for identical subexpressions in the code and makes sure they are only evaluated once.

Constant propagation propagates scalar constant values into all subexpressions. For arrays, even small constant arrays, constant propagation would be counter-productive as arrays are instantiated in heap memory at runtime. Here, we provide alternative means to convey the value information, e.g. for the case that elements are selected from a constant vector.

Constant folding does partial evaluation of code as far as constants become operands to built-in functions and operators.

Copy propagation is a very simple optimisation that removes the binding of multiple variables to the same value and effectively avoids chains of assignments like `a = b;`.

Algebraic simplification is a whole collection of optimisations, from simple to challenging, that range from avoiding multiplication by one or addition with zero towards large-scale code transformations based on the associative and distributive laws of algebra.

Loop unrolling replaces a loop with a statically known small number of iterations by the corresponding sequence of properly instantiated copies of the loop body. We still call this transformation *loop unrolling* for clarity, although strictly speaking all loops have already been replaced by tail-recursive functions during the earlier functionalisation phase. In addition to saving loop overhead, loop unrolling typically triggers a plethora of further optimisations by replacing induction variables with constants.

Loop invariant code motion is a typical text book optimisation adapted to our tail-recursive intermediate representation. We implemented both variants: moving code ahead of the tail-recursion and below it.

Type upgrade and specialisation reruns the type system during optimisations to infer stronger array types as an effect of other optimisations and to dispatch more functions statically.

Signature simplification removes superfluous parameters from tail-recursive functions and the corresponding applications. Such superfluous parameters typically originate from other optimisations such as loop unrolling.

While many of these optimisations are common in industrial-strength compilers for imperative languages, the functional semantics of SAC allows us to apply them much more aggressively.

6.2 Organisation of the Optimisation Process

As the bottom-up arrow in Fig. 22 suggests, we organise the optimisation phase as a bounded fixed point iteration. All optimisations are carefully designed to avoid cycles in this fixed point iteration. Still, the organisation of the optimisation cycle is far from trivial because we must be careful with respect to efficient use of resources. Namely, the memory required for the intermediate representation of program code and the time spent in compilation are crucial. Some optimisations expand the intermediate code representation while others reduce its size. Applying a sequence of code expanding optimisations in a row to the intermediate representation of a non-trivial program may exceed the available memory. The other issue is compilation time. Even if an optimisation does not find any optimisation case, it must traverse the entire syntax tree to figure this out. This becomes time-consuming as codes turn non-trivial.

To make good use of both compilation time and memory we run one complete sequence of optimisations (Actually, some optimisations, like for instance dead code elimination, appear multiple times in the sequence.) for each function definition. We count the number of optimisation cases and can, thus, detect function-specific fixed points. Only after having completed one entire sequence of optimisations for each of the function definitions do we start into the next iteration of the optimisation cycle. Of course, this is restricted to those functions that have not yet reached a fixed point. Some of our optimisations have cross-function effects. Consequently, optimisation of one function may reactivate the optimisation of other functions that in turn will again be included in further iterations of the optimisation cycle.

Our compiler design ensures that code expanding optimisations are only applied to a single function definition before code shrinking optimisations, such as dead code elimination or constant folding, make sure that overall memory consumption remains within acceptable bounds. At the same time, we support cross-fertilisation of optimisations across function definitions.

6.3 Array Optimisations

The compositional programming methodology advocated by SaC creates a particular compilation challenge. Without dedicated compiler support it inflicts the creation of numerous temporary arrays at runtime. This adversely affects performance: large quantities of data must be moved through the memory hierarchy to perform often minor computations per array element. We quickly hit the memory wall and see our cores mainly waiting for data to be brought in from memory rather than performing productive computations. With individual WITH-loops as basis for parallelisation, compositional specifications also incur high synchronisation and communication overhead.

As a consequence, the major theme of array optimisation lies in condensing many light-weight array operations, more technically WITH-loops, into much fewer heavy-weight array operations/WITH-loops. Such techniques universally improve a number of ratios that are crucial for performance: the ratio between computations and memory operations, the ratio between computations and loop overhead and, in case of parallel execution, the ratio between computations and synchronisation and communication overhead.

We identified three independent optimisation cases and address each one with a tailor-made program transformation:

Vertical composition describes the case where the result of one WITH-loop is consumed as an argument by one or more subsequent WITH-loops. A good example is the convergence check in Fig. 15. Naive compilation would yield three temporary intermediate arrays before the final reduction is computed. To avoid the actual creation of such temporary arrays we devised the WITH-loop-folding optimisation described in Sect. 6.4 below.

Horizontal composition describes the case where two WITH-loops independently define two values (i.e. values unrelated in the data flow graph) based on at least partially the same original argument values and the same or at least very similar overall index space. Such compositions are taken care of by the WITH-loop-fusion optimisation introduced in Sect. 6.5 below.

Nested composition describes the case of two nested WITH-loops where the result of the inner WITH-loop describes the value of one element of the outer WITH-loop. This scenario likewise introduces a large quantity of temporary arrays. It usually cannot, and thus should not, be avoided in the code, but thoroughly taken care of by the compiler. We devised the WITH-loop-scalarisation optimisation to this effect and describe it in Sect. 6.6 below.

These optimisations are essential for making the compositional programming style advocated by SAC feasible in practice with respect to performance.

We illustrate all three composition styles and the corresponding optimisations by a running example. In order to demonstrate complexity and versatility of the individual optimisations without making the example overly complicated, we use the synthetic SAC function `foo` shown in Fig. 23. It takes a 9×9-element matrix of complex numbers as an argument and yields two 9×9-element matrices of complex numbers in return. On the right hand side of the figure we illustrate the corresponding index space partitions.

```
complex[9,9], complex[9,9] foo (complex[9,9] A)
{
  B = with {
        ([0,0] <= iv < [5,9]): A[iv];
      }: genarray( [9,9], toc(1.0));

  C = with {
        ([1,2] <= iv < [8,7]): A[iv] + B[iv-1];
      }: genarray( [9,9], toc(0.0));

  D = with {
        ([0,0] <= iv < [9,7]): B[iv];
      }: genarray( [9,9], toc(0.0));

  return (C, D);
}
```

Fig. 23. Synthetic code example to illustrate SAC high-level array optimisation

Both result arrays `C` and `D` are defined in terms of the argument array `A` and an intermediate array `B`. We use the conversion function `toc` ("to complex") to create default elements of type `complex`.

Before applying any optimisations, all WITH-loops are transformed into an internal representation that makes the default elements explicit by adding further generators as shown in Fig. 24.

```
C = with {
      ([0,0] <= iv < [1,9]): toc(0.0);
      ([1,0] <= iv < [8,2]): toc(0.0);
      ([1,2] <= iv < [8,7]): A[iv] + B[iv-1];
      ([1,7] <= iv < [8,9]): toc(0.0);
      ([8,0] <= iv < [9,9]): toc(0.0);
    }: genarray( [9,9]);
```

Fig. 24. Creating a full partition for the second WITH-loop of the running example introduced in Fig. 23

6.4 With-Loop Folding Optimisation

Our first optimisation technique, WITH-loop-folding, addresses vertical compositions of WITH-loops. In the running example introduced in the previous section, we have vertical compositions between the first and the second WITH-loop and again between the first and the third WITH-loop. Technically spoken, WITH-loop-folding aims at identifying array references within the generator-associated expressions in WITH-loops. If the index expression is an affine function of the WITH-loop's index variable and if the referenced array is itself defined by another WITH-loop, the array reference is replaced by the corresponding element computation. Instead of storing an intermediate result in a temporary data structure and taking the data from there when needed, we forward-substitute the computation of the intermediate value to the place where it is actually needed.

```
complex[9,9], complex[9,9] foo (complex[9,9] A)
{
  C = with {
        ([0,0] <= iv < [1,9]): toc(0.0);
        ([1,0] <= iv < [8,2]): toc(0.0);
        ([1,2] <= iv < [6,7]): A[iv] + A[iv-1];
        ([1,7] <= iv < [8,9]): toc(0.0);
        ([6,2] <= iv < [8,7]): A[iv] + toc(1.0);
        ([8,0] <= iv < [9,9]): toc(0.0);
      }: genarray( [9,9]);

  D = with {
        ([0,0] <= iv < [5,7]): A[iv];
        ([0,7] <= iv < [5,9]): toc(0.0);
        ([5,0] <= iv < [9,7]): toc(1.0);
        ([5,7] <= iv < [9,9]): toc(0.0);
      }: genarray( [9,9]);

  return (C, D);
}
```

Fig. 25. Running example after WITH-loop-folding

The challenge of WITH-loop-folding lies in the identification of the correct expression to be forward-substituted. Usually, the referenced WITH-loop has multiple generators each being associated with a different expression. Hence, we must decide which of the index sets defined by the generators is actually referenced. To make this decision we must take into account the entire generator sequence of the referenced WITH-loop, the generator of the referencing WITH-loop associated with the expression that contains the array reference under consideration, and the affine function defining the index. As demonstrated by the example in Fig. 25, this process generally involves intersection of generators. For example, folding the first WITH-loop into the second one requires splitting the index range of the generators in lines 3, 4 and 5 in Fig. 24.

For a more in-depth coverage of the ins and outs of WITH-loop-folding we refer the interested reader to [42,43].

6.5 With-Loop Fusion Optimisation

WITH-loop-fusion addresses horizontal composition of WITH-loops. Horizontal composition is characterised by two or more WITH-loops without data dependencies that iterate over the same index space or, at least, over similar index spaces. In our running example the WITH-loops defining the result arrays `C` and `D` in Fig. 25 form such a horizontal composition. The idea of WITH-loop-fusion is to combine horizontally composed WITH-loops into a more versatile internal representation named *multi-operator* WITH-loop. The major characteristic of multi-operator WITH-loops is their ability to simultaneously define multiple array comprehensions and multiple reduction operations as well as combinations thereof.

Figure 26 shows the effect of WITH-loop-fusion on the running example. As a consequence of the code transformation both result arrays `C` and `D` are computed in a single sweep. This allows us to share the overhead inflicted by the multi-dimensional loop nest among computing both array `C` and array `D`.

Furthermore, we change the order of array references. The intermediate code as shown in Fig. 25 accesses large parts of array `A` in both WITH-loops. Assuming array sizes typical for numerical computing, elements of `A` are extremely likely not to reside in cache memory any more when they are needed for execution of the second WITH-loop. With the fused code in Fig. 26 both array references `A[iv]` occur in the same WITH-loop iteration and, hence, the second one always results in a cache hit.

Technically, WITH-loop-fusion requires systematically computing intersections of generators in a way similar to WITH-loop-folding. After identification of suitable WITH-loops, we compute the intersections of all pairs of generators. Whereas in the worst case this leads to a quadratic increase in the number of generators, many of the new generators in practice turn out to be empty as demonstrated by our running example.

For a more complete coverage of the ins and outs of WITH-loop-fusion we refer the interested reader to [44].

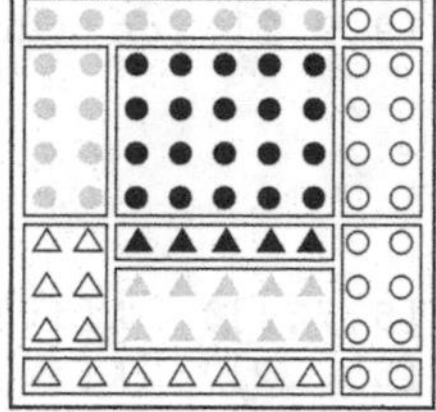

```
complex[9,9], complex[9,9] foo (complex[9,9] A)
{
  C, D =
   with {
    ([0,0] <= iv < [1,7]): toc(0.0),          A[iv];
    ([0,7] <= iv < [1,9]): toc(0.0),          toc(0.0);
    ([1,0] <= iv < [5,2]): toc(0.0),          A[iv];
    ([5,0] <= iv < [8,2]): toc(0.0),          toc(1.0);
    ([1,2] <= iv < [5,7]): A[iv] + A[iv-1],   A[iv];
    ([5,2] <= iv < [6,7]): A[iv] + A[iv-1],   toc(1.0);
    ([6,2] <= iv < [8,7]): A[iv] + toc(1.0),  toc(1.0);
    ([1,7] <= iv < [5,9]): toc(0.0),          toc(0.0);
    ([5,7] <= iv < [8,9]): toc(0.0),          toc(0.0);
    ([8,0] <= iv < [9,7]): toc(0.0),          toc(1.0);
    ([8,7] <= iv < [9,9]): toc(0.0),          toc(0.0);
   }: (genarray( [9,9]),
       genarray( [9,9]));

  return (C, D);
}
```

Fig. 26. Running example after WITH-loop-fusion with graphical illustration of the final iteration space on top

6.6 With-Loop Scalarisation Optimisation

So far, we have not paid any attention to the element types of the arrays involved. In SAC, complex numbers are not built-in, but they are defined as vectors of two elements of type `double`. As a consequence, our 9×9 arrays of complex numbers are in fact three-dimensional arrays of shape `[9,9,2]`, and the addition operation on complex numbers, in fact, is defined by a WITH-loop over vectors of two elements. The idea of WITH-loop-scalarisation is to eliminate such nestings of WITH-loops and to transform them into WITH-loops that exclusively operate on scalar values. This is achieved by concatenating the bound and shape expressions of the WITH-loops involved and by adjusting the generator variables accordingly. For our example we obtain an intermediate code representation equivalent to the code shown in Fig. 27.

```
double[9,9,2], double[9,9,2] foo (double[9,9,2] A)
{
  C, D =
   with {
     ...
     ([1,2,0] <= iv < [5,7,1]): A[iv] + A[iv-1], A[iv];
     ([1,2,1] <= iv < [5,7,2]): A[iv] + A[iv-1], A[iv];
     ...
     ([6,2,0] <= iv < [8,7,1]): A[iv] + 1.0, 1.0;
     ([6,2,1] <= iv < [8,7,2]): A[iv] + 0.0, 0.0;
     ...
   }: (genarray( [9,9,2]),
       genarray( [9,9,2]));

  return (C, D);
}
```

Fig. 27. Running example after WITH-loop-scalarisation.

When comparing this code against the code of Fig. 26, we can observe several benefits. There are no more two-element vectors which results in less memory allocations and deallocations at runtime. Furthermore, the individual values are directly written into the result arrays without any copying from temporary vectors. The fine grain skeletons for the additions of complex numbers have been absorbed within the coarse grain skeleton that constitutes the entire function body now. For a more complete coverage of the ins and outs of WITH-loop-scalarisation we refer the interested reader to [45].

6.7 Further Array Optimisations

The SAC compiler features a plethora of further array optimisations. Some are merely WITH-loop-specific variations of otherwise fairly standard code transformations. For instance, WITH-loop-unrolling or WITH-loop invariant code motion exactly do what their names suggest and what their conventional loop counterparts do. Another group of array optimisation aims at improving the utilisation of multi-level cache memories, e.g. array padding [46] and WITH-loop-tiling [47].

7 Lowering Towards Code Generation

Following target-independent code optimisation we now start our descent towards code generation. While in the SAC-compiler this involves a plethora of smaller and bigger steps, we concentrate our presentation here on three essential conceptual steps: WITH-loop lowering, index vector elimination and memory management. Figure 28 illustrates this part of the compiler in greater detail.

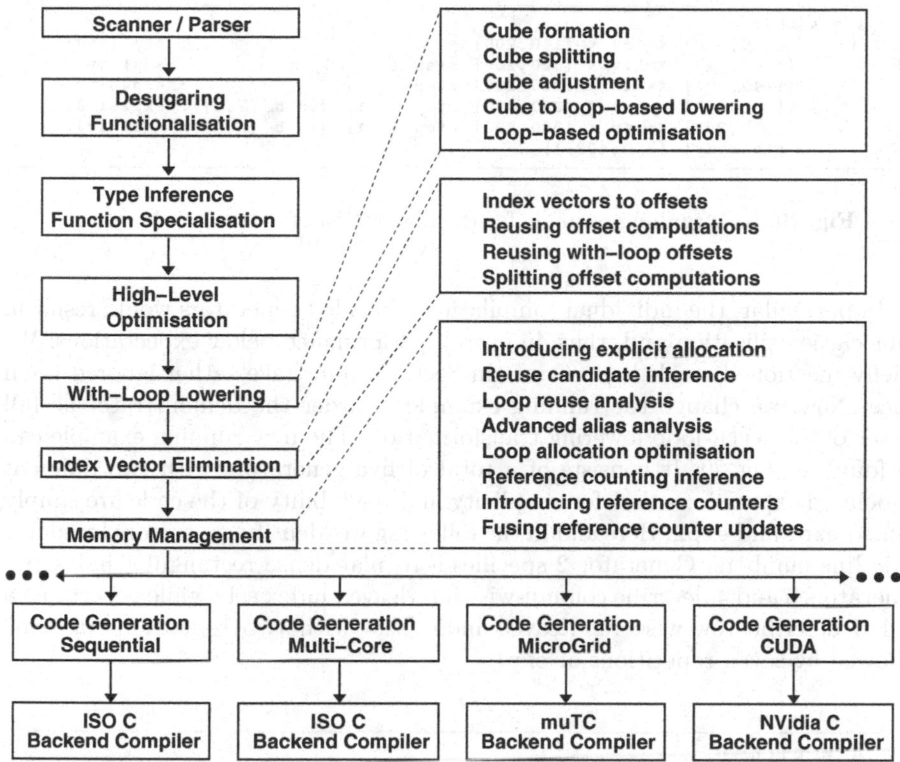

Fig. 28. Compilation process with focus on backend lowering subsystem

7.1 Transforming Complex Generator Sets

It has become clear by now that compiling WITH-loops into efficiently executable code is of paramount importance for overall success. WITH-loops are responsible for the by far largest share of execution time in typical application programs. Unfortunately, generating efficiently executable code for WITH-loops with complex generator sets is far from trivial. The last stages of the running example, as shown in Fig. 26 and in Fig. 27, nicely demonstrate this.

Compiling each generator in isolation into a nesting of C `for`-loops in the target code would be the most straightforward solution. However, the deep cache hierarchies of modern compute systems demand memory to be accessed in linear storage order to exploit spatial locality. As a consequence, the SAC compiler puts considerable effort into compiling complex generator sets first into an abstract intermediate representation that dispenses with the source-language motivated generator-centric view of WITH-loops. Instead, it resembles a tree of fairly simple conventional loops with one loop layer per dimension of the WITH-loop's index space. We call this intermediate representation *canonical order* representation.

```
1  A = with {
2        ([  0,   0] <= iv < [140,200]                          ): exp1(iv);
3        ([140,   0] <= iv < [320,200] step [1,2]               ): exp1(iv);
4        ([140,   1] <= iv < [320,200] step [1,2]               ): exp2(iv);
5        ([  0,200] <= iv < [320,400] step [9,1] width [2,1]): exp2(iv);
6        ([  2,200] <= iv < [320,400] step [9,1] width [7,1]): exp1(iv);
7     }: genarray( [320,400]);
```

Fig. 29. New running example for the illustration of WITH-loop lowering

In particular, the individual compilation of strided generators would result in poor cache utilisation and, thus, in overall performance below expectations. We briefly mentioned strided generators in Sect. 2.3, but have rather ignored them since. Now, we change the running example in order the demonstrate the full power of the WITH-loop lowering transformation. The new running example can be found in Fig. 29. It consists of a total of five generators with two different associated expressions that for simplicity and readability of the code are simply named `exp1` and `exp2`. Here and in the following we identify generators by source code line numbers. Generator 2 specifies a regular dense rectangular index set, generators 3 and 4 describe column-wise interleaved index sets while generators 5 and 6 describe row-wise interleaved index sets with two repetitions of `exp2` followed by seven repetitions of `exp1`.

```
A = with {
      cube ([  0,   0] <= iv < [140,200] step [1,1]) {
        (width [1,1] offset [0,0]): exp1(iv);
      }
      cube ([140,   0] <= iv < [320,200] step [1,2]) {
        (width [1,1] offset [0,0]): exp1(iv);
        (width [1,1] offset [0,1]): exp2(iv);
      }
      cube ([  0,200] <= iv < [320,400] step [9,1]) {
        (width [2,1] offset [0,0]): exp2(iv);
        (width [7,1] offset [2,0]): exp1(iv);
      }
    }: genarray( [320,400]);
```

Fig. 30. Running example after cube formation

WITH-loop lowering in itself is organised as a multi-step process. Its effect on the running example is illustrated in Fig. 35, but we first go through the example step by step. In a first transformation step, named *cube formation*, we identify interleaved generators. Note that all generators form a set, and hence their textual order is semantically irrelevant. Thus, cube formation identifies generators that spatially belong together. Figure 30 demonstrates the effect of cube formation on the running example, using pseudo code notation.

Note the three cubes that directly reflect the above text. Instead of slightly varying lower bounds, we now use *offsets* in (pseudo) generators. Lower bound, upper bound and step specifications become properties of the cube rather than properties of the individual generator. At this time we also introduce missing default step and width expressions which we set to default values.

```
A = with {
      cube ([  0,   0] <= iv < [140,200] step [1,1]) {
        (width [1,1] offset [0,0]): exp1(iv);
      }
      cube ([140,   0] <= iv < [320,200] step [1,2]) {
        (width [1,1] offset [0,0]): exp1(iv);
        (width [1,1] offset [0,1]): exp2(iv);
      }
      cube ([  0,200] <= iv < [140,400] step [9,1]) {
        (width [2,1] offset [0,0]): exp2(iv);
        (width [7,1] offset [2,0]): exp1(iv);
      }
      cube ([140,200] <= iv < [320,400] step [9,1]) {
        (width [4,1] offset [0,0]): exp1(iv);
        (width [2,1] offset [4,0]): exp2(iv);
        (width [3,1] offset [6,0]): exp1(iv);
      }
    }: genarray( [320,400]);
```

Fig. 31. Running example after cube splitting

In the next step, named *cube splitting*, we split cubes such that no cube spans multiple other cubes in an outer dimension. For example, cube 3 in Fig. 30 is split into cubes 3 and 4 in Fig. 31 (numbering in textual order). Cube 3 now spans the upper 140 rows while cube 4 spans the lower 180 rows. Since the row step of 9 does not divide the cube size of 140, cube 4 looks different from cube 3 internally: instead of 2 rows with `exp2` followed by 7 rows with `exp1`, we now see 4 rows with `exp1` followed by 2 rows with `exp2` followed by 3 rows again with `exp1`.

In the next step we adjust cubes that are adjacent in inner dimensions to match each other's stride. For instance, the dense cube 1 in Fig. 31 is a horizontal neighbour of cube 3 with stride `[9,1]`. After the cube adjustment transformation in Fig. 32 cube 1 also shows stride `[9,1]` with the same two partitions inside as cube 3. With one dense cube this is, of course, fairly straightforward, but the example of the horizontally adjacent cubes 2 and 4 is more complex. In fact, we need to fully intersect strided cubes. In the running example cube 2 is adjusted to cube 4 and now has stride `[9,2]` and the corresponding 6 partitions inside.

In the next step we switch from the cube-based representation used so far to a loop-oriented representation that forms a tree-shaped nesting of pseudo `for`-loops, as shown in Fig. 33. In the general case we generate two nested loops per

```
A = with {
      cube ([  0,   0] <= iv < [140,200] step [9,1]) {
        (width [2,1] offset [0,0]): exp1(iv);
        (width [7,1] offset [2,0]): exp1(iv);
      }
      cube ([140,   0] <= iv < [320,200] step [9,2]) {
        (width [4,1] offset [0,0]): exp1(iv);
        (width [4,1] offset [0,1]): exp2(iv);
        (width [2,1] offset [4,0]): exp1(iv);
        (width [2,1] offset [4,1]): exp2(iv);
        (width [3,1] offset [6,0]): exp1(iv);
        (width [3,1] offset [6,1]): exp2(iv);
      }
      cube ([  0,200] <= iv < [140,400] step [9,1]) {
        (width [2,1] offset [0,0]): exp2(iv);
        (width [7,1] offset [2,0]): exp1(iv);
      }
      cube ([140,200] <= iv < [320,400] step [9,1]) {
        (width [4,1] offset [0,0]): exp1(iv);
        (width [2,1] offset [4,0]): exp2(iv);
        (width [3,1] offset [6,0]): exp1(iv);
      }
    }: genarray( [320,400]);
```

Fig. 32. Running example after cube adjustment

dimension: an outer strided loop and an inner loop covering the stride. Likewise, indexing into the target array A as well as within the associated right hand side expressions now use the sum of outer strided index and inner step index.

To make the common case fast, we deviate from the general transformation scheme in the case of dense partitions and generate only a single loop per dimension. We deliberately use a pseudo notation for `for`-loops to improve the readability of code, here and throughout the remainder of the paper.

Of course, the current form of representation lowering raises the question where the memory used to represent the target array A might be allocated. To decouple the problem of memory management from the generation of loop nests we will continue with the latter aspect for now and entirely focus on memory management in the following Sect. 7.3.

As demonstrated in Fig. 34, the loop-based representation gives rise to a number of optimisations. Namely, we eliminate step-1 loops (lines 35–36, 44–45, 53–54) and we merge adjacent loops with the same associated expression (lines 11–13). We also apply loop peeling whenever the size of a cube is not a multiple of its stride (lines 17–30).

```
for (iv_0 = 0 to 140 step 9) {
  for (step_0 = 0 to 2) {
    for (iv_1 = 0 to 200) {
      A[iv_0+step_0, iv_1] = exp1(iv_0+step_0, iv_1);
    }
    for (iv_1 = 200 to 400) {
      A[iv_0+step_0, iv_1] = exp2(iv_0+step_0, iv_1);
    }
  }
  for (step_0 = 2 to 9) {
    for (iv_1 = 0 to 200) {
      A[iv_0+step_0, iv_1] = exp1(iv_0+step_0, iv_1);
    }
    for (iv_1 = 200 to 400) {
      A[iv_0+step_0, iv_1] = exp1(iv_0+step_0, iv_1);
    }
  }
}

for (iv_0 = 140 to 320 step 9) {
  for (step_0 = 0 to 4) {
    for (iv_1 = 0 to 200 step 2) {
      for (step_1 = 0 to 1) {
        A[iv_0+step_0, iv_1+step_1] = exp1(iv_0+step_0, iv_1+step_1);
      }
      for (step_1 = 1 to 2) {
        A[iv_0+step_0, iv_1+step_1] = exp2(iv_0+step_0, iv_1+step_1);
      }
    }
    for (iv_1 = 200 to 400) {
      A[iv_0+step_0, iv_1] = exp1(iv_0+step_0, iv_1);
    }
  }
  for (step_0 = 4 to 6) {
    for (iv_1 = 0 to 200 step 2) {
      for (step_1 = 0 to 1) {
        A[iv_0+step_0, iv_1+step_1] = exp1(iv_0+step_0, iv_1+step_1);
      }
      for (step_1 = 1 to 2) {
        A[iv_0+step_0, iv_1+step_1] = exp2(iv_0+step_0, iv_1+step_1);
      }
    }
    for (iv_1 = 200 to 400) {
      A[iv_0+step_0, iv_1] = exp2(iv_0+step_0, iv_1);
    }
  }
  for (step_0 = 6 to 9) {
    for (iv_1 = 0 to 200 step 2) {
      for (step_1 = 0 to 1) {
        A[iv_0+step_0, iv_1+step_1] = exp1(iv_0+step_0, iv_1+step_1);
      }
      for (step_1 = 1 to 2) {
        A[iv_0+step_0, iv_1+step_1] = exp2(iv_0+step_0, iv_1+step_1);
      }
    }
    for (iv_1 = 200 to 400) {
      A[iv_0+step_0, iv_1] = exp1(iv_0+step_0, iv_1);
    }
  }
}
```

Fig. 33. Running example after switching from the cube based representation to a pseudo loop-based representation

```
for (iv_0 = 0 to 135 step 9) {
  for (step_0 = 0 to 2) {
    for (iv_1 = 0 to 200) {
      A[iv_0 + step_0, iv_1] = exp1(iv_0 + step_0, iv_1);
    }
    for (iv_1 = 200 to 400) {
      A[iv_0 + step_0, iv_1] = exp2(iv_0 + step_0, iv_1);
    }
  }
  for (step_0 = 2 to 9) {
    for (iv_1 = 0 to 400) {
      A[iv_0 + step_0, iv_1] = exp1(iv_0 + step_0, iv_1);
    }
  }
}

iv_0 = 135;

for (step_0 = 0 to 2) {
  for (iv_1 = 0 to 200) {
    A[iv_0 + step_0, iv_1] = exp1(iv_0 + step_0, iv_1);
  }
  for (iv_1 = 200 to 400) {
    A[iv_0 + step_0, iv_1] = exp2(iv_0 + step_0, iv_1);
  }
}
for (step_0 = 2 to 5) {
  for (iv_1 = 0 to 400) {
    A[iv_0 + step_0, iv_1] = exp1(iv_0 + step_0, iv_1);
  }
}

for (iv_0 = 140 to 320 step 9) {
  for (step_0 = 0 to 4) {
    for (iv_1 = 0 to 200 step 2) {
        A[iv_0 + step_0, iv_1] = exp1(iv_0 + step_0, iv_1);
        A[iv_0 + step_0, iv_1 + 1] = exp2(iv_0 + step_0, iv_1 + 1);
    }
    for (iv_1 = 200 to 400) {
      A[iv_0 + step_0, iv_1] = exp1(iv_0 + step_0, iv_1);
    }
  }
  for (step_0 = 4 to 6) {
    for (iv_1 = 0 to 200 step 2) {
        A[iv_0 + step_0, iv_1] = exp1(iv_0 + step_0, iv_1);
        A[iv_0 + step_0, iv_1 + 1] = exp2(iv_0 + step_0, iv_1 + 1);
    }
    for (iv_1 = 200 to 400) {
      A[iv_0 + step_0, iv_1] = exp2(iv_0 + step_0, iv_1);
    }
  }
  for (step_0 = 6 to 9) {
    for (iv_1 = 0 to 200 step 2) {
        A[iv_0 + step_0, iv_1] = exp1(iv_0 + step_0, iv_1);
        A[iv_0 + step_0, iv_1 + 1] = exp2(iv_0 + step_0, iv_1 + 1);
    }
    for (iv_1 = 200 to 400) {
      A[iv_0 + step_0, iv_1] = exp1(iv_0 + step_0, iv_1);
    }
  }
}
```

Fig. 34. Running example after WITH-loop lowering pseudo loop-based optimisation

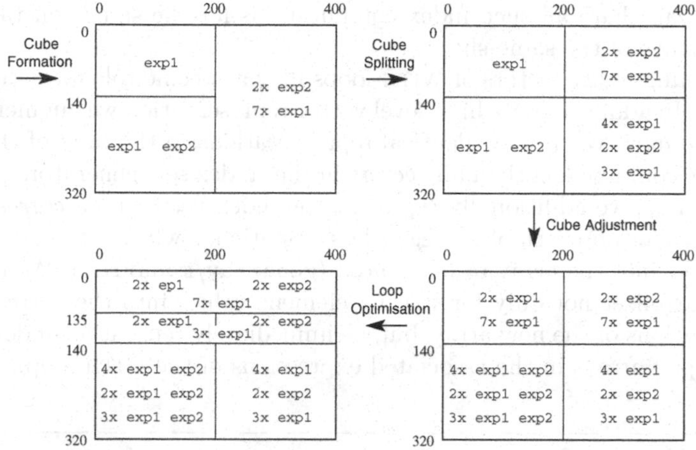

Fig. 35. Illustration of WITH-loop lowering steps for our running example

Figure 35 illustrates the entire compilation process of the running example as explained so far. A more formal description of the compilation scheme for WITH-loops and its implementation can be found in [47, 48].

7.2 Index Vector Elimination

As a characteristic feature SAC introduces the array indexing operation `sel` (or the corresponding square bracket notation) that uniformly has two parameters, regardless of the indexed array's rank. Instead of an unbounded collection of rank-specific indexing operations, as is common in other languages, SAC makes use of vector values for indexing into arrays. See Sect. 2.2 for details.

It comes at no surprise that dynamically creating such index vectors in heap memory would be prohibitively expensive. Hence, elimination of index vectors is an important lowering step for SAC. Index vector elimination systematically replaces vector-based selection operations by one that expects a single scalar index into the flat memory representation of the array concerned. Computing this scalar index into a flat array representation is an inevitable step anyhow, but up to now it has been hidden within `sel`. Index vector elimination makes this computation explicit in the intermediate representation, and thereby opens up a whole avenue towards further optimisation.

For example, index computations using the same index vector for different arrays that are known to have the same shape, even if the shape itself is unknown to the compiler, can be shared. Moreover, the common situation of an index vector with a constant offset can be optimised by splitting it into the sum of a scalar index derived from the statically unknown index vector and a scalar index derived from the constant offset. Should the shape of the indexed array be known to the compiler, the latter constituent of the scalar index can be entirely evaluated at compile time. If the array's shape is not known at compile time, we at least can share all such index computations for the same constant offset across all arrays of the same shape.

The running index vectors of WITH-loops play a specific role for index vector elimination. In addition to its high-level vector representation we augment WITH-loops by two more value-wise identical representations: If the rank of the WITH-loop, i.e. the common length of all vectors in the (index set) generators, is known at compile time, we additionally represent the index vector by a corresponding number of scalar loop variables. Regardless of static knowledge, we maintain the running offset into the array to be created (**genarray**/**modarray**). We make use of this scalar offset not only for writing element values into the corresponding element locations of the new array, but we immediately reuse it for indexing into equally shaped arrays in the associated expressions of the WITH-loop.

```
int offset = 0;
for (iv_0 = 0 to 135 step 9) {
  for (step_0 = 0 to 2) {
    for (iv_1 = 0 to 200) {
      A[offset] = exp1(iv_0 + step_0, iv_1, offset);
      offset++;
    }
    for (iv_1 = 200 to 400) {
      A[offset] = exp2(iv_0 + step_0, iv_1, offset);
      offset++;
    }
  }
  for (step_0 = 2 to 9) {
    for (iv_1 = 0 to 400) {
      A[offset] = exp1(iv_0 + step_0, iv_1, offset);
      offset++;
    }
  }
}
...
```

Fig. 36. Effect of index vector elimination on running example (excerpt)

We illustrate (parts of) index vector elimination by continuing the running example from the previous section. Figure 36 shows the resulting code corresponding to the first loop nesting in Fig. 34. In addition to the dimension-wise induction variables of the pseudo `for`-loops (`i` and `j`) we maintain a scalar offset (named **offset**) into the linear memory representation of target array `A`. This offset is likewise available to the right hand side expressions in the WITH-loop-bodies, where index vector elimination leads to further code transformations that we will describe in more detail in Sect. 9.7.

In many cases, index vector elimination makes the original vector representation of the index vector obsolete, and we entirely avoid its costly creation and maintenance at runtime. However, we also must care for the odd case where, for instance, the index vector is passed as an argument to a function. We refer the interested reader to [49] for a much more in-depth motivation and explanation of index vector elimination.

7.3 Memory Management

Functional arrays require memory resources to be managed automatically at runtime. Automatic garbage collection is a key ingredient of any functional language and meanwhile well understood [50–52]. For array programming, however, many design decisions in memory management must be reconsidered. For example, single arrays can easily stretch hundreds of MegaBytes (and more) of contiguous memory. This pretty much rules out copying garbage collectors with respect to runtime performance.

Another aspect of memory management for arrays is the *aggregate update problem* [53]. Often, an array is computed from an existing array by only changing a few elements. Or, imagine a recurrence relation where vector elements are computed in ascending index order based on their left neighbour. A straightforward functional implementation would need to copy large quantities of data unchanged from the "old" to the "new" array. As any imperative implementation would simply overwrite array elements as necessary, the functional code could never achieve competitive performance.

As a domain-specific solution for array processing, SAC uses *non-deferred reference counting* [54] for automatic garbage collection. At runtime each array is augmented with a reference counter, and the generated code is likewise augmented with reference counting instructions that dynamically keep track of how many conceptual copies of an array exist. Compared with other garbage collection techniques non-deferred reference counting has the unique advantage that memory can immediately be reclaimed as soon as it turns into garbage. All other known techniques in one way or another decouple the identification and reclamation of dead data from the last operation that makes use of the data.

Only reference counting supports a number of optimisations that prove to be crucial for achieving high performance in functional array programming. The ability to dynamically query the number of references of an array prior to some eligible operation creates opportunities for immediate memory reuse. Take for example a simple arithmetic operator overloaded for arrays like rank-generic element-wise subtraction as introduced in Fig. 12 in Sect. 3.1. Both argument arrays `A` and `B` are so-called *reuse candidates* for the result array named `R` in the following.

In Fig. 37 we show pseudo code representative for what the SAC compiler generates for the memory allocation part of the WITH-loop. The memory holding array `A` could be reused for the representation of result array `R` if and only if the reference counter is 1 and both arrays have the same shape and, thus, the same memory footprint. Should the first test be negative, we try the same with argument array `B`. Third, we try the special case where `A` and `B` actually refer to the same array (pointer equality) and the joint reference counter is 2,

```
if (RC(A) == 1 && shape(A) == shp) R = A;
else if (RC(B) == 1 && shape(B) == shp) R = B;
else if (RC(A) == 2 && A == B) R = A;
else R = SAC_malloc(shp);
```

Fig. 37. Pseudo code generated by the SAC compiler for the memory allocation part of the compiled WITH-loop implementing element-wise subtraction as defined in Fig. 12 in Sect. 3.1

which again means nothing but that A and B become obsolete after the current operation. Only if all three options fail, do we allocate fresh memory of required size. Immediate memory reuse does not only avoid a costly memory allocation, but also reduces the overall memory footprint of the operation, which improves memory locality through more effective cache utilisation.

Moreover, we frequently observe code scenarios where we may not only be able to reuse the memory of argument arrays but even some of the data that already resides in that memory. Consider for example the WITH-loop in Fig. 38. Here, an array B is computed from an existing array A such that every element in the upper left quadrant (in the further assumed 2-dimensional case) is incremented by 1 while all remaining elements are copied from array A proper. If we figure out at runtime (at the latest) that the memory of array A can safely be reused to store array B, we can effectively avoid to copy all those elements that remain the same in B as in A.

```
B = with {
      (. <= iv < shape(A) / 2): A[iv] + 1;
    }: modarray(A);
```

Fig. 38. SAC code example illustrating our data reuse optimisation

In Fig. 39 we illustrate, by means of pseudo code, how the SAC compiler deals with this example. We can clearly identify the case distinction between array A becoming garbage at the end of the operation or not. The example additionally illustrates both the canonical order code generation scheme as well as index vector elimination (use of additional scalar `offset` instead of loop induction variables). We call this compiler transformation *immediate data reuse optimisation.*

Memory management techniques, as we have described in this section, are important prerequisites to compete with imperative languages in terms of performance. A survey on SAC memory management techniques with further static code analyses and a number of additional optimisations to reduce memory requirements as well as memory management overhead can be found in [55].

```
if (RC(A) == 1) {
  B = A;
  for(i = 0 to shape(A)[0]/2) {
    for (j = 0 to shape(A)[1]/2) {
      B[offset] = A[offset] + 1;
      offset++;
    }
  }
}
else {
  B = SAC_malloc(shape(A));
  for (i = 0 to shape(A)[0]/2) {
    for (j = 0 to shape(A)[1]/2) {
      B[offset] = A[offset] + 1;
      offset++;
    }
    for (j = shape(A)[1]/2 to shape(A)[1]) {
      B[offset] = A[offset];
      offset++;
    }
  }
  for (i = shape(A)[0]/2 to <shape(A)[0]) {
    for (j = 0 to shape(A)[1]) {
      B[offset] = A[offset];
      offset++;
    }
  }
  RC(A) -= 1;
}
```

Fig. 39. Pseudo code illustration of the immediate data reuse optimisation

Unlike other garbage collection techniques, non-deferred reference counting still relies on a heap manager for allocations and de-allocations. Standard heap managers are typically optimised for memory management workloads characterised by many fairly small chunks. In array processing, however, extremely large chunks are common, and they are often handled inefficiently by standard heap managers. Therefore, SAC comes with its own heap manager tightly integrated with compiler and runtime system and properly equipped for multithreaded execution [56].

8 Code Generation

It is one of the strengths of the SAC compiler and the whole SAC approach to generate executable code for a variety of architectures from the very same target-agnostic source code. So far the entire compilation process has been (mostly)

target-agnostic, but now we reach the point to apply one of multiple target-specific code generators to our intermediate code representation. The SAC compiler supports a number of different compilation targets that we will describe in the remainder of this section. Space limitations preclude any in-depth discussion of technical details, but we refer the interested reader to additional resources for further reading.

In fact, the SAC compiler does not generate architecture-specific machine code but rather architecture-specific variations of C code. The final step of machine code generation is left to a backend compiler, configurable for any a given computing platform. While this design choice foregoes certain machine-level optimisation opportunities, we found it to be a reasonable compromise between engineering effort and support for a variety of computing architectures and operating systems. This flexibility also allows us to choose the best performing C compiler among various alternatives, e.g. the Intel compiler for Intel processors, the Oracle compiler for Niagara systems or GNU gcc for AMD Opteron based systems. It would be extremely challenging to compete with these compilers in terms of binary code quality.

Our first code generator produces purely sequential C code. It is of special relevance as it serves as a blue print for all other code generators. After all, substantial parts of any parallel program are nonetheless run in a single-threaded way, and many aspects of code generation are simply independent of the concrete backend choice and parallelisation approach. The various lowering steps described in the preceding Sect. 7 have already brought us reasonably close to (C) code generation. The remaining code generation steps are not trivial, but more of a technical than of a conceptual nature. Hence, we omit any further details here and refer the interested reader to [39] for more details.

8.1 Compiler-Directed Parallelisation for Multi-core Systems

An important (non-coincidental) property of WITH-loops is that by definition evaluation of the associated expression for any element of the union of index sets is completely independent of any other. This allows the compiler to freely choose any suitable evaluation order. We thoroughly exploit this property in the various WITH-loop-optimisations described in Sect. 6, but at the end of the day our main motivation for this design is entirely compiler-directed parallelisation.

In contrast to auto-parallelisation in the imperative world, our problem is not to decide *where* code can safely be executed in parallel, but we still need to decide *where* and *when* parallel execution is beneficial to reduce program execution times. The focus on data-parallel computations and arrays helps here: We do know the index space size of an operation before actually executing it, which is better than in typical divide-and-conquer scenarios.

It is crucial to understand that WITH-loops do not prescribe parallel execution. Instead, they merely open up parallelisation opportunities for compiler and runtime system. They still take the autonomous decision as whether to make use of this opportunity or not. This design sets SAC apart from many other approaches, may they be as explicit as OPENMP directives [30] or as implicit as `par` and `seq` in HASKELL [57].

For symmetric multi-core multi-processor systems we target ANSI/ISO C with occasional calls to the PThread library. Conceptually, the SAC runtime system follows a fork-join approach, where a program is generally executed by a single *master thread.* Only computationally-intensive kernels are effectively run in parallel by temporarily activating a team of *worker threads* created at program startup. In intermediate SAC code these kernels are uniformly represented by WITH-loops already enhanced and condensed through high-level optimisation. The synchronisation and communication mechanisms implementing the transition between single-threaded and multi-threaded execution modes and vice versa are highly optimised to exploit cache coherence protocols in today's multi-core multi-processor systems.

As demonstrated in Sect. 7.1 the SAC compiler may generate very complex loop nestings for individual WITH-loops. Therefore, we aim at orthogonalising loop nest generation from parallelisation aspects as far as possible. In multithreaded execution each thread must take care of a mutually disjoint index subset such that the union of all these subsets is equal to the complete index set. In Fig. 40 we illustrate our code generation approach by continuing the running example from Fig. 34 in Sect. 7.1.

```
run, lo, hi = scheduler( thread_id, num_threads, shape);

while (run) {
  for (iv_0 = max(0,lo[0]) to min(135,hi[0]) step 9) {
    ...
  }

  if (lo[0] <= 135 && 135 < hi[0]) {
    iv_0 = 135;
    ...
  }

  for (iv_0 = max(140,lo[0]) to min(320,hi[0]) step 9) {
    ...
  }

  run, lo, hi = scheduler( thread_id, num_threads, shape);
}
```

Fig. 40. Pseudo code illustrating the generation of multithreaded target code

We add a separate *loop scheduler* in front of the loop nesting. Based on the current thread's id, the total number of threads and the shape of the index set this oracle computes a Boolean flag `run` and the lower and upper bound vectors defining a multi-dimensional, rectangular index subset. The following `while`-loop as well as the second call to the loop scheduler at the bottom of the `while`-loop body are motivated to support oracles that repeatedly assign (disjoint) index subsets to the same thread. Such a feature is a prerequisite for supporting dynamic load balancing. Each (non-step) loop generated from the original WITH-loop is further augmented by code that restricts the effectiveness of the loop to the intersection between its original lower and upper bound and the lower and upper bounds computed by the loop scheduling oracle.

At the time of writing the SAC compiler supports multiple loop scheduling strategies similar to those of OpenMP, both static and dynamic, both with and without data locality awareness. Unfortunately, an automatic choice of the best loop scheduler based on static code analysis is still subject to future work.

Whether it is beneficial to actually execute some WITH-loop in parallel or whether it might be better to fall back to sequential execution critically depends on the code generated for the expressions associated with the various index set generators, but even more so on the shape and size of the index set. In the presence of shape- and rank-generic codes this information may not always be available to the compiler, even with sophisticated static analysis. Therefore, we generally create fat binaries that contain both sequential and multithreaded code variants for WITH-loops. Decisions are taken at compile time as far as possible and at runtime as far as necessary. We refer the interested reader to [58,59] for all further information regarding generation of multi-threaded code.

8.2 Compiler-Directed Parallelisation for Many-Core GPGPUs

Our support for GPGPUs is based on NVidia's CUDA framework [60]. In this case, our design choice to leave binary code generation to an independent C compiler particularly pays off because one is effectively bound to NVidia's custom-made CUDA compiler for generation of binary code.

A number of issues need to be taken into account when targeting graphics cards in general and the CUDA framework in particular, that are quite different from generating multithreaded code as before. First CUDA kernels, i.e. the code fragments that actually run on the accelerator, are restricted by the absence of a runtime stack. Consequently, WITH-loops whose bodies contain function applications that cannot be eliminated by the compiler, e.g. through inlining, disqualify for being run on the graphics hardware. Likewise, there are tight restrictions on the organisation of C-style loop nestings that (partially) rule out the transformations for traversing arrays in linear order that are vital on standard multi-core systems. This requires a fairly different path through the compilation process early on.

Last not least, data must be transferred from *host memory* to *device memory* and vice versa before the GPU can participate in any computations, effectively creating a distributed memory. It is crucial for achieving good performance to avoid superfluous memory transfers. We take a type-based approach here and attribute every type in SAC intermediate code with an additional *host* or *device* tag. This way transfers between host and device memory turn into type conversions. By taking these particularities of GPGPU computing into account in the compiler, SAC drastically facilitates the utilisation of GPGPUs for non-expert programmers in practice. More details can be found in [61].

8.3 Compiler-Directed Parallelisation for Heterogeneous Systems

This still rather experimental code generator aims at systems equipped with multiple, possibly different GPUs as well as at systems where we may want to use both the CPU cores and the GPGPUs. Already the CUDA code generator described before results in binary code that runs on both the CPU and the GPU, namely all suitable WITH-loops are run on the GPU and the remaining mostly scalar and/or auxiliary code is executed on the CPU by a single core in a sequential fashion. However, in the plain GPGPU compiler generator any WITH-loop is either executed by the GPGPU or by the CPU cores in its entirety.

Using our heterogeneous code generator we actually employ multiple CPU cores and multiple GPUs to jointly execute a single WITH-loop. Technically, we combine aspects of both the multi-core and the CUDA backend. Nonetheless, the plethora of organisational decisions that arise justify naming this approach a fully-fledged backend in its own right.

As mentioned before, code generation for CPUs and code generation for GPGPUs require different paths through the compilation process from the optimisation stage onwards. For this purpose we extend our internal representation of WITH-loops (once more) to accommodate two alternative representations that are independently and differently optimised and later lowered towards code generation. We reuse the loop scheduler of the multithreaded code generation backend to decide which parts of an index space to compute on the various CPU cores and which parts to compute on the multiple GPGPUs attached. For the latter purpose, each GPGPU is represented by one (special) worker thread in the multithreaded runtime system of SAC.

We still aim at transferring the minimal amount of data between the various memories needed to perform the computations assigned to each compute unit. To this end we compute the inverse index functions to determine the subsets of indices of each array referred to in the body of a heterogeneously computed WITH-loop. For the time being this is restricted to constant offsets to the index (vector). This actually suffices for many relevant numerical codes. Where we fail to compute the precise inverse index function, we make sure the entire argument array is available in the memory where it is needed. In many cases we do succeed in computing problem sizes that would not fit into the memory of a single GPGPU. We refer the interested reader to [20] for an in-depth motivation and discussion of this compiler backend.

8.4 Compiler-Directed Parallelisation for the MicroGrid

The MicroGrid is an experimental general-purpose many-core processor architecture developed by the Computer Systems Architecture group at the University of Amsterdam [18]. The MicroGrid combines, among others, single-cycle thread creation/deletion with an innovative network-on-chip memory architecture. An architecture-specific programming language, named μTC, and the corresponding compiler tool chain form the basis of our work [62].

The MicroGrid, or more precisely μTC, allows (or better requires) us to expose fine-grained concurrency to the hardware. This is in sharp contrast to our multithreaded code generator, described in Sect. 8.1. There we take considerable effort to adapt the fine-grained concurrency exposed by SAC intermediate code to the (generally) much coarser-grained actually available concurrency on the executing hardware platform. Now, the MicroGrid efficiently deals with fine-grained concurrency in the hardware itself. Details on code generation for the MicroGrid architecture can be found in [63–65].

8.5 Compiler-Directed Parallelisation for Workstation Clusters

Most recently we added support for workstation clusters, or, more generally, symmetric parallel distributed memory architectures. Our approach is based on our custom-designed software distributed shared memory solution (Software DSM). Our approach resembles a cache-only architecture where data needed to compute parts of a WITH-loop is dynamically mapped into local memory on demand. Instead of individual values, we always transfer entire memory pages (of configurable size) from the owning compute node to the one in need. Assuming a certain level of spatial and temporal locality in memory access, we expect the caching effect to largely mitigate the performance penalty of on demand data fetching from remote nodes. As the alert reader will expect by now, we once more restrict parallel execution to WITH-loops of our choice while all other code is executed in a replicated manner.

Among others, our approach was triggered by recently growing general interest in Software DSM solutions due to the fundamental changes in relative performance characteristics of network and memory access latency and throughput of today compared to two decades ago when Software Distributed Shared Memory was initially proposed, explored and eventually rejected [66]. Having our own tailor-made Software DSM subsystem allows us to exploit SAC's functional semantics as well as the very controlled parallel execution model of WITH-loops. While other arrays can be referred to in the body of a WITH-loop in many ways, these ccesses are solely in read mode. All writing to memory is restricted to result array(s) of WITH-loops, which is under complete control of the compiler. In contrast, modern general-purpose SDSM implementations go to great lengths to perform correctly and efficiently when used to implement synchronisation facilities.

It may be interesting to note the difference in design choice we made here as compared to the heterogeneous code generator. There we relied on static analysis of memory access patterns. Where our analysis failed we retreated to data replication across memories. We deemed this undesirable but nonetheless acceptable for a scenario of a host computer equipped with a small number of accelerators. In contrast, we deem data replication unacceptable on an otherwise scalable architecture. Or, in other words, we aim at a solution that is for sure capable of running computations that would no fit into the memory of any individual compute node. We refer the interested reader to [19] for an in-depth motivation, discussion and evaluation of this compiler backend.

9 Compilation Case Study: Convolution

In this section we illustrate the major steps of the compilation process, and in particular the impact of the various compiler optimisations, by means of a small case study. For this we directly connect to the programming case study on convolution in Sect. 4 and demonstrate step by step how that code example is transformed into efficiently executable code.

```
double[9,9] convolution (double[9,9] A,
                         double[5] weights
                           = [0.4, 0.2, 0.2, 0.1, 0.1],
                         double eps)
{
  double[9,9] B;

  do {
    B = A;
    A = convolution_step( B, weights);
  }
  while (!is_convergent( A, B, eps));

  return A;
}

double[9,9] convolution_step (double[9,9] A,
                              double[5] weights
                                = [0.4, 0.2, 0.2, 0.1, 0.1])
{
  double[9,9] R = weights[[0]] * A;

  for (i=0; i<dim(A); i++) {
    R +=   weights[[2*i+1]] * rotate( i,  1, A)
         + weights[[2*i+2]] * rotate( i, -1, A);
  }

  return R;
}
```

Fig. 41. Specialised convolution implementation from Fig. 19

9.1 Type Inference and Function Specialisation

To improve readability we omit the desugaring and functionalisation steps described in Sect. 5 and commence with type inference and specialisation. To make the example more concrete we specialise the code shown in Fig. 19 for an application to 9×9-matrices with the weight vector `[0.4,0.2,0.2,0.1,0.1]`.

We keep the threshold eps symbolic because compile time knowledge of its concrete value, although not unlikely in practice, would not affect the compilation process. We use an example shape as small as 9×9 solely for the purpose of illustration.

Figure 41 shows the corresponding specialisations of our functions convolution and convolution_step, as originally introduced in Fig. 17 and in Fig. 19, respectively. We deliberately omit the similar specialisations of is_convergent and rotate for now. Note the inferred types for arrays B and R.

9.2 Optimisation Prologue

In an initial step we inline the function convolution_step into the function convolution, which yields the representation shown in Fig. 42 Thanks to the specialisation to rank 2, the iteration count of the for-loop in line 11 is known to the compiler. Our compiler decides to unroll this loop, which yields the intermediate representation shown in Fig. 43.

```
1  double[9,9] convolution (double[9,9] A,
2                             double[5] weights
3                               = [0.4, 0.2, 0.2, 0.1, 0.1],
4                             double eps)
5  {
6    double[9,9] B, R;
7    do {
8      B = A;
9
10     R = weights[[0]] * A;
11     for (i=0; i<dim(A); i++) {
12       R +=    weights[[2*i+1]] * rotate( i,  1, A)
13             + weights[[2*i+2]] * rotate( i, -1, A);
14     }
15
16     A = R;
17   }
18   while (!is_convergent( A, B, eps));
19
20   return A;
21 }
```

Fig. 42. Convolution case study after inlining the convolution step

We now tend to the rotation function for a moment. Following the unrolling of the for-loop in the previous step, all four applications of the rotate function are characterised by constant axis and offset values. This enables specialisation of rotate as shown in Fig. 44 for the first of the four applications.

```
double[9,9] convolution (double[9,9] A,
                         double[5] weights
                           = [0.4, 0.2, 0.2, 0.1, 0.1],
                         double eps)
{
  double[9,9] B;

  do {
    B = A;

    A =   weights[[0]] * B
        + weights[[1]] * rotate( 0,  1, B)
        + weights[[2]] * rotate( 0, -1, B)
        + weights[[3]] * rotate( 1,  1, B)
        + weights[[4]] * rotate( 1, -1, B);

  }
  while (!is_convergent( A, B, eps));

  return A;
}
```

Fig. 43. Convolution case study after unrolling the `for`-loop for its two iterations and applying variable propagation

Static knowledge of rotation axis and rotation offset triggers an avalanche of partial evaluation at whose end only the WITH-loop at the bottom of the original implementation of `rotate` remains. This is shown in Fig. 45. Further inlining the four applications of the `rotate` function yields the still fairly compact convolution code in Fig. 46.

Looking back at Sect. 3, however, we understand that the five element-wise multiplications of intermediate arrays with the corresponding scalar coefficients are nothing but five more WITH-loops, at least after inlining the corresponding function definition from the SAC standard library. Likewise, but slightly hidden within the assignment operator `+=`, a syntactic heritage of C proper, we have four more WITH-loops derived from the definition of element-wise addition. The resulting intermediate code representation is shown in Fig. 47. However, for space reasons we only show about the first half of the `do-while` loop's body.

9.3 With-Loop Folding

At this stage, the first of our array optimisations kicks in. WITH-loop-folding manages to condenses all 13 WITH-loops in Fig. 47 into a single one as shown in Fig. 48. This step leads to a complete reorganisation of the WITH-loop's index space into a total of nine partitions: the central part, the four edges and the four corners. This is achieved by systematic intersection of the various generator sets

```
double[9,9] rotate (int axis = 0,
                    int offset = 1,
                    double[9,9] A)
{
  if (offset == 0  axis >= dim(A)  axis < 0) {
    R = A;
  }
  else {
    max_rotate = shape(A)[axis];

    if( max_rotate == 0) {
      R = A;
    }
    else {
      offset = offset % max_rotate;
      if (offset < 0) {
        offset = offset + max_rotate;
      }

      lower = 0 * shape(A);
      lower[axis] = offset;

      upper = shape(A);
      upper[axis] = offset;

      R = with {
            (lower <= iv <=    .   ): A[iv-lower];
            (  .   <= iv <  upper): A[iv+shape(A)-upper];
          }: modarray( A );
    }
  }

  return R;
}
```

Fig. 44. Specialised intermediate representation of rotation as introduced in Fig. 20 with constant arguments propagated according to the first application in Fig. 42

present in the previous representation. At the same time the index offsets into the argument array A are adapted accordingly.

Each of the nine partitions has an associated expression that is very similar to the one of the central partition shown in Fig. 48. Only the constant 2-element offset vectors for accessing array elements in A differ according to the cyclic boundary pattern chosen. For space reasons we only show the associated expression of the central partition here and in the following intermediate code examples.

So far, we haven't really looked at the convergence check. In fact, WITH-loop-folding can also very successfully be applied to the implementation of the

```
double[9,9] rotate (int axis = 0,
                    int offset = 1,
                    double[9,9] A)
{
  return with {
            ( [1,0] <= iv < [9,9] ): A[iv-[1,0]];
            ( [0,0] <= iv < [1,9] ): A[iv+[8,0]];
          }: modarray( A );
}
```

Fig. 45. Specialised rotation after thorough optimisation: with axis and offset known the entire definition can be partially evaluated to the single WITH-loop originally at the end of the function

convergence check. Figure 49 shows the resulting intermediate representation that comes along with a single WITH-loop for the reduction with Boolean conjunction while all other array operators have been moved to the scalar level.

9.4 With-Loop Fusion

Assuming the convergence check to also be inlined, we are in the situation that two WITH-loops suffice to implement the entire convolution with cyclic boundary conditions and convergence check. However, this is still one too many. Any experienced imperative programmer would combine computing the convolved array and computing the convergence check in a single traversal of the memory space. With our current intermediate code, in contrast, we go twice over the whole memory involved in every iteration: once to compute the one step convolved array `R` from array `A`, and once more to compute the element-wise difference of `R` and `A` for the convergence check.

Our second array optimisation, WITH-loop-fusion makes an end to this situation and successfully fuses the two remaining WITH-loops into the single one shown in Fig. 50. Technically, we first split the index space representation of the convergence check WITH-loop to comply with that of the convolution WITH-loop and then fuse the two. This results in a multi-operator WITH-loop that defines both an array comprehension (`genarray`) and a reduction (`fold`).

The fact that we can actually fuse the two WITH-loops in Fig. 49 requires further explanation. In Sect. 6.5 we explained the optimisation case of WITH-loop-fusion to be two WITH-loops *unrelated* in the data flow graph. This is clearly not the case in Fig. 49, where the result of the convolution WITH-loop clearly is an argument of the convergence check WITH-loop. This scenario marks the most advanced application case of WITH-loop-fusion: The second WITH-loop only refers to the result of the first WITH-loop *at index location*, i.e. without any further computing on the index vector variable of the WITH-loop. In this case we can still fuse the two WITH-loops because the access to the intermediate array in the second WITH-loop can be replaced by the scalar variable referring to that value in the new combined associated expression, as demonstrated in Fig. 50.

```
double[9,9] convolution (double[9,9] A,
                         double[5] weights
                           = [0.4, 0.2, 0.2, 0.1, 0.1],
                         double eps)
{
  double[9,9] B;

  do {
    B = A;

    A = 0.4 * B

    A += 0.2 * with {
                 ( [1,0] <= iv < [9,9] ): B[iv-[1,0]];
                 ( [0,0] <= iv < [1,9] ): B[iv+[8,0]];
               }: modarray( A );

    A += 0.2 * with {
                 ( [8,0] <= iv < [9,9] ): B[iv-[8,0]];
                 ( [0,0] <= iv < [8,9] ): B[iv+[1,0]];
               }: modarray( A );

    A += 0.1 * with {
                 ( [0,1] <= iv < [9,9] ): B[iv-[0,1]];
                 ( [0,0] <= iv < [9,1] ): B[iv+[0,8]];
               }: modarray( A );

    A += 0.1 * with {
                 ( [0,8] <= iv < [9,9] ): B[iv-[0,8]];
                 ( [0,0] <= iv < [9,8] ): B[iv+[0,1]];
               }: modarray( A );
  }
  while (!is_convergent( A, B, eps));

  return A;
}
```

Fig. 46. Convolution case study after inlining the four applications of the `rotate` function, each partially evaluated for the individual combination of axis and offset

Accordingly, each partition becomes associated with two expressions, or better say: a pair of expressions. For this we use a pseudo syntax similar to that introduced in Sect. 3.2 with pairs in the trailing return statement reusing the syntax of functions with multiple return values.

```
double[9,9] convolution (double[9,9] A,
                         double[5] weights
                           = [0.4, 0.2, 0.2, 0.1, 0.1],
                         double eps)
{
  double[9,9] B, R, P, T;

  do {
    B = A;

    A = with {
          ( [0,0] <= iv < [9,9] ): 0.4 * B[iv];
        }: genarray( [9,9] );

    T = with {
          ( [1,0] <= iv < [9,9] ): B[iv-[1,0]];
          ( [0,0] <= iv < [1,9] ): B[iv+[8,0]];
        }: modarray( A );

    P = with {
          ( [0,0] <= iv < [9,9] ): 0.2 * T[iv];
        }: genarray( [9,9] );

    A = with {
          ( [0,0] <= iv < [9,9] ): A[iv] + P[iv];
        }: genarray( [9,9] );

    T = with {
          ( [8,0] <= iv < [9,9] ): B[iv-[8,0]];
          ( [0,0] <= iv < [8,9] ): B[iv+[1,0]];
        }: modarray( A );

    P = with {
          ( [0,0] <= iv < [9,9] ): 0.2 * T[iv];
        }: genarray( [9,9] );

    A = with {
          ( [0,0] <= iv < [9,9] ): A[iv] + P[iv];
        }: genarray( [9,9] );

        ...
  ]
  while (!is_convergent( A, B, eps));

  return A;
}
```

Fig. 47. Convolution case study after following the inlining of element-wise sum and product operations

```
double[9,9] convolution (double[9,9] A,
                         double[5] weights
                           = [0.4, 0.2, 0.2, 0.1, 0.1],
                         double eps)
{
  double[9,9] B;

  do {
    B = A;

    A = with {
          ( [0,0] <= iv < [1,1] ): ... ;
          ( [0,1] <= iv < [1,8] ): ... ;
          ( [0,8] <= iv < [1,9] ): ... ;
          ( [1,0] <= iv < [8,1] ): ... ;
          ( [1,1] <= iv < [8,8] ): 0.4 * B[iv]
                                   + 0.2 * B[iv-[0,1]]
                                   + 0.2 * B[iv+[0,1]]
                                   + 0.1 * B[iv-[1,0]]
                                   + 0.1 * B[iv+[1,0]];
          ( [1,8] <= iv < [8,9] ): ... ;
          ( [8,0] <= iv < [9,1] ): ... ;
          ( [8,1] <= iv < [9,8] ): ... ;
          ( [8,8] <= iv < [9,9] ): ... ;
        }: genarray( [9,9] );
  }
  while (!is_convergent( A, B, eps));

  return A;
}
```

Fig. 48. Convolution case study after aggressive WITH-loop-folding

```
bool is_convergent (double[9,9] A, double[9,9] B,
                    double eps)
{
  return with {
          ([0,0] <= iv < [9,9]): abs(A[iv] - B[iv]) < eps;
         }: fold( &&);
}
```

Fig. 49. Specialised convergence check after WITH-loop-folding

9.5 Optimisation Epilogue

The far-reaching reorganisation of the intermediate code is now complete, but the expressions associated with the in total nine partitions of our final WITH-loop allow for some further optimisation. For example, common

```
double[9,9] convolution (double[9,9] A,
                         double[5] weights
                           = [0.4, 0.2, 0.2, 0.1, 0.1],
                         double eps)
{
  do {
    A, p = with {
             ( [0,0] <= iv < [1,1] ): ... ;
             ( [0,1] <= iv < [1,8] ): ... ;
             ( [0,8] <= iv < [1,9] ): ... ;
             ( [1,0] <= iv < [8,1] ): ... ;
             ( [1,1] <= iv < [8,8] ): {
                t1 =   0.4 * A[iv]
                     + 0.2 * A[iv-[0,1]]
                     + 0.2 * A[iv+[0,1]]
                     + 0.1 * A[iv-[1,0]]
                     + 0.1 * A[iv+[1,0]];
                t2 = abs(t1 - A[iv]) < eps;
                return (t1, t2);
             }
             ( [1,8] <= iv < [8,9] ): ... ;
             ( [8,0] <= iv < [9,1] ): ... ;
             ( [8,1] <= iv < [9,8] ): ... ;
             ( [8,8] <= iv < [9,9] ): ... ;
           }: (genarray( [9,9]), fold( && ));
  }
  while (!p);

  return A;
}
```

Fig. 50. Convolution case study after inlining the convergence check and applying WITH-loop-fusion

subexpression elimination finds the repeated indexing into array `A` with index vector `iv` and avoids a repeated load of the same value from memory by storing it in a fresh variable `t0`. Another optimisation concerns the identical coefficients for the left and right neighbour as well as the top and bottom neighbour, respectively. Here, algebraic simplification based on the distributive law avoids two multiplications. The resulting intermediate code for the central partition can be found in Fig. 51; all other partitions' associated expressions undergo equivalent transformations.

9.6 With-Loop Lowering

We eventually leave the realm of optimisation and start the lowering process towards final code generation. This process in reality is much more complicated than illustrated here, but we sketch out the main ideas.

```
{
  t0 = A[iv];
  t1 =   0.4 * t0
       + 0.2 * (A[iv-[0,1]] + A[iv+[0,1]])
       + 0.1 * (A[iv-[1,0]] + A[iv+[1,0]]);
  t2 = abs(t1 - t0) < eps;
  return (t1, t2);
}
```

Fig. 51. Fused WITH-loop body for inner indices following epilogue optimisations

As our first major lowering step the WITH-loop-lowering code transformation systematically transforms multi-dimensional partition generator sets into nested one-dimensional pseudo `for`-loops, as outlined in Sect. 7.1. All other aspects of the WITH-loop, namely the codes associated with each nested generator, for now remain exactly as they are.

In Fig. 52 we demonstrate the combined effect of all three (major) lowering steps, namely WITH-loop-lowering, index vector elimination and memory management, on the running example. The effects of these three code transformations are largely orthogonal to each other. Hence, we make use of a single figure and highlight the individual lowering effects in the textual description hereafter.

In the convolution example it is not straightforward to establish the canonical traversal order, but nonetheless simpler than in the running example of Sect. 7.1. The first nesting of generators takes care of the upper left corner of the matrix, the upper edge and the upper right corner. The same holds for the third nesting of generators covering the last row of the matrix, including the two lower corners. For these 6 generators the canonical order could also be achieved by simple reordering.

However, this is not always the case as the remaining three generators demonstrate: one covers the left-most column, one the right-most column and one the bulk of the index space of all non-boundary elements. Instead we aim at an organisation of the 2-dimensional index space where for each row we first compute the element of the first column according to the 4th partition, then the middle part of the row according to the 5th partition and, at last, the final element of the right-most column according to the 6th partition. Note in Fig. 52 that we deliberately refrain from unrolling single-iteration loops to retain the structural similarity with the original nine generators obtained from the optimisation compilation phase.

9.7 Index Vector Elimination

Our next major lowering step is index vector elimination, as introduced in Sect. 7.2. Here, we start accompanying the running index vector of a WITH-loop, i.e. `iv`, and the scalar induction variables, i.e. `i` and `j` in our running example, by a scalar offset into the flat memory representation of the array being computed.

As can be seen in lines 20 to 33 of Fig. 52, we completely scalarise the index computation, including the constant (vector) offsets. With static knowledge of the accessed arrays' shapes the compiler can compute the corresponding scalar offset difference in the flat memory representation of arrays. For reasons of illustration we still use the same square bracket notation for indexing as before. Of course, the compiler internally distinguishes between index operations with vectors and with scalars.

We now potentially have three runtime representations of the WITH-loop index: the original 2-element vector, two individual scalar indices and, third, the scalar offset into the flat memory representation added during index vector elimination. As can be seen in Fig. 52, only the offset is actually used in the right hand side expressions. We already eliminated the (costly) vector representation, but it is important to understand that this is not per sé superfluous as the index vector could be passed as an argument to a function that does expect a vector no matter what and cannot or should not be inlined. We refrain from eliminating the scalar induction variables as well because that would make the construction of the loops considerably more complex at limited performance gain.

9.8 Memory Management

While memory management with its multitude of analyses and optimisations as detailed in Sect. 7.3 is a comprehensive lowering step, the case study example code leaves little opportunity for far-reaching optimisation. In essence, we do need two chunks of memory, one is occupied by the incoming argument array `A`, the other is freshly allocated in the first iteration of the `do-while`-loop (line 9). The WITH-loop essentially computes the new array `T` stored in the newly allocated memory chunk from the data in the incoming memory chunk representing array `A`. Immediate reuse of the memory of array `A` for array `T` is not possible due to the access pattern in lines 25 and 26.

Following the WITH-loop, the `SAC_tryfree(A)` in line 41 acknowledges the fact that while we no longer need array `A` in function `convolution` and thus could de-allocate the corresponding chunk of memory, the original function argument could still be needed in the calling context and, thus, may need to be preserved throughout the evaluation of `convolution`. If so, the next iteration of the `do-while`-loop leads to the allocation of a third chunk of memory; otherwise, we immediately re-use the argument memory.

In either case, already in the first iteration of the `do-while`-loop, or at the latest in the second iteration, we end up with a scenario where two chunks of memory alternately represent arrays `A` and `T`, and pointers are effectively swapped between iterations. Further optimisation of the memory management structure would only be possible by either separating the first iteration of the `do-while`-loop at the expense of considerable code duplication or by analysis of all potential call sites of function `convolution`, should that be technically feasible in the presence of multiple modules and separate compilation.

Instead of pursuing either of the above ways forward we very much optimised the de-allocation/allocation in the SAC private heap manager, which guarantees an effective pointer swapping with only a few machine cycles overhead.

```
double[9,9] convolution (double[9,9] A,
                         double[5] weights
                           = [0.4, 0.2, 0.2, 0.1, 0.1],
                         double eps)
{
  double[9,9] T;

  do {
    T = SAC_malloc( 9 * 9 * sizeof(double));

    p = true;
    offset = 0;

    for (i=0; i<1; i++) {
      for (j=0; j<1; j++) { ... }
      for (j=1; j<8; j++) { ... }
      for (j=8; j<9; j++) { ... }
    }

    for (i=1; i<8; i++) {
      for (j=0; j<1; j++) { ... }
      for (j=1; j<8; j++) {
        t0 = A[offset];
        t1 =   0.4 * t0
             + 0.2 * (A[offset-1] + A[offset+1])
             + 0.1 * (A[offset-9] + A[offset+9]);
        t2 = abs(t1 - t0) < eps;
        T[offset] = t1;
        p = p && t2;
        offset++;
      }
      for (j=8; j<9; j++) { ... }
    }

    for (i=8; i<9; i++) {
      for (j=0; j<1; j++) { ... }
      for (j=1; j<8; j++) { ... }
      for (j=8; j<9; j++) { ... }
    }

    SAC_tryfree( A);
    A = T;
  }
  while (!p);

  return A;
}
```

Fig. 52. Convolution case study after applying WITH-loop-lowering, index vector elimination and memory management transformations

9.9 Code Generation and Final Words

The code shown in Fig. 52 is our final word on the compilation case study. It goes (almost) without saying that the C code actually emitted by the SAC compiler is hardly readable even for domain experts. Hence, showing that makes little sense. Instead, we conclude this section with some outlook what else could still be done. We already mentioned that the single-iteration `for`-loops are merely still there for readability, whereas we would normally expect them to have been eliminated in the course of WITH-loop-lowering as described in Sect. 7.1.

What else could we do from here?

We could, for instance consider to apply loop unrolling or loop invariant removal on the level of the generated `for`-loops. At the time of writing the SAC compiler still lacks such capacity and instead relies on the backend C compiler to exploit such opportunities, for good or for bad.

As mentioned before, we could avoid maintaining the loop indices `i` and `j` altogether as our code exclusively uses the flat index `offset` instead. Again, we expect any decent C compiler to do this job for us at the right optimisation level.

Another optimisation opportunity would be the detection of the fixed point where `p` equals false in the Boolean computations of lines 27 and 29. Again we hope for the C compiler to this effect. Alternatively, the SAC features an experimental `foldfix` WITH-loop-operator that generalises the notion of a fixed point in fold-like computations from the usual Boolean operators to any operator. However, we didn't make use of this feature here due to its experimental nature and incomplete code generators for some target architectures.

At last, it might be tempting to unroll the `for`-loop in line 20, but be aware that the small number of iterations is merely an artefact of our illustration while any production code would come with a number of iterations here and elsewhere in the code that would immediately preclude any idea of loop unrolling.

10 Experimental Evaluation: An Annotated Bibliography

Many publications on SAC, if not most, contain some form of experimental evaluation of the concrete subject matter described. In addition to these publications we have over the years conducted a number of larger-scale case studies that demonstrate the applicability of SAC in various application domains and put the performance achieved by SAC into the perspective of other high-level and low-level programming models and their compilers and runtime systems. Instead of reproducing essential results, we rather provide a certainly non-exhaustive annotated bibliography. This is not only owed to the limitation of space here but at least as much to the fact that any experimental investigation is a snapshot in time since not only the SAC compiler is continuously evolving, but likewise other compilers, operating systems and last not least computer architectures.

Motivated by the SICSA Multi-core Challenge we investigate SAC implementations of the all-pairs N-body problem and compare performance on CPUs and GPUs in [67]. In [68] we experiment with anisotropic filters and single-class support vector machines from an industrial image processing pipeline again both on multi-core CPUs and GPGPUs. In [69] we investigate the scalability of the SAC multithreaded code generator and runtime system on the 4-socket 16-core Oracle T3-4 server with up to 512 hardware threads. We analyse the performance of the GPGPU code generator for a variety of benchmarks in [61].

In [70] we compare SAC with FORTRAN-90 in terms of programming productivity and performance on multi-core multi-processor systems for unsteady shock wave interactions. We again compare SAC with FORTRAN-90 in [71], this time based on the Kadomtsev-Petiviashvili-I equations (KP-I) that describe the propagation of non-linear waves in a dispersive medium. In [72] and [73] we describe SAC implementations of the NAS benchmarks [74] FT (3-dimensional fast-Fourier transforms) and MG (multigrid), respectively, on multi-processor systems of the pre-multi-core era. Last not least, [75] contains an early comparison between SAC and High Performance Fortran.

11 Related Work

Given the wide range of topics around the design and implementation of SAC that we have covered in this article, there is a plethora of related work that is impossible to do justice in this section. Hence, the selection inevitably is subjective and incomplete.

General-purpose functional languages such as HASKELL, CLEAN, SML or OCAML all support arrays in one way or another on the language level. Or more precisely, they support (potentially nested) vectors (1-dimensional arrays) in our terminology. However, as far as implementations are concerned, arrays are rather side issues; design decisions are taken in favour of list- and tree-like data structures. This largely rules out achieving competitive performance on array-based compute-intensive kernels.

The most radical step is taken by the ML family of languages: arrays come as stateful, not as functional data structures. To the same degree as this choice facilitates compilation, it looses the most appealing characteristics of a functional approach. The lazy functional languages HASKELL and CLEAN both implement fully functional arrays, but investigations have shown that in order to achieve acceptable runtime performance arrays must not only be strict and unboxed (as in SAC), but array processing must also adhere to a stateful regime [76–78]. While conceptually more elaborate than the ML approach to arrays, monads and uniqueness types likewise enforce an imperative programming style where arrays are explicitly created, copied and removed.

Data Parallel Haskell [79,80] is an extension of vanilla HASKELL with particular support for nested vectors (arrays in HASKELL speak). Data Parallel Haskell aims at irregular and sparse array problems and inhomogeneous nested vectors in the tradition of NESL [81]. Likewise, it adopts NESL's flattening optimisation that turns nested vectors into flat representations.

One project that deserves acknowledgement in our context is SISAL [82,83]. SISAL was the first approach to high-performance functional array programming, and, arguably, it is the only other approach that aims at these goals as stringently as SAC. SISAL predates SAC, and consequently, we studied SISAL closely in the beginning of the SAC project. Unfortunately, the development of SISAL effectively ended with version 1.1 around the time the first SAC implementation was available. Further developments, such as SISAL 2.0 [84] and SISAL-90 [85], were proposed, but have to the best of our knowledge never been implemented.

SAC adopted several ideas of SISAL, e.g. dispensing with many great but implementation-wise costly functional features, e.g. currying, higher-order functions or lazy evaluation. In many aspects, however, SAC goes significantly beyond SISAL. Examples are support for truly multi-dimensional arrays instead of 1-dimensional vectors (where only vectors of the same length can be nested in another vector), the ability to define generic abstractions on array operations or the compositional programming style. This list could be extended, but then the comparison is in a sense both unfair and of limited relevance given that development of SISAL ended many years ago.

An interesting offspring from the SISAL project is SAC's namesake SA-C also called Sassy [86,87]. Independently of us and around the same time the originators of SA-C had the idea of a functional language in the spirit of SISAL but with a C-inspired syntax. Thus, we came up with same name: Single Assignment C. Here, the similarities end, even from a syntactic perspective. Despite the almost identical name, SAC and SA-C are in practice very different programming languages with SA-C mainly targeting programmable hardware.

SAC's implementation of the calculus of multi-dimensional arrays is closely related to interpreted array languages like APL [14,15], J [16] or NIAL [17]. In [88] Bernecky argues that array languages are in principle well suited for data parallel execution and thus should be appropriate for high-performance computing. In practice, language implementations have not followed this path. The main show stopper seems to be the interpretive nature of these languages that hinders code-restructuring optimisations on the level of SAC (Sect. 6). While individual operations could be parallelised, the ratios between productive computation and organisational overhead are often unfavourable.

Dynamic (scripting) languages like PYTHON are very popular these days. Consequently, there are serious attempts to establish such languages for compute-intensive applications [89,90]. Here, however, it is very difficult to achieve high performance. Like the APL-family of languages the highly dynamic nature of programs renders static analysis ineffective. It seems that outside the classical high-performance community, programmers are indeed willing to sacrifice performance in exchange for a more agile software engineering process. Often this is used to explore the design space, and once a proper solution is identified, it is re-implemented with low-level techniques to equip production code with the right performance levels. This is exactly where we see opportunities for SAC: combine agile development with high runtime performance through compilation technology and save the effort of re-implementation and the corresponding consistency issues. Much of the above likewise holds for the arguably most used array language of our time: MatLab and its various clones.

12 Conclusions and Perspectives

We have presented the ins and outs of the compilation technology of the functional programming language Single Assignment C (SAC), developed over more than two decades. SAC combines array programming technology with functional programming principles and a C-like look-and-feel. By means of a case study, namely rank-generic convolution with cyclic boundary conditions and convergence check, we have first illustrated how the SAC approach facilitates the engineering of concise, abstract, high-level, reusable code. Then, we have proceeded to illustrate step-by-step how such concise, abstract, high-level, reusable code may nonetheless systematically be compiled into highly efficiently executable code without additional programmer intervention. This code forms the basis of fully automatic parallelisation for a variety of architectures from multi-socket, multi-core systems to GPGPU accelerators, heterogeneous systems, multi-node clusters and beyond. Unfortunately, space limitations only allowed us to briefly sketch out these aspects of the compilation technology. Likewise, we could only provide pointers for further reading with respect to performance evaluation and comparison.

The ability to fully automatically generate code for various parallel architectures, from symmetric multi-core multi-processors to GPGPU accelerators is arguably one of SAC's major assets. In a standard software engineering process the job is less than half done when a first sequential prototype yields correct results. Every targeted parallel architecture requires a different parallelisation approach using different APIs, tools and expertise. Explicit parallelisation is extremely time-consuming and error-prone. Typical programming errors manifest themselves in a non-deterministic way that makes them particularly hard to find. Targeting different kinds of hardware, say multi-core systems and GPGPU-accelerators inevitably clutters the code and creates particular maintenance issues. With SAC the job is done as soon as a sequential program is ready. Multiple parallel target architectures merely require recompilation of the same source code base with different compiler flags.

While much has been achieved already, our work at the crossroads of language design and compiler technology is far from finished. The continuous development of new parallel architectures keeps us busy just as further improvements of the language and of our compilation technology as well as of our compiler infrastructure.

Acknowledgements. The work described in this paper is the result of more than 15 years of research and development conducted by an ever changing group of people working at a variety of places. From the nucleus at the University of Kiel, Germany, in the mid-1990s the virus spread to the University of Lübeck, Germany, the University of Hertfordshire, England, the University of Toronto, Canada, the University of Amsterdam, Netherlands, and recently to Heriot-Watt University, Scotland. Apart from the internal funds of these universities, three European projects have been instrumental in supporting our activities: ÆTHER, APPLE-CORE and ADVANCE.

First and foremost, I would like to thank Sven-Bodo Scholz for many years of intense and fruitful collaboration. The original proposal of a no-frills functional language with a C-like syntax and particular support for arrays was his [91]. Apart from the name and these three design principles not too much in today's SAC resembles the original proposal, though.

My special thanks go to those who helped to shape SAC by years of continued work: Dietmar Kreye, Robert Bernecky, Stephan Herhut, Kai Trojahner and Artem Shinkarov. Over the years many more have contributed to advancing SAC to its current state. I take the opportunity to thank (in roughly temporal order) Henning Wolf, Arne Sievers, Sören Schwartz, Björn Schierau, Helge Ernst, Jan-Hendrik Schöler, Nico Marcussen-Wulff, Markus Bradtke, Borg Enders, Michael Werner, Karsten Hinckfuß, Steffen Kuthe, Florian Massel, Andreas Gudian, Jan-Henrik Baumgarten, Theo van Klaveren, Daoen Pan, Sonia Chouaieb, Florian Büther, Torben Gerhards, Carl Joslin, Jing Guo, Hraban Luyat, Abhishek Lal, Santanu Dash, Daniel Rolls, Zheng Zhangzheng, Aram Visser, Tim van Deurzen, Roeland Douma, Fangyong Tang, Pablo Rauzy, Miguel Diogo, Heinz Wiesinger, Jaroslav Sykora, Raphaël Poss, Victor Azizi, Stuart Gordon, Hans-Nikolai Viessmann, Thomas Macht, Cédric Blom, Nikolaos Sarris for their invaluable work.

References

1. Sutter, H.: The free lunch is over: a fundamental turn towards concurrency in software. Dr. Dobb's J. **30**, 202–210 (2005)
2. Intel: Product Brief: Intel Xeon Processor 7500 Series. Technical report (2010)
3. AMD: AMD Opteron 6000 Series Platform Quick Reference Guide. Technical report, AMD (2011)
4. Sun/Oracle: Oracle's SPARC T3-1, SPARC T3-2, SPARC T3-4 and SPARC T3-1B Server Architecture. Whitepaper, Oracle (2011)
5. Shin, J.L., Huang, D., Petrick, B., et al.: A 40 nm 16-core 128-thread SPARC SoC processor. IEEE J. Solid-State Circ. **46**, 131–144 (2011)
6. Strohmaier, E., Dongarra, J., Simon, H., Meuer, M.: 48th top500 list. Technical report (2016). www.top500.org
7. Greenhalgh, P.: Big.LITTLE Processing with ARM Cortex-A15 and Cortex-A7. Technical report, EE Times (2011)
8. Jeff, B.: big.LITTLE Technology Moves Towards Fully Heterogeneous Global Task Scheduling. Arm whitepaper, ARM (2013)
9. Chrysos, G.: Intel Xeon Phi coprocessor (codename Knights Corner). In: Hot Chips 24 Symposium (HCS 2012), Cupertino, USA. IEEE (2012)
10. Chrysos, G.: Intel Xeon Phi Coprocessor: The Architecture. Technical report, Intel Corp. (2013)
11. Jeffers, J., Reinders, J.: Intel Xeon Phi Coprocessor High Performance Programming. Morgan Kaufmann, San Francisco (2013)
12. Grelck, C., Scholz, S.B.: SAC: a functional array language for efficient multithreaded execution. Int. J. Parallel Program. **34**, 383–427 (2006)
13. Grelck, C., Scholz, S.B.: SAC: off-the-shelf support for data-parallelism on multicores. In: Glew, N., Blelloch, G. (eds.) 2nd Workshop on Declarative Aspects of Multicore Programming (DAMP 2007), Nice, France, pp. 25–33. ACM Press (2007)
14. Falkoff, A., Iverson, K.: The design of APL. IBM J. Res. Dev. **17**, 324–334 (1973)
15. International Standards Organization: Programming Language APL, Extended. ISO N93.03. ISO (1993)

16. Hui, R.: An Implementation of J. Iverson Software Inc., Toronto (1992)
17. Jenkins, M.: Q'Nial: a portable interpreter for the nested interactive array language Nial. Softw. Pract. Exp. **19**, 111–126 (1989)
18. Bousias, K., Guang, L., Jesshope, C., Lankamp, M.: Implementation and evaluation of a microthread architecture. J. Syst. Archit. **55**, 149–161 (2009)
19. Macht, T., Grelck, C.: SAC goes cluster: from functional array programming to distributed memory array processing. In: Knoop, J. (ed.) 18th Workshop on Programming Languages and Foundations of Programming, Pörtschach am Wörthersee, Austria, Technical University of Vienna (2015)
20. Diogo, M., Grelck, C.: Towards heterogeneous computing without heterogeneous programming. In: Loidl, H.-W., Peña, R. (eds.) TFP 2012. LNCS, vol. 7829, pp. 279–294. Springer, Heidelberg (2013). https://doi.org/10.1007/978-3-642-40447-4_18
21. Grelck, C.: Single Assignment C (SAC) high productivity meets high performance. In: Zsók, V., Horváth, Z., Plasmeijer, R. (eds.) CEFP 2011. LNCS, vol. 7241, pp. 207–278. Springer, Heidelberg (2012). https://doi.org/10.1007/978-3-642-32096-5_5
22. Schildt, H.: American National Standards Institute, International Organization for Standardization, International Electrotechnical Commission, ISO/IEC JTC 1: The annotated ANSI C standard: American National Standard for Programming Languages C: ANSI/ ISO 9899-1990. McGraw-Hill (1990)
23. Kernighan, B., Ritchie, D.: The C Programming Language, 2nd edn. Prentice-Hall, Englewood Cliffs (1988)
24. Iverson, K.: A Programming Language. Wiley, Hoboken (1962)
25. Iverson, K.: Programming in J. Iverson Software Inc., Toronto (1991)
26. Burke, C.: J and APL. Iverson Software Inc., Toronto (1996)
27. Jenkins, M., Jenkins, W.: The Q'Nial Language and Reference Manual. Nial Systems Ltd., Ottawa (1993)
28. Mullin, L.R., Jenkins, M.: A comparison of array theory and a mathematics of arrays. In: Arrays, Functional Languages and Parallel Systems, pp. 237–269. Kluwer Academic Publishers (1991)
29. Mullin, L.R., Jenkins, M.: Effective data parallel computation using the Psi calculus. Concurr. - Pract. Exp. **8**, 499–515 (1996)
30. Dagum, L., Menon, R.: OpenMP: an industry-standard API for shared-memory programming. IEEE Trans. Comput. Sci. Eng. **5**, 46–55 (1998)
31. Chapman, B., Jost, G., van der Pas, R.: Using OpenMP: Portable Shared Memory Parallel Programming. MIT Press, Cambridge (2008)
32. Gropp, W., Lusk, E., Skjellum, A.: Using MPI: Portable Parallel Programming with the Message Passing Interface. MIT Press, Cambridge (1994)
33. Douma, R.: Nested arrays in single assignment C. Master's thesis, University of Amsterdam, Amsterdam, Netherlands (2011)
34. Trojahner, K., Grelck, C.: Dependently typed array programs don't go wrong. J. Log. Algebraic Program. **78**, 643–664 (2009)
35. Trojahner, K.: QUBE – array programming with dependent types. Ph.D. thesis, University of Lübeck, Institute of Software Technology and Programming Languages, Lübeck, Germany (2011)
36. Grelck, C., Tang, F.: Towards hybrid array types in SAC. In: Stolz, V., Trancón Widemann, B. (eds.) 7. GI Arbeitstagung Programmiersprachen (ATPS 2014), Software Engineering Workshops (SE-WS 2014), Kiel, Germany, CEUR Workshop Proceedings, vol. 1129 (2014)

37. Chamberlain, B., Callahan, D., Zima, H.: Parallel programmability and the Chapel language. Int. J. High Perform. Comput. Appl. **21**, 291–312 (2007)
38. Grelck, C., Scholz, S.B., Shafarenko, A.: Asynchronous stream processing with S-Net. Int. J. Parallel Prog. **38**, 38–67 (2010)
39. Scholz, S.B.: Single Assignment C—efficient support for high-level array operations in a functional setting. J. Func. Program. **13**, 1005–1059 (2003)
40. Grelck, C., van Deurzen, T., Herhut, S., Scholz, S.B.: Asynchronous adaptive optimisation for generic data-parallel array programming. Concurr. Comput.: Pract. Exp. **24**, 499–516 (2012)
41. Grelck, C., Wiesinger, H.: Next generation asynchronous adaptive specialization for data-parallel functional array processing in SAC. In: Plasmeijer, R., Achten, P., Koopman, P. (eds.) 25th International Symposium Implementation and Application of Functional Languages (IFL 2013), Nijmegen, Netherlands. ACM (2014)
42. Scholz, S.B.: With-loop-folding in SAC - condensing consecutive array operations. In: Clack, C., Hammond, K., Davie, T. (eds.) IFL 1997. LNCS, vol. 1467, pp. 72–91. Springer, Heidelberg (1998). https://doi.org/10.1007/BFb0055425
43. Scholz, S.B.: A case study: effects of with-loop-folding on the NAS benchmark MG in SAC. In: Hammond, K., Davie, T., Clack, C. (eds.) IFL 1998. LNCS, vol. 1595, pp. 216–228. Springer, Heidelberg (1999). https://doi.org/10.1007/3-540-48515-5_14
44. Grelck, C., Hinckfuß, K., Scholz, S.B.: With-loop fusion for data locality and parallelism. In: Butterfield, A., Grelck, C., Huch, F. (eds.) IFL 2005. LNCS, vol. 4015, pp. 178–195. Springer, Heidelberg (2006). https://doi.org/10.1007/11964681_11
45. Grelck, C., Scholz, S.B., Trojahner, K.: With-loop scalarization – merging nested array operations. In: Trinder, P., Michaelson, G.J., Peña, R. (eds.) IFL 2003. LNCS, vol. 3145, pp. 118–134. Springer, Heidelberg (2004). https://doi.org/10.1007/978-3-540-27861-0_8
46. Grelck, C.: Improving cache effectiveness through array data layout manipulation in SAC. In: Mohnen, M., Koopman, P. (eds.) IFL 2000. LNCS, vol. 2011, pp. 231–248. Springer, Heidelberg (2001). https://doi.org/10.1007/3-540-45361-X_14
47. Grelck, C., Kreye, D., Scholz, S.B.: On code generation for multi-generator with-loops in SAC. In: Koopman, P., Clack, C. (eds.) IFL 1999. LNCS, vol. 1868, pp. 77–94. Springer, Heidelberg (2000). https://doi.org/10.1007/10722298_5
48. Kreye, D.: Zur Generierung von effizient ausführbarem Code aus SAC-spezifischen Schleifenkonstrukten (1998)
49. Bernecky, R., Herhut, S., Scholz, S.B., Trojahner, K., Grelck, C., Shafarenko, A.: Index vector elimination – making index vectors affordable. In: Horváth, Z., Zsók, V., Butterfield, A. (eds.) IFL 2006. LNCS, vol. 4449, pp. 19–36. Springer, Heidelberg (2007). https://doi.org/10.1007/978-3-540-74130-5_2
50. Wilson, P.R.: Uniprocessor garbage collection techniques. In: Bekkers, Y., Cohen, J. (eds.) IWMM 1992. LNCS, vol. 637, pp. 1–42. Springer, Heidelberg (1992). https://doi.org/10.1007/BFb0017182
51. Jones, R.: Garbage Collection: Algorithms for Automatic Dynamic Memory Management. Wiley, New York City (1999)
52. Marlow, S., Harris, T., James, R.P., Peyton Jones, S.: Parallel generational-copying garbage collection with a block-structured heap. In: 7th International Symposium on Memory Management (ISMM 2008), pp. 11–20. ACM (2008)
53. Hudak, P., Bloss, A.: The aggregate update problem in functional programming systems. In: 12th ACM Symposium on Principles of Programming Languages (POPL 1985), New Orleans, Louisiana, USA, pp. 300–313. ACM Press (1985)

54. Collins, G.E.: A method for overlapping and erasure of lists. Commun. ACM **3**, 655–657 (1960)
55. Grelck, C., Trojahner, K.: Implicit memory management for SAC. In: Grelck, C., Huch, F. (eds.) 16th International Workshop Implementation and Application of Functional Languages, IFL 2004, University of Kiel, Institute of Computer Science and Applied Mathematics, Technical Report 0408, pp. 335–348 (2004)
56. Grelck, C., Scholz, S.B.: Efficient heap management for declarative data parallel programming on multicores. In: Hermenegildo, M., Peterson, L., Glew, N. (eds.) 3rd Workshop on Declarative Aspects of Multicore Programming (DAMP 2008), San Francisco, CA, USA, pp. 17–31. ACM Press (2008)
57. Trinder, P., Hammond, K., Loidl, H.W., Jones, S.P.: Algorithm + Strategy = Parallelism. J. Funct. Program. **8**, 23–60 (1998)
58. Grelck, C.: A multithreaded compiler backend for high-level array programming. In: Hamza, M.H. (eds.) 2nd International Conference on Parallel and Distributed Computing and Networks (PDCN 2003), Innsbruck, Austria, pp. 478–484. ACTA Press (2003)
59. Grelck, C.: Shared memory multiprocessor support for functional array processing in SAC. J. Funct. Program. **15**, 353–401 (2005)
60. Kirk, D., Hwu, W.: Programming Massively Parallel Processors: A Hands-on Approach. Morgan Kaufmann, San Francisco (2010)
61. Guo, J., Thiyagalingam, J., Scholz, S.B.: Breaking the GPU programming barrier with the auto-parallelising SAC compiler. In: 6th Workshop on Declarative Aspects of Multicore Programming (DAMP 2011), Austin, USA, pp. 15–24. ACM Press (2011)
62. Bernard, T., Grelck, C., Jesshope, C.: On the compilation of a language for general concurrent target architectures. Parallel Process. Lett. **20**, 51–69 (2010)
63. Grelck, C., et al.: Compiling the functional data-parallel language SAC for microgrids of self-adaptive virtual processors. In: 14th Workshop on Compilers for Parallel Computing (CPC'09). IBM Research Center, Zürich (2009)
64. Herhut, S., Joslin, C., Scholz, S.B., Grelck, C.: Truly nested data-parallelism: compiling SAC to the microgrid architecture. In: 21st Symposium on Implementation and Application of Functional Languages (IFL 2009), South Orange, NJ, USA. Number SHU-TR-CS-2009-09-1, Seton Hall University (2009)
65. Herhut, S., Joslin, C., Scholz, S.B., Poss, R., Grelck, C.: Concurrent non-deferred reference counting on the microgrid: first experiences. In: Hage, J., Morazán, M.T. (eds.) IFL 2010. LNCS, vol. 6647, pp. 185–202. Springer, Heidelberg (2011). https://doi.org/10.1007/978-3-642-24276-2_12
66. Ramesh, B., Ribbens, C.J., Varadarajan, S.: Is it time to rethink distributed shared memory systems? In: 17th IEEE International Conference on Parallel and Distributed Systems (ICPADS 2011), pp. 212–219, ID 1 (2011)
67. Šinkarovs, A., Scholz, S., Bernecky, R., Douma, R., Grelck, C.: SAC/C formulations of the all-pairs N-body problem and their performance on SMPs and GPGPUs. Concurr. Comput.: Pract. Exp. **26**, 952–971 (2014). https://doi.org/10.1002/cpe.3078
68. Wieser, V., et al.: Combining high productivity and high performance in image processing using Single Assignment C on multi-core CPUs and many-core GPUs. J. Electr. Imaging **21**, 021116 (2012)
69. Grelck, C., Douma, R.: SAC on a Niagara T3-4 server: lessons and experiences. In: de Bosschere, K., D'Hollander, E., Joubert, G., Padua, D., Peters, F., Sawyer, M. (eds.) Applications, Tools and Techniques on the Road to Exascale Computing.

Advances in Parallel Computing, vol. 22, pp. 289–296. IOS Press, Amsterdam (2012)

70. Rolls, D., Joslin, C., Kudryavtsev, A., Scholz, S.B., Shafarenko, A.: Numerical simulations of unsteady shock wave interactions using SAC and Fortran-90. In: Malyshkin, V. (ed.) PaCT 2009. LNCS, vol. 5698, pp. 445–456. Springer, Heidelberg (2009). https://doi.org/10.1007/978-3-642-03275-2_44
71. Shafarenko, A., Scholz, S.B., Herhut, S., Grelck, C., Trojahner, K.: Implementing a numerical solution of the KPI equation using single assignment C: lessons and experiences. In: Butterfield, A., Grelck, C., Huch, F. (eds.) IFL 2005. LNCS, vol. 4015, pp. 160–177. Springer, Heidelberg (2006). https://doi.org/10.1007/11964681_10
72. Grelck, C., Scholz, S.B.: Towards an efficient functional implementation of the NAS benchmark FT. In: Malyshkin, V.E. (ed.) PaCT 2003. LNCS, vol. 2763, pp. 230–235. Springer, Heidelberg (2003). https://doi.org/10.1007/978-3-540-45145-7_20
73. Grelck, C.: Implementing the NAS benchmark MG in SAC. In: Prasanna, V.K., Westrom, G. (eds.) 16th International Parallel and Distributed Processing Symposium (IPDPS 2002), Fort Lauderdale, USA. IEEE Computer Society Press (2002)
74. Bailey, D., et al.: The NAS parallel benchmarks. Int. J. Supercomput. Appl. **5**, 63–73 (1991)
75. Grelck, C., Scholz, S.B.: HPF vs. SAC—a case study. In: Bode, A., Ludwig, T., Karl, W., Wismüller, R. (eds.) Euro-Par 2000. LNCS, vol. 1900, pp. 620–624. Springer, Heidelberg (2000). https://doi.org/10.1007/3-540-44520-X_87
76. Groningen, J.H.G.: The implementation and efficiency of arrays in Clean 1.1. In: Kluge, W. (ed.) IFL 1996. LNCS, vol. 1268, pp. 105–124. Springer, Heidelberg (1997). https://doi.org/10.1007/3-540-63237-9_21
77. Zörner, T.: Numerical analysis and functional programming. In: Hammond, K., Davie, T., Clack, C. (eds.) 10th International Workshop on Implementation of Functional Languages (IFL 1998), pp. 27–48. University College, London (1998)
78. Chakravarty, M.M.T., Keller, G.: An approach to fast arrays in Haskell. In: Jeuring, J., Peyton Jones, S. (eds.) AFP 2002. LNCS, vol. 2638, pp. 27–58. Springer, Heidelberg (2003). https://doi.org/10.1007/978-3-540-44833-4_2
79. Chakravarty, M.M.T., Leshchinskiy, R., Peyton Jones, S., Keller, G., Marlow, S.: Data parallel Haskell: a status report. In: 2nd Workshop on Declarative Aspects of Multicore Programming (DAMP 2007), Nice, France. ACM Press (2007)
80. Peyton Jones, S., Leshchinskiy, R., Keller, G., Chakravarty, M.: Harnessing the multicores: nested data parallelism in Haskell. In: IARCS Annual Conference on Foundations of Software Technology and Theoretical Computer Science (FSTTCS 2008), Bangalore, India (2008) 383–414
81. Blelloch, G., Chatterjee, S., Hardwick, J., Sipelstein, J., Zagha, M.: Implementation of a portable nested data-parallel language. J. Parallel Distrib. Comput. **21**, 4–14 (1994)
82. McGraw, J., Skedzielewski, S., Allan, S., Oldehoeft, R., et al.: SISAL: Streams and Iteration in a Single Assignment Language: Reference Manual Version 1.2. M 146. Lawrence Livermore National Laboratory, Livermore, California, USA (1985)
83. Cann, D.: Retire Fortran? A debate rekindled. Commun. ACM **35**, 81–89 (1992)
84. Oldehoeft, R.: Implementing arrays in SISAL 2.0. In: 2nd SISAL Users Conference, San Diego, CA, USA, pp. 209–222. Lawrence Livermore National Laboratory (1992)
85. Feo, J., Miller, P., Skedzielewski, S.K., Denton, S., Solomon, C.: SISAL 90. In: Böhm, A., Feo, J. (eds.) Conference on High Performance Functional Computing

(HPFC 1995), Denver, Colorado, USA, pp. 35–47. Lawrence Livermore National Laboratory, Livermore (1995)
86. Hammes, J.P., Draper, B.A., Böhm, W.: Sassy: a language and optimizing compiler for image processing on reconfigurable computing systems. ICVS 1999. LNCS, vol. 1542, pp. 83–97. Springer, Heidelberg (1999). https://doi.org/10.1007/3-540-49256-9_6
87. Najjar, W., Böhm, W., Draper, B., Hammes, J., et al.: High-level language abstraction for reconfigurable computing. IEEE Comput. **36**, 63–69 (2003)
88. Bernecky, R.: The role of APL and J in high-performance computation. APL Quote Quad **24**, 17–32 (1993)
89. van der Walt, S., Colbert, S., Varoquaux, G.: The NumPy array: a structure for efficient numerical computation. Comput. Sci. Eng. **13**, 22–30 (2011)
90. Kristensen, M., Vinter, B.: Numerical Python for scalable architectures. In: 4th Conference on Partitioned Global Address Space Programming Model (PGAS 2010), New York, NY, USA. ACM Press (2010)
91. Scholz, S.B.: Single Assignment C - functional programming using imperative style. In: Glauert, J., (ed.) 6th International Workshop on Implementation of Functional Languages (IFL 1994), Norwich, England, UK, pp. 21.1-21.13. University of East Anglia, Norwich (1994)

Type-Safe Functions and Tasks in a Shallow Embedded DSL for Microprocessors

Pieter Koopman(✉) and Rinus Plasmeijer

Institute for Computing and Information Sciences, Radboud University, Nijmegen, The Netherlands
{pieter,rinus}@cs.ru.nl

Abstract. The Internet of Things, IoT, brings us large amounts of connected computing devices that are equipped with dedicated sensors and actuators. These computing devices are typically driven by a cheap microprocessor system with a relatively slow processor and a very limited amount of memory. Due to the special input-output capabilities of IoT devices and their connections it is very attractive to execute (parts of) programs on these microcomputers.

Task-oriented programming, as introduced in the iTask framework, offers a very convenient abstraction level to construct distributed programs at a high level of abstraction. The task concept basically introduces lightweight threads. Tasks can be composed to more powerful tasks by a flexible set of combinators. These tasks can communicate with each other via shared data sources and inspect intermediate task values of other tasks.

The IoT devices considered here are far from powerful enough to execute programs made within the standard iTask system. To facilitate the execution of simple tasks using the special capabilities of the IoT devices from the iTask environment, we introduce a type-safe multi-view extendable domain-specific language to specify tasks for IoT devices. This domain specific language is embedded in the iTask system to facilitate the integration of both systems, but those systems are very useful on their own.

Keywords: Task oriented programming · Embedded systems · Internet of Things · Domain specific language · Shallow embedding · User-defined functions

1 Introduction

The Internet of Things, IoT, is a trending name for the large collection of interconnected smart devices. The IoT apparatus are smart in the sense that they can be programmed. Most of these devices are microprocessor-based systems. These microcomputers are usually equipped with special purpose sensors for quantities

V. Zsók et al. (Eds.): CEFP 2015, LNCS 10094, pp. 283–340, 2019.
https://doi.org/10.1007/978-3-030-28346-9_8

like temperature, pressure, GPS position, distance to the nearest object and so on. On the output side, the IoT devices can often control lights, the heating system, open doors and windows, etcetera. These special input–output capabilities and the fact that they can be programmed make those devices very valuable despite their limited computing power. Our long-term goal is to incorporate IoT devices in distributed task-oriented programs to execute tasks that require their special input–output options.

Task Oriented Programming, TOP [32], uses tasks as basic building blocks of software construction. The tasks perform real world or artificial units of work, like providing information, make decisions based on information (provided by other tasks), start other tasks, or change something in the real world. Currently the iTask system [31] is the main implementation of this paradigm. Interaction of TOP software with users is done via the browser. The required web-pages are automatically generated and updated. On an IOT device tasks repeatedly check the value of inputs, can decide to invoke other tasks based on these measurements, or use the outputs to induce changes in the real world.

In this paper, we construct a TOP system embedded in the iTask system to program IoT devices. The behaviour of microprocessors is specified in a Domain Specific Language, DSL, with type-safe user-defined functions and simple tasks. This DSL is intended to enable TOP on small embedded systems like an Arduino [2,6]. The 8-bit 16 MHz ATmega328P microprocessor of the Arduino Uno R3 is very suited for simple control tasks, but it is not particularly speedy. It provides just 32 Kb of program store and 2 Kb of RAM. Other microprocessors have more memory and a faster processor, but they are all very modest systems compared to desktops and laptops. The Arduino is the archetype of microcomputers. It is widely used due to the large number of input–output equipment available and the associated software infrastructure (IDE and libraries) that is portable to most other microcomputers. Due to the limited capabilities of such systems, it is unfeasible to implement a complete higher order and lazy functional programming language on these embedded systems. Despite the limited processing power of such microprocessor-based systems, these devices are very useful for simple control tasks.

Since microcomputers cannot execute full iTask programs, we use an embedded DSL. This ensures that the programs for the IoT devices are part of the iTask programs. Using a DSL has as additional advantage that we can piggyback on the parser and a type checker of the host language. We use Clean [33], the implementation language of the iTask system as the host language. We call our DSL for TOP of microprocessors mTask.

To achieve TOP on a tiny microprocessor we have to impose significant restrictions on the DSL used to specify tasks compared to the iTask system. The available memory makes it impossible to use a standard heap. This implies that we can neither have lazy evaluation nor higher-order functions. It is possible to transform higher-order functions to a first-order language by defunctionalization, [11,35], but that introduces many new functions. Due to the very limited amount of flash memory to store programs, additional functions are undesirable.

We must restrict the use of data types rigorously. Any data structure that uses large or uncontrolled amounts of memory will cause problems. Currently, we support only primitive data types, but this will be extended as future work.

We require that the type system of the functional host language checks the types in the DSL. This is achieved by a shallow embedded DSL: the DSL is a set of functions. The types of these functions ensure that the expressions in the DSL are correctly typed. To allow different interpretations (like pretty printing, code generation and simulation) of the DSL, we use type classes of functions instead of plain functions. Each interpretation, or *view*, is constructed as a new instance of the type classes.

To prevent that we silently inherit the complete host language in our DSL, we need a clearly bounded DSL. This is achieved by providing primitives to lift elements of the host language to the DSL, but not the other way around. This is accomplished by using type constructor classes instead of plain type classes. Only language elements of the type constructor class belong to our DSL.

The class-based DSL can be extended by new language constructs or new views without changing any existing code. The type system of the host language checks that the required constructs and views are defined for an application.

In the translation view, mTask programs are compiled to C++ programs for the Arduino dialect. The Arduino infrastructure has as advantages that code generation is relative simple (compared to generating machine code for individual microprocessors), the generated code is applicable to all microcomputers supported by the Arduino platform, it is easy to reuse existing libraries, and suited for portable optimizations.

Unfortunately, simple compilation to C++ imposes some additional restrictions on mTask. In particular, mTask is a first-order strict language. We use additional type constraints in mTask to prevent that statements will be generated in a context that only allows expressions.

We first give a brief introduction to Arduino programming in C in Sect. 2. In Sect. 3 we discuss various ways to make an embedded DSL and make a motivated choice for the rest of this paper. Based on our requirements for strong typing, multiple views, and extendibility we show that a shallow embedding based on type constructor classes is the best fit. The next Sect. 4, introduces our type-safe extendable shallow embedded DSL. Section 5 shows how we can generate directly C++ code in a tailor-made view of our DSL. Section 6 shows how we can simulate programs in our DSL using a view that transforms DSL programs into expressions in its host language. An iTask program is used to interactively show and update the state and to execute the tasks generated by the simulation view. Section 7 shows briefly two different approaches to optimize DSL programs. Since these optimization views yield a new program in our DSL, all other views can profit from the optimizations. Finally, we discuss related work in Sect. 8, and discuss the obtained results in Sect. 9.

The contributions of this paper are:

- It defines the notion of task-oriented programming that can run on small microprocessors. The tasks can communicate via shared data sources, but run interleaved like light-weight threads.
- The examples show that this TOP paradigm yields concise programs for these microcomputers. This enables the fast and dynamic creation and assignment of tasks to IoT devices.
- The implementation technique of the mTask DSL using type constructor classes is interesting on its own; it yields a type-safe multi-view extendable DSL. The type checker of the host language also checks the types in the DSL. It guarantees that all identifiers in the DSL are well defined and used in a type-safe way. A preliminary version of this implementation technique was used in [26].

  The extendibility of the mTask system is used to add libraries controlling input-output shields of the microprocessors as primitives to the language without requiring any changes, or even recompilation, of the existing DSL.

2 Arduino Programming

An Arduino is typically programmed in its own dialect of C++. The Arduino IDE supports programming. It can translate such a C++ program to machine code for the selected board. This code is uploaded to the microprocessor via a USB cable and a tiny boot loader on the board. Apart from the various Arduino variants, the IDE also supports many other microprocessors.

An Arduino does not run an operating system, nor offers support from some runtime system. This implies that the user program is all on its own on the microcomputer. Therefore, every Arduino program in C++ contains two basic functions. The function **void** setup() is called once at startup of the microprocessor. After this initialization, the function **void** loop () is repeated forever. Each of these functions can be empty.

The "hello world" example for the Arduino blinks the onboard LED connected to digital pin 13.

```
void setup() {
  pinMode(13, OUTPUT);                    // initialize pin 13 as output
}

void loop() {
  digitalWrite(13, HIGH);                 // switch LED on (HIGH voltage)
  delay(1000);                            // wait a second
  digitalWrite(13, LOW);                  // switch LED off (LOW voltage)
  delay(1000);                            // wait a second
}
```

The pins of the Arduino can be used as input and output. It is required to set the pin in the right input–output mode before using it in that mode. In this example setup() configures pin 13 as an output. The loop switches on the LED, waits for a second, switches of the LED, and waits another second. Since there is no operating system, there are no other threads or programs on the Arduino. This implies that the delay(1000) call blocks any program execution for one second. For more advanced programs it is better to prevent blocking by long delays. The use of delay is easily to circumvent by introducing some state variables and looking repeatedly at the clock with millis(), a function returning the milliseconds since start-up of the microprocessor.

```
#define DELAY 1000
boolean ledOn = false;                  // status of LED
long lastTime = 0;                      // last status switch

void setup() {
  pinMode(LED_BUILTIN, OUTPUT);
}

void loop() {
  if (millis() - DELAY > lastTime) {  // time to change?
    ledOn = not ledOn;
    digitalWrite(LED_BUILTIN, ledOn );
    lastTime += DELAY;
  }
}
```

2.1 Shields

Shields are boards that can be plugged on top of the Arduino main board offering additional functionality. For this purpose, the Arduino main board has connectors giving access to the analogue and digital ports of the microprocessor as well as some power lines. Many of these shields contain connectors to plug in another shield on top of this shield; these shields are stackable. There are shields for purposes like WiFi and Bluetooth connections, sensors (like temperature and heartbeat), actuators (like motor drivers and relays), displays and many more. These shields typically come with a library that offers a class to control that shield. The availability of a wide range of stackable shields and associated libraries are an important factor in the success of the Arduino development platform.

Figure 1 displays a picture of an Arduino with a 1602 LCD-shield executing the program sonar from Sect. 4.10. At the bottom of the figure, there is an ultrasonic distance sensor. A small servo with moving arms is displayed on the right side of the picture. The big blue cable is a USB connection providing power to the microprocessor. After loading a program via the Arduino-IDE it is perfectly possible to run this microprocessor without USB connection. Power can be provided by a DC-adapter, or battery.

One of the most used shields contains an LCD of two lines of 16 characters each. It is called a 1602 LCS shield. The corresponding library can control many different LCD-shields. The library is included in an Arduino program by

Fig. 1. An Arduino Uno with a LCD-shield, an ultrasonic sensor and a servo.

#include <LiquidCrystal.h>. A LCD control object is made by the constructor `LiquidCrystal lcd(8,9,4,5,6,7)`. The numbers are the Arduino pins used to control the actual LCD hardware, see [5] for a complete description. A simple program that shows the message `Hello World!` on the display and scrolls it back and forth is:

```
#include <LiquidCrystal.h>              // LCD library
#define STEPS 10                        // max scroll steps
int pos = 0;                            // scroll steps done
int inc = 1;                            // step inc
LiquidCrystal lcd(8,9,4,5,6,7);         // define lcd object

void setup() {
  lcd.begin(16, 2);                     // set LCD size
  lcd.print("Hello world!");            // display message
}

void loop() {
  if (inc > 0)                          // scroll right?
    lcd.scrollDisplayRight();           // scroll one step right
  else                                  // scroll left
    lcd.scrollDisplayLeft();            // scroll one step left
  step();                               // count step
  delay(400);
}

void step() {
  pos += inc;                           // increment steps
  if (pos < -STEPS || pos > STEPS)      // outside bounds?
```

```
    inc = -inc;                              // turn around
}
```

Part of the message is scrolled outside the display, but remembered by the `LiquidCrystal` object `lcd`. Note that this program uses the variables `pos` and `inc` to store the state between subsequent calls of `loop()`. This is a very common pattern in Arduino programs. This example also uses a simple user-defined function.

The final example combines an ultrasonic distance sensor, a LCD, a servo [3]. The method `ping_cm()` of the `sonar` object returns the echo time of a short ultrasonic burst in centimetres [4]. The measured distance is shown on the LCD. The angle of servo in degrees is set to the distance limited between 10 and 170° by `servo.write(deg)`.

```
#include <LiquidCrystal.h>                   // LCD library
#include <Servo.h>                           // servo library
#include <NewPing.h>

#define trigPin A1                           // pin names
#define echoPin A2
#define servoPin A5
#define maxDist 250

LiquidCrystal lcd(8, 9, 4, 5, 6, 7);
Servo servo;                                 // no constructor parameters
NewPing sonar(trigPin, echoPin, maxDist);

void setup() {
  servo.attach(servoPin);                    // servo at A5
  lcd.begin(16, 2);                          // set LCD size
  lcd.print("echo distance");
}

void loop() {
  int dist = sonar.ping_cm();                // measure distance in cm
  lcd.setCursor (0, 1);                      // print it on lcd
  lcd.print(dist);
  lcd.print(" cm   ");
  int deg = min(max(dist, 10), 170);
  servo.write(deg);                          // set servo
  delay(250);
}
```

These examples give a good first impression of possibilities of microprocessor programming in C++.

3 DSL Implementation Techniques

In this section, we motivate the implementation technique chosen for the DSL to implement task-oriented programming on microprocessors. The simplest way to add functionality to a programming language is by a library with tailor-made functions and data types that directly implement the desired functionality. Most libraries, including the iTask system, are implemented in this way. In our situation this cannot be applied; the microprocessors are too small to execute Clean programs. Adding a library makes the programs bigger and hence does not solve the memory and speed problems.

It is possible to communicate with the microprocessor via various channels, for instance, serial communication over the USB-connection. The Firmata protocol can implement this solution [16]. The actual task is running on an ordinary computer. This task controls the ports of the microprocessor via this Firmata protocol. HArduino is a Haskell library that demonstrates that this approach works [12]. A drawback of this approach is that it requires quite some communication between the task program on the ordinary computer and the microprocessor. We aim for a solution where the task is actually executed on the microprocessor itself.

Since we cannot execute a high-level task-oriented Clean program on a microprocessor and we do not want to execute such programs on an ordinary computer that remotely controls the microprocessor, we need a special language to specify the task-oriented program. We want that this special DSL is part of our high-level task-oriented system. It is convenient to have only a single source for programs that are distributed between an ordinary computer and a microprocessor. It is easier for the programmer and prevents problems with versions and language interfaces. Moreover, this allows the main program on the host computer to analyse the task oriented program executed on the microprocessor. The way to realize such a special DSL is by using an *embedded DSL*. Fowler gives a solid introduction to DSLs [14]. There is a long tradition of DSLs and functional programming, e.g. Hudak [17]. Gibbons gives a recent overview of the use of functional programming in DSL construction [15]. We give here a brief overview of approaches for DSL construction in functional programming languages tailored to task-oriented approach for microprocessor programming (see also [26]).

3.1 Deep Embedding of the DSL

The simplest approach to make an embedded DSL is by a data structure to represent the DSL. This is called a *deep embedding*. This data structure is, of course, an algebraic data type in a functional programming language. In this section, we use a very simple language with integer constants, Boolean constants, identifiers, integer addition, logical AND, and an overloaded equality for integers as well as Booleans. The algebraic data type DeepExp is an appropriate deep representation of this simple DSL in Clean.

```
:: DeepExp
    = Int  Int                           // integer constants
    | Bool Bool                          // Boolean constants
    | Id   Name                          // integer identifiers
    | Add  DeepExp DeepExp               // integer addition
    | And  DeepExp DeepExp               // Logical AND for Booleans
```

```
  | Eq   DeepExp DeepExp               // equality for integers and Booleans

:: Name := String                      // identifier names
```

For a syntactical more appealing DSL we will probably use infix operators instead of the prefix constructors of this algebraic data type. In this situation we can even make an instance of the ordinary + for the expressions in our DSL.

```
instance + DeepExp where (+) x y = Add x y
```

For the equality operator, ==, this is not possible since its result is always `Bool` while we need a `DeepExp` here.

It is straightforward to write interpretations, called *views*, of this representation of the DSL. Typical interpretations are the evaluation, pretty printing, optimization and so on. In this section, we use the views to evaluate, `eval`, and to pretty print, `show`, a program in the DSL.

For evaluation, we need an environment that maps variables to their value. we use only integer variables for simplicity. A simple environment, `Env`, is defined as a function from names to integer values.

```
:: Env  := Name → Int          // environment is function from name to integer

new :: Env                     // new environment
new = \name.0                  // every name is bound is initially bound to 0

(↦) infix 0 :: Name Int → Env → Env // environment update operator
(↦) name val = λenv name2.if (name == name2) val (env name2)
```

Using this environment we can write an evaluator for our DSL. We restrict this evaluator to well-typed programs. For instance, we do not include an alternative for the addition of integers and Booleans. Such a case is allowed by the data type, e.g., `Add ("Id "x") (Bool True)`, but should not occur in our DSL.

```
eval :: DeepExp Env → DeepExp
eval (Id name) env = Int (env name)
eval (Add x y) env =
    case (eval x env, eval y env) of
        (Int  a, Int  b) = Int (a + b)
eval (And x y) env =
    case (eval x env, eval y env) of
        (Bool a, Bool b) = Bool (a && b)
eval (Eq x y) env =
    case (eval x env, eval y env) of
        (Int  a, Int  b) = Bool (a == b)
        (Bool a, Bool b) = Bool (a == b)
eval exp env = exp // constants Int and Bool
```

In the same style we define a pretty printer that produces a list of strings. We use a continuation argument that represents the rest of the representation. This continuation prevents the use of a large number of append operators.

```
show :: DeepExp [String] → [String]
show (Int i  ) cont = [toString i:cont]
show (Bool b ) cont = [toString b:cont]
show (Id name) cont = [name:cont]
show (Add x y) cont = ["(","Add ":show x [" ":show y [")":cont]]]
show (And x y) cont = ["(","And ":show x [" ":show y [")":cont]]]
show (Eq  x y) cont = ["(","Eq " :show x [" ":show y [")":cont]]]
```

As an example we define the expression `e1`. The `Start` expression initiates its evaluation and pretty printing.

```
e1 :: DeepExp
e1 = And (Bool False) (Eq (Add (Int 2) (Id "x")) (Int 7))

env1 :: Env
env1 = ("x" ↦ 6) new           // bind x to 6 in a new environment

Start = (eval e1 env1, show e1 [ ])
```

The result of evaluation `e1` is `Bool False`. Pretty printing this expression with `show` yields `(And False (Eq (Add 2 x) 7))`.

Although this deep embedding of the DSL works fine for correct programs and is familiar to most functional programmers, it has a huge drawback; the type system of the host language, here Clean, is unable to spot all the type errors in a DSL program. Expressions like `Add (Int 7) (Bool True)` are proper instances of the type `DeepExp`, but evaluation of such a statement will produce a runtime type error like *Cannot add integers and Booleans.* It is very well possible to write a function that checks the types of a DSL program, but such a function will discover the type problems in the DSL program when it is executed; at runtime. Detecting type problems in the DSL programs at compile time (statically), by the type system of the host language, is very desirable. In such a statically typed DSL, the compiler of the host language rejects common type errors in DSL programs, like the equivalent of `Add 7 True` in that DSL.

Making the type of the expression an argument of the algebraic data type prevents some of the problems, but there is no proper way to handle the overloaded equality. Neilson and Neilson show in their example language While how to make a separate data type `AExpr` for arithmetic expressions and `BExpr` for Boolean expressions [29]. This enables the type checker of the host language to check the types in DSL programs. This requires a separate constructor for each type of arguments of an operation, e.g., there must be an equality for integers, separate equality for Booleans, yet another equality operator for equality of characters and so on. In our DSL we require at least overloading for the basic operations like equality to prevent a huge number of operators for the same operation that only differ in the type of arguments.

Another problem with this representation is that it is hard to extend. Adding a language construct requires a change of the algebraic data type `DeepExp` and all functions manipulating it. The host language compiler offers at best-limited support to check whether all views are correctly adapted.

3.2 Generalized Algebraic Data Types for the DSL

A way to prevent the type problems of the previous representation is to use Generalized Algebraic Data Types, GADTs [22], instead of algebraic data types. Even in a language without GADT support, we can achieve the effect of a GADT by introducing some type conversion functions.

The record `BM` contains a bimap between the types `x` and `y`. There are functions `f` and `t` for transformations in both directions.

```
:: BM x y = {f :: y→x, t :: x→y}

bm :: BM t t
bm = {f = id, t = id}
```

The only bimaps we will use are the identities from `bm`. Here we need only the function `f`. In more complex situations, like program transformations, one needs also transformations of kind ⋆→⋆. This means we need functions like `f2 :: (v x)→v y`.

We extend our representation of the DSL with a type parameter `a`. The cases for `Int` and `Bool` can now be mapped to a single literal definition `Lit`. In all other cases, we add an instance of the bimap to convince the type system that the resulting type matches the required type `a`.

```
:: GadtExp a
    =       Lit              a
    |       Id   (BM a Int)  Name
    |       Add  (BM a Int)  (GadtExp Int)  (GadtExp Int)
    |       And  (BM a Bool) (GadtExp Bool) (GadtExp Bool)
    | ∃b: Eq   (BM a Bool) (GadtExp b)    (GadtExp b)    & toString, == b
```

Note that we use an existentially quantified type `b` for the arguments of the equality operator `Eq`. Since we need instances of the classes `toString` and `==` in the show and eval views later on, we have to state those class restrictions here. This is the only place where we can impose such restrictions.

Pretty printing those expressions is simple. We do not need the argument type `a` of `GadtExp` in this view. Hence, we do not need the bimap at all.

```
show :: (GadtExp a) [String] → [String] | toString a
show (Lit i)        cont = [toString i: cont]
show (Id bm name) cont = [name: cont]
show (Add bm x y) cont = ["(","Add ": show x [" ": show y [")": cont]]]
show (And bm x y) cont = ["(","And ": show x [" ": show y [")": cont]]]
show (Eq  bm x y) cont = ["(","Eq " : show x [" ": show y [")": cont]]]
```

Evaluating those expressions changes. Note that this evaluator yields a result of type `a` instead of `GadtExp a`. This eliminates the need to remove the constructor `Lit`, like we removed and inserted the constructors `Int` and `Bool` in the previous representation.

```
eval :: (GadtExp a) Env → a
eval (Id {f} name) env = f (env name)
```

```
eval (Add {f} x y) env = f (eval x env +  eval y env)
eval (And {f} x y) env = f (eval x env && eval y env)
eval (Eq  {f} x y) env = f (eval x env == eval y env)
eval (Lit a)       env = a // constants Int and Bool
```

Here we need the type transforming function f from the bimap. The actual types are always correct, applying f is just needed to convince the Hindley-Milner type system that this is indeed correct. A GADT implementation will insert these functions without user interaction.

Our example and associated Start rule becomes:

```
e1 :: GadtExp Bool
e1 = And bm (Lit False) (Eq bm (Add bm (Lit 2) (Id bm "x")) (Lit 7))

Start = (eval e1 env1, show e1 [ ])
```

We use the environment env1 from the previous encoding in all examples in this Section. The obtained results are identical to the previous example.

3.3 Shallow Embedding of the DSL

In a shallow embedding, the DSL is represented as a set of functions. An expression is a function that takes the environment as its argument and produces a value of the indicated type. All operations become functions of this type. For compatibility, we use here function names that start with an uppercase character, note that these are really functions and not constructors used as functions. In Clean it is allowed to start function names with an uppercase character.

```
:: Exp a :== Env → a

Lit :: a → Exp a                              // literals of any type
Lit a = λe.a

Add :: (Exp Int) (Exp Int) → Exp Int
Add x y = λe.x e + y e

And :: (Exp Bool) (Exp Bool) → Exp Bool
And x y = λe.x e && y e

Eq :: (Exp a) (Exp a) → Exp Bool | == a
Eq x y = λe.x e == y e

Id :: Name → Exp Int
Id n = λe.e n
```

It is possible to hide the passing of the environment in a monad. Especially when the operations are able to change the environment, this is more elegant than explicitly passing this environment around.

In the shallow embedding our standard example and invoking evaluation by a Start rule looks like:

```
e1 :: Exp Bool
e1 = And (Lit False) (Eq (Add (Lit 2) (Id "x")) (Lit 7))

Start = e1 env1
```

The advantage of the shallow embedding is that the type system of the host language can check all types in the DSL very well. Moreover, it is very easy to extend the DSL without touching the existing code. By just defining the desired functions the DSL is extended, the type system of the host language checks whether everything is properly defined. This blend very well with the usual way to extend programs; one can add functions and tailor-made abbreviations by need. This is the reason this embedding is used in many libraries adding new functionality to the host languages. For instance, the iTask DSL is added in this way to the host language Clean.

A substantial limitation of this shallow embedding is that it provides just one view. Typically, this view is the evaluation of the DSL. The elements of the DSL just implement the desired behaviour. Adding another view like pretty printing, compile-time optimization, or code generation in another language requires a significant change of design.

3.4 Shallow Embedding of the DSL with Multiple Views

Type classes provide a way to assign different views to a shallow embedded DSL. Actually, a type class allows us to define different functions with identical names. The actual type used for the type variables of the class determines the function used. This is fully integrated with every modern functional programming language; the system selects the desired function based on the available type information, or gives an error message that such a function cannot be found.

Based on these type classes we define a DSL with multiple views. The language itself becomes a type class. The view v is the type variable of this class. The functions in this class are the constructs in our DSL. For our running example this becomes:

```
class Exp v where
    Lit :: t                    → v t     | toString t
    Id  :: Name                 → v Int
    Add :: (v Int)  (v Int)     → v Int
    And :: (v Bool) (v Bool)    → v Bool
    Eq  :: (v t)    (v t)       → v Bool | ==, toString t
```

The type t of the actual language construct in the DSL is not a parameter of the type class. This connotes that any class restriction needed in the views must be stated in the class definition. This explains the class restrictions of Lit and Eq in this DSL definition. The toString is needed in the show view and the equality is needed in eval.

Adding more classes with the same type variable can extend the DSL at need. In an extreme case, any function in the class above becomes its own class. We just group operations of the DSL in a class to express their relation. Whenever one of the functions in such a class is needed in a particular view, all other functions must also be implemented. Note that the type argument v for the view requires the type of the DSL construct as its argument. So, it is a type constructor class.

The views are just instances of this type class. The Clean type system cannot distinguish functions with different types as instances of a class. Hence, we use a data type containing such a function as an instance. For the evaluation view, we define the type Eval. Apart from adding and removing the constructors Eval this definition is identical to the shallow embedding presented above.

```
:: Eval t = Eval (Env→t)

instance Exp Eval where
    Lit a                     = Eval λe.a
    Id  n                     = Eval λe.e n
    Add (Eval x) (Eval y) = Eval λe.x e +  y e
    And (Eval x) (Eval y) = Eval λe.x e && y e
    Eq  (Eval x) (Eval y) = Eval λe.x e == y e

eval :: (Eval t) → t
eval (Eval f) = f env1
```

We still use uppercase identifiers for functions to stay compatible with the deep embedded DSL names.

In contrast to the ordinary shallow embedding, it is here very easy to add a new view. Showing DSL expressions is just another instance of the class Exp. Just like the evaluation we define a data type Show for this instance of Exp. In line with the previous show views we use a continuation of type [String] to prevent appends in this view.

```
:: Show a = Show ([String]→[String])

instance Exp Show where
    Lit x                     = Show λc.[toString x: c]
    Id  name                  = Show λc.[name: c]
    Add (Show x) (Show y) = Show λc.["(","Add ":x [" ":y [")":c]]]
    And (Show x) (Show y) = Show λc.["(","And ":x [" ":y [")":c]]]
    Eq  (Show x) (Show y) = Show λc.["(","Eq " :x [" ":y [")":c]]]

show :: (Show a) → [String]
show (Show f) = f [ ]
```

The plumbing with the additional constructors and environments in these views is very standard. With a few auxiliary functions, this can be nicely hidden.

The definition of our running example and the Start rule looks again very familiar.

```
e1 :: v Bool | Exp v
e1 = And (Lit False) (Eq (Add (Lit 2) (Id "x")) (Lit 7))

Start = (eval e1, show e1)
```

This class-based way to define a DSL combines best of both worlds. The type system of the host language checks types as well as for any other function. One can always supply additional language constructs in the DSL by adding a new class. This requires no changes to the existing code at all. The type system of the host language will check whether the required instances of these classes are available. The views themselves can be made by need, but the host language compiler checks their availability at compile time of a DSL program. Like a deep embedded DSL, it is always possible to add a new view without touching existing code. Unlike a deep embedding, the host language compiler will check whether all the required parts of the DSL are defined. Apart from type constructor classes, which are part of modern functional programming languages for many years, no fancy type extension are needed for this powerful methodology to implement embedded domain-specific languages. Hence, we use this class–based architecture to construct a DSL for microprocessors.

4 The mTask DSL

As outlined in the introduction we want to create a task-oriented programming language to program microprocessors. In the long run, it should interoperate smoothly with the iTask system, such that parts of an iTask application can run on a microprocessor.

Due to the small amount of memory on a microprocessor (e.g., 2 KB RAM on an Arduino UNO), it is impossible to port the entire iTask system to microprocessors. A typical iTask program requires 100 MB of heap space. To run a task-based program in the limited memory of a microprocessor we reject the heap. Hence, we cannot have lazy evaluation and standard higher-order functions. Transforming higher-order functions to first order functions by defunctionalization introduces too many new functions for the limited flash memory available. Hence, we restrict our language to first order functions. We obtain a first order, strict language. This strictness matches very well with the imperative nature of controlling the input/output ports of the microprocessor.

The examples in Sect. 2 use shares to store state information. In our DSL this information is stored in a state that is passed around in a monadic style. Program specific fields of the state are defined by need.

Our DSL should be equipped with the possibility to define recursive functions. These functions will be used to express repetition. The functions also enable abstraction and code reuse.

The actions of the program can be grouped into tasks. These tasks are parameterized, just like functions, to tune their actions. Unlike functions, tasks are not executed immediately when they are encountered during program execution, but somewhere in the future. It is perfectly possible to schedule different tasks or multiple instances of the same task for future execution. Since we have no heap the current program cannot wait for the result of an invoked task. Task invocation immediately returns a value of type `Task`.

Instead of the functions `setup` and `loop`, our programs execute a single `main` expression. After executing the main expression, the system repeatedly takes a task from the pool of scheduled tasks and executes it. Executing a task can initiate any number of new tasks.

The Arduino examples above show that it is very common to wait for some time in programs interacting with their environment. To facilitate this, every task definition specifies a custom delay. The task will not be executed before the given time is passed. Whenever it is necessary, the actual task invocation can have a customized delay.

The DSL is defined by a set of type classes. The functions in the classes define the allowed constructs in the mTask language. There is one instance of these classes for each view of the DSL. In this paper, we will use code generation and translation to the host language Clean as views. This can be extended with views like pretty printing and partial evaluation.

4.1 Expressions

The basic class of our DSL is `arith`. It contains a function `lit` to lift a constant from the host language to mTask, and some basic operations. Like any class in the DSL, `arith` is based on a type constructor type `v t p`, where `v` is the view, `t` is the type of the mTask construct, and `p` indicates whether the expression is an updatable position, an arbitrary expression or a statement.

```
class arith v where
    lit :: t → v t Expr | toCode t
    (+.) infixl 6 :: (v t p) (v t q) → v t Expr
                   | type, + t & isExpr p & isExpr q
    (-.) infixl 6 :: (v t p) (v t q) → v t Expr
                   | type, - t & isExpr p & isExpr q
    (*.) infixl 7 :: (v t p) (v t q) → v t Expr
                   | type, * t & isExpr p & isExpr q
    (/.) infixl 7 :: (v t p) (v t q) → v t Expr
                   | type, / t & isExpr p & isExpr q
```

The names of these operators are slightly different from the usual operator names in Clean. Since the types are different from the usual operators we cannot use instances of these operators. We do not redefine the operators in Clean since they coexist in programs with embedded DSL components. By convention, we add a dot to the operator name. The class restrictions `toCode t` and `type t` guarantee that we can only lift types that can become code to the DSL level, and use DSL type of arguments for the operators respectively. Currently there are instances of `toCode` for the basic types and `String`. There are instances of the basic types for `type`. The class restriction to the corresponding operator in Clean guarantees that we can apply the corresponding operator in the DSL simulator.

These class members yield an expression of type `Expr`. The mTask language has three kinds of constructs: updatable state elements, expressions, and statements. These kinds are identified by single constructor types.

```
:: Update = Update
:: Expr   = Expr
:: Stmt   = Stmt
```

The difference between expressions and statements is guided by the generated code. The arguments of the binary operations should be compilable to expression instead of statements. This implies that only updatable elements and expressions are allowed. This is checked at compile time by the class `isExpr`. The function `isExpr` is never used, its only purpose is to guarantee the contents restriction.

```
class isExpr a :: a → Int
instance isExpr Update where isExpr _ = 0
instance isExpr Expr   where isExpr _ = 1
```

The class `boolExpr` contains the Boolean operators, the overloaded equality and comparison operators. The new class shows that the DSL is extendable. More operators can be added by need without changing existing code.

```
class boolExpr v where
  (&.) infixr 3 :: (v Bool p) (v Bool q) → v Bool Expr
                 | isExpr p & isExpr q
  (|.) infixr 2 :: (v Bool p) (v Bool q) → v Bool Expr
                 | isExpr p & isExpr q
  Not :: (v Bool p) → v Bool Expr | isExpr p
  (==.) infix 4 :: (v a p) (v a q) → v Bool Expr
                 | ==, type a & isExpr p & isExpr q
  (!=.) infix 4 :: (v a p) (v a q) → v Bool Expr
                 | ==, type a & isExpr p & isExpr q
  (<.)  infix 4 :: (v a p) (v a q) → v Bool Expr
                 | Ord, type a & isExpr p & isExpr q
  (>.)  infix 4 :: (v a p) (v a q) → v Bool Expr
                 | Ord, type a & isExpr p & isExpr q
  (≤.) infix 4 :: (v a p) (v a q) → v Bool Expr
                 | Ord, type a & isExpr p & isExpr q
  (≥.) infix 4 :: (v a p) (v a q) → v Bool Expr
                 | Ord, type a & isExpr p & isExpr q
```

4.2 Arduino Data Types

The Arduino programming language comes with a rich set of basic data types. Characters and Booleans nicely match the corresponding data types in our host language Clean. There are only some minor syntax differences that are handled by the class `toCode` that transforms values to their string representation.

Integers on the Arduino come in various sizes: **byte** of 8 bits, **int** of 16 bits, and **long** of 32 bits. These types come in a signed as well as in an unsigned variant. In our DSL we will use the Clean type `Int` as the representation of the default type **int** of the Arduino. Currently, we ignore differences due to overflow on the Arduino and in the simulation view. In addition, we introduce a type `Long` to mimic the 32-bit integers of the Arduino.

```
:: Long = L Int
```

To use this type in both views of our DSL we define instances of the arithmetic operations for this type. Some typical examples are:

```
instance + Long where (+) (L x) (L y) = L (x + y)
instance one Long where one = L one
```

For the conversion of ordinary integers to longs we define the class `long`.

```
class long v t :: (v t p) → v Long Expr | isExpr p
```

The inverse transformation from **long** to **int** looses information and is hence much less used. For the sake of compactness, we restrict ourselves here to the types `Int` and `Long` and the single transformation `long`. More types and conversions can be added in the same style. Using functional dependencies it is possible to use the arithmetic operations of a class like `arith` with mixed integer representations [23]. In the Arduino C++ version this mixed used of integer representations and the implicit insertion of the required conversions is hard-wired into the language.

Similar representation issues apply for the floating-point numbers and more complex native types like strings and arrays. Currently, the basic type `Real` of the host language is used as the type of floating-point numbers in our DSL. Whenever the need for various representations arises, they will be introduced similar to the various types for integers. Note that also these changes of the DSL are incremental, there is no need to change existing views.

4.3 Conditionals

The class `If` contains only the conditional expression of the DSL. The `If` has a DSL expression of the `Bool` as argument and two DSL expressions of type `t`. Any expression/statement type for the last two arguments is allowed. The result is a DSL component of type `t`. Whether the conditional yields an expression or a statement is determined by the kind of the argument using a functional dependency. The `~s` indicates that this class variable is dependent on the other class variables. There is also an infix conditional that has only a then part. It is a statement with a void result ().

```
class If v q r ~s where
  If :: (v Bool p) (v t q) (v t r) → v t s | isExpr p
class IF v where
  (?) infix 1 :: (v Bool p) (v t q) → v () Stmt | isExpr p
```

4.4 Shared Data Sources

As outlined above, it is necessary to have user-defined fields in the state that passed around. In an imperative language adding a field to the state is just a variable definition. For small embedded systems defining variables in the DSL is quite convenient, but it is not required by our approach to constructing DSLs at all. In the mTask system, we use a shared data source, SDS, for the communication between tasks. This way of task communication is directly copied from the iTask system. Since the mTask system uses strict evaluation, the state containing these shares can be implicitly passed around. There is no need for a state monad to obtain referential transparency. Although the shares are intended for task communication, they can also be used to store parts of the state of individual tasks. Using task arguments is the preferred functional approach, but the shares can be used as ordinary variables.

Shares in mTask can be introduced by the class sds. The first argument is the initial value of the share. This value determines the type of the share. The second argument is a function that takes the share in the current view as argument and yields an arbitrary construct in the DSL. The introduced share can be updated as indicated by the kind Update. There is also a con to define constants. Its kind is Expr instead of Update to indicate that a constant cannot be updated.

```
class sds v where
  sds :: t ((v t Update)→(Main (v c s))) → (Main (v c s)) | type t
  con :: t ((v t Expr)  →(Main (v c s))) → (Main (v c s)) | type t
```

The type Main packs a value in a record. It is defined as:

```
:: Main a = { main :: a }

unMain :: (Main a) → a
unMain m = m.main
```

Its only purpose is to make the main expression of mTask programs recognizable by the type system. The use of a record provides the desirable curly braces. shares are introduced by a function. The argument represents the share in the DSL program. Its type v t Update ensures that it is used only in a well-typed manner. There is no other way to specify shares; hence, all shares in the DSL are properly defined.

We can assign a new value to such a share in the DSL by the class assign. The first argument is the share that is required to be updatable by Update. It is required that the new value given by the second argument has the same type t as the share.

```
class assign v where
  (=.) infixr 2 :: (v t Update) (v t p) → v t Expr | type t
```

A minimal example is:

```
e1 =
  sds 6 λx.
  {main =
    x =. x *. lit 7
  }
```

Here we define a share with the name x. Its initial value is 6. This program assigns the value x multiplied by 7 to this share.

We omit the types of our example programs in mTask. The host language compiler is perfectly capable to derive these types. In the current example this is v Int Expr | arith & sds & assign v. For larger examples, there is generally a long list of class restrictions. This list contains all classes that contain mTask constructs used in the example.

4.5 Monadic Bind

There is a monadic bind operator, ≫= , in mTask. In the variant :. the second argument does not need the result of the first argument. This is just the semicolon from imperative programming, or the sequence operator >>.

```
class bind v where
  (≫=) infixr 0 :: (v t p) ((v t Expr) → (v u q)) → v u Stmt
                   | type t & type u
  (:.)   infixr 0 :: (v t p) (v u q) → v u Stmt | type t & type u
```

There is no explicit return, all results are implicit returns. See Sect. 4.9 for the first example.

4.6 Input–Output Pins

A distinguished property of microprocessor programming is the direct access to the input and output pins of the microprocessor. Often this access will be done by the library controlling the shields stacked on the Arduino, or connected to the microprocessor. In simple situations, like the control of a LED or relay, the pins are usually directly controlled by the user program. To this end, we define some data types and classes.

The input–output pins of the Arduino come into two flavours. The digital pins are either low or high, represented as false or true. An Arduino Uno has 14 of these pins. Each of these pins can be used as input or output. The 6 analogue pins contain a 10-bit analogue to digital converter. Any input voltage between 0 and 5 V is mapped to an integer between 0 and 1023. Writing an integer value between 0 and 255 to these pins results in a pulse width modulated, PWM, output signal. This is a steady square wave output signal with the specified duty cycle. It can be used to vary the brightness of a LED or speed of a motor without generating heat in the microprocessor of the attached motor driver. By quickly switching the digital pins on and off we can achieve a similar PWM output effect on any output pin. There are special libraries implementing conveniently the generation of PWM signals on arbitrary output pins. These libraries use the native Arduino timers instead of a simple loop with blocking delays.

We can indicate the pins by an integer pin number. This simple scheme has as drawback that the integers can also indicate non-existing pins. To prevent this we have created enumeration types for the digital and analogue pins. The number of pins is tailor-made for the Arduino Uno, but can easily be changed for any other microprocessor. The PinMode indicates either input, output, or input where an unconnected pin is connected internally to positive power voltage, INPUT_PULLUP, by a pull-up resistor.

```
:: DigitalPin
   = D0 | D1 | D2 | D3 | D4 | D5 |D6 | D7 | D8 | D9 | D10 | D11 | D12 | D13
:: AnalogPin = A0 | A1 | A2 | A3 | A4 | A5
:: PinMode   = INPUT | OUTPUT | INPUT_PULLUP
:: Pin       = Digital DigitalPin | Analog AnalogPin
```

The class pin can be used to convert any pin to the unified Pin type.

```
class pin p | type, == p where
   pin :: p → Pin
instance pin DigitalPin where pin p = Digital p
instance pin AnalogPin  where pin p = Analog  p
```

With these primitives, we can make classed to set the mode of any pin, to read and write digitally to any pin, and set the described input and output to the analogue pins.

```
class pinMode v where
   pinmode :: p PinMode → v () Expr | pin p
class digitalIO v where
   digitalRead  :: p → v Bool Expr | pin, readPinD p
   digitalWrite :: p (v Bool q) → v Bool Expr | pin, writePinD  p
class analogIO v where
   analogRead  :: AnalogPin → v Int Expr
   analogWrite :: AnalogPin (v Int p) → v Int Expr
```

Instead of digitalWrite and analogWrite it would be possible to use a variant of the assignment operator for these output actions, or state changes. We have chosen for the current architecture to stay close to the Arduino C++ primitives and to avoid overloading of the assignment operator.

4.7 Shield Control

To lift the C++ classes controlling a shield to mTask we introduce a class containing the shield manipulations in the host language. As an example, we show how to control an LCD. The LCD object is created by liquidCrystal. This object is introduced very similar to shares. The manipulation functions take this object as its first argument. Hence, they always act on a properly defined LCD object. In contrast to the plain Arduino constructor, this constructor takes the size of the display as an argument. This eliminates the need for a method call begin with this size as argument in the main expression. The other arguments correspond one-to-one with the arguments of the methods in the C++ class.

```
class lcd v where
  print          :: (v LCD Expr) (v t p) → v Int Expr|stringQuotes t
  setCursor      :: (v LCD Expr) (v Int p) (v Int q) → v () Expr
  scrollLeft     :: (v LCD Expr) → v () Expr
  scrollRight    :: (v LCD Expr) → v () Expr
  liquidCrystal ::
    Int Int [DigitalPin] ((v LCD Expr)→Main (v b q))→Main (v b q)
```

Example 1. Hello world

The program that prints a message on a 16 × 2 LCD looks like:

```
helloLCD =
  liquidCrystal 16 2 [ ] λlcd.
```

```
  {main =
     print lcd (lit "Hello world")
  }
```

The list of digital pins in the argument of the constructor specifies to which pins the LCD is connected. An empty list is automatically converted to the most common list of pins.

In the same style we add a servo-control class.

```
:: Servo = {pin :: String , pos :: Int }

class servo v where
  attachS :: (v Servo q) (v p r)→v () Expr|pin p & isExpr r
  writeS  :: (v Servo q) (v Int q) → v () Expr
  servo   :: ((v Servo p)→(Main (v t q))) → (Main (v t q))
```

There are embeddings for the classes `Serial`, and `newPing` in the same fashion. Other classes from the large collection of available libraries are added to mTask by need.

4.8 Function Definitions

Function definitions are implemented similarly to shares. The main difference is that the function introducing the function name needs two arguments: the function body and the main expression. These elements are grouped by the infix constructor `def In main` of type `In def main`. The function body needs the name of the function in recursive functions. The function body itself is a function in the host language taking the function arguments in the host language as arguments. The class for function definitions in mTask is:

```
class fun v t where
  fun :: ((t→v s Expr)→In (t→v s p) (Main (v u q))) → Main (v u q)
      | type s

:: In def main = In infix 0 def main
```

Note that this class has two class arguments; the familiar view `v` and the type of the function argument `t`. By making the type of the function argument a type class argument, we can control the function arguments allowed in mTask, and create the desired instances of the function definition. Moreover, the type of the argument of the mTask function is available in Clean. Below we will see that this type is required in the views.

Example 2. Factorial Function

Using these definitions we can define the famous factorial function and the main expression applying it to 5 as:

```
e2 =
  fun
    λfac.(\n.If (n ≤. One) One (n *. fac (n -. One)))
```

```
  In
  {main =
    fac (lit 5)
  }

One :: v Int Expr | arith v
One = lit 1
```

Currently, there are instances of the class `fun` allowing basic types, i.e. instances of the class `type`, and tuples with zero, two, three and four of these types as arguments. Since there is no instance of `type` for functions the type system of Clean prevents higher order functions in mTask programs.

4.9 Task Definitions

Task definitions are very similar to function definitions. The result of such a task is of type `Task` instead of an instance of `type`. Remember that the operational semantics of a task is different than of a function. Functions are evaluated immediately in our imperative DSL. Tasks are evaluated somewhere in the future. The additional integer argument in task definitions is the minimal delay in milliseconds between task invocation and actual task execution.

```
class mtask v a where
 task :: Int ((a→v MTask Expr)→In (a→v u p) (Main (v t q)))
         → Main (v t q) | type t & type u
```

Example 3. Blinking Task

The task blink switches the LED on digital pin 13 every 500 ms. The argument `b` of the task indicates the new state of the LED. The main expression makes pin `D13` an output and starts the blink task.

```
blink =
    task 500 λblink.
      (λb. digitalWrite D13 b :.
           blink (Not b)) In
    {main =
        pinmode D13 OUTPUT :.
        blink (lit True)
    }
```

This example illustrates that, in contrast to the Arduino `loop ()`, tasks are not repeated by default. When repetition is needed, a task can call any number of tasks in its body. Here, the task `blink` is called with the inverted Boolean value. Tasks can have the same type of arguments as functions.

The type `MTask` is different from the ordinary type `Task a` in the `iTask` system. Since these types coexist in programs, like the simulator in Sect. 6, we use different names. In our DSL the type `MTask` just carries the information needed by the simulator described in Sect. 6. This happens to be just the index in the list of task invocations. Hence, we define:

```
:: MTask = MTask Int
```

Tasks have a default delay. This delay can be zero, but in many situations it is required to wait some time. For instance, the program has to wait until a signal becomes stable, to wait until the system can switch to the next state, and so on. Sometimes it is useful to change the default delay to a specific value in an individual invocation. This can be done with the function `setDelay`.

```
class setDelay v where
  setDelay :: (v Long p) (v MTask Expr) → (v MTask Expr) | isExpr p
```

Since `MTask` is not an instance of `type`, it is not possible to store task-ids in the state. We have designed `mTask` such that the delay can only be set during the creation an instance if the task.

Example 4. Clock with multiple instances of a task

The clock example shows that it is perfectly possible to have multiple instances of the same task. Here the same task is used to update hours, minutes and seconds. The different delays and position are arguments of the task.

```
clock =
  liquidCrystal 16 2 [ ] λlcd.
  fun λprintWithZero.
    (\n. n <. lit 10 ? print lcd Zero :. print lcd n) In
  task 0 \tick.
    (λ(n, max, pos, delay).
      setCursor lcd pos Zero :.
      printWithZero n :.
      setDelay (long delay *. lit (L 1000))
        (tick (If (n ==. max -. One) Zero (n +. One), max, pos, delay))
    ) In
  {main =
    print lcd (lit "00:00:00") :.
    tick (lit 0, lit 24, lit 0, lit (60*60)) :.
    tick (lit 0, lit 60, lit 3, lit 60) :.
    tick (lit 0, lit 60, lit 6, lit 1)
  }
```

4.10 Mutual Recursion

The scope of functions and tasks is determined by the scope of the functions getting their name. Typically these are nameless functions with the rest of the `mTask` program as a body. This implies that it is impossible to make mutual recursive functions and tasks. By defining two of them in one go this limitation can be circumvented.

```
class mtasks v a b where
  tasks :: Int Int ((a→v MTask Expr, b→v MTask Expr)→
              In (a→v t p, b→v u p) (Main (v s q))) → Main (v s q) | type s
```

Example 5. Mutual Recursion

A simple mTask program that scrolls the text `Hello World!` back and forth without using any state shares with two mutual recursive tasks is:

```
scroll =
  liquidCrystal 16 2 [ ] λlcd.
  tasks 400 600 λ(left, right).
    (\n. If (n <. lit (~steps))
          (right n)
          (scrollLeft lcd :. left (n -. One))
    ,\n. If (n >. lit steps)
          (left n)
          (scrollRight lcd :. right (n +. One))
    ) In
  {main =
    print lcd (lit "Hello world!") :.
    right Zero
  }
  where
    steps = 10
```

The sonar example illustrates the use of the host language Clean as "macro" language in the mTask DSL.

```
sonar maxDist =
  liquidCrystal 16 2 [ ] λlcd.
  servo λservo.
  newPing trigPin echoPin (max maxDist 5) λsonar.
  task 250 λping. (λ().
    ping_cm sonar ≫= .λdist.
    printAt lcd Zero One dist:. print lcd (lit " cm  "):.
    writeS servo (Limit minDegree maxDegree dist):.
    ping ()
  ) In
  {main =
     attachS servo servoPin :.
     print lcd (lit "echo distance") :.
     ping ()
  }

trigPin    = A1
echoPin    = A2
servoPin   = lit A5
minDegree  = lit 10
maxDegree  = lit 170

printAt :: (v LCD Expr) (v Int b) (v Int c) (v t e) → v Int Stmt
        | lcd, bind v & stringQuotes t
printAt lcd x y z = setCursor lcd x y :. print lcd z
```

```
Limit :: (v t p) (v t q) (v t r) → v t s
    | boolExpr v & Ord, toCode t
    & isExpr p & isExpr q & isExpr u & isExpr r & If v p r u & If v u q s
Limit low up x = Min (Max x low) up

Min :: (v t p) (v t q) → v t r
    | boolExpr v & Ord, toCode t & isExpr p & isExpr q & If v p q r
Min x y = If (x <. y) x y

Max :: (v t p) (v t q) → v t r
    | boolExpr v & Ord, toCode t & isExpr p & isExpr q & If v q p r
Max x y = If (x <. y) y x
```

Fortunately, the elaborated types of the auxiliary DSL definitions `printAt`, `Limit`, `Min`, and `Max` are derived by the host language compiler. It is not necessary to write these types manually.

This concludes our description of the language mTask. There are few other classes in our DSL containing additional operators and convenience definitions. Due to the architecture that builds the language as a set of classes, it is easy to add classes without influencing the existing code.

4.11 Examples

To illustrate task-oriented programming on microprocessors we present a few additional examples. The program `demo1` shows that it is very well possible to have related as well as unrelated tasks running concurrently on a microprocessor. In the Arduino examples of Sect. 2 this is problematic since the programs contain explicit `delay` statements. When we simply combine the `setup` and `loop` functions of several programs these delays add up to a long delay in the `loop`. The timing of the various components changes much more as necessary based on pure processing time. Our setup with minimum waiting times does not suffer from this problem.

Example 6. Clock

In this example, there are three instances of the task `tick` implementing a clock similar to the one presented above. The task `tick` invokes itself recursively with the appropriate delay passed as parameter. In addition, there is un uncoupled task `swing` that swings the position of a servo repeatedly from a minimum number of degrees to the maximum and back. When the servo turns it invokes a task `count` that counts the number of turns and displays it on the same LCD as the clock. The task `count` uses the share `turns` to count the number of turns.

```
demo1 =
  liquidCrystal 16 2 [] λlcd.
  task 0 \tick.
    (λ(n, max, pos, delay).
      setCursor lcd pos Zero :.
      n <. lit 10 ? print lcd Zero :.
```

```
      print lcd n :.
      setDelay (long delay *. lit (L 1000))
        (tick (If (n ==. max -. One) Zero (n +. One), max, pos, delay))
    ) In

  sds 0 \turns.
  task 0 λcount.
    (λ().
        turns =. turns +. One :.
        setCursor lcd Zero One :.
        print lcd turns
    ) In

  servo λservo.
    task 100 λswing.
    (λ(pos, step).
      step +. pos >>= .\new.
      If (new <. minDegree |. new >. maxDegree)
        (swing (pos, Zero -. step):.
         count ())
        (writeS servo new :.
       swing (new, step))
    ) In
  {main =
    print lcd (lit "00:00:00") :.
    tick (lit 0, lit 24, lit 0, lit (60*60)) :.
    tick (lit 0, lit 60, lit 3, lit 60) :.
    tick (lit 0, lit 60, lit 6, lit 1) :.
    attachS servo servoPin :.
    swing (lit 90, One)
  }
```

In this example the task `count` is started every now and then by the task `swing`, but apart from that there is no task communication.

Example 7. Servo Sweep

The next example shows that it is very well possible to have communicating tasks. The task `sweep` repeatedly increments the share `pos` by `step` and sets the servo position to this number of degrees. The task `turn` turns the direction of this sweep ever 25 s by inverting the value of the share `step`. Finally, there is a task `key` that repeatedly checks whether a key of the LCD-shield is pressed. Whenever a key is pressed the input voltage on pin A0 drops below 5v. Hence, the AD converter will produce a number below 1023 when we execute an `analogRead`. Here the value 900 is used as the threshold to prevent that small voltage fluctuation might accidentally trigger an action. When pressing a key is detected the position and direction of the servo are reset to their initial position by changing the shares.

```
demo2 =
   sds 1 λstep.
   task 25000 \turn.
   (λ().
      step =. Zero -. step:.
      turn ()
   ) In

   sds initPos λpos.
   task 500 λkey.
   (λ().
      analogRead A0 <. lit 900 ? (pos =. lit initPos :. step =. One) :.
      key ()
   ) In

   servo λservo.
   task 250 λsweep.
   (λ().
      pos =. pos +. step:.
      writeS servo pos :.
      sweep ()
   ) In
   {main =
      attachS servo servoPin :.
      key () :.
      turn () :.
      sweep ()
   }
where
   initPos = 30
```

Example 8. Displaying Temperature and Humidity

One of the many ways to measure the temperature with an Arduino is by using one of the DHT sensors. The DHT11 is a relatively cheap sensor for measuring temperature and humidity [8]. The DHT22 is similar to the DHT11 but has greater accuracy. Both sensors have a (different) single-wire digital serial interface. Apart from the power and ground connections, only one single wire is used for the digital communication between the sensor and the microprocessor. This communication is handled by a library offering a tailor-made C++ class. We will use the DHT-sensor-library from Adafruit [1]. The embedding of this library is very similar to the library for liquid crystal displays:

```
class dht v where
  dht :: p DHTtype ((v DHT Expr)→Main (v b q)) → Main (v b q) | pin p
  temperature :: (v DHT Expr) → v Real Expr
  humidity    :: (v DHT Expr) → v Real Expr

:: DHTtype = DHT11 | DHT21 | DHT22
```

In this example we create a dht object handling the sensor and an lcd object handling the 1602 LCD. There is a single task that reads and displays every second the temperature and the humidity.

```
displayTemp =
  dht A1 DHT11 λdht =
  liquidCrystal 16 2 [] λlcd =
  task 1000 \t = (λ().
    printAt lcd Zero Zero (lit "Temp ") :.
    print lcd (temperature dht) :.
    print lcd (lit " C") :.
    printAt lcd Zero One (lit "Humidity ") :.
    print lcd (humidity dht) :.
    print lcd (lit "% ") :.
    t ()
  ) In
  {main = t Zero ()}
```

Example 9. Thermostat

Based on this DHT11 temperature sensor we construct a simple thermostat. Just like the previous example, there is a dht and an lcd object controlling the sensor and the display respectively. There is a share goal for the target temperature. The task temp just measures and displays the temperature every second. The task keys checks every 250 ms if the up-key or the down-key is pressed. When a key is pressed, the goal temperature is adjusted accordingly. The task control compares the actual temperature with the goal temperature and switches the heating whenever desired. The Boolean argument of this task is the current state of the heating system controlled by pin D13. When the state changes, the task waits the corresponding minimum on or off time. Without a state switch, the task is repeated every 500 ms. Even when the control task is blocked due to a recent state switch, the temp task adjusts the display and the keys task updates the goal temperature at their own rate.

```
thermostat =
  dht A1 DHT11 λdht =
  liquidCrystal 16 2 [] λlcd =
  sds λgoal = 20.0 In
  task 1000 \temp = (λ().        // adjust current temperature on LCD
    printAt lcd Zero Zero (lit "temp ") :.
    print lcd (temperature dht) :.
    temp ()) In
  task 250 λkeys = (λ().        // adjust goal temperature and adjust display
    IF (pressed upButton) (
      goal =. goal +. step
    ) ((pressed downButton) ? (goal =. goal -. step)) :.
    printAt lcd Zero One (lit "goal ") :.
    print lcd goal :.
    keys ()
    ) In
```

```
  task 500 λcontrol = (λon.   // switch the heating whenever required
    temperature dht ≫=. \temp.
    IF (goal >. temp &. Not on) (
      digitalWrite D13 true :.
      printAt lcd (lit 11) Zero (lit "On ") :.
      setDelay minOnTime (control true)
    ) (IF (goal <. temp &. on) (
        digitalWrite D13 false :.
        printAt lcd (lit 11) Zero (lit "Off") :.
        setDelay minOffTime (control false)
      ) (control on)
    )
  ) In
  {main =
    temp () :.
    keys () :.
    control false
  }
where
  step = lit 0.5                    // change in goal temperature when button is pressed
  minOnTime  = lit (L 60000)  // 60 seconds
  minOffTime = lit (L 90000)  // 90 seconds
```

These examples show that we have achieved task-oriented programming of microprocessors. Tasks are parameterized by their argument and have a user-defined standard delay. It is perfectly possible for tasks to invoke each other or call themselves recursively, they can even be mutually recursive. It is also possible to execute several unrelated and related tasks simultaneously. In the next section, we show that this can be implemented within a fixed amount of memory. Whenever desired, tasks can be made so that they communicate via custom defined shares.

4.12 Software Download

The software described in this paper is used in our research and education. The system is actively maintained and developed. The current version can always be found at https://gitlab.science.ru.nl/mlubbers/mTask. This site contains an installation guide and explains how the system should be used. It is intended to work on Windows, Linux as well as on Mac OS X. This version of the mTask system works with the most recent version of the Clean system which is available at https://clean.cs.ru.nl/Download_Clean.

5 The Code Generation View of mTask

The most important view of mTask generates code of DSL programs that can be executed on a microprocessor. In this paper, we will generate C++ code from the mTask constructs directly. Functions and expressions in our DSL will be mapped rather directly to corresponding C++ constructs. This is a rather extraordinary implementation route for functional programming languages. In general, the need for heap manipulations, especially garbage collection, make a direct translation of a functional language to C++ impractical. In mTask we carefully avoided a heap due to memory size restrictions. The distinction between `Expr` and `Stmt` ensures that all mTask expressions of kind `Expr` can be translated to C++ expressions (without the need to introduce additional helper functions). Since there are only first-order functions with proper names on the outermost level, the functions of our DSL can be directly mapped to functions in C++.

This architecture comes with some clear advantages. **(1)** It is easier to generate C++ code than low-level machine code for a microprocessor. We profit from all optimizations of the existing compiler from C++ to microprocessor code. **(2)** The code generation is to a large extent microprocessor independent. The Arduino system contains code generators for various microprocessors. **(3)** It is obvious how the existing ecosystem of shields and associated C++ libraries can be used in mTask. We just have to extend our DSL with a one-to-one mapping of the relevant methods of the C++ class. The LCD library in Sect. 4.7 illustrates this. **(4)** Whenever necessary C gives enough low-level control to implement additional optimization in the future.

5.1 Data Type for Compilation

Any view `v` of our DSL requires two arguments: the type `t` and the kind `k`. The data type `Code` uses neither of these arguments. This type contains just a function changing the state, `CODE`, of the code generation. In this state we store the actual code in four different flavours: functions, shares, code for the `setup` function, and code for the `loop` function. In addition, it stores book-keeping fields for generating fresh identifiers for names in the generated code, the appropriate indentation in the various contexts, the kind of code currently generated in `def`, and the `mode` whether we need to decorate the code with a `return` or a semicolon.

```
:: Code t k = C (CODE → CODE)
:: CODE =
    { fresh     :: Int          // to generate id's
    , freshTask :: Int          // to generate task id's
    , funs      :: [String]     // code for functions
    , ifuns     :: Int          // indentation for functions
    , sdss      :: [String]     // code for shares
    , isdss     :: Int          // indentations for shares
    , setup     :: [String]     // code for setup() function
    , isetup    :: Int          // indentation in setup()
    , loop      :: [String]     // code for loop() function
    , iloop     :: Int          // indentation foor loop()
    , includes  :: [String]     // names of included libraries
    , def       :: Def          // definition switch: where the code goes in
this state
```

```
  , mode        :: Mode                      // decoration mode of translation
  }

:: Def  = SDS | Fun | Setup | Loop
:: Mode = NoReturn | Return String | SubExp | Assign String
```

There is a set of manipulation functions. For instance, the function c adds code to the current definition, and the operator +.+ composes two code generation functions.

```
c :: a → Code b p | toCode a
c a =  C λc.case c.def of
       Fun    = {c & funs  = [toCode a: c.funs]}
       SDS    = {c & sdss  = [toCode a: c.sdss]}
       Setup  = {c & setup = [toCode a: c.setup]}
       Loop   = {c & loop  = [toCode a: c.loop]}

(+.+) infixl 5 :: (Code a p) (Code b q) → Code c r
(+.+) (C f) (C g) = C (g o f)
```

The mode of the code-state controls the generation of embedding C++ keywords like return and the semicolon. Subexpressions do not need any embedding. As everywhere else, the definition switch of the code state controls to what part of the code the output goes.

```
embed :: (Code a p) → Code a p
embed e =
  getMode λm. case m of
    NoReturn = setMode SubExp +.+ e +.+ c ";"
     Return t = c "return " +.+ setMode SubExp +.+ e +.+ c ";"
    Assign s = c (s+" = ") +.+ setMode SubExp +.+ e +.+ c ";"
    SubExp   = e
```

The actual compilation applies the code generation function to the initial CODE state and composes all code strings in the right order. The simplified version without predefined shares and the loop function reads like:

```
compile :: (Main (Code a p)) → [String]
compile {main=(C f)} =
  reverse c.sdss ++
  reverse c.funs ++
  ["void setup () {\n"
  ,"  Serial.begin(9600);\n"
  :reverse c.setup
  ] ++ ["\n}\n"]
where c = f newCode
```

The actual compile function is about 90 lines long and listed in Appendix A.

5.2 Code Generation for Expressions

These preparations enable code generation for expressions as:

```
instance arith Code where
  lit a = embed (c a)
  (+.) x y = codeOp2 x " + " y
  (-.) x y = codeOp2 x " - " y
  (*.) x y = codeOp2 x " * " y
  (/.) x y = codeOp2 x " / " y

codeOp2 :: (Code a p) String (Code b q) → Code c r
codeOp2 x n y = embed (brac (x +.+ c n +.+ y))

brac :: (Code a p) → Code b q
brac e = c "(" +.+ e +.+ c ")"
```

The code generation for the operators from the class `BoolExpr` is very similar and omitted for brevity.

5.3 Code Generation for Arduino Data Types

The Arduino code does all the hard work. When a 16-bit integer has to be transformed to a 32-bit version, we insert `long`. Transforming a `Long` to a `Long` done by the identity function, an efficient implementation requires no generated code at all.

```
instance long Code Int where
    long x = embed (c "long" +.+ brac x)
instance long Code Long where
    long x = embed (toE x)
```

The auxiliary class `toE` ensures that the kind of the result is an expression. For expressions, this is just the identity function. For shares that all have kind `Update`, the kind is replaced by `Expr`:

```
class toE v :: (v t p) → v t Expr | isExpr p

instance toE Code where toE (C c) = C c
```

For the simulation view, we have a similar instance of this class.

There is a class `toCode` that transforms basic values to their representation in the Arduino variant of C++. For integers, this is just the accompanying `toString` instance. For Booleans, we have to take care of the lowercase in the constant name. For a `Long` we add the letter `L` to the end of the integer value.

```
class toCode a :: a → String

instance toCode Int where toCode a      = toString a
instance toCode Bool where toCode b     = if b "true" "false"
instance toCode Long where toCode (L i) = toCode i + "L"
```

All other types are handled similarly.

5.4 Code Generation for Conditionals

Code generation for conditionals distinguishes two situations. We generate a conditional statement when one or more of the branches is a statement. Otherwise, we generate the C++ conditional expression `c ? t : e`. The functional dependency in the class definition ensures that the type entire conditional construct has kind `Stmt` when one of the branches is a statement. When none of the branches is a statement, the conditional itself is an expression.

```
instance If Code Stmt Stmt Stmt where If c t e = IfStm c t e
instance If Code e    Stmt Stmt where If c t e = IfStm c t e
instance If Code Stmt e    Stmt where If c t e = IfStm c t e
instance If Code x    y    Expr where If c t e = IfExp c t e

IfExp b t e =
     embed (brac (b +.+ indent +.+ nl +.+ c " ? " +.+ t +.+ nl +.+
                  c " : " +.+ e +.+ unindent))
```

Code generation for a statement with `IfStm` is similar, but slightly bigger, to code generation for expressions.

```
IfStmt b t e =
  getMode λmode.
    let
      sds = sdsName t
      newMode =
        case mode of
          Return s = Return s
          _        = if (sds == "") NoReturn (Assign sds)
    in
      setMode SubExp +.+
      c "if " +.+ brac b +.+ c " {" +.+
        indent +.+ nl +.+ setMode newMode +.+ t +.+ unindent +.+ nl +.+
        c "} else {" +.+ indent +.+ nl +.+ setMode newMode +.+ e +.+
        unindent +.+ nl +.+ c "}" +.+ setMode mode +.+
      case newMode of
        Assign _ = embed (c sds) // return value only if newMode = Assign
        _        = C id
```

5.5 Code Generation for Share Definitions

For share and constant definitions, we generate exactly the same code. The difference between those definitions in mTask is made due to the kind argument by the type system of the host language. It is possible to add the keyword `const` to generate C++ code of a constant definition, but this is not required. The actual work is done by `defCode`. It generates a fresh share name, `name`. The actual definition of a global variable is added to the share definition part of the code. In the value `embed name` is used as actual value for applied occurrences of this share in this view. This is achieved by supplying this value to the function f that produces the main expression. The code for main is directed towards the body of the setup function.

```
instance sds Code where
  sds v f = defCode v f
  con v f = defCode v f

defCode :: t ((Code t p)→Main (Code u q)) → Main (Code u r) | type t
defCode v f =
  {main = fresh \n.
    let
      name = c ("v" + toCode n)
    in
      setCode SDS +.+ c (type2string v + " ") +.+ name +.+
      c (" = " + toCode v + ";\n") +.+
      setCode Setup +.+ unMain (f (embed name))
  }
```

Code generation for an assignment just generates the code for the share (generated by the share definition above), an equals sign and the code for the expression.

```
instance assign Code where
    (=.) v e = embed (setMode SubExp +.+ v +.+ c " = " +.+ e)
```

For instance, for example e1 from Sect. 4.4 the following code is generated:

```
int v0 = 6;

void setup () {
  v0 = (v0 * 7);
}
```

5.6 Code Generation for the Monadic Bind

For a monadic bind, we define a constant to store the result of the first argument. We use the name of this constant as an argument to the function on the right-hand side. By design, the kind of the introduced identifier is Expr instead of Update. This implies that it is not possible to update this identifier. In the code, we generate a constant to hold the value of the lefthand-side of the bind operator, if we would use the kind Update for the generated identifier, the variable would be updatable. In the code generation, we have to juggle a little with modes to ensure that a potential return goes to the second statement and the first statement gets just a semicolon.

```
instance bind Code where
  (>>=.) x f =
    getMode λmode. fresh \n.
      let
        v = c ("b" + toCode n)
```

```
    in
    sdsType x +.+ c " " +.+ setMode NoReturn +.+ v +.+
    c " = " +.+ x +.+ nl +.+ setMode mode +.+ f (embed v)
(:.) x y = getMode λmode. setMode NoReturn +.+ embed x +.+
          nl +.+ setMode mode +.+ y
```

5.7 Code Generation for Input–Output Pins

We have chosen to have the digital and analogue pins as separate fields in the evaluator state instead of ordinary values in the list of shares. Since there are a small number of pins we can use a simple association list between pin names and values. To keep the length of this list as short as possible in the GUI, we only store values actually used. All other pins get a default value when they are used.

Moreover, the read and write functions clearly distinguish whether we want to read or write to a pin. This eliminates the need for a type like `RW a` which was needed to distinguish the read and write contexts of the shares.

```
instance pinMode Eval where
  pinmode p m = rtrn ()
instance digitalIO Eval where
  digitalRead  p   = E λrw s=:{dpins, apins}.(readPinD p dpins apins, s)
  digitalWrite p b = b >>= λa. E λrw s.(a, writePinD p a s)
instance analogIO Eval where
  analogRead  p    = E λrw s=:{apins}. (readPinA p apins, s)
  analogWrite p b = b >>= λa. E λrw s.(a, writePinA p a s)
```

Reading and writing of analog pins is defined by two simple helper functions.

```
readPinA :: AnalogPin [(AnalogPin, Int)] → Int
readPinA p lista
  = case [b \\ (q, b) ← lista | p == q] of
    []    = 0
    [a:x] = a

writePinA :: AnalogPin Int State → State
writePinA p x s
  = {s & apins = [(p, x):[(q, y) \\ (q, y) ← s.apins | p ≠ q]]}
```

For the digital pins we need two classes to distinguish whether we are handling an analog pin or a digital pin.

5.8 Code Generation for Shield Classes

The object definition goes to the share part. Its name is given to the function generating the main expression. The manipulation functions take this name as first argument and yields code calling the appropriate methods in C++.

```
instance lcd Code where
  begin         v x y = embed (v +.+ c ".begin" +.+ codeOp2 x "," y)
  print         v x   = embed (v +.+ c".print("+.+quotes x+.+c ")")
  scrollLeft    v     = embed (v +.+ c ".scrollDisplayLeft()")
  scrollRight   v     = embed (v +.+ c ".scrollDisplayRight()")
  setCursor     v x y = embed (v +.+ c ".setCursor" +.+ codeOp2 x "," y)
  liquidCrystal x y [] f = liquidCrystal x y [D8, D9, D4, D5, D6, D7] f
  liquidCrystal x y pins f =
    {main =
      getCode λcd. fresh \n.
      let
        name = "lcd" + toString n
        rest = f (c name)
      in
        include "LiquidCrystal" +.+
        setCode SDS +.+
          c ("LiquidCrystal " + name + "(" + argList pins + ");\n") +.+
        setCode Setup +.+
          c (name + ".begin(" + toCode x + "," + toCode y +");") +.+ nl +.+
        setCode cd +.+
          rest.main
    }
```

5.9 Code Generation for Function Definitions

Our DSL is designed such that functions in mTask can be mapped directly to functions in C++. We designed the class `fun` such that we have to make an instance for every number of arguments allowed. Currently, we allow zero to four arguments. As an example, we show the code generation for a two-argument function. Based on a fresh number we generate names for the function, `fname`, and its arguments, `aname` and `bname`. The class `argTypes` yields the types of the arguments needed in the C++ function definition. Applied occurrences of the function take a Clean tuple of mTask expressions as an argument. The nameless function we supply as argument to `f` converts this to code for C++ arguments. In the function section of the code, we generate the C++ version of our DSL function. In the obtained function body `g` we use the generated formal arguments as actual arguments.

```
instance fun Code (Code a p, Code b q) | type a & type b where
  fun f =
    {main =
      getMode λmode. fresh \n.
      let
        fname = c ("f" + toCode n + " ")
        aname = c ("a" + toCode n + " ")
        bname = c ("b" + toCode n + " ")
        (atype, btype) = argTypes f
        (g In main) = f (λ(x,y).embed (fname +.+ codeOp2 x ", " y))
```

```
    in setCode Fun +.+ nl +.+ resType f +.+ fname +.+
       codeOp2 (atype +.+ aname) "," (btype +.+ bname) +.+
       funBody (setMode (Return (toCode (resType2 f))) +.+
                  g (embed aname, embed bname)) +.+
       setCode Setup +.+ setMode mode +.+ unMain main
    }
```

For the mTask program

```
e22 =
  con 6 λsix.
  fun λf.(λ(a,b).a +. One ≫=. λx. x *. b) In
  { main = serialPrint (f (six, six)) }
```

our compiler generates:

```
int v0 = 6;

int f1 (int a1, int b1);{
  int  b2 = (a1 + 1);
  return (b2 * b1);
}

void setup () {
  Serial.begin(9600);
  Serial.print(f1 (v0, v0));
}
```

5.10 Code Generation for Task Definitions

Although the definition of tasks is very similar to the definition of functions, the operational behaviour is quite different. Functions are evaluated strictly by compiling them directly to C++ functions. Tasks are scheduled for execution somewhere in the future.

Executing task in the future is implemented by a small array, `tasks`, of task activation records of C++ type `Task`. Each record contains the task-id (a small number that fits in a byte), a waiting time in milliseconds, and an array containing the arguments.

```
typedef union Arg {int i; bool b; char c; word w;} ARG;
typedef struct Task {byte id; long wait; ARG a[M_ARG];}TASK;

TASK tasks[MAX_TASKS];
```

The generated `loop()` function scans this array of tasks. When the next task in the array needs to wait before it may start, the task record is copied to the end of the sequence of waiting tasks in a round-robin arrangement. When the waiting time of the current task in the array has expired, the task body is executed. The generated `loop` function contains a case construct to select the proper task body. The task-id is used to find the appropriate code fragment.

The compilation scheme for `mtask` is very similar to the one for `fun`. Since we have also an `mtasks` class we distribute the code generation slightly different to reuse more code.

```
instance mtask Code a | taskImp a & types a where
  task i f =
   {main =
     freshTask \n.
       let
         (app, a)     = taskImp n types
         (b In main) = f (app i)
       in
         codeTaskBody (loopCode n (b a)) (unMain main)
   }
```

The class `taskImp` generates the task application and the formal arguments of the definition. A task application boils down to a call of `newTask` in the generated code with appropriate task-id, waiting time, and arguments. The instance for a two-argument task is:

```
class taskImp a :: Int a → (Int a→Code MTask Expr, a)

instance taskImp (Code a p, Code b q) where
  taskImp n (type1, type2) = (app, (ta1, ta2)) where
    ta1 = c "t0p→a[0]" +.+ type1
    ta2 = c "t0p→a[1]" +.+ type2
    app i (a1, a2) =
      embed (c "newTask(" +.+ c n +.+ c ", " +.+  c i +.+
      c ", " +.+ a1 +.+ c ", " +.+ a2 +.+ c ", 0, 0)")
```

The `loopCode` generates the appropriate case in the switch statement for this task. It just puts the code generated for the task body between a **case** and a **break**.

```
loopCode :: Int (Code a b) → Code c d
loopCode n b =
  nl +.+ c "case " +.+ c n +.+ c ": {" +.+ indent +.+ nl +.+
  setMode NoReturn +.+ b +.+ nl +.+ c "break;" +.+
  unindent +.+ nl +.+ c "} "
```

The function `codeTaskBody` ensures that the generated code goes to the right part of the produced C++ program.

In order to delay task execution, we change the waiting time of a task invocation in the array `tasks`. The generated code invokes the C++ function `setDelay` from our own library.

```
instance setDelay Code where
  setDelay d t = embed (c "setDelay" +.+ brac (t +.+ c ", " +.+ d))
```

The C++ function to change a delay gets the task index in the array of tasks and the new waiting time as arguments and updates the task record in the array of tasks with the given waiting time.

```
byte setDelay(byte t, long d) {
  tasks[t].wait = d;
  return t;
}
```

It would be better to set the desired waiting time directly in the C++ code. This requires the transformation of the generated code `setDelay(newTask(id, w1, a0, a1, a2, a3), w2)` by `newTask(id, w2, a0, a1, a2, a3)`. This is beyond the capabilities of our code generation view. In Sect. 7 we discuss optimizations that are capable to achieve this kind of transformations.

The generated `loop` for the `scroll` example from Sect. 5 is:

```
void loop () {
  if (t0 != tn) {
    if (t0 == tc) {          // update delta for all tasks
      unsigned long time2 = millis();
      delta = time2 - time;
      time = time2;
      tc = tn;               // update delta at a new task
    };
    TASK* t0p = &tasks[t0];
    t0p->wait -= delta;
    if (t0p->wait > 0L) { // task has to wait longer?
      newTask(t0p->id, t0p->wait, t0p->a[0].w, t0p->a[1].w,
              t0p->a[2].w, t0p->a[3].w);
    } else {                 // waiting is done: execute task
      switch (t0p->id) {  // select task
        case 0: {            // task left
          if ((t0p->a[0].i < -10)) {
            newTask(1, 600, t0p->a[0].i, 0, 0, 0);
          } else {
            lcd0.scrollDisplayLeft();
            newTask(0, 400, (t0p->a[0].i - 1), 0, 0, 0);
          }
          break;
        }
        case 1: {            // task right
          if ((t0p->a[0].i > 10)) {
            newTask(0, 400, t0p->a[0].i, 0, 0, 0);
          } else {
            lcd0.scrollDisplayRight();
            newTask(1, 600, (t0p->a[0].i + 1), 0, 0, 0);
          }
          break;
        }
      default:
        t0 = tn; // no known task: force termination
        return;
      };
    }
```

```
    t0 = NEXT_TASK(t0);
  }
}
```

The somewhat peculiar way to decrement all waiting times of tasks with the same `delta` ensures that all tasks that are created in `main` and all tasks started in that expression stay in sync. This is used for instance in our clock example in Sect. 4. When each task looks at the timer itself, we would get small deviations in accumulated waiting times since the actual timer of the Arduino counts in nanoseconds. Since tasks might consume an arbitrary amount of computation time, we can only ensure that task will not start before the waiting time is passed. When one task takes much computation time, the next task in the queue is delayed.

After 50 days the timer in the Arduino hardware will overflow. The calculation of `delta` should be somewhat more sophisticated to prevent problems at that moment.

6 The Simulation View

The next view translates mTask programs to plain Clean programs. This is very useful in a simulation of mTask programs. Since it is hard to debug programs running on an Arduino, simulation is an important tool to spot execution problems. In this section, we outline how to translate our DSL to the host language and we indicate how this can be simulated with an iTask program.

6.1 Data Type for Simulation

Similar to the code view, the evaluation view is a state transformer. The state in this view contains the relevant parts of the Arduino and the task queue. As Arduino parts, we have the declared shares, an abstraction of the IO-pins, the timer and the serial output.

```
:: State
  { mtasks :: [(Int, State→State)]    // delay and actual mtask
  , store  :: [Dyn]                   // user defined fields
  , dpins  :: [(DigitalPin, Bool)]    // used digital pins
  , apins  :: [(AnalogPin, Int)]      // used analog pins
  , serial :: [String]                // serial output
  , millis :: Int                     // the milli seconds of the Arduino clock
  }
```

The state transition takes a read/write value of type `RW t` as argument. This value determines whether a share occurs in a read, `R`, or write context, `W t`. The write context occurs on the left-hand side of assignments, everywhere else we have the read context. The function `F` value is used to update objects in the store.

```
:: Eval t p = E ((RW t) State → (t, State))
:: RW    t  = R | W t | F (t→t)
```

For convenience we define a tailor-made monadic bind, ≫=, and return, `rtrn`, for `Eval`. Since the usual names ≫= and `return` are used by the iTask system we use slightly different names.

```
(≫=) infixl 1 :: (Eval a p) (a→Eval b q) → Eval b r
(≫=) (E f) g = Eλr s.let (a,t) = f R s in unEval (g a) R t

rtrn :: a → Eval a q
rtrn a = E λr s → (a, s)

yield :: t (Eval s p) → Eval t Expr // effect of rtrn in Expr
yield a (E f) = E λr s.(a, snd (f R s))
```

6.2 Evaluating Expressions

The evaluation view of expression computes their value in the context of the monad introduced above.

```
instance arith Eval where
  lit  a   = rtrn a
  (+.) x y = x ≫= λa. y ≫= λb. rtrn (a + b)
  (-.) x y = x ≫= λa. y ≫= λb. rtrn (a - b)
  (*.) x y = x ≫= λa. y ≫= λb. rtrn (a * b)
  (/.) x y = x ≫= λa. y ≫= λb. rtrn (a / b)
```

6.3 Evaluation of Arduino Data Types

We have designed the DSL such that the types in the DSL match the types of the host language. This implies that no actions are required for the simulation of those data types.

The explicit type conversion to long integers is the only exception. Since these operations are part of our DSL, we need to provide an instance for their simulation. For ordinary integers this is just a type conversion from `Int` to `Long`. Long integers are already of the desired type, the code generator does not produce anything at all.

```
instance long Eval Int where
    long x = x ≫= rtrn o L
instance long Eval Long where
    long x = toE x
```

6.4 Evaluation of Conditionals

The evaluation of conditionals starts with the usual computation of the value of the condition in the monad. Based on the value of the condition either the **then**-branch or the **else**-branch will be chosen. For the operator ? there is no **else**-branch, we just return void if the condition evaluates to `False`. The `toExpr` in the `If` is necessary to ensure that the kind of the result is an expression.

```
instance If Eval p q Expr where
  If  c t e = c >>= λb.if b (toExpr t) (toExpr e)
instance IF Eval where
  IF  c t e = c >>= λb.if b (yield () t) (yield () e)
  (?) c t   = c >>= λb.if b (yield () t) (rtrn ())

toExpr :: (Eval t p) → (Eval t Expr)
toExpr (E f) = E f
```

6.5 Evaluation of Share Definitions

A share becomes an element in the list store. Since we have different type of share (e.g. `Int` and `Bool`), we store a dynamic representation of these values, a list of strings, instead of the values themselves. The element number in this list becomes the share identifier. Each applied occurrence of the identifier `v` is replaced by a piece of code that reads the value of store element n, `refer n`, form the value store. The value n is the position of the next share at the end of the store. The number n of the next share is computed by `length s.store`.

```
instance sds Eval where
  sds v f = defEval v f
  con v f = defEval v f

defEval v f =
  {main =
    E (λr s.(length s.store, {s & store = s.store ++ [toDyn v]}))
    >>= \n.unMain (f (E (refer n)))
  }
```

The handling of shares in expressions is somewhat challenging. On the left-hand side of an assignment, the share indicates the position to be updated. Any other occurrence of a share indicates a read access of this position. In such expressions, we want to write a plain share name, like `x`, instead of an explicit read operation, like `read x`. This is realized by the argument `RW t` of the evaluation function. This argument is nearly always `R` for reading. Only on the left-hand side of an assignment, we replace it by `W a` to write value `a`. In an object update, for shields, we replace the `R` by `F f`, where `f` the object update function is.

The function `refer` selects the appropriate element form the `store`. The read-write context, of type `RW t`, indicates the desired action with this share: `R` read, `W a` write value `a`, and `F f` apply function `f` to update the object:

```
refer :: Int (RW a) State → (a,State) | dyn a
refer n R     s = (fromJust (fromDyn (s.store !! n)), s)
refer n (W a) s = (a, {s&store=updateAt n (toDyn a) s.store})
refer n (F f) s = (obj, {s & store = updateAt n (toDyn obj) s.store})
where obj = f (fromJust (fromDyn (s.store !! n)))
```

As outlined above, the read-write context `RW a` of shares is always read `R`, except in an assignment. In an assignment we write the new value a with the read-write context `W a`. The new value is obtained by evaluating the expression `e` on the right-hand side of the assignment.

```
instance assign Eval where
  (=.) (E v) e = e >>= λa. E λr s.v (W a) s
```

This view of shares illustrates that the shares do respect the functional semantics. Due to the strict evaluation order of mTask programs the handling of the shares obeys referential transparency. The monad containing the values of the shares is passed around implicitly, but give mTask programs the desired functional semantics. This holds also for the class `bind` treated in the next subsection.

6.6 Evaluation of the Monadic Bind

The bind operators ≫= . and :. are directly translated to the corresponding operators in Clean.

```
instance bind Eval where
  (>>=.) x f = x >>= f o rtrn
  (:.)   x y = x >>= λ_. y
```

Since the values bound by these operators are constants in the mTask DSL, there is no reason to introduce a share for them in the store (as we did in the compilation view).

6.7 Evaluation of Input–Output Pins

The classes `pinMode`, `digitalIO`, and `analogIO` directly reflect the operations available in Arduino C++. Hence, code generation is very easy. The corresponding functions in C++ are called directly.

```
instance pinMode Code where
  pinmode      p m =
    embed (c ("pinMode(" + toCode p + ", " + consName{|*|} m + ")"))
instance digitalIO Code where
  digitalRead  p   = embed (c ("digitalRead(" + toCode p + ")"))
  digitalWrite p b =
    embed (c ("digitalWrite(" + toCode p + ", ") +.+ b +.+ c ")")
instance analogIO Code where
  analogRead   p   = embed (c ("analogRead(" + toCode p + ")"))
  analogWrite  p b =
    embed (c ("analogWrite(" + toCode p + ", ") +.+ b +.+ c ")")
```

6.8 Evaluation of Shield Control

In the iTask system, the simulation of shields can be as fancy as one can imagine. Here we present a very simple version where the objects controlling a shield are elements in the `store`.

The `servo` definition adds the object to the store and yields the appropriate selection function. The `attach` and `write` methods update the object in the store.

```
instance servo Eval where
 attachS (E v) x = x >>= λp.yield () (E λr.v (F λs.{s & pin = toCode p}))
 writeS  (E v) x = x >>= λp.yield () (E λr.v (F λs.{s & pos = p}))
 servo f         = defEval {pin = "", pos = 0} f
```

In a similar way the `liquidCrystal` constructor of the class `lcd` adds a LCD object to the store.

```
instance lcd Eval where
  print     (E v) x   =
    x >>= λa. let str = toCode a in
    yield (size str) (E λr.v (F λlcd.lcdPrintStr str lcd))
  setCursor (E v) x y =
    x >>= λw.
    y >>= λh.
    yield () (E λr.v (F λlcd.{lcd & cursorRow = h, cursorCol = w}))
  liquidCrystal w h pins f = defEval lcd f where
    lcd =
         { cursorRow = 0
         , cursorCol = 0
         , sizeH = h
         , sizeW = w
         , lcdtxt = repeatn h (toString (repeatn w ' '))
         }
```

6.9 Evaluation of Functions Definitions

Also functions are directly converted to functions in Clean:

```
instance fun Eval x | arg x where
  fun f = e where (g In e) = f (λa.toExpr (g a))
```

6.10 Evaluation of Task Definitions

Task definitions are slightly more complicated since every invocation is stored as `State→State` function with its delay `d` in a separate field in the state. The function `toS2S` transforms an eval function to a plain state transformation.

```
instance mtask Eval x | arg x where
 task d f = e where
  (t In e) =
    f (λa.Eλr s.(MTask (length s.mtasks)
                ,{s & mtasks = s.mtasks ++ [(i, toS2S (t a))]}))
```

6.11 An mTask Simulator

The translation of a program in mTask by this view yields a state transformation function in Clean. By construction, the tasks wait in the state to get evaluated.

The function step collects the task from the state increments the time by the smallest delay of these tasks and apply the tasks in their creation order. In general, this will create new tasks. This step function has the same effect as evaluating all currently available tasks in the generated loop of the compilation.

```
step :: State → State
step s =
  foldr appTask {s & millis = s.millis + delta, mtasks = []}
        [(w - delta, f) \\ (w, f) ← s.mtasks]
where delta = foldl1 min (map fst s.mtasks) // smallest wait
```

A simple iTask program can be used as an interactive simulator for mTask programs. This is very useful in the construction of mTask programs; in the simulator, we can execute the tasks step by step, inspect the store and outputs, and manipulate the inputs of the system. In an actual microprocessor debugging is very troublesome. We cannot inspect the state and we have limited control over the input-output of the system. Producing trace information over the serial port changes the timing of tasks and it can change the behaviour of the mTask program. Controlling the inputs in time is often next to impossible. In the simulator, all these desirable things can be done easily.

By a push of the loop button in the simulator, we apply the step function, this executes a single step of all currently available tasks. New tasks, including recursive calls of a task, are just collected instead of being directly executed. The iTask defining the simulator is:

```
simulate :: (Main (Eval a p)) → Task ()
simulate {main=(E f)} = setup state0 where
  setup s =
    updateInformation "State" [] (toView s)
    >>* [ OnAction ActionFinish (always shutDown)
        , OnAction (Action "setup" []) (hasValue
          (λsi.simloop (snd (f R (mergeView s si)))))
        ]
  simloop s =
    updateInformation "State" [] (toView s)
    >>* [ OnAction ActionFinish (always shutDown)
        , OnAction ActionNew (always (setup state0))
        : if (isEmpty s.mtasks)
            []
            [OnAction (Action "loop" []) (hasValue
            λsi.simloop (step (mergeView s si)))
          ]
        ]
```

In this simulator we used a type StateInterface and the conversion functions toView :: State → StateInterface and mergeView :: State StateInterface → State to obtain a nicer view of the machine state in the iTask simulation.

```
:: StateInterface =
  { serialOut   :: Display [String]
  , analogPins  :: [(AnalogPin, Int)]
  , digitalPins :: [(DigitalPin, Bool)]
  , shares      :: [DisplaySDS]
  , timer       :: Int
  , taskCount   :: Display Int
  }
```

A screenshot of this simulator executing the sweep program below is depicted in Fig. 2. This program is using the serial port, the onboard LED, as well as a servo.

```
sweep =
  liquidCrystal 16 2 [] λlcd.
  servo λs.
  sds ((max - min) / 2) λpos.
  sds 1  λstep.
  task 50 \task.(λ().
    pos =. pos +. step :.
    lit max <. pos |. pos <. lit min ? step =. Zero -. step :.
    writeS s pos :.
    printAt lcd Zero Zero pos :.
    print lcd (lit " ") :.
    task ())
  In {main =
    serialPrint (lit "Hello World!"):.
    serialPrint (lit "This is sweep.") :.
    attachS s (lit A5) :.
    task ()
  }
where
  max = 170
  min = 10
```

Unfortunately, it is not possible to show the code of these tasks easily since they are functions. In a better simulator, we would include a separate view to display the code of the tasks. Then it makes also sense to execute the tasks one by one, and even to execute tasks step by step.

This simulation of the Arduino is by design not accurate to the last bit. For instance, we do not update the values of the input–output pins controlling the shields, hence interferences of shields with other pin manipulations cannot be detected in the simulator. The simulator also does not check whether the memory of the actual microprocessor is capable of handling all actions, overflows might happen unnoticed in the simulator. Nevertheless, the simulation is very useful to observe and test the behaviour of mTask programs. Debugging any program running on a microprocessor is cumbersome since the program to debug is designed to occupy the whole machine. Changing the program to write trace information to the serial port is often the simplest approach. There are libraries and IDE extensions to facilitate this, e.g., [38]. Despite the mentioned limitations,

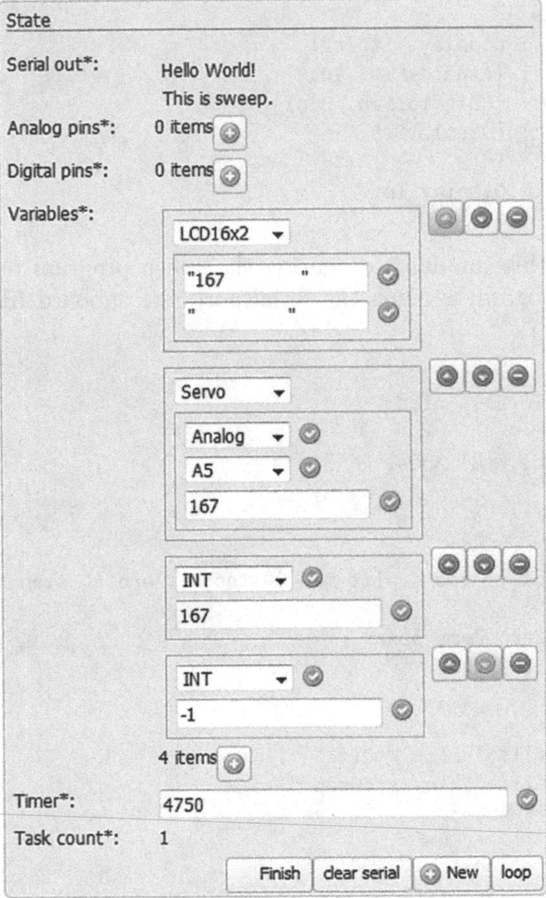

Fig. 2. Screenshot of the simulation.

the simulation presented here provides an easy to use alternative. The simulator provides information about the state and tasks to be executed at the abstraction level of tasks instead of individual instructions and memory addresses of the microprocessor.

7 Optimization

The given code generator and transformation to the host language Clean follow the given definitions in the mTask very directly. Since Clean can be used as the macro language of the mTask DSL this is often sufficient. In general, it is desirable to make more sophisticated views that do transformations and optimizations of the given DSL program.

There are at least two approaches to consider: partial evaluation of mTask programs to new mTask programs, and view-dependent optimizations. We will briefly discuss both possibilities.

7.1 Partial Evaluation

Partial evaluation transforms a program to an equivalent program in the same language that can be executed more efficiently [7,24]. Typical transformations are the execution of computation that only depend on static information, like arithmetic expressions of statically known constants.

In our approach, the basic steps are the definition of a data type PE that hold potentially a compile-time value, Val t, as well as a language component in an arbitrary view, v t p. The function pe performs partial evaluation. Whenever a value x is known, it is produced by lit x. Otherwise, the given view is the result.

```
:: PE v t p = PE (Val t) (v t p)
:: Val  t   = Val t | NoVal

pe :: (PE v t p)→v t Expr|expr,toE v & toCode t & isExpr p
pe (PE (Val x) v) = lit x
pe (PE _       v) = toE v
```

Producing partial evaluation of literals and addition is defined as:

```
instance arith (PE v) | toE, arith v where
    lit a = PE (Val a) (lit a)
    (+.) a=:(PE mx vx) b=:(PE my vy) =
        case (mx, my) of
            (Val x, Val y) = PE (Val (x + y)) (pe a +. pe b)
            (Val x, _)     | x == zero
                           = PE NoVal (pe b)
                           = PE NoVal (lit x +. pe b)
            (_    , Val y) | y == zero
                           = PE NoVal (pe a)
                           = PE NoVal (pe a +. lit y)
            (_    , _)     = PE NoVal (pe a +. pe b)
```

The advantage of this approach is that an mTask expression in an arbitrary view is generated. Each and every other view of the DSL can be optimized by this transformation.

Since we have currently no plain view of mTask that yields a textual representation of DSL programs, we can only observe the effect of partial evaluation indirectly (for instance in the generated code). As a tiny example we partially evaluate and compile the following minimal program.

```
pe1 = {main = pe (output (lit 6 *. lit 7))}
```

The generated code for the setup() function shows that lit 6 *. lit 7 is indeed replaced by 42 in the partial evaluation:

```
void setup () {
  Serial.begin(9600);
  Serial.println(42);
}
```

Partial evaluation of the complete mTask system is an ongoing endeavour. It seems definitely possible, but it deserves some attention to handle the carefully constructed types correctly.

7.2 Syntax Tree Manipulation

Instead of partial evaluation, we can also make view specific transformations. For the most flexible transformations, it is convenient to transform mTask programs to an equivalent abstract syntax tree of type AST. When we limit ourselves to integers and Booleans the required basis is:

```
:: AST = VAR String | Ap String [AST] | Int Int | Bool Bool
:: Ast t p = Ast ([Int]→([Int],AST))

class ast t :: t → AST
instance ast Int  where ast i = Int i
instance ast Bool where ast b = Bool b
```

The view that produces an optimized AST of lit and +. is:

```
instance arith Ast where
  lit x = Ast λl.(l,ast x)
  (+.) (Ast x) (Ast y)
    = Ast λl.
        let
          (m, a) = x l
          (n, b) = y m
        in (n, (case (a, b) of
                    (Int i, Int j) = Int (i + j)
                    (Int 0, b)     = b
                    (a    , Int 0) = a
                    (a    , b)     = Ap "+" [a,b]))
```

A constant definition can be replaced by inlining the value as the literal in the AST. For a share definition, this is not allowed since the value can change dynamically.

```
instance sds Ast where
  sds v f =
    {main =
      Ast λ[a:x].(λ(Ast g).g x)
                 (unMain (f (Ast λl.(l, VAR ("x"+fromInt a)))))
    }
  con v f = f (lit v)
```

Applying this transformation to

```
ast = con 6 λs.sds 1 λx.{main = s *. (s +. One) +. x}
```

yields (Ap"+" [(Int 42),(VAR "x0")]) for the main expression.

The obtained AST is very suited for view specific transformations like tail-call optimization of recursive functions.

Basically, we transform the shallow embedded version of mTask here to a deeply embedded version of the DSL. It is still worthwhile to make a shallow embedded version of the language for the user. In contrast to the deeply embedded version, the shallow embedded version enables the type checker of the host language to verify types in mTask with a plain Hindley-Milner type system [10]. The shallow embedded version also ensures the proper definition of identifiers, functions and tasks.

8 Related Work

There are several groups of related work. We discuss approaches to control microprocessors with high-level languages, the generation of C code to implement function languages directly, and related representations of DSLs.

8.1 High-Level Languages for Microprocessors

There are many microprocessors with various capabilities. Many languages are ported to some microprocessors. The Clean compiler is currently ported to the ARM-processor driving the Raspberry Pi. With the announcement of the Pi Zero [34] as the $5 computer, this can become a serious alternative for many microprocessor applications, especially in the IoT.

The package hArduino allows Haskell programs to control Arduino boards and peripherals, using the Firmata [16] protocol. The Haskell program is not running on the Arduino itself. The Haskell package frp-arduino offers Functional Reactive Programming, FRP, for the Arduino [28]. It is implemented as a deeply embedded DSL that compiles to C. Our task-based approach is more flexible than the FRP paradigm.

Microscheme is an implementation of a subset of Scheme for the Arduino [36]. This implementation uses a simple heap in the 2K of RAM of the Arduino. It implements proper tail calls and it offers the exception handling required by Scheme's dynamic nature. Microscheme contains a last-resort primitive for memory recovery of the form (free! ...), instead of a garbage collector.

Lua [18,19] is a powerful, fast, lightweight, embeddable scripting language ported to the ESP8266 microprocessor. The ESP8266 is far more powerful than the ATmega328P driving the Arduino, both is memory size and clock-speed. Since it costs only a few dollars and has WiFi support, it is a very interesting platform.

The Espruino project projects provides a JavaScript interpreter on single chips microprocessor boards [40]. This JavaScript interpreter is also ported to the ESP8266. The interpreter is originally designed for 128 kb of Flash and 8 kb of RAM. This is small in JavaScript terms, about 1000 times smaller than an ordinary interpreter, but still a factor 4 bigger than an Arduino Uno.

The SAPL approach compiles functional programming languages to small executables, typically executing in a browser [20,21]. It is interesting to investigate whether it is possible to generate C code with a very small footprint to allow execution on a microprocessor in this way.

8.2 Generating C-Code

Generating C code from functional languages is quite common, e.g. [13,25,37]. Until version 6 GHC compiled Haskell to C code [30]. These implementations use C has a high-level assembly. Functions in the source language are not directly mapped to functions in C.

Filet-o-fish is a tool to build DSLs to write operating systems [9]. Like mTask the DSL generates C code. The abstraction level of the DSLs constructed is typically lower than in our mTask system. The implementation route is quite different; the filet-o-fish approach uses standalone compiler instead of an embedded DSL.

8.3 Shallow Embedding of DSLs with Multiple Views

Carette et al. use a class-based approach to construct a DSL with multiple views like we do [7]. One of the views is the partial evaluation. Their language is basically λ-calculus. Their work is missing the fancy type system used here as well as C code generation. Lämmel and Ostermann discuss the possibilities to use type classes for an extendable software and integration [27]. This shows that the class-based approach used here solves Wadler's expression problem [39]. Their approach to making an extendable DSL is far less sophisticated as the technique described in the current paper.

8.4 Future Work

Although we are now able to execute task-oriented programs on a tiny microprocessor system like the Arduino, this work is not finished. The first thing to be done is making a connection between the mTask and the iTask system. The goal is that an iTask program can specify subtasks in mTask and delegate them to a microprocessor. The iTask system should be able to monitor and influence task execution on the mTask system, similar to its own tasks.

The current mTask system is able to interact with other systems over the serial port by sending and receiving messages. To make it a better IoT language we will add communication over WiFi as well as Bluetooth.

The mTask system itself should be completed with data types. It is desirable to add at least strings and arrays. Currently, the mTask system is lacking primitives for task management. Any task coordination must be implemented using shares. It is desirable to introduce constructors to implement frequently occurring communication patterns between tasks.

9 Discussion

The goal of this work was to construct a system for task-oriented programming on tiny microprocessors like the Arduino. We built a shallow embedded domain-specific language based on type classes. This shallow embedding defines the DSL as a set of functions. The tasks in our system are light-weight threads that run interleaved and communicate via shared data sources. The examples show that out mTask system yields concise and flexible programs.

We showed that the advantage of shallow embedding over deep embedding is that a plain Hindley-Milner type system ensures well-typed DSL programs. Moreover, a shallow embedded DSL is easily extendable by adding new functions in the host language as elements of the DSL. This paper shows how one can introduce type-safe and well-defined shares, functions, as well as tasks, in a shallow embedded DSL by (nameless) functions in the host language. Guaranteeing well-defined identifiers at compile time is usually problematic in a DSL. This paper provides a simple and elegant solution.

Since we defined the DSL as a set of classes instead of a set of plain functions, it is easy to introduce new interpretations, called views, of the DSL. In this paper, we showed how to compile our DSL to compact C++ code for the Arduino ecosphere. This makes the generated C++ programs portable to a family of microprocessors. By targeting the smallest member, the Arduino Uno R3, of the family the generated programs can be ported easily to all other similar microprocessors.

Despite the high-level C++ intermediate language, the generated code is rather compact. The largest examples in this paper use about 25% of the available flash memory. The shares and task table use about 25% of the dynamic memory. This usually leaves enough space for function calls and the associated local shares. The memory usage is similar to memory needs of handwritten C++ code for those tasks.

The second view translates programs from the DSL with shares to a monadic expression in the pure host language. A concise iTask program simulates the DSL programs interactively. The user can inspect and change the state of the DSL program between the execution of DSL tasks.

Finally, we have briefly shown how to optimize DSL programs. The partial evaluation view optimizes programs within the DSL. The obtained program can be used in any of the views available. For view specific transformations a view of the DSL that yields an abstract syntax tree is more appropriate. This combines best of both worlds; we have an extendable and a type-safe DSL in the primary shallow embedding, while the generated data structure of the deep embedding is convenient for analysis and transformation.

Our example programs show that task-oriented programming in the introduced mTask system is very suitable for programming microprocessor systems. Using parameterized tail-calls in the tasks the use of shares can often be circumvented. This results in concise, well-typed, elegant, and portable high-level programs for microprocessor systems. We can run any number of independent tasks on the microprocessor, as well as tasks that invoke each other. Whenever necessary tasks can communicate via shares. The advantage of our DSL over C++ for microprocessor programming is that it provides high-level task-oriented programming. In our approach, it is much easier to recognize the tasks and to compose them.

Acknowledgements. The authors thank Ralf Hinze and Peter Achten from the Radboud University for inspiring discussions about the architecture of the DSL used. Special thanks to the anonymous referees for their feedback on the draft version of this paper.

A The Function `compile`

For completeness, this appendix contains the complete function `compile` discussed in Sect. 5.

```
compile :: (Main (Code a p)) → [String]
compile {main=(C f)} =
  ["/*\n"
  ,"  Generated code for Arduino\n"
  ,"  Pieter Koopman, pieter@cs.ru.nl\n"
  ,"*/\n"
  ,"\n"
  ,"#define MAX_ARGS 4\n"
  ,"#define MAX_TASKS 20\n"
  ,"#define MAX_TASK_NO MAX_TASKS - 1\n"
  ,"#define NEXT_TASK(n) ((n) == MAX_TASK_NO ? 0 : (n) + 1)\n"
  ,"\n"
  ,"typedef union Arg {\n"
  ,"  int i;\n"
  ,"  bool b;\n"
  ,"  char c;\n"
  ,"  word w;\n"
  ,"} ARG;\n"
  ,"\n"
  ,"typedef struct Task {\n"
  ,"  byte id;\n"
  ,"  long wait;\n"
  ,"  ARG a[MAX_ARGS];\n"
  ,"} TASK;\n"
  ,"\n"
  ,"boolean pressed(int b) {\n"
  ,"  pinMode(A0, INPUT);\n"
  ,"  int a0 = analogRead(A0);\n"
  ,"  switch (b) {\n"
  ,"  case ",toCode RightButton,": return a0 < "
    ,toString RightBound,";        // right\n"
  ,"  case ",toCode UpButton,": return ",toString RightBound
    ," < a0 && a0 < ",toString UpBound,"; // up\n"
  ,"  case ",toCode DownButton,": return ",toString UpBound
```

```
    ," < a0 && a0 < ",toString DownBound,";// down\n"
  ,"  case ",toCode LeftButton,": return ",toString DownBound
    ," < a0 && a0 < ",toString LeftBound,";//left\n"
  ,"  case ",toCode SelectButton,": return ",toString LeftBound
    ," < a0 && a0 < ",toString SelectBound,";//select\n"
  ,"  default: return ",toString SelectBound," < a0;       //no button\n"
  ,"  }\n"
  ,"}\n"
  ] ++
  foldr (λlib c.["♯include <":lib:".h>\n":c]) [[]] (mkset c.includes) ++
  ["\n// --- Shared Data Source definitions ---\n"
  ,"TASK tasks[MAX_TASKS];\n"
  ,"byte t0 = 0, tc = 0, tn = 0;\n"
  ,"long delta;\n"
  ,"\n"
  ,"int vInt;\n"
  ,"bool vBool;\n"
  ,"char vChar;\n"
  ,"float vFloat;\n"
  ,"unsigned long time = 0;\n"
  :reverse c.sdss
  ] ++
  ["\n// --- functions ---\n"
  ,"byte newTask(byte id, long wait, word a0, word a1, word a2, word a3) {\n"
  ,"  TASK *tnp = &tasks[tn];\n"
  ,"  tnp→id = id;\n"
  ,"  tnp→wait = wait;\n"
  ,"  tnp→a[0].w = a0;\n"
  ,"  tnp→a[1].w = a1;\n"
  ,"  tnp→a[2].w = a2;\n"
  ,"  tnp→a[3].w = a3;\n"
  ,"  byte r = tn;\n"
  ,"  tn = NEXT_TASK(tn);\n"
  ,"  return r;\n"
  ,"}\n"
  ,"\n"
  ,"byte setDelay(byte t, long d) {\n"
  ,"  tasks[t].wait = d;\n"
  ,"  return t;\n"
  ,"}\n"
  :reverse c.funs
  ] ++
  ["\n// --- setup --- \n"
  ,"void setup () {\n"
  ,"  Serial.begin(9600);\n"
  ,"  "
  :reverse c.setup
  ] ++
  ["\n}\n"
  ,"\n// --- loop --- \n"
```

```
,"void loop () {\n"
,"  if (t0 != tn) {\n"
,"    if (t0 == tc) {\n"
,"      unsigned long time2 = millis();\n"
,"      delta = time2 - time;\n"
,"      time = time2;\n"
,"      tc = tn;\n"
,"    };\n"
,"    TASK* t0p = &tasks[t0];\n"
,"    t0p→wait -= delta;\n"
,"    if (t0p→wait > 0L) {\n"
,"      newTask(t0p→id, t0p→wait"
               ,", t0p→a[0].w, t0p→a[1].w, t0p→a[2].w, t0p→a[3].w);\n"
,"    } else {\n"
,"      switch (t0p→id) {"
:reverse c.loop
] ++
["\n"
,"      default:\n"
,"        Serial.println(\"stopped\");\n"
,"        t0 = tn; // no known task: force termination of tasks\n"
,"        return;\n"
,"      };\n"
,"    }\n"
,"    t0 = NEXT_TASK(t0);\n"
,"  }\n"
,"}\n"
]
where c = f newCode
```

References

1. Ada, L.: adafruit/DHT-sensor-library (2017). https://github.com/adafruit/DHT-sensor-library
2. Arduino.cc: (2015). https://www.arduino.cc
3. Arduino.cc: Arduino LiquidCrystal Library (2015). https://www.arduino.cc/en/Reference/LiquidCrystal
4. Arduino.cc: Arduino NewPing Library (2015). http://playground.arduino.cc/Code/NewPing
5. Arduino.cc: Arduino Servo Library (2015). https://www.arduino.cc/en/Reference/Servo
6. Arduino.org (2015). http://www.arduino.org/
7. Carette, J., Kiselyov, O., Shan, C.: Finally tagless, partially evaluated: tagless staged interpreters for simpler typed languages. J. Funct. Program. **19**(5), 509–543 (2009). https://doi.org/10.1017/S0956796809007205
8. D-Robotics: DHT11 humidity & temperature sensor (2010). http://www.micro4you.com/files/sensor/DHT11.pdf

9. Dagand, P.E., Baumann, A., Roscoe, T.: Filet-o-fish: practical and dependable domain-specific languages for OS development. SIGOPS Oper. Syst. Rev. **43**(4), 35–39 (2010). https://doi.org/10.1145/1713254.1713263
10. Damas, L., Milner, R.: Principal type-schemes for functional programs. In: Proceedings of the 9th ACM SIGPLAN-SIGACT Symposium on Principles of Programming Languages, POPL 1982, pp. 207–212. ACM, New York (1982). https://doi.org/10.1145/582153.582176
11. Danvy, O., Nielsen, L.R.: Defunctionalization at work. In: Proceedings of the 3rd ACM SIGPLAN International Conference on Principles and Practice of Declarative Programming, PPDP 2001, pp. 162–174. ACM, New York (2001). https://doi.org/10.1145/773184.773202
12. Erkok, L.: hArduino (2014). https://hackage.haskell.org/package/hArduino
13. Feeley, M., Miller, J.S., Rozas, G.J., Wilson, J.A.: Compiling higher-order languages into fully tail-recursive portable C. Technical report (1997)
14. Fowler, M.: Domain Specific Languages, 1st edn. Addison-Wesley Professional, Boston (2010)
15. Gibbons, J.: Functional programming for domain-specific languages. In: Zsók, V., Horváth, Z., Csató, L. (eds.) CEFP 2013. LNCS, vol. 8606, pp. 1–28. Springer, Cham (2015). https://doi.org/10.1007/978-3-319-15940-9_1
16. Hoefs, J.: Firmata protocol (2014). http://firmata.org/wiki/Main_Page
17. Hudak, P.: Building domain-specific embedded languages. ACM Comput. Surv. **28**(4es) (1996). https://doi.org/10.1145/242224.242477
18. Ierusalimschy, R., de Figueiredo, L.H., Filho, W.C.: Lua - an extensible extension language. Softw. Pract. Exper. **26**(6), 635–652 (1996)
19. Ierusalimschy, R., de Figueiredo, L.H., Celes, W.: Lua 5.1 Reference Manual (2006). Lua.org
20. Jansen, J.M.: Programming in the λ-calculus: from Church to Scott and back. In: Achten, P., Koopman, P. (eds.) The Beauty of Functional Code. LNCS, vol. 8106, pp. 168–180. Springer, Heidelberg (2013). https://doi.org/10.1007/978-3-642-40355-2_12
21. Jansen, J.M., Koopman, P., Plasmeijer, R.: From interpretation to compilation. In: Horváth, Z., Plasmeijer, R., Soós, A., Zsók, V. (eds.) CEFP 2007. LNCS, vol. 5161, pp. 286–301. Springer, Heidelberg (2008). https://doi.org/10.1007/978-3-540-88059-2_8
22. Johann, P., Ghani, N.: Foundations for structured programming with GADTs. SIGPLAN Not. **43**(1), 297–308 (2008)
23. Jones, M.P., Diatchki, I.S.: Language and program design for functional dependencies. In: Proceedings of the First ACM SIGPLAN Symposium on Haskell, Haskell 2008, pp. 87–98. ACM, New York (2008). https://doi.org/10.1145/1411286.1411298
24. Jones, N.D., Gomard, C.K., Sestoft, P.: Partial Evaluation and Automatic Program Generation. Prentice-Hall, Inc., Upper Saddle River (1993)
25. Kameyama, Y., Kiselyov, O., Shan, C.: Combinators for impure yet hygienic code generation. In: Proceedings of the ACM SIGPLAN 2014 Workshop on Partial Evaluation and Program Manipulation, pp. 3–14, PEPM 2014. ACM, New York (2014). https://doi.org/10.1145/2543728.2543740
26. Koopman, P., Plasmeijer, R.: A shallow embedded type safe extendable DSL for the Arduino. In: Serrano, M., Hage, J. (eds.) TFP 2015. LNCS, vol. 9547, pp. 104–123. Springer, Cham (2016). https://doi.org/10.1007/978-3-319-39110-6_6

27. Lämmel, R., Ostermann, K.: Software extension and integration with type classes. In: Proceedings of the 5th International Conference on Generative Programming and Component Engineering, GPCE 2006, pp. 161–170. ACM, New York (2006). https://doi.org/10.1145/1173706.1173732
28. Lindberg, R.: frp-arduino (2015). https://github.com/frp-arduino/frp-arduino#contributing
29. Nielson, H.R., Nielson, F.: Semantics with Applications: A Formal Introduction. Wiley, New York (1992)
30. Peyton Jones, S.L.: The Implementation of Functional Programming Languages. Prentice-Hall International Series in Computer Science. Prentice-Hall, Inc., Upper Saddle River (1987)
31. Plasmeijer, R., Achten, P., Koopman, P.: iTasks: executable specifications of interactive work flow systems for the web. In: Hinze, R., Ramsey, N. (eds.) Proceedings of the ICFP 2007, pp. 141–152. ACM, Freiburg (2007)
32. Plasmeijer, R., Lijnse, B., Michels, S., Achten, P., Koopman, P.: Task-oriented programming in a pure functional language. In: Proceedings of the 14th Symposium on Principles and Practice of Declarative Programming, PPDP 2012, pp. 195–206. ACM, New York (2012). https://doi.org/10.1145/2370776.2370801
33. Plasmeijer, R., van Eekelen, M., van Groningen, J.: Clean language report (version 2.2) (2011). http://clean.cs.ru.nl/Documentation
34. Raspberrypi.org: Pi zero description (2015). https://www.raspberrypi.org/products/pi-zero/
35. Reynolds, J.C.: Definitional interpreters for higher-order programming languages. In: Proceedings of the ACM Annual Conference, ACM 1972, vol. 2, pp. 717–740. ACM, New York (1972). https://doi.org/10.1145/800194.805852
36. Suchocki, R., Kalvala, S.: MicroScheme: functional programming for the Arduino. In: Scheme Workshop (2014)
37. Sumii, E.: MinCaml: a simple and efficient compiler for a minimal functional language. In: Proceedings of the 2005 Workshop on Functional and Declarative Programming in Education, FDPE 2005, pp. 27–38. ACM, New York (2005). https://doi.org/10.1145/1085114.1085122
38. visualmicro.com: Debugging tutorial (2015). http://www.visualmicro.com/page/User-Guide.aspx?doc=Debugging-Walkthrough-Start.html
39. Wadler, P.: The expression problem (1998). http://www.daimi.au.dk/~madst/tool/papers/expression.txt
40. Williams, G.: The espruino project (2015). http://www.espruino.com/

Static and Dynamic Visualisations of Monadic Programs

Jurriën Stutterheim(✉), Peter Achten(✉), and Rinus Plasmeijer(✉)

Institute for Computing and Information Sciences, Radboud University Nijmegen, P.O. Box 9010, 6500 GL Nijmegen, The Netherlands
{j.stutterheim,p.achten,rinus}@cs.ru.nl

Abstract. iTasks is a shallowly embedded monadic domain-specific language written in the lazy, functional programming language Clean. It implements the Task-Oriented Programming (TOP) paradigm. In TOP one describes, on a high level of abstraction, the tasks that distributed collaborative systems and end users have to do. It results in a web application that is able to coordinate the work thus described. Even though iTasks is defined in the common notion of "tasks", for stake holders without programming experience, textual source code remains too difficult to understand. In previous work, we introduced Tonic (Task-Oriented Notation Inferred from Code) to graphically represent iTasks programs using *blueprints*. Blueprints are designed to bridge the gap between domain-expert and programmer. In this paper, we add the capability to graphically trace the dynamic behaviour of an iTasks program at run-time. This enables domain experts, managers, end users and programmers to follow and inspect the work as it is being executed. Using *dynamic blueprints* we can show, in real-time, who is working on what, which tasks are finished, which tasks are active, and what their parameters and results are. Under certain conditions we can predict which future tasks are reachable and which not. In a way, we have created a graphical tracing and debugging system for the TOP domain and have created the foundation for a tracing and debugging system for monads in general. Tracing and debugging is known to be hard to realize for lazy functional languages. In monadic contexts, however, the order of evaluation is well-defined, reducing the challenges Tonic needs to overcome.

Keywords: Dynamic program visualisation · Purely functional programming · Monads · iTasks · Clean

1 Introduction

When developing non-trivial software, one frequently needs to gather the correct requirements and frequently evaluate whether the right software is being built. This can be a hard and time-consuming activity when stakeholders with different backgrounds are involved. This is in part due to the communication gap that exists between experts in unrelated fields.

V. Zsók et al. (Eds.): CEFP 2015, LNCS 10094, pp. 341–379, 2019.
https://doi.org/10.1007/978-3-030-28346-9_9

Task-oriented programming (TOP) is a style of functional programming that, amongst other things, aims to reduce the communication gap between various parties by developing programs in terms of the common notion of *tasks.* TOP is implemented by iTasks [11], a *shallowly embedded* monadic domain-specific language in the general-purpose, lazy, purely functional programming language Clean [12]. iTasks is used to compose multi-user web-based applications. Common technical issues related to distributed client-server settings, such as communication, synchronization, user interface generation, and user interaction, are handled automatically by applying advanced functional programming techniques. These include type driven generic functions, and the ability to store, load and communicate closures in a type safe way using Clean's dynamic system.

As a result, the iTasks application writer is able to concentrate on the main issues: the tasks that have to be done by the end users in collaboration with the computer systems they use. Although one can now, when writing the application code, concentrate on the things that matter, there still exists a communication gap between various stakeholders. Commonly, domain experts, managers and end users are not used to read and understand textual source code. They prefer pictures, diagrams and natural language instead. Yet it is vital that they are able to evaluate the software that has been built, preferably more quickly than by simply running the program in a testing or production environment.

One way to bridge the communication gap between stakeholders and programmers is to utilise graphical notations. Well-known examples of such notations are BPMN [7] and UML [10]. However, such notations have as disadvantage that they are not part of the actual implementation and cannot practically be used as such. Additionally, since they are not part of the implementation, commonly manual labour is required to keep the models synchronized with the implementation. In practice, these models are prone to becoming outdated, because the cost of maintaining them may be higher than the benefit gained from the up-to-date documentation [3].

In previous work [18] we introduced our own graphical notation, called Tonic (Task-Oriented Notation Inferred from Code). Rather than specifying programs graphically, however, we made a specialised version of the Clean compiler[1], the Clean-Tonic compiler, which *generates* a graphical representation, called a *blueprint*, of the tasks that have been defined in Clean. Since blueprints are generated, they always provide up-to-date documentation of the source code. Implementing Tonic in the Clean compiler is necessary, since iTasks is shallowly embedded in Clean. As a result, programmers can use any Clean language construct to write iTasks programs. Implementing Tonic in the Clean compiler allows us to capture these language constructs in the blueprints we generate.

It is neither practical nor informative to show all the details of the original source code in the blueprints; they would become huge and unreadable. Instead we abstract from certain details yet provide enough information such that one should be able to understand by looking at the pictures which tasks have been

[1] Available in the latest development releases at https://clean.cs.ru.nl/Download_Clean.

defined and understand how these tasks depend on each other. We hope that by doing so, blueprints are easier to understand for non-programmers than the (Clean) code they are generated from.

The first version of the Clean-Tonic compiler, however, did suffer from a number of drawbacks. For one, we could only generate *static* blueprints. Secondly, it had a hard-coded connection between the compiler and iTasks, which is not desirable for a general-purpose compiler. Thirdly, since the compiler was modified specifically for iTasks, Tonic's features were not usable in other contexts. Lastly, there was no way to customize the rendering of specific tasks without modifying both the compiler and iTasks.

In this paper, we set out to solve all of the aforementioned problems. We transform monadic programs such that dynamic information can be added to blueprints at run-time, creating *dynamic blueprints*. With these one can monitor what is happening with the monad during execution. In principle this can be done for any monad, but some programming effort is required to link its execution at run-time to the blueprints generated at compile-time. Our focus in this paper is one specific yet challenging example, the dynamic blueprints for iTasks, which is a highly complex and dynamic system.

iTasks is a challenging example because it is used for developing complex distributed systems. In the real world, people and systems often don't do their work as planned. Therefore it would be of great help if one were able to inspect what is going on at run-time. This aids, for example, programmers in debugging, domain experts in seeing whether the application works as designed, and managers and end users in tracking progress of workflows.

In essence, we have developed a kind of monitoring, tracing and debugging tool. This is commonly known to be a very challenging tool to make for a lazy functional language, particularly if one realizes that Clean applications are not interpreted, but compiled.

The Clean compiler is a state-of-the-art compiler, well known for the efficient code it generates. Due to the many transformations performed by the compiler to obtain such efficient code, and the laziness of the language, it is in general near to impossible to relate the execution of an application to a specific part of the original source code. The advantage we have here is that, since we restrict ourselves to monadic contexts, we statically know their order of evaluation.

A particular challenge is how to relate run-time behaviour to the corresponding parts of static blueprints. The difficulty comes from run-time calculations and higher order functions. To do so, we modify the generated code by adding wrapper functions to the monadic applications. These wrappers tell which part of the original source code is being evaluated, so that it can be related to the correct part of the static blueprint.

With the dynamic blueprints we can show, at run-time, for any iTasks application, dynamic aspects such as: which tasks have been started, which are finished, which are running, how are they instantiated, what are the actual arguments, who is working on what, and which information is currently being produced by a specific task. The graphical representation of dynamic blueprints has to be modified at run-time to reflect the current program state.

In this paper we address the issues mentioned above and make the following contributions:

- We generalise the notion of blueprints to not only capture iTasks programs, but monadic programs in general. Using this new-found generalisation, we remove the hard connection between the Clean-Tonic compiler and iTasks, making Tonic a general solution.
- We show how static and dynamic blueprints are being made for the Task monad. Furthermore we discuss how our approach can be used for any monad, such as e.g. the IO Monad.
- We explain what kind of code transformations are made by the compiler such that we are able to map run-time behaviour to static information generated from the source program.
- We explain how we created a Tonic Task which allows an end-user of any iTasks application to browse through the dynamic blueprints, and to inspect values of arguments and results of any task executed in the past or currently under evaluation.
- We explain that with a simple control-flow analysis and code transformation we can show the reachability of information (monads/task) in the blueprints. In this way we are able to show which future task can or cannot be executed given the current state of affairs.
- Tonic's end users can now customize how tasks are rendered using the declarative `Graphics.Scalable` library [1].

The rest of this paper is structured as follows: Sect. 2 shows several examples of static blueprints, after which Sect. 3 shows how these are made. Section 4 shows how we instantiate blueprints at run-time and incorporate run-time information in them, using an example in iTasks. Finally, Sect. 6 discusses related work, and Sect. 7 discusses current challenges and concludes.

2 Static Blueprints: Examples

In this section we explain, with the help of a number of examples, what kind of *static blueprints* we generate from Clean source text[2]. In the introduction we already made clear that it is not a good idea to turn a complete Clean program into a graphical counterpart. First of all, Clean, much like Haskell, contains many language constructs. A pictorial representation isomorphic with the source code would only be huge and would not contribute to a better understanding of the code than the text of the source program itself. Secondly, there are technical obstacles that currently prevent us from showing all language features in a meaningful, graphical way. This is due to the fact that the Clean compiler generates highly efficient code, applying many transformations during compilation. Some of the original code is simply no longer available.

---

[2] All blueprints in this paper are generated from the example programs.

For all these reasons, we decided to restrict ourselves to generating graphical representations for certain top level abstractions and a limited number of language primitives. We want to capture the major structure of the application being defined; we don't want nor need to provide all details of the application. We therefore decided to focus on monads. Monads are a frequently used abstraction in functional programming. In Haskell, for example, the `IO` monad is the principal way to perform side-effecting operations. As well as being useful, monads provide the ability to hide tedious book-keeping operations under the bind combinator, making code easier to read and reason about. In addition, the evaluation order of sequentially composed monadic computations is well defined and strict. The laziness of the language does not provide problems here.

We distinguish two sets of monads: one for which we want to generate a blueprint, and one for which we don't want to generate blueprints, but that may be *part* of a blueprint. We call the first set *blueprint* monads and the second *contained* monads. A blueprint monad is always a contained monad, but not the other way around. For iTasks, for example, the set of blueprint monads contains the `Task` monad, while the set of contained blueprints contains both the `Task` and the `Maybe` monad. To distinguish between the two sets of monads, we introduce two new type classes. We discuss the implementation and application of these classes in Sect. 3.

What makes generating blueprints challenging is that in any combinator definition, any Clean language construct may be used as well. As explained above, and further illustrated in the examples below, we limit ourselves to Clean language constructs which we are able to visualize in a meaningful manner, and hide those which are too complicated to visualize. We support `if`-blocks, `case`-blocks, pattern matching, `let`-blocks, recursion, higher-order functions and list definitions in the case that the number of list elements are statically known. For all other language constructs and cases we do not offer special graphical support in a blueprint. If we cannot graphically represent an expression, we pretty-print the original source code. Let's have a look at some examples.

2.1 Static Blueprints of the I/O Monad

The example in Fig. 1 shows a simple interactive program implemented in Clean's IO monad[3]. It asks the user to enter a number, confirms which number has been entered and then tells the user whether the number is prime or not. An example of its output is shown in Fig. 2.

Figure 3(a) shows the blueprint we generate for this program. The graphical representation of the top-level `primeCheck` computation acts as a container for the other graphical elements. Each `IO` function application is represented by its own function-application box. The applied function's name is presented in bold on the top of the box, while its arguments are presented below it. Binds are represented by edges between two boxes. If the right-hand side of a bind is a lambda, the expression in the lambda is pretty-printed as edge-label.

[3] Clean does not have `do`-notation, so binds are explicitly written out.

```
primeCheck :: IO ()
primeCheck =         putStrLn "Enter␣number:"
        >>|          getLine
        >>= \numStr -> putStrLn ("Entered:␣" +++ numStr)
        >>|          if (isPrime (toInt numStr))
                        (putStrLn ("Is␣prime:␣" +++ numStr))
                        (putStrLn ("Isn't␣prime:␣" +++ numStr))
```

Fig. 1. IO implementation of the primeCheck example.

```
Enter number:
42
You have entered 42
42 is not prime
```

Fig. 2. Example of IO performed by primeCheck

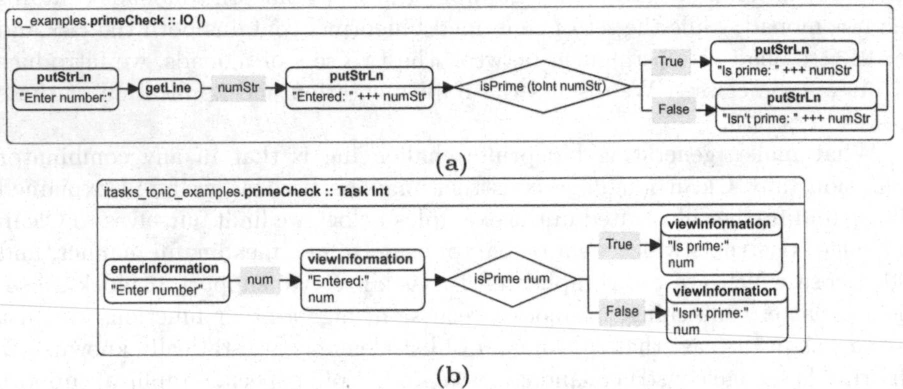

Fig. 3. Static blueprints of the primeCheck function implemented in both the IO and the Task monad.

2.2 Static Blueprints of the Task Monad

In this subsection we look at several example iTasks programs and the blueprint we generate for each of them. The goal of this subsection is to give an intuition for Tonic and its blueprints, while at the same time explaining the basics of iTasks. The basic tasks used in this section are also listed in Appendix B.

Prime Number Checker. An iTasks version of the primeCheck program is shown in Fig. 4, with its output shown in Fig. 5 and its corresponding blueprint shown in Fig. 3(b). iTasks' bind combinator automatically adds a "Continue" button to the user interface to progress to the right-hand side task. Since iTasks is *shallowly* embedded in Clean, *all* Clean language features can be used to construct iTasks programs. Some of these, e.g. conditionals, we also want to include in the blueprints. Tasks are defined as functions with monadic result type (Task a) for some a. Sequential task composition is accomplished with the monadic bind combinator. enterInformation and viewInformation are examples of basic predefined *editor* tasks, which generate a web-based graphical user interface for a given type using generic programming techniques. The former editor allows the user to enter data using generically generated web forms, while the latter editor renders a textual read-only representation of the data.

```
primeCheck :: Task Int
primeCheck
  =           enterInformation "Enter␣number" []
  >>= \num -> viewInformation "Entered:" [] num
  >>|         if (isPrime num)
                (viewInformation "Is␣prime:" [] num)
                (viewInformation "Isn't␣prime:" [] num)
```

Fig. 4. iTasks implementation of the primeCheck example.

Despite the fact that the previous two programs are defined in different monads, their blueprints are similar, since they share the common abstraction level of a monad.

Step. User definable buttons can be created by using the *step* combinator (>>*), shown in Fig. 6 (with its output in Fig. 10(a) and blueprint in Fig. 7). The step's left-hand side is a task that is executed first, while its right-hand side is a *list* of conditions paired with a follow-up task. If a condition is met, the corresponding follow-up task is executed.

In this example one such condition is provided in the form of an OnAction condition, which causes a button to be rendered in the left-hand side task's user interface. OnAction takes two arguments: an *action*, which describes the button's text and a list of button meta-data, and a continuation to proceed to the next task once the corresponding button is pressed. The continuation is of type (TaskValue a) -> Maybe (Task b). If the continuation returns Nothing the button is disabled, if it returns Just, the button is enabled and pressing it will progress the work-flow to the inner Task b. Several convenience functions are available to write these continuation functions. In this example, the ifValue function is used. It takes a predicate (isPalindrome) over the left hand-side task's value, enabling the corresponding button only if the predicate returns True.

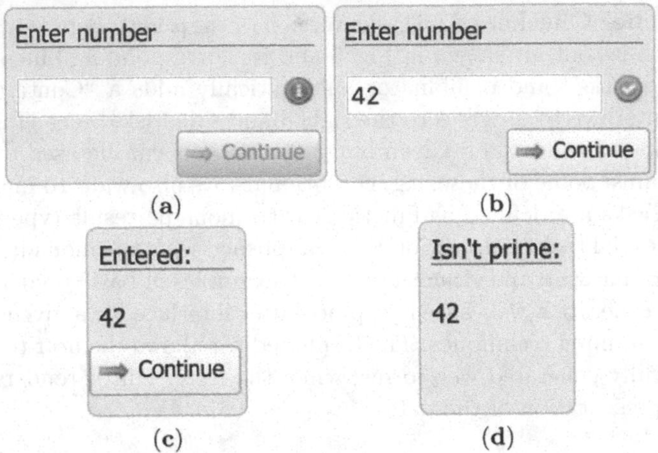

Fig. 5. Example of the web forms generated by primeCheck

```
palindrome :: Task String
palindrome
  =  enterInformation "Enter␣a␣palindrome" []
  >>* [ OnAction (Action "Ok" [])
         (ifValue isPalindrome (\palindrome -> return palindrome))]
  where
  isPalindrome :: String -> Bool
  isPalindrome s = let s‘ = [toLower c \\ c <-: s | c <> '␣']
                   in  s‘ == reverse s‘
```

Fig. 6. iTasks implementation of the palindrome example.

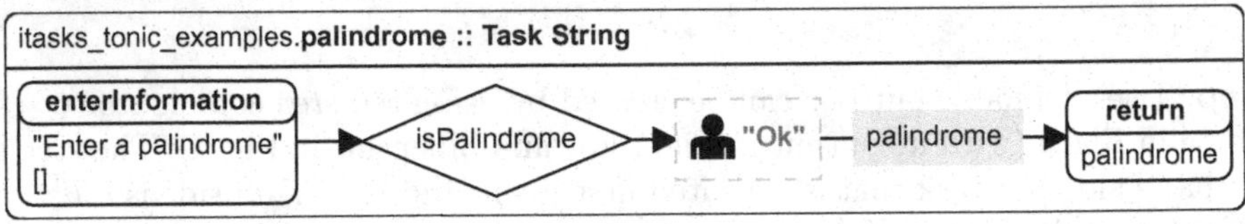

Fig. 7. Static blueprint of palindrome

The step combinator is strictly more powerful than the bind combinator. In fact, the bind combinator is implemented in terms of the step combinator, as shown in Fig. 8.

```
(>>=) :: (Task a) (a -> Task b) -> Task b | iTask a & iTask b
(>>=) taska taskbf = taska >>* [ OnAction (Action "Continue" []) (hasValue taskbf)
                               , OnValue  (ifStable taskbf) ]
```

Fig. 8. Implementation of the bind combinator.

If the left-hand side task has a value, the "Continue" button is enabled. Additionally, if the left-hand side task has a *stable* value, i.e., if the value is guaranteed to never change again, it also proceeds to the right-hand side task.

Recursion and Higher-Order Tasks. Tasks can be passed as argument to other tasks: one can define higher-order tasks. Other functional concepts translate to TOP as well, such as recursive tasks. Both of these concepts are demonstrated in Fig. 9 in the `add1by1` task. Its blueprint is shown in Fig. 11. One new graphical element is that of the `let` binding; they are rendered as sign-posts.

Here we see that `add1by1` has two arguments; a higher order task, called `task`, of type `(Task a)`, and an accumulator `listSoFar` of type `[a]`. On demand of the end user, `add1by1` recursively evaluates the higher order task and accumulates the results. When finished, the accumulator is yielded as result. Notice that `add1by1` is not polymorphic in `a`, but overloaded. In Clean, context restrictions are specified at the end of a type definition (`| iTask a`). This context restriction is synonymous for several generic functions that take care of the type driven rendering of GUIs and the communication between the web server and the client (i.e. the web browser). This can automatically be derived by the Clean compiler for any first order type. Context information is considered to be too much detail to mention in a blueprint and is therefore left out in the types shown in the blueprint.

The task `add1by1` also has a step function. In this particular example, we can see that step functions are rendered differently from binds. Each condition in the step's right-hand side's list is rendered in its own branch. Continuation convenience functions as found in iTasks' standard libraries are rendered in a special way as well. Here, the `hasManyElems` predicated is rendered as a diamond, implying that this condition should be met before the work-flow can continue. The action is rendered as well, together with a small figure showing that it relates to a user action. It is possible to customize the way blueprints are rendered (see Sect. 4.2).

The higher order task `task` is executed first. Statically we only know the type of `task`, but we do not know what its concrete value will be. For this we use a dashed frame. We do know that the task yields a value of proper type `a`. This value can be added to the accumulator (when the "Add another" button is pressed), after which `add1by1` recursively calls itself. Alternatively, the task can be terminated by pressing "Done", but this option can only be chosen when at least two values are collected in the list.

```
add1by1 :: (Task a) [a] -> Task [a] | iTask a
add1by1 task listSoFar
  =         task
  >>= \elem -> let newList = [elem : listSoFar] in
              viewInformation "New␣list:␣" [] newList
  >>*         [ OnAction (Action "Add␣another" [])
                       (always (add1by1 task newList))
              , OnAction (Action "Done" [])
                       (ifValue hasManyElems (\xs -> return xs))
              ]
  where
  hasManyElems :: [a] -> Bool
  hasManyElems xs = length xs > 1

addPalindromes :: Task [String]
addPalindromes = add1by1 palindrome []
```

Fig. 9. Implementation of the `add1by1` task.

Parallel Tasks. iTasks allows several tasks to be executed in parallel. In the `parallelChat` example, shown in Fig. 13, the user of the task (`currentUser`) starts a chat by first selecting n friends to chat with from a list of administrated users. Next, $n + 1$ `makeChat` tasks are started in parallel using the library combinator `allTasks`. This function expects a lists of tasks to be executed in parallel and ends when all its tasks are ended. `parallelChat`'s output is shown in Fig. 12 and its blueprint is shown in Fig. 14.

Each `makeChat` task enables user i to have a chat with the others via a shared data source `chatBox` of type `Shared [String]`. Shared Data Sources (SDS) [?] allow tasks to share information. The shared list used here contains as many strings as there are chatting users, where the i-th element of the list represents the information typed in by the i-th chat user. In iTasks, shared data structures are maintained automatically. Whenever someone is changing the content of a shared data structure, any task that is looking at its structure is informed and updated automatically. This notification system works for any first order data type, not just shared strings of text. In this example, chatting users automatically see what is written by someone else. Chat users can only update their part of the shared structure. In `updateSharedInformation` the i-th element is selected (`selectChat`) to be updated in the function defined in `UpdateWith` while in `viewSharedInformation` the other elements are selected (`dropChat`) in `ViewWith` and shown read-only.

In this particular example it is statically undecidable how many parallel task there will be, since it depends on the number of chosen friends. We will later see that at run-time we can in fact show these tasks in a dynamic blueprint, and see who is chatting with whom and inspect what they are chatting about.

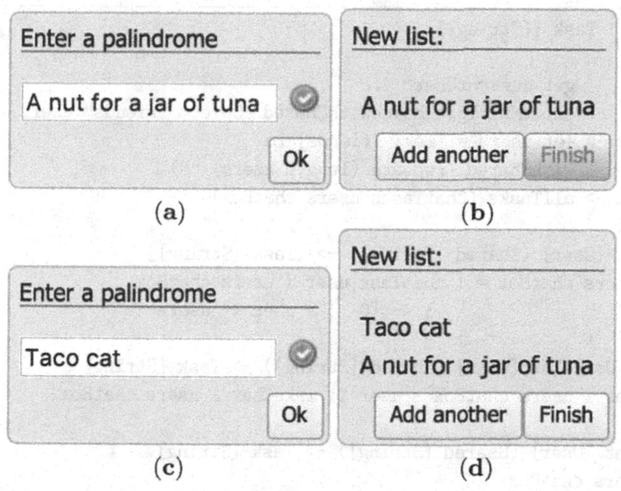

Fig. 10. GUIs when applying add1by1 to the palindrome task

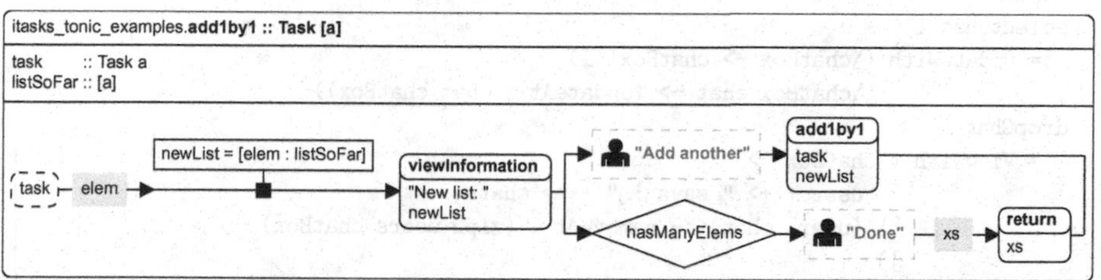

Fig. 11. Static blueprint of add1by1 with a higher-order task and recursion

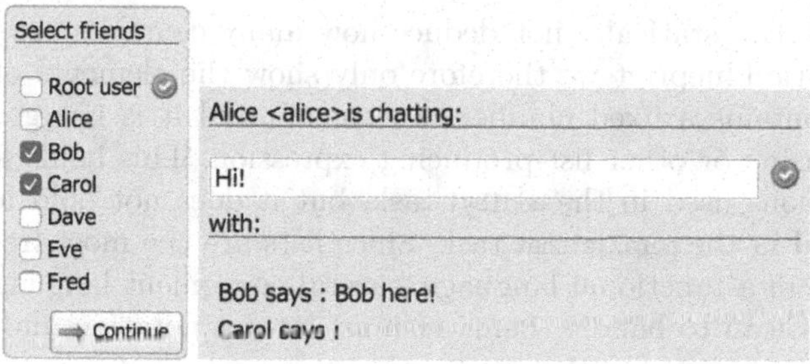

Select friends
Root user
Alice
Bob
Carol
Dave
Eve
Fred
Continue

Alice <alice>is chatting:
Hi!
with:
Bob says : Bob here!
Carol says :

Fig. 12. parallelChat program execution

```
parallelChat :: Task [[String]]
parallelChat
  =              get currentUser
  >>= \me      -> enterMultipleChoiceWithShared "Select␣friends" users
  >>= \friends -> let users = [me : friends] in
                 withShared (repeatn (length users) "")
     (\chatBox -> allTasks (chatTasks users chatBox))
  where
  chatTasks :: [User] (Shared [String]) -> [Task [String]]
  chatTasks users chatBox = [ chatTask user i users chatBox
                            \\ i <- [0 ..] & user <- users
                            ]
  chatTask :: User Int [User] (Shared [String]) -> Task [String]
  chatTask user i users chatBox = user @: makeChat i users chatBox

makeChat :: Int [User] (Shared [String]) -> Task [String]
makeChat i users chatBox
  =   updateSharedInformation [selectChat i]
        (users !! i +++> "is␣chatting:␣") chatBox
  ||- viewSharedInformation [dropChat i] "with:␣" chatBox
  where
  selectChat i
    = UpdateWith (\chatBox -> chatBox!!i)
                 (\chatBox chat -> (updateAt i chat chatBox))
  dropChat i
    = ViewWith (\chatBox ->
               [  user +++> "␣says␣:␣" +++> chat
               \\ (user, chat) <- removeAt i (zip2 users chatBox)
               ])
```

Fig. 13. Implementation of the `parallelChat` task.

In general, one can statically not deduce how many elements are contained in a list. In a static blueprint we therefore only show the elements of a list when it statically contains a fixed number of elements and it is not generated by a list-comprehension or other list-producing expression. This holds for the list of step continuations used in the `add1by1` task, but it does not hold for the list of chat tasks used in the `parallelChat` task. Since lists are the most frequently used data structure in a functional language, several convenient language constructs are offered in Clean to handle them, such as dot-dot notation and list comprehensions.

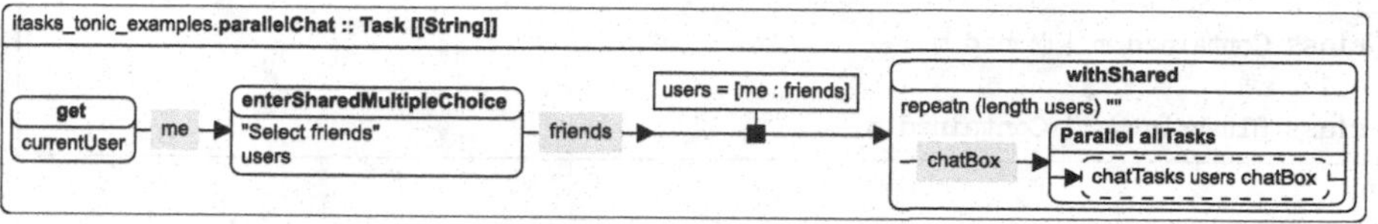

Fig. 14. Static blueprint of parallel chat example in iTasks

3 Building Static Blueprints

Figure 15 shows the architecture of the modified Clean-Tonic compiler. In addition to the code the compiler normally generates (Intel, Arm and JavaScript), it now also generates a file containing blueprint information for each Tonic-enabled Clean module. This information can be read in by a tool called the *Tonic Viewer*. The viewer is implemented in iTasks itself and can render blueprints in any HTML5 compatible browser.

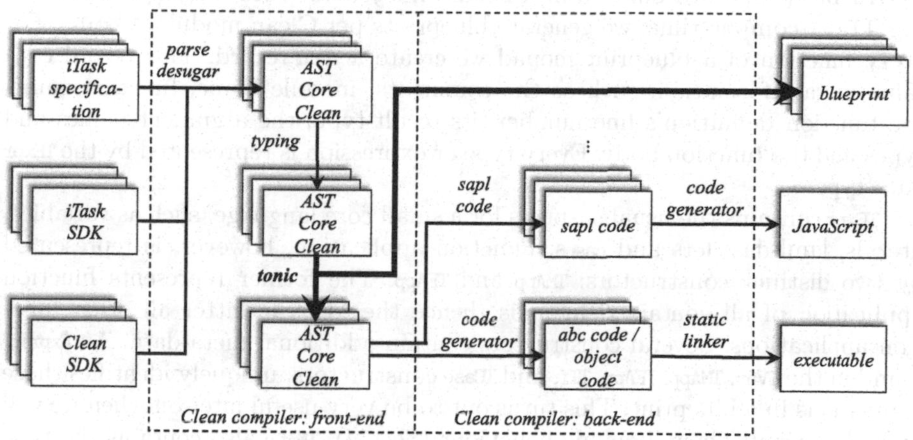

Fig. 15. Global architecture of the clean - tonic compiler

As explained in the previous section, not all functions are automatically turned into a blueprint, only those with a blueprint monadic return type. Likewise, not all monadic function applications are turned into blueprint nodes, only those with a contained monadic return type. To differentiate between these sets of monads we introduce two type classes, `Blueprint` and `Contained`, both shown in Fig. 16.

```
class Contained m | Monad m

class Blueprint m | Contained m
```

Fig. 16. Class signatures for `Contained` and `Blueprint` type classes.

Whenever a programmer provides an instance of the `Blueprint` class for a certain type, a blueprint is generated by the compiler for every function which returns a monad of that type. Whenever an instance of the class `Contained` is provided, the application of the function in a blueprint is treated special. Any type with a `Blueprint` instance also requires a `Contained` instance, which is enforced by the former class' context restriction. Not all modules are considered for blueprint generation. Only modules that explicitly import the Tonic framework are searched for top-level blueprints. This approach offers a course-grained control over the blueprint generation process. For example, none of the iTasks core modules import the Tonic framework, so no core tasks are turned to blueprint.

All blueprints are built from a small and *general* core language, shown in Fig. 17. At compile-time, we generate blueprints per Clean module (`TModule`). For every function of a blueprint monad we create a `TFun` record. This record contains meta-information, such as the comments, module name, function name, the function definition's line number, its result-type, the argument names and types and the function body. Every type or expression is represented by the `TExpr` data type.

`TExpr` contains the usual suspects for a small core language, such as variables, literals, lambdas, `let`s and `case`s. Function application, however, is represented by two distinct constructors: `TMApp` and `TFApp`. The former represents function application of all contained monads (hence the M), the latter all other function applications. Several constructors contain additional meta-data. An `ExprId`, found in the `TVar`, `TMApp`, `TFApp`, `TIf`, and `TCase` constructors, uniquely identifies those expressions in a blueprint. This turns out to be very useful later on when we will make blueprints show dynamic behaviour (Sect. 4). `TMApp` also contains the type of the monad (if the function is monomorphic in its monadic return type) and the name of the module in which the function being applied is defined. This is to disambiguate functions with the same name. In addition to the function's arguments and priority, it has an optional `VarPtr` in case the function being applied is variable.

```
:: ModuleName  :== String
:: FuncName    :== String
:: Pattern     :== TExpr
:: TypeName    :== String
:: PPExpr      :== String
:: ExprId      :== [Int]
:: VarName     :== String
:: VarPtr      :== Int

:: TModule    = { tm_name  :: ModuleName
                , tm_funcs :: Map FuncName TFun }

:: TFun       = { tf_comments  :: String
                , tf_module    :: ModuleName
                , tf_name      :: FuncName
                , tf_iclLineNo :: Int
                , tf_resty     :: TExpr
                , tf_args      :: [(TExpr, TExpr)]
                , tf_body      :: TExpr }

:: TExpr      = TVar    ExprId PPExpr VarPtr
              | TPPExpr PPExpr
              | TMApp   ExprId (Maybe TypeName) ModuleName
                        FuncName [TExpr] TPriority (Maybe VarPtr)
              | TFApp   ExprId FuncName [TExpr] TPriority
              | TLam    [TExpr] TExpr
              | TLet    [(Pattern, TExpr)] TExpr
              | TIf     ExprId TExpr TExpr TExpr
              | TCase   ExprId TExpr [(Pattern, TExpr)]

:: TPriority = TPrio TAssoc Int | TNoPrio

:: TAssoc    = TLeftAssoc | TRightAssoc | TNoAssoc
```

Fig. 17. Algebraic data type definitions for blueprints.

To get an intuition of what a static blueprint looks like in code, lets look at a blueprint for the iTasks `primeCheck` example (Sect. 2.2). The blueprint code is shown in Fig. 18. Note how the unique node numbering allows for a deterministic lookup of a node's parents and siblings. Despite the presence of meta data such as the unique node identifiers and the unique variable identifiers, the blueprint remains compact, making it suitable for transmission over a network.

```
{ TFun
| tf_comments  = ""
, tf_module    = "itasks_tonic_examples"
, tf_name      = "primeCheck"
, tf_iclLineNo = 36
, tf_resty     = TFApp [] "Task" [TPPExpr "_String"] TNoPrio
, tf_args      = []
, tf_body      =
  TMApp [0] Nothing "iTasks.API.Core.Types" ">>="
    [ TMApp [0, 0] (Just "Task") "itasks_tonic_examples" "enterNumber"
        [] TNoPrio Nothing
    , TLam [TVar [] "num" 4566313280]
        (TLet [ ( TVar [] "numStr" 4566313512
                , TFApp [0, 1, 1] "toString" [TVar [] "num" 4566313280] TNoPrio)]
          (TMApp [0, 1, 0] Nothing "iTasks.API.Core.Types" ">>|"
            [ TMApp [0, 1, 0, 0] (Just "Task")
                "iTasks.API.Common.InteractionTasks" "viewInformation"
                [TPPExpr "Entered:", TVar [] "numStr" 4566313512] TNoPrio Nothing
            , TIf [0, 1, 0, 1, 0]
                (TFApp [0, 1, 0, 1, 0, 0] "isPrime"
                  [TVar [] "num" 4566313280] TNoPrio)
                (TMApp [0, 1, 0, 1, 0, 1] (Just "Task")
                  "iTasks.API.Common.InteractionTasks" "viewInformation"
                  [TPPExpr "Is␣prime:", TVar [] "numStr" 4566313512]
                  TNoPrio Nothing)
                (TMApp [0, 1, 0, 1, 0, 2] (Just "Task")
                  "iTasks.API.Common.InteractionTasks" "viewInformation"
                  [TPPExpr "Isn't␣prime:", TVar [] "numStr" 4566313512]
                  TNoPrio Nothing)
            ] (TPrio TLeftAssoc 1) Nothing))]
    (TPrio TLeftAssoc 1) Nothing
}
```

Fig. 18. Concrete blueprint value.

4 Dynamic Blueprints

A static blueprint gives a graphical view of how the monad combinators are defined in the source code. Now we want to be able to trace and inspect the execution of the resulting application, making use of the static blueprints. Although the monad parts of the program may be just a small part of the source code, they are an important part and they commonly form the backbone of the architecture of the application. If we can follow their execution and see how their corresponding blueprints are being applied, we will already have a good impression of the run-time behaviour of the application. We want to show which monadic computation is currently being executed, how far along the program's flow we currently are, the current value for a given argument or variable, the result of a completed computation, and which program branches will be taken in the future. Before delving into the technical challenges associated with addressing these requirements, lets look at our previous examples and how their static blueprints are used at run-time.

When a function with a `Blueprint`-monadic type is applied, we make an instantiation (a copy) of its corresponding static blueprint, creating a *dynamic blueprint.* On top of it we can show who is calling it, we can inspect its actual arguments, and visualize the progress in the flow when the body is being executed. The Tonic viewer can show and inspect these dynamic blueprints. Notice that the Tonic viewer can show the blueprints in real-time, i.e. when the application is being executed. The Tonic viewer also allows inspecting the past, and it can sometimes predict the future. Since we output blueprints in SVG, most blueprints in this section are imported SVG files. In some cases, however, we use a screen-shot instead. This is so we can include other DOM elements, such as the Tonic viewer's value inspector windows, as well.

4.1 Dynamic Blueprints of the Task Monad

In this section we will look at how we augment the blueprints of the previous examples with run-time information.

Prime Number Checker. In the `primeCheck` example we saw sequential composition using a bind combinator. Since bind determines the order in which computations are executed, it is a great place for us to track progress in a program's flow. Figure 19 shows the dynamic blueprints for the `primeCheck` iTasks program as it is executed.

When the program starts and the user is presented with the input field, its corresponding blueprint instance is that of Fig. 19(a). Immediately the blueprint is different from its static incarnation in several ways. A pair of numbers is added in the top bar, next to the task name. This is the *task ID*, uniquely identifying this task instance within the iTasks run-time system. Next to it is the image of a person, together with the name of the person that is currently executing this particular task instance. Going to the lower half of the blueprint, we see that the upper area of the task-application node is coloured green. Green means that the task is currently actively being worked on. We also say that the `enterNumber` node is *active.* Additionally, the task ID of the `enterNumber` task instance is added to the blueprint and positioned next to the task name.

Next to each node, a square is drawn. Clicking on this square allows us to inspect the task's value in real-time. Its colour also indicates the stability of the task's value. In Fig. 19(a), there is no value yet, hence the square is white. This is confirmed by a pop-up window when we click the white square. However, as soon as a number is entered by the end user in the editor's text field, or whenever the number is changed, the current input is directly shown in the inspection window (Fig. 19(b)).

On the right side of the blueprint there is a diamond-shaped conditional node, followed by two `viewInformation` nodes, which now have green borders. These border

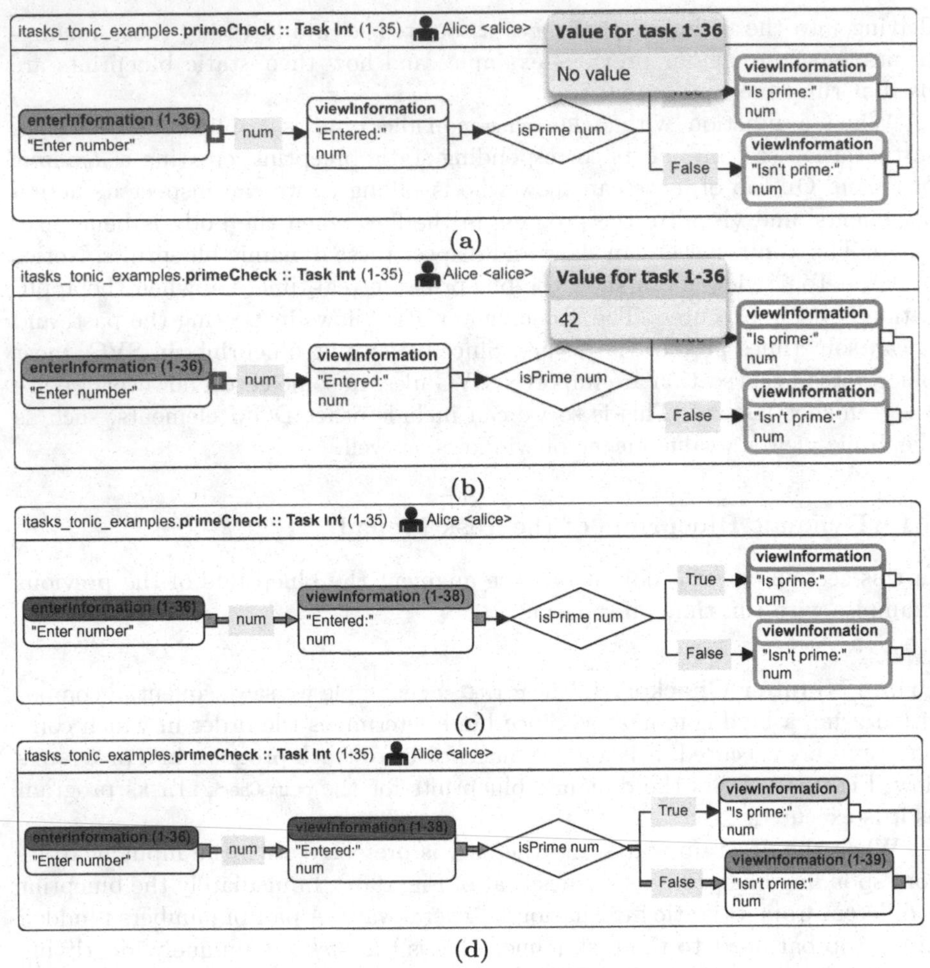

Fig. 19. Dynamic blueprints of `primeCheck` showing monadic progress tracking and value inspection (Color figure online)

colours tell us something about the future, in particular which program branch might be taken. Since the program has only just started, all branches might still be reached. However, when we enter the number 42 to the `enterNumber` task's text field – which is not a prime number – we can already predict that the `True` branch will not be reached. This is represented by red borders, as seen in Fig. 19(b). If we would change the number in the box to, e.g., 7 the tasks in the `False` branch would receive a red border instead. We call this feature *dynamic branch prediction*. Once the user has entered a number and has pressed "Continue", the work-flow progresses to the second task and the blueprint instance is updated accordingly (Fig. 19(c)). The first node is no longer highlighted. Instead, it is *frozen* and given a blue colour. A frozen blueprint node for a given task instance will not change again. Additionally, the edge between the first and second node is now coloured green. For edges, green does not indicate activity, but the *stability* of the previous task's value. A green edge means an unstable value, while a blue edges means a stable value. In iTasks, tasks may have a stable or unstable value, or even no value at all. It reflects the behaviour of an end user filling in a form. The form may be empty to start with or some information may be entered which can be changed over time. Once values are stable they can no longer change over time. When the "Continue" button is pressed again, we reach the `False` branch, as predicated earlier. Since the `True` branch is no longer reachable, its nodes now get a grey header (Fig. 19(d)).

Recursion and Higher-Order Tasks. Yet other dynamic behaviour is found in the blueprints of `add1by1` (as applied in `addPalindromes`), in which we have to deal with a task as argument, a step combinator, and recursion. Its dynamic blueprints are shown in Fig. 20. Notice that the `task` variable is now replaced by a task-application node containing the name of the `palindrome` task (Fig. 20(a)). When a valid palindrome has been entered, the workflow continues to the `viewInformation` task. The step combinator at that point presents the user with two buttons: "Add another" and "Done". The former can always be pressed, whereas the latter is only enabled when at least two values are accumulated in `newList`. Since we only have one palindrome so far, only the "Add another" button is enabled. This is reflected in the blueprint (Fig. 20(b)). Recursion is simply yet another task-application node (Fig. 20(c)). Entering the recursion creates a new blueprint instance for the `add1by1` task in which another `palindrome` task is executed (Fig. 20(d)). When the user submits another valid palindrome, we encounter `viewInformation` again. This time, however, the "Done" button is enabled, because the `hasManyElems` predicate holds. (Figure 20(e)). Pressing "Done" finishes the `add1by1` task and returns the list of palindromes (Fig. 20(f)).

Parallel Chat Tasks. In the `parallelChat` example we saw that the function application of `chatTasks` can only be pretty printed. There are two reasons for this: (1) we don't have a `Contained` instance for lists (for the sake of this example), and (2) `chatTasks` is a function application. We cannot compute any kind of function statically. At run-time, however, we would like to know which tasks are being executed in parallel, so we need to replace the pretty-printed expression with a list of task-application nodes dynamically. We can see how Tonic deals with this situation in Fig. 21.

Figure 21(a) shows that we select two friends to chat with: Bob and Carol. Next, the `parallelChat` task delegates three chat tasks: one to the current user, Alice, and one to each of her friends. Since the `chatTasks` function application is now evaluated, we can substitute a list of task application nodes for the pretty-printed expression. Each of the nodes contain the parallel task's name and task ID. For each of these nodes a corresponding blueprint instance is created, which can be inspected as well (Fig. 21(a)).

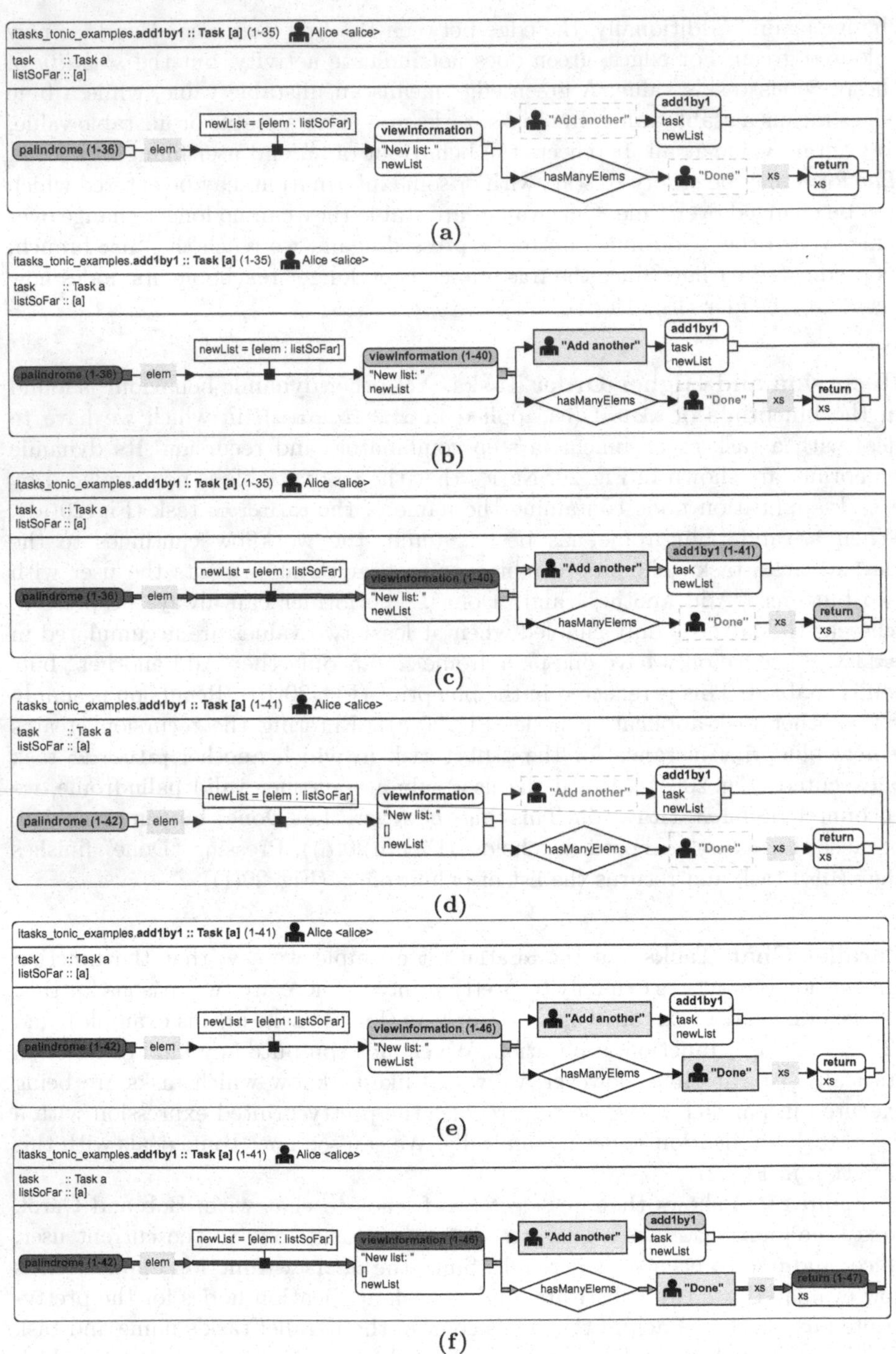

Fig. 20. Dynamic blueprints of add1by1

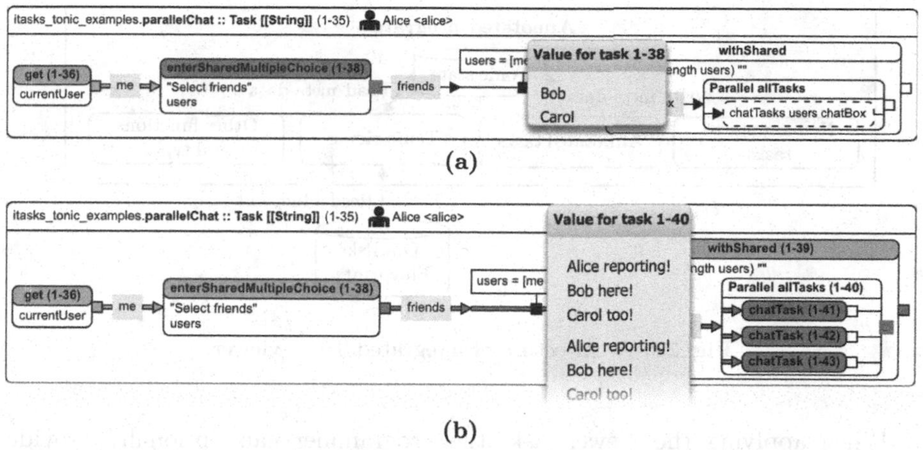

Fig. 21. Dynamic blueprints for the parallel chat example

4.2 Tonic Architecture

To enable such dynamic features, we need to make a connection between the static blueprints and the program's run-time. With this connection, we can pass additional information from the original program to the Tonic run-time system. This is similar to standard tracing and debugging tools. Connecting blueprints and a program's run-time is done by extending the `Contained` and `Blueprint` classes with *wrapper functions* that we apply to the original program at compile-time. These wrapper functions are executed at the same time as the program's original functions. It is up to the programmer to provide sensible instances for these classes. We have already provided instances for both classes for the `Task` type that can be used in any iTasks program. Section 4.4 shows how these classes are defined for iTasks.

Figure 22 shows the architecture of a Tonic-enabled iTasks application. Tonic maintains a central SDS with run-time information. When a wrapper function is applied, it writes additional information to this SDS, allowing us to track the program's progress and inspect its values. The specifics of what data the wrappers contain are discussed later in this section. Writing to the share triggers an update that refreshes the dynamic blueprint in the Tonic viewer.

The Tonic viewer is written in iTasks itself and is therefore yet another task. Using the Tonic viewer in an iTasks application requires the programmer to make sure the viewer task is reachable by the program's end-user. Having the viewer built into the application that is going to be visualized has certain advantages. In iTasks' particular case, this allows us to easily inspect nearly all function arguments and task values using iTasks' own generic editors. This even works for complex types. Section 4.5 shows how this integrated viewer is used by an end-user. Section 5.1 talks about a solution that does not require the viewer to be integrated with the original application.

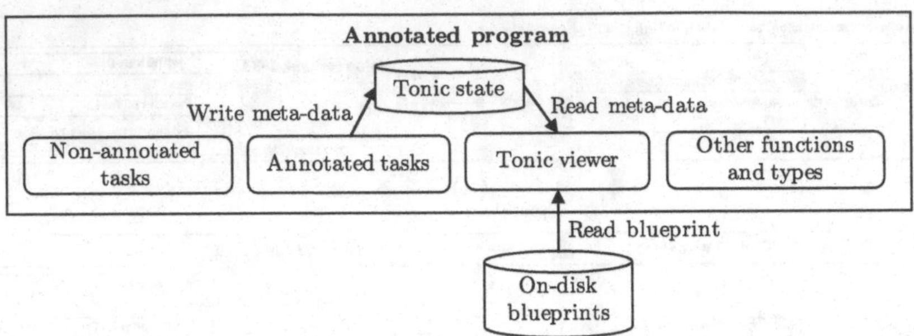

Fig. 22. Architecture of integrated Tonic viewer.

When applying the viewer-task, the programmer can optionally provide additional render functions with which the rendering of individual function-application nodes can be customized. The programmer can use our fully declarative SVG library [1] to define alternative visualizations. This library is a general-purpose tool to draw arbitrary vector images. As such, the programmer is not constrained in what the custom rendering looks like.

Contained Monads. The `Contained` class is what identifies interesting function applications. It is therefore the right place to gather more information about the functions being applied. For example, which function is being applied? To which blueprint node does this function application correspond? How does the value of the underlying function application influence the program's workflow? We extend the `Contained` class with only one function: `wrapFunApp`, as shown in Fig. 23.

```
class Contained m | Monad m where
  wrapFunApp :: ModuleName FuncName ExprId [(ExprId, a -> Int)]
                (m a) -> m a | iTask a
```

Fig. 23. Complete definition of the `Contained` type class.

It is here that the Tonic system is notified of the execution of individual computations, where the current value of these computations is inspected, where blueprints are updated dynamically, etcetera. `wrapFunApp` takes five arguments, the first two of which are the module and function name of the function being applied. The third argument is an `ExprId`, which together with the module and function name of the function application's context (obtained via the `Blueprint` class and passed through by iTasks; see also Sect. 4.2), uniquely identifies this function application. The same `ExprId` is also found in the blueprint of the parent function, allowing us to relate run-time execution to the static blueprint. The fourth argument allows us to do dynamic branch prediction. It is a list of pairs, the first element of which is the `ExprId` that refers to the `case` block of which we want to predict its future. The second element is a function that, given the value of type `a` of the wrapped task (`Task a`), gives the index number of the branch that will be chosen, should that value be used. Before discussing how the `Contained` class is used we need to understand how dynamic branch prediction works.

Tonic's dynamic branch prediction feature utilizes the fact that Tonic is implemented as a compiler pass in the Clean compiler. During the Tonic pass, we copy `case` blocks and lift them to a newly generated function. We transform the right-hand side of the individual cases and return the *index* of the branch as integer. We call this entire procedure *case lifting.* By applying this fresh function, we known, using the original case expression, the index of the branch that will be taken, should that expression be evaluated with an identical context. Definition 1 formalizes this process.

Definition 1. *Case lifting transformation. Given a* `case` *expression*

$$\begin{aligned}&\textbf{case } f\ x_1 \ldots x_i \textbf{ of}\\ &\quad p_1 \rightarrow e_1\\ &\quad \ldots\\ &\quad p_j \rightarrow e_j\end{aligned}$$

Generate a fresh function

$$\begin{aligned}&dbpf :: a_1 \ldots a_i \rightarrow Int\\ &dbpf\ x_1 \ldots x_i = \textbf{case } f\ x_1 \ldots x_i \textbf{ of}\\ &\qquad p_1 \rightarrow 1\\ &\qquad \ldots\\ &\qquad p_j \rightarrow j\end{aligned}$$

As mentioned earlier, wrappers are not always applied. In particular, it might be necessary to forego wrapping certain expressions when they are an argument to another function. Consider again the `add1by1` example. Should we wrap the recursive call as well as the `task` variable, the recursive instance would effectively have two wrappers around `task` due to laziness. When `task` is evaluated, both wrappers would be evaluated as well, polluting Tonic's run-time state with wrong data. Still, in some cases we do want to wrap higher-order arguments. The most prominent case for this is the bind combinator. An iTasks-specific case are the parallel combinators. They are rendered as a container within which we want to keep following the workflow's progress. We need the wrappers to do so. To support this case, we only wrap function arguments when the function itself comes from a module that does not enable Tonic. In addition, a function-level pragma, either `TONIC_CONTEXT` or `TONIC_NO_CONTEXT`, can be provided. When the former pragma is used, the function's arguments are wrapped. With the latter, they are not. The pragmas override the default module-based wrapping behaviour and allow custom domain-specific behaviour to be specified instead. Definition 2 formalizes the transformations the Tonic compiler applies to utilize the `Contained` class.

Definition 2. *Contained transformation. For all function applications $f e_1 \ldots e_i$ where $f :: \alpha_1 \ldots \alpha_i \rightarrow m\ \alpha_n$ and f is in module M, and for which holds* **instance Contained** m:

$[\![f e_1 \ldots e_i \gg\!= \lambda v \rightarrow e_j]\!]$
iff module `M` *does not enable Tonic or f has* `TONIC_CONTEXT`
$\Rightarrow$
wrapFunApp "M" "f" $exprId(f)\ dbpC(v, e_j)\ (f [\![e_1]\!] \ldots [\![e_i]\!])$
$\gg\!= \lambda x \rightarrow [\![e_j]\!]$

$[\![f e_1 \ldots e_i \gg\!= \lambda v \rightarrow e_j]\!]$
otherwise
$\Rightarrow$
wrapFunApp "M" "f" $exprId(f)\ dbpC(v, e_j)\ (f e_1 \ldots e_i)$
$\gg\!= \lambda x \rightarrow [\![e_j]\!]$

$[\![f e_1 \ldots e_i]\!]$
iff module `M` *does not enable Tonic or f has* `TONIC_CONTEXT`
$\Rightarrow$
wrapFunApp "M" "f" $exprId(f)\ \square\ (f [\![e_1]\!] \ldots [\![e_i]\!])$

$[\![f e_1 \ldots e_i]\!]$
otherwise
$\Rightarrow$
wrapFunApp "M" "f" $exprId(f)\ \square\ (f e_1 \ldots e_i)$

$[\![e]\!]$
$\Rightarrow$
e

Two additional functions are used during this transformation: *exprId* and *dbpC*. *exprId*(f) returns a unique identifier for the application of f to its arguments. *dbpC* enables dynamic branch prediction for contained monads as follows. For all lifted case functions $dbpf_k\ x_1 \ldots x_i, x_{i+1}$ from e_j, if $v \equiv x_{i+1}$ and $x_1 \ldots x_i$ are bound, then $[(caseExprId(dbpf_1), dbpf_1\ x_1 \ldots x_i), \ldots, (caseExprId(dbpf_n), dbpf_n\ x_1 \ldots x_i)]$. Here, *caseExprId* returns the unique identifier for the original case expression that was used to create *dbpf*. Implementing dynamic branch prediction in a bind is possible because the monad right-identity law guarantees that for a bind expression $e_1 \gg\!= \lambda x \rightarrow e_2$, x will always bind e_1's result value.

Blueprint Monads. The `Blueprint` class already allows us to identify functions for which to generate a blueprint. This class is therefore well suited to capture some meta data for blueprint functions that would otherwise be lost at run-time. We extend the `Blueprint` class with two functions: `wrapFunBody` and `wrapFunArg`, as shown in Fig. 24.

```
class Blueprint m | Contained m where
  wrapFunBody :: ModuleName FuncName [(VarName, m ())]
                 [(ExprId, Int)] (m a) -> m a | iTask a
  wrapFunArg  :: VarName a -> m () | iTask a
```

Fig. 24. Complete definition of the `Blueprint` type class.

The `wrapFunBody` function is statically applied to the body of a blueprint function. It has several goals: to make the blueprint function's module and function name available at run-time, to provide a way to inspect the blueprint function's arguments, and to do future branch prediction based on the function's arguments. The `wrapFunArg` function is used in the third argument of `wrapFunBody`. It is statically applied to all function arguments to enable their inspection at run-time. In general, the compiler applies the following transformation rule:

Definition 3. *Blueprint transformation. For all function definitions* $f :: \alpha_1 \ldots \alpha_i \rightarrow m\ \alpha_n$ *in module* M*, for which holds* **instance Blueprint** m*:*

$$
\begin{array}{l}
\llbracket f x_1 \ldots x_i = e \rrbracket \\
\Rightarrow \\
f\ x_1 \ldots x_i = \textit{wrapFunBody}\ \text{“M”}\ \text{“f”} \\
\qquad\qquad\qquad [(\text{“}x_1\text{”}, \textit{wrapFunArg}\ x_1) \\
\qquad\qquad\qquad ,\ldots \\
\qquad\qquad\qquad ,(\text{“}x_i\text{”}, \textit{wrapFunArg}\ x_i)] \\
\qquad\qquad\qquad dbpB(x_1 \ldots x_i, e) \\
\qquad\qquad\qquad \llbracket e \rrbracket
\end{array}
$$

dbpB works subtly different from *dbpC*. Rather than being associated with a variable bound by a lambda in a bind, it works on the function's arguments, which are all bound as soon as the blueprint is instantiated.

The `iTask` constraint on the `Contained` and `Blueprint` class members is used extensively in iTasks. Unfortunately, due to limitations in Clean's type system, we are currently forced to include this context restriction in our two classes, even though they might be instantiated for monads that have nothing to do with iTasks. We will come back to this limitation in Sect. 7.

4.3 Tonic Wrappers in Action

Applying all transformations to the `primeCheck` example transforms it to the code in Fig. 25 (manually simplified for readability). Module names passed to the wrappers are fully qualified. The lists of numbers are the unique expression identifiers from the *exprId* function. The `_f_case` function is an instance of the *dbpf* function.

```
primeCheck :: Task String
primeCheck = wrapFunBody "itasks_tonic_examples" "primeCheck" [] []
  wrapFunApp "itasks_tonic_examples" "enterNumber" [0, 0]
    [([0, 1, 0, 1, 0], _f_case_4566316320)] enterNumber
>>= \num -> let numStr = toString num in
  wrapFunApp "iTasks.API.Common.InteractionTasks" "viewInformation"
    [0, 1, 0, 0] [] (viewInformation "Entered:" [] numStr)
>>| if (isPrime num)
      (wrapFunApp "iTasks.API.Common.InteractionTasks"
        "viewInformation" [0, 1, 0, 1, 0, 0] []
        (viewInformation "Is␣prime:" [] numStr)
      (wrapFunApp "iTasks.API.Common.InteractionTasks"
        "viewInformation" [0, 1, 0, 1, 0, 1] []
        (viewInformation "Isn't␣prime:" [] numStr)
```

Fig. 25. Example of the transformed `primeCheck` program.

4.4 Dynamic Blueprints in iTasks

To demonstrate how these wrappers can be used, we show their concrete implementation for iTasks. A task in iTasks is represented by the `Task` type (Fig. 26).

```
:: Task a = Task (TaskAdministration TonicAdministration *IWorld
                 -> *(TaskResult a, *IWorld))
```

Fig. 26. The `Task` type.

A task is implemented as a continuation which takes some internal task-administration and some Tonic administration and passes it down the continuation. It chains a unique `IWorld` through the continuation, which allows interaction with SDSs and provides general IO capabilities, amongst other things. The continuation produces a `TaskResult`, which, amongst other things, contains the task's result value.

The wrappers we place in the code unpack the continuation from a `Task` constructor and use it to define a new task, as shown in Fig. 27. In the case of the `Blueprint` class, the wrapper's job is to create a new blueprint instance for the task that is being started (line 7), while in the case of `Contained`, the wrapper's job is to update the blueprint instance in which the task-application takes place. In that case, a blueprint instance already exists and just needs to be loaded from Tonic's internal administration (line 23). Both wrapper classes perform similar operations: the relevant blueprint instance is loaded and updated, after which it is stored again, triggering a redraw event. One of the differences between the two classes is in when the original continuation is executed. In `wrapFunBody`, it is the last thing the wrapper does (line 12). In `wrapFunApp`, the original continuation

```
1  instance Blueprint Task where
2    wrapFunBody :: ModuleName FuncName [(VarName, Task ())] [(ExprId, Int)]
3                   (Task a) -> Task a | iTask a
4    wrapFunBody modNm funNm args dbp (Task oldEval) = Task newEval
5      where
6      newEval taskAdmin tonicAdmin iworld
7        # (blueprint, iworld) = instantiateBlueprint modNm funNm taskAdmin
8                                   args iworld
9        # blueprint           = processCases dbp blueprint
10       # iworld              = storeBlueprint blueprint iworld
11       # tonicAdmin          = updateTonicAdminFun blueprint tonicAdmin
12       = oldEval taskAdmin tonicAdmin iworld
13
14   wrapFunArg :: String a -> Task () | iTask a
15   wrapFunArg descr val = viewInformation descr [] val @! ()
16
17 instance Contained Task where
18   wrapFunApp :: ModuleName FuncName ExprId [(ExprId, a -> Int)]
19                 (Task a) -> Task a | iTask a
20   wrapFunApp modNm funNm exprId dbp (Task oldEval) = Task newEval
21     where
22     newEval taskAdmin tonicAdmin iworld
23       # (blueprint, iworld) = getBlueprintInstance tonicAdmin iworld
24       # (blueprint, iworld) = preEvalUpdate modNm funNm exprId blueprint iworld
25       # iworld              = storeBlueprint blueprint iworld
26       # tonicAdmin          = updateTonicAdminApp modNm funNm tonicAdmin exprId
27       # (result, iworld)    = oldEval taskAdmin tonicAdmin iworld
28       # (blueprint, iworld) = getBlueprintInstance tonicAdmin iworld
29       # blueprint           = processCases dbp result blueprint
30       # (blueprint, iworld) = postEvalUpdate result modNm funNm exprId
31                                  blueprint iworld
32       # iworld              = storeBlueprint blueprint iworld
33       = (result, iworld)
```

Fig. 27. Wrapper implementation for iTasks.

is executed half-way in the wrapper (line 27). After executing the original continuation, the blueprint instance is loaded again, since it may have been updated by other wrappers in the mean time. Another thing both class instances have in common is that they both do future branch prediction (lines 9 and 29).

4.5 The Integrated Tonic Viewer

The integrated Tonic viewer is written in iTasks, for iTasks. To use the viewer for viewing dynamic blueprints, the programmer has to import it in the application that needs to be inspected, thereby including it as part of the original program. Implementing the viewer in iTasks is advantageous, because it allows us to develop it quickly and to leverage our Graphics.Scalable library for drawing the blueprints. Another advantage is that we can easily integrate SDSs in our iTasks programs and refresh the correct tasks when the SDSs are changed. Tonic uses SDSs to store its blueprint instances and run-time meta-data. Any time an instance or its meta-data is updated, the Tonic viewer gets a signal and is able to redraw the corresponding blueprint. Yet another advantage of implementing Tonic in iTasks, for iTasks, is that we have iTasks' generic machinery at our disposal with which we can easily inspect the data that is being passed around in the program. With the generic instances derived for the data, inspecting the data has become equivalent to applying a `viewInformation` editor.

Figure 28 shows a screen-shot of the integrated dynamic Tonic viewer. Both the original application and the Tonic viewer are running in the browser. The latter has its own url. The viewer offers two modes, represented by two tabs: a mode with which one can view static blueprints and a mode with which one can view dynamic blueprints. When viewing static blueprints, one can browse through all static blueprints for that particular application. Viewing static blueprints is useful when using Tonic as a means of communication with stakeholders. In this mode, Tonic is akin to static UML or BPMN viewers. When viewing dynamic blueprints, the user is presented with a list of active tasks, i.e. with a list of blueprint instances. Each of these tasks can be selected, in order to view the instance. Meta-data such as a task's unique identifier, start time, modification time, optional end time, and which is working on it is also presented.

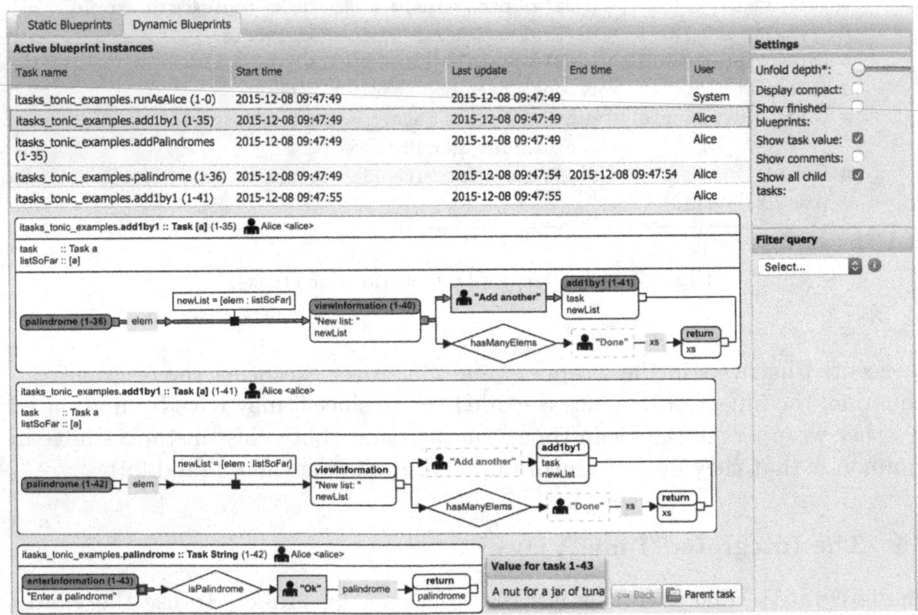

Fig. 28. A screenshot of the integrated Tonic viewer

Below the list of blueprint instances is a large space for rendering the dynamic blueprints. Exactly what is visualized can be customized in a settings panel on the right side of the screen. For example, the "Unfold depth" slider determines how many levels of child tasks are shown together with the selected task. In the screen-shot in Fig. 28 we have selected the "Show all child tasks" option, so all child tasks to the currently selected task are shown recursively. Another option is "Show task value". This opens a floating window in which one can see the task value of a selected task. Tasks can be selected for this purpose by clicking the small square on the right-hand side of the task-application node. Other features of the viewer include viewing the doc-block comments associated with a particular function, showing all finished blueprints, and a compact-mode, in which task-application arguments are not rendered.

One of the challenges in making a viewer for dynamic blueprints is designing a way to navigate through all active blueprints. Even in a small application such as this `add1by1` example, the number of blueprint instances quickly rises. To manage a potentially large number of blueprint instances, the Tonic viewer offers a means to filter the list of dynamic blueprints. This is done in the "Filter query" panel on the right side of the screen. Active blueprints can be filtered by substring matching on any of the columns in the blueprint list. Complex filters can be constructed using conjunction and disjunction operators.

5 Blueprints for All

In the previous sections we have looked in great detail at the way Tonic is implemented for iTasks programs. One of the claims we have made earlier is that we now support blueprints for any monad. To solidify this claim, we shall look at an example of dynamic blueprints of a program in the `IO` monad. Showing a dynamic blueprint for non-iTasks programs requires a new Tonic viewer, which we will discuss as well.

5.1 Dynamic Blueprints of the I/O Monad

Lets look at how Tonic handles the `IO` variant of the `primeCheck` example. Figure 29 shows the dynamic blueprints for `primeCheck`. This dynamic blueprint is produced by an experimental stand-alone Tonic viewer, which serves as a proof-of-concept that such a stand-alone viewer can be constructed. As such, we are currently limited in the kind of information that we can dynamically show. The next section will elaborate on the implementation of the stand-alone viewer and talk about how the Tonic classes are implemented for the `IO` monad. We will also discuss some of the challenges we have encountered.

Creating a *general* (i.e. iTasks-agnostic) stand-alone viewer largely requires solving the same problems as for writing an embedded viewer: how does one load and draw the blueprints? How does one receive and process dynamic updates? How does one inspect dynamic data? It turns out that these questions become significantly more challenging when answering them for a general and stand-alone Tonic viewer. We will look at these aspects next.

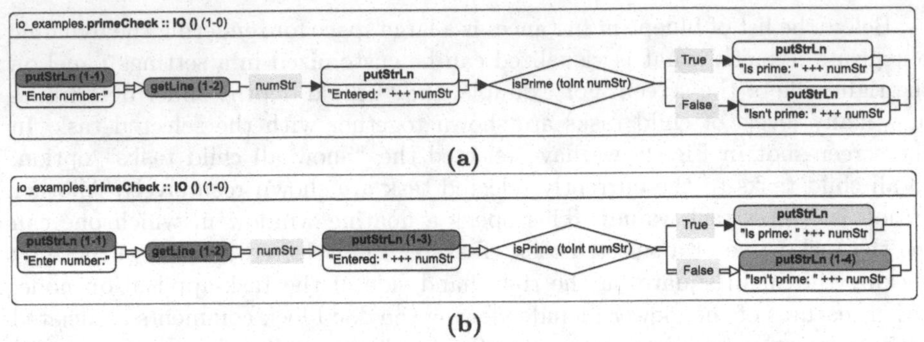

Fig. 29. Dynamic blueprint for IO variant of primeCheck.

5.2 Stand-Alone Viewer Architecture

Instead of including the Tonic viewer as part of an iTasks program, the stand-alone viewer communicates with the to-be-inspected program via a TCP protocol. Figure 30 shows its architecture. There is a two-way communication channel between the original application (the server) and the Tonic viewer (the client).

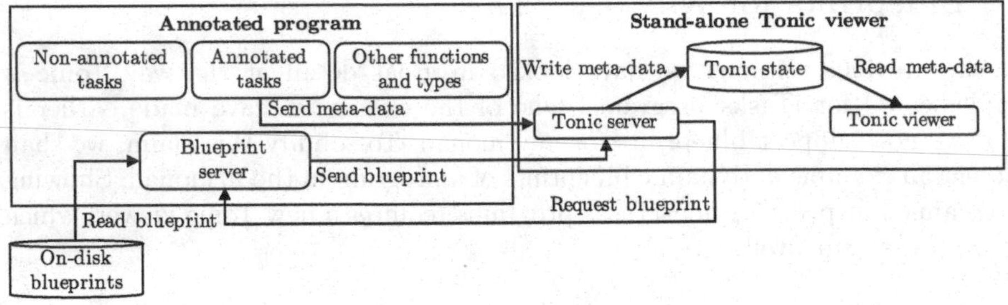

Fig. 30. Architecture of the stand-alone Tonic viewer

Blueprints are stored on disk in the same directory as the application for which they are generated. This allows the embedded Tonic viewer to locate them. The stand-alone viewer is not necessarily located in the same directory as the program that needs to be inspected, however. As a result, it cannot access the blueprints directly. Instead, it requests blueprints from the server and caches them, after which they can be drawn. The stand-alone viewer uses the same drawing mechanism as the built-in viewer.

Dynamic updates are provided by the Tonic wrappers. In the iTasks implementation, these wrappers write directly to the Tonic SDS. Wrappers for the stand-alone viewer write to a TCP connection instead. On the client-side, this data is stored again in an SDS.

5.3 Drawing Dynamic Blueprints

Figure 31 shows the protocol the Tonic viewer uses to instantiate blueprints and update them. When starting the client, it connects to exactly one server. The server registers the client, so it knows it can send updates to it when the program is executed. These updates are received by the client. If a given blueprint instance does not exist yet, the client tries to instantiate it. If the blueprint is not available on the client yet, it requests it from the server. Finally, the blueprint instance is updated and the client waits for the next update.

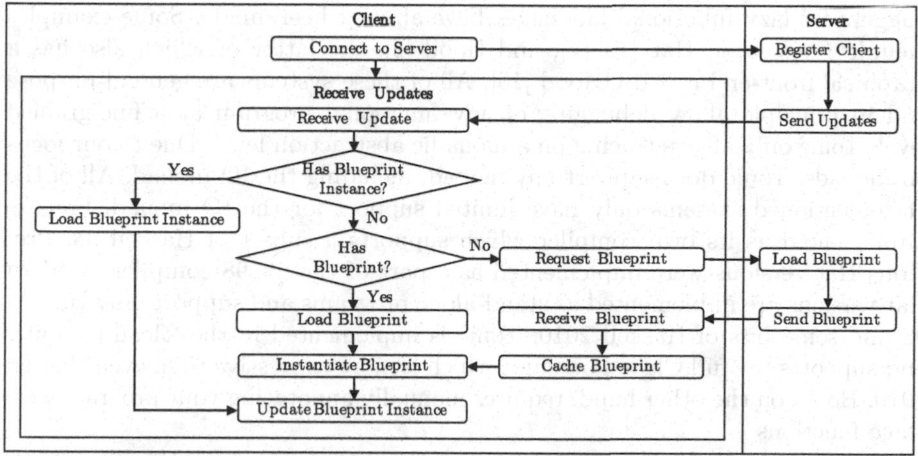

Fig. 31. Client/server protocol for the stand-alone Tonic viewer.

In the integrated Tonic viewer, blueprints are identified by a task's unique identifier. In the stand-alone viewer, we abstract over this identifier by allowing it to be anything for which equality is defined. It is up to the implementation of the `Blueprint` and `Contained` classes to determine what the identifier is.

Inspecting values at run-time is another challenge in the stand-alone Tonic viewer. In the integrated viewer, we simply imposed the `iTask` constraint on anything that could be inspected, allowing rich visualizations. In general, we cannot rely on this constraint being fulfilled. In the stand-alone viewer, we therefore currently disallow inspection of run-time values. One could take a first step towards dynamic value inspection by, for example, impose JSON (de)serialization constraints. Inspecting raw JSON data structures quickly becomes unwieldy for complex data structures, however.

5.4 Discussion

A clear downside to the approach presented above is that for each monad for which one wants to have dynamic blueprints, one needs to implement a blueprint server. The current implementation of the stand-alone Tonic viewer also has several limitations. It is currently not possible to inspect values or do dynamic branch prediction, nor is it possible to select which blueprint instance you are interested in; the viewer only ever shows the blueprint instance for which the latest update arrived. Still, we feel like this is an important step towards positioning Tonic as a general tool.

6 Related Work

Tonic can be seen as a graphical tracer/debugger. Several attempts at tracer/debuggers for lazy functional languages have already been made. Some examples include Freja [5,6], Hat [16,17], and Hood [2], the latter of which also has a graphical front-end called GHood [15]. All of these systems are general-purpose and in principle allow debugging of any functional program at a fine-grained level. Tonic only allows tracing on a monadic abstraction level. Due to our focus on monads, Tonic does support any monad, including the IO monad. All of the aforementioned systems only have limited support for the IO monad. Freja is implemented as its own compiler which supports a subset of Haskell 98. Previous Hat versions were implemented as a part of the nhc98 compiler. Modern Hat versions are implemented as stand-alone programs and support only Haskell 98 and some bits of Haskell 2010. Tonic is implemented in the Clean compiler and supports the full Clean language, which is more expressive than even Haskell 2010. Hood, on the other hand, requires manually annotating your program with trace functions.

GHood is a graphical system on top of Hood that visualizes Hood's output. Its visualizations are mostly aimed at technical users. Graphical programming language, such as VisaVis [13] and Visual Haskell [14] suffer from similar problems. Tonic explicitly aims at understandability by laymen by choosing a higher level of abstraction, hiding details that do not contribute significantly to understanding the program, and by utilizing coding conventions.

Another way to look at Tonic is as a graphical communication tool. In this sense it fulfills a role similar to UML [8,9] and BPMN [19]. Both of these technologies also offer a means to *specify* programs and workflows. This is something Tonic is *not* designed to do. Previous work from our group, GiN – Graphical iTasks Notation [4] can be used for that.

7 Discussion and Conclusion

In this paper we generalised and expanded our original Tonic idea. Any monadic program can now be statically visualized by Tonic. While dynamic visualization is currently mostly limited to iTasks, we have laid the foundation for dynamically visualizing any monadic program.

So far, we have extensively experimented with using Tonic for iTasks. Our approach of using type classes for defining how dynamic behaviour should be captured allows for an almost completely orthogonal implementation for iTasks;

the core system only required very minimal changes. The biggest change was made to the way iTasks handles task IDs. These IDs are not generated deterministically, so we had to implement a form of stack-tracing in iTasks to capture which tasks had already been executed. Systems with deterministic identifiers will not have to resort to such measures.

Section 5.1 shows the results of experiments aimed at supporting dynamic blueprints for the `IO` monad. The fact that we can successfully generate these blueprints suggests that Tonic can be used in contexts other than iTasks as well. While this experimental Tonic viewer works reasonably well for simple IO programs, it lacks many of the features shown in Sect. 4.5 and is not very user-friendly. In the future we want to expand this stand-alone viewer to the point where it can replace the built-in iTasks Tonic viewer.

Complete iTasks Agnostisism
Even though we have made the Tonic compiler completely iTasks-agnostic, Tonic itself still is tied to iTasks by means of the `iTask` context restriction in the `Blueprint` and `Contained` classes. The `iTask` class is used to be able to generically inspect values. Its presence in the classes means that, even when using Tonic for non-iTasks programs, we require an iTasks-specific class to be instantiated for all types that we want to inspect. Clean's type-system, however, offers no elegant solution to this problem. GHC in particular could solve this problem elegantly using its `ConstraintKinds` and `TypeFamilies` extensions, as shown in the code snippet in Fig. 32. Here, the context restriction depends on the type of the `Blueprint` monad.

For Clean, we could require values to be serializable to JSON so we can display data as, for example, a set of key-value pairs. While this approach would generalise the Tonic classes in the short term, it limits the ways in which we can present the inspected values. For example, we can currently render interactive graphics in the Tonic inspector. A true solution would be to implement variable context restrictions in type classes in Clean, similar to GHC.

Portability
By generalising Tonic it becomes clear that it could be implemented in a context different from Clean as well. Acknowledging that GHC in particular offers elegant solutions to improve Tonic's type classes, it would be interesting to explore porting Tonic to GHC.

Dynamic Blueprint Modification
Tonic's blueprints, whether static or dynamic, are currently read-only. We cannot influence the execution of programs or change a program's implementation. In the future we would like to explore such possibilities.

Wrapping Up
Tonic, as presented in this paper, lays the foundation for a plethora of distinct but related tools. On the one hand, blueprints can be seen as automatic program documentation. Each time the program is compiled, its blueprints are generated too, giving the programmer up-to-date documentation for free. Furthermore, dynamic instances of these blueprints document the program's dynamic behaviour. Due to the blueprint's high level of abstraction, this free documentation can serve as the

```
class Monad m => Contained m where
  type CCtxt m a :: Constraint
  type CCtxt m a = ()
  wrapFunApp  :: CCtxt m a
              => (ModuleName, FuncName) -> ExprId -> m a -> m a

class Contained m => Blueprint m where
  type BpCtxt m a :: Constraint
  type BpCtxt m a = ()
  wrapFunBody :: BpCtxt m a
              => ModuleName -> FuncName -> [(VarName, m ())]
              -> m a -> m a
  wrapFunArg  :: BpCtxt m a => String -> a -> m ()

instance Contained Task where
  type CCtxt Task a = ITask a
  wrapFunApp  = ..

instance Blueprint Task where
  type BpCtxt Task a = ITask a
  wrapFunBody = ..
  wrapFunArg  = ..

instance Contained Maybe where
  wrapFunApp  = ..
```

Fig. 32. GHC definition of Tonic type classes.

basis of communication between various project stakeholders as well, enabling rapid software development cycles. Whether Tonic succeeds in being a suitable communication tool is a subject for future work.

Another way to look at Tonic is as a graphical tracer and debugger. Dynamic blueprints trace the execution of the program, while Tonic's inspection and future branch prediction capabilities add features desirable in a debugger. Even for programmers, having such information visualized may aid in understanding the behaviour of the programs they have written better. It may also aid in constructing the required program faster or with less effort.

Yet another avenue worth exploring is education. We are currently including blueprints in the lecture slides of functional programming courses. In our experience, students struggle with the concept of monads, so we want to see if and how Tonic can reduce these problems.

A Using Tonic

In this section we will look at how to use Tonic in iTasks programs. Tonic consists of two parts: the Tonic compiler and the Tonic framework. iTasks ships with preconfigured Tonic environment files, which you can load into the Clean IDE. The Tonic environment then ensures the correct compiler is used.

Tonic uses an opt-in mechanism to determine which modules to visualize. Opting a module in is done by importing the `iTasks._Framework.Tonic` module. By default, importing this module will import instances for the `Contained` and `Blueprint` type classes for the following types: `Task`, `Maybe`, `Either`, and `IO`. At this point, you can also define your own instances for these classes.

In order to see the blueprints, you still need to include a path to the built-in Tonic viewer. This is done in the `startEngine` rule of your program, as shown in Fig. 33. The built-in Tonic viewer is exported via another module, which will need to be imported first.

```
import iTasks._Framework.Tonic
import iTasks.API.Extensions.Admin.TonicAdmin

Start :: *World -> *World
Start world = startEngine [ publish "/"       (\_ -> myMainTask)
                          , publish "/tonic" (\_ -> tonic) ] world
```

Fig. 33. Using Tonic.

Navigating to the `/tonic` URL presents the user with a screen similar to Fig. 34. Two tabs on the top of the screen allow the user to choose between viewing static or dynamic blueprints. Initially, the "Static Blueprints" tab is selected. The user can browse the static blueprints by first selecting the module for which to view the blueprints. After selecting the module, a list with the task names for which a blueprint has been generated appears. Selecting a task name from that list will cause the corresponding blueprint to be rendered.

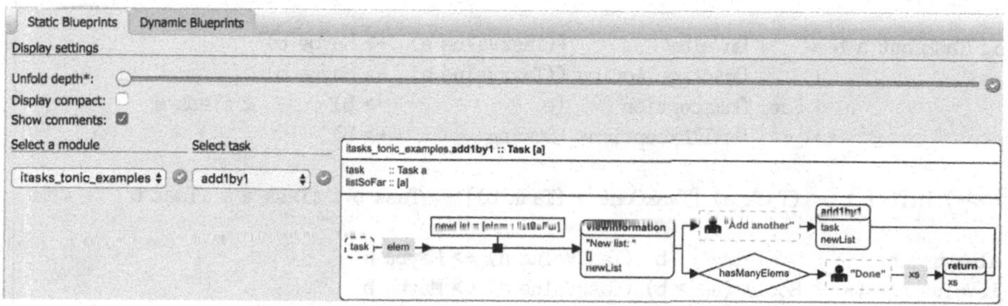

Fig. 34. Built-in static blueprint browser

To view runtime progress, the user can select the "Dynamic Blueprints" tab. This is shown in Sect. 4.5, Fig. 28.

B iTasks Combinators

In this appendix we list common task combinators. All of the combinators used in this paper are presented here. Additional combinators are presented as well. We encourage the reader to experiment with them. Because the iTasks system is a work in progress, it is inevitable that definitions may change in the future. Please use the dedicated search engine *Cloogle*[4] to get access to up-to-date definitions and documentation, not only of iTasks but also of Clean and all other libraries.

B.1 Type Classes

```
class Functor f where
  fmap :: (a -> b) (f a) -> f b

class TApplicative f | Functor f where
  (<#>)  :: (f (a -> b)) (f a) -> f b | iTask a & iTask b
  return :: a -> f a | iTask a

class TMonad m | TApplicative m where
  (>>=) infixl 1 :: (m a) (a -> m b) -> m b | iTask a & iTask b
  (>>|) infixl 1 :: (m a) (      m b) -> m b | iTask a & iTask b

instance Functor Task
instance TApplicative Task
instance TMonad Task
```

B.2 Step Combinator and Utility Functions

```
:: Action       = Action ActionName [ActionOption]
:: ActionOption = ActionKey  Hotkey
                | ActionIcon String

:: TaskCont a b =       OnValue          ((TaskValue a)  -> Maybe b)
                |       OnAction Action  ((TaskValue a)  -> Maybe b)
                | E.e:  OnException      (e              -> b)        & iTask e
                |       OnAllExceptions  (String         -> b)

(>>*) infixl 1 :: (Task a) [TaskCont a (Task b)] -> Task b | iTask a & iTask b

always   ::                      b (TaskValue a) -> Maybe b
ifValue  :: (a -> Bool) (a -> b) (TaskValue a) -> Maybe b
hasValue ::             (a -> b) (TaskValue a) -> Maybe b
ifStable ::             (a -> b) (TaskValue a) -> Maybe b
```

[4] Cloogle resides at https://cloogle.org/.

B.3 Parallel Combinators

```
allTasks :: [Task a]              -> Task [a]      | iTask a
anyTask  :: [Task a]              -> Task a        | iTask a
(-||-) infixr 3 :: (Task a) (Task a) -> Task a     | iTask a
(||-)  infixr 3 :: (Task a) (Task b) -> Task b     | iTask a & iTask b
(-||)  infixl 3 :: (Task a) (Task b) -> Task a     | iTask a & iTask b
(-&&-) infixr 4 :: (Task a) (Task b) -> Task (a, b) | iTask a & iTask b
```

B.4 Editors

```
:: ViewOption a   = E.v: ViewAs  (a -> v) & iTask v

:: EnterOption a  = E.v: EnterAs (v -> a) & iTask v

:: UpdateOption a b = E.v: UpdateAs       (a -> v) (a v -> b)             & iTask v
                    | E.v: UpdateSharedAs (a -> v) (a v -> b) (v v -> v) & iTask v

:: ChoiceOption o  = E.v: ChooseFromDropdown   (o -> v) & iTask v
                   | E.v: ChooseFromCheckGroup (o -> v) & iTask v
                   | E.v: ChooseFromList       (o -> v) & iTask v
                   | E.v: ChooseFromGrid       (o -> v) & iTask v

viewInformation   :: d [ViewOption m]     m -> Task m | toPrompt d & iTask m
enterInformation  :: d [EnterOption m]      -> Task m | toPrompt d & iTask m
updateInformation :: d [UpdateOption m m] m -> Task m | toPrompt d & iTask m

viewSharedInformation          :: d [ViewOption r]        (ReadWriteShared r w)
                               -> Task r | toPrompt d & iTask r
enterMultipleChoiceWithShared  :: d [ChoiceOption a]      (ReadWriteShared [a] w)
                               -> Task [a] | toPrompt d & iTask a & iTask w
updateSharedInformation        :: d [UpdateOption r w]    (ReadWriteShared r w)
                               -> Task r | toPrompt d & iTask r & iTask w
```

B.5 Share Combinators

```
withShared :: b        ((Shared b) -> Task a) -> Task a | iTask a & iTask b
get        ::          (ReadWriteShared a w)  -> Task a | iTask a
set        :: a        (ReadWriteShared r a)  -> Task a | iTask a
upd        :: (r -> w) (ReadWriteShared r w)  -> Task w | iTask r & iTask w
watch      ::          (ReadWriteShared r w)  -> Task r | iTask r
```

B.6 Task Assignment

```
(@:) infix 3 :: worker (Task a) -> Task a | iTask a & toUserConstraint worker
```

References

1. Achten, P., Stutterheim, J., Domoszlai, L., Plasmeijer, R.: Task oriented programming with purely compositional interactive scalable vector graphics. In: Tobin-Hochstadt, S. (ed.) Proceedings of the 26Nd 2014 International Symposium on Implementation and Application of Functional Languages, IFL 2014, pp. 7:1–7:13. ACM, New York (2014). https://doi.org/10.1145/2746325.2746329
2. Andy, G.: Debugging haskell by observing intermediate data structures. Electron. Notes Theor. Comput. Sci. **41**(1), 1 (2001). http://www.sciencedirect.com/science/article/pii/S1571066105805389
3. Arisholm, E., Briand, L.C., Hove, S.E., Labiche, Y.: The impact of UML documentation on software maintenance: an experimental evaluation. IEEE Trans. Softw. Eng. **32**(6), 365–381 (2006). http://ieeexplore.ieee.org/xpl/articleDetails.jsp?tp=&arnumber=1650213&contentType=Journals+
4. Henrix, J., Plasmeijer, R., Achten, P.: GiN: a graphical language and tool for defining iTask workflows. In: Peña, R., Page, R. (eds.) TFP 2011. LNCS, vol. 7193, pp. 163–178. Springer, Heidelberg (2012). https://doi.org/10.1007/978-3-642-32037-8_11
5. Nilsson, H.: Information: declarative debugging for lazy functional languages (1998). http://books.google.nl/books?id=nQQ9AAAACAAJ&dq=intitle:Declarative+Debugging+for+Lazy+Functional+Languages&hl=&cd=1&source=gbs_api. Science, U.i.L.D.o.C
6. Nilsson, H., Sparud, J.: The evaluation dependence tree as a basis for lazy functional debugging. Autom. Softw. Eng. **4**(2), 121–150 (1997). http://link.springer.com/10.1023/A:1008681016679
7. Object Management Group: Business process model and notation (BPMN) version 1.2. Technical report, Object Management Group (2009)
8. Object Modeling Group: OMG unified modeling language specification. Technical report, March 2000. http://www.omg.org/spec/UML/1.3/PDF/index.htm
9. Object Modeling Group: OMG unified modeling language (OMG UML), infrastructure. Technical report, March 2012. http://www.omg.org/spec/UML/2.4.1/Infrastructure/PDF/
10. OMG: OMG unified modeling language (OMG UML), superstructure, Version 2.4.1, August 2011. http://www.omg.org/spec/UML/2.4.1
11. Plasmeijer, R., Achten, P., Koopman, P., Lijnse, B., Van Noort, T., Van Groningen, J.: iTasks for a change: type-safe run-time change in dynamically evolving workflows. In: PEPM '11: Proceedings Workshop on Partial Evaluation and Program Manipulation, PEPM 2011, Austin, TX, USA, pp. 151–160. ACM, New York (2011)
12. Plasmeijer, R., van Eekelen, M.: Clean language report (version 2.1) (2002). http://clean.cs.ru.nl
13. Poswig, J., Vrankar, G., Morara, C.: VisaVis: a higher-order functional visual programming language. J. Vis. Lang. Comput. **5**(1), 83–111 (1994). http://linkinghub.elsevier.com/retrieve/pii/S1045926X84710056
14. Reekie, H.J.: Visual haskell: a first attempt. Technical report (1994). http://citeseerx.ist.psu.edu/viewdoc/download?doi=10.1.1.56.1582&rep=rep1&type=pdf
15. Reinke, C.: GHood–graphical visualisation and animation of Haskell object observations. In: 2001 ACM SIGPLAN (2001). http://www.haskell.org/haskell-workshop/2001/proceedings.pdf#page=127

16. Sparud, J., Runciman, C.: Tracing lazy functional computations using redex trails. In: Glaser, H., Hartel, P., Kuchen, H. (eds.) PLILP 1997. LNCS, vol. 1292, pp. 291–308. Springer, Heidelberg (1997). https://doi.org/10.1007/BFb0033851
17. Sparud, J., Runciman, C.: Complete and partial redex trails of functional computations. In: Clack, C., Hammond, K., Davie, T. (eds.) IFL 1997. LNCS, vol. 1467, pp. 160–177. Springer, Heidelberg (1998). https://doi.org/10.1007/BFb0055430
18. Stutterheim, J., Plasmeijer, R., Achten, P.: Tonic: an infrastructure to graphically represent the definition and behaviour of tasks. In: Hage, J., McCarthy, J. (eds.) TFP 2014. LNCS, vol. 8843, pp. 122–141. Springer, Cham (2015). https://doi.org/10.1007/978-3-319-14675-1_8
19. White, S.A.: Business process model and notation, V1.1 pp. 1–318, January 2008. http://www.omg.org/spec/BPMN/1.1/PDF/

Analyzing Scale-Free Properties in Erlang and Scala

Gábor Oláh, Gergely Nagy, and Zoltán Porkoláb(✉)

Department of Programming Languages and Compilers, Eötvös Loránd University, Pázmány Péter sétány 1/C, Budapest 1117, Hungary
{olikas,njeasus,gsd}@caesar.elte.hu

Abstract. The optimal modularization and the right level of coupling between components are important for the overall quality of software systems. Although the generic suggestion is to minimize the coupling between modules, earlier research on object-oriented programming showed that there is a natural limit to eliminating dependencies between classes. In our research we extend these findings for non-OOP systems and show that this limitation seems to be paradigm-independent. For this purpose we define paradigm-agnostic metrics for coupling and evaluate them. Our results, measuring Scala and Erlang sources, prove that the coupling behavior shows scale-free properties. Our contribution could be useful to avoid unnecessary or harmful code refactors to chase overall low coupling in systems.

1 Introduction

A good software system is said to be loosely coupled between components [1]. This general software engineering advice does not specify the nature of coupling. We define coupling in a generic way, stating that two separate entities are coupled if they are connected by some kind of dependency. This still leaves freedom in defining the entities and the dependency relation. From scientific point of view, any kind of directed connection can be considered a dependency (e.g. one function calls another, one class inherits from another, etc.), and any kind of grouping of pieces of code can be an entity (e.g. function, class, module and package).

In our paper we focus on a common subset of the artifacts and dependencies of two programming paradigms, namely object-oriented (OOP) and functional paradigms (FP). We have chosen these as they are both separately and independently gaining popularity in scientific and industrial applications [2]. We investigate the scale-free property of large software systems from both OOP and FP. In our investigation, entities will be classes for OOP and modules for FP, and function call as the dependency for both of them. To apply our measurements we have chosen Scala [3] and Erlang [4] programming languages. Function call dependency naturally defines two metrics, that we precisely describe in Sect. 3. It is important to note that our analysis considers static and not dynamic calls.

V. Zsók et al. (Eds.): CEFP 2015, LNCS 10094, pp. 380–393, 2019.
https://doi.org/10.1007/978-3-030-28346-9_10

Dynamic binding can happen only at run-time, and it can depend on previous program state or user input. It leads to a completely separate problem space that this paper doesn't intend to solve.

Our paper is organized as follows: Sect. 2 overviews the related works on scale-free networks and metrics. Section 3 describes two metrics and proves that they are coupling metrics. Section 4 lists our measurements and findings on how the scale-free property is paradigm-agnostic considering coupling metrics. Section 5 discusses the possible future works. Our paper concludes in Sect. 6.

2 Related Works

In this section we summarize already-existing key findings on scale-free properties of software metrics.

2.1 On Scale-Free Networks

Considerable amount of effort has been recently put into researching the structure of networks, their transformations over time and properties describing them [5]. Networks that originate in real-world systems rather than follow a mathematically designed structure have been found to usually follow a degree distribution described by a *power-law distribution* [6]. This opposes previous findings of networks generated by algorithms that tend to have a Poisson degree distribution [7]. Network properties of large computer programs were investigated for several publicly available computer programs written in various programming languages including Java, C, C++, Erlang, etc. [8–10]. Moreover, the scale-free property was justified for large scale test systems as well [11].

The Power-Law Distribution

Definition (Scale-free Network) [12]. A graph is called a scale-free network, if its degree distribution follows a power-law distribution, that is for all nodes in the graph having k connections to other nodes, the following must be true for large enough k values:

$$P(k) \sim Ck^{-\lambda} \tag{1}$$

where λ is typically in the range of $2 < \lambda < 3$ and C is the normalization constant that needs to satisfy

$$\sum_{n=1}^{\infty} Cn^{-\lambda} = 1 \tag{2}$$

Properties of Scale-Free Networks. In practice, this describes two key characteristics of these networks:

1. The graph has a set of vertices possessing the number of degrees that is considerably above the mean of the whole network. These nodes are usually called "hubs" of the graph.

2. The clustering coefficient tends to correlate with the node degree: as the degree decreases, the local clustering coefficient decreases as well. This also declares that the coefficient needs to follow a power-law distribution.

The aforementioned properties are thought to be descriptive of how fault-tolerant the network is [13–15] (if this can be considered regarding the network in question), percolation theory had been used to analyze the fault tolerance of scale-free networks previously. Findings in these studies have identified hubs as both the weaknesses and the strengths of networks. If the graph has mostly low-degree vertices and failures randomly affect nodes, losing a hub is less likely. Although, the fall of a hub can mean severe loss of connectedness of the graph, this effect is still negligible compared to a random graph.

While matching the power-law distribution to a data-set can become resource-intensive, there is a much easier (although less precise) method to analyze empirical data. By transforming the definition of power-law distribution as described in [16], we can arrive to a practical solution to analyze data. After plotting the data-set in the fashion of degrees assigned to frequencies on a log-log graph (that is to have a logarithmic scale on both the x- and y-axes), this graph should show a linear regression. This method has been shown to be statistically imprecise [17], although it matches our practical requirements, since it is between the error limits.

There is also a need to ignore some points in the data-set, as these tend to corrupt the linearity of the plot. Our definition takes this into consideration, the condition to check *large enough* k values is to avoid noise at the ends of the graph. This is studied and explained in detail in [17].

Lastly, we make an observation on the naming of these networks. Scale-freeness can be caught when one considers nodes at different levels of degree distribution. These nodes tend to "look familiar" at all levels, thus providing the self-similar nature of the network.

2.2 Metrics

Software metrics is a thoroughly investigated research area. Metrics come from mathematics where the abstract notion of metrics is based on some axioms. All relations satisfying the set of axioms are considered valid metrics. Although software metrics are originated from industrial experiences [18] later Weyuker [19] defined nine axioms that every software metric should satisfy. Although they provided a solid theoretical foundation for the field, these axioms themselves did not provide useful hints for neither the usefulness nor the categorization of metrics. It seems obvious that software metrics can be grouped in categories based on the investigated property of the software. A useful categorization was described in [20]. They defined a simple mathematical background for the theory where non-specified parts of the software are described with nodes, connections between the parts with directed edges and sets as "abstract containers" for the parts. This simplification is useful for achieving full language-independence, which is a requirement to compare different paradigms. In our paper we define nodes as functions, edges as function calls (the starting node of the edge is the calling function; the ending node is the called function) and sets as modules or classes. Five categories were defined for metrics:

- *size*: a straightforward property describing the number of elements or lines in a program;
- *length*: it describes the distance between two elements;
- *complexity*: it is a system level property describing the relationship between components (modules, classes etc.) of the system;
- *cohesion*: it describes how the related program entities are grouped together (e.g. how modules are self-contained in a modularized system);
- *coupling*: it captures the amount of relationship between the modules of the system.

There are different kinds of coupling metrics in the literature, based on this we only list here axioms directly related to them:

1. *Non-negativity.* The coupling value of a module is non-negative.
2. *Null value.* The coupling of a module is zero, if there are no connections to other modules through function calls. (If the module is denoted by m, then let $Outer_o(m)$ denote the number of function calls towards other modules, and $Outer_i(m)$ the number of function calls towards m. The distinction between incoming and outgoing calls is not necessary.)
3. *Monotonicity.* Let $Outer(m) := Outer_i(m) + Outer_o(m)$ and $Coupling(m)$ be the function that assigns the Coupling metrics result to module m. In this case, if we add a new inter-module relationship to m (let us denote this modified module by m'), its coupling will not decrease:

$$Outer(m) \leq Outer(m') \Rightarrow Coupling(m) \leq Coupling(m')$$

4. *Merging of modules.* If two modules are merged together (all functions from one module is moved to the other) then the coupling of the merged module is not greater than the sum of the individual modules.
5. *Disjoint module additivity.* If two modules, m and m' are not connected (i.e. there exists no function call between the two modules) and there is no module m'' such that it connects to both m and m', then the sum of the coupling of the individual modules equals to the coupling of the merged module.

3 Formal Evaluation

In this section we formally define the metrics we use and prove that they comply with the previously defined axioms of coupling. The metrics do not depend on the programming paradigm, we only suppose that there are functions, functions are grouped in sets (modules or classes) and function calls are possible among these sets.

Firstly, we define Aggregated Coupling Metric (ACG)[1] as the sum of incoming and outgoing function calls to a module: $ACG(m) = ACG_i(m) + ACG_o(m)$ If we have modules a and b, and one function call from a to b, then $ACG_i(b) = 1$ and $ACG_o(a) = 1$. We also define a variant of ACG that considers the cardinality of function calls: $WACG$ in the case of multiple function calls existing between a and b, the number of these function calls will be the result of the metric.

Let us denote a module or class by m. Suppose that function f is defined in module m. Denote a function call from f to a function g in module m' by $m.f \rightarrow m'.g$. Denote M as the set of modules of the software system. Let us denote χ a characteristic function that returns 1 if the parameter set is non-empty and 0 otherwise. Furthermore, # will be used as the cardinality of a set.

3.1 Definitions

The ACG metric is the sum of the number of incoming calls from other modules and the number of outgoing calls of the module.

Definition 1. *(Incoming function calls)*

$$S_i(m) = \{(f,g) | \exists f \in m, \exists g \in m' : m'.f \rightarrow m.g\} \tag{3}$$

Definition 2. *(Outgoing function calls)*

$$S_o(m) = \{(f,g) | \exists f \in m, \exists g \in m' : m.f \rightarrow m'.g\} \tag{4}$$

Definition 3. *(ACG metric)*

$$ACG(m) := ACG_i(m) + ACG_o(m) \tag{5}$$

where

$$ACG_i(m) = \chi(S_i(m)) \tag{6}$$

$$ACG_o(m) = \chi(S_o(m)) \tag{7}$$

Definition 4. *(WACG metric)*

$$WACG(m) := WACG_i(m) + WACG_o(m) \tag{8}$$

where

$$WACG_i(m) = \#(S_i(m)) \tag{9}$$

$$WACG_o(m) = \#(S_o(m)) \tag{10}$$

The following theorem shows the coupling nature of the incoming and outgoing components of metrics based on the coupling axioms mentioned previously.

[1] ACG stands for *A*ggregated *C*ouplin*g* to avoid the acronym ACM.

Theorem 1. *$WACG_i$ and $WACG_o$ as well as ACG_i and ACG_o are coupling metrics.*

Proof. It is enough to prove for ACG_i and $WACG_i$. The proof for ACG_o and $WACG_o$ is analogous. We check the five properties of coupling metrics.

1. Trivially true, since both χ and $\#$ return non-negative values.
2. $Outer(m) = 0$ implies that there exists no $g \in n$ so that $n.g \rightarrow m.f$, hence the resulting set is always empty. It makes both χ and $\#$ equal to 0.
3. To prove monotonicity, we need to consider two cases:
   (a) Let us suppose that we add a function call to module m and S_i in (1) was not empty. In this case, the number of elements in S_i increases, but the characteristic functions χ and $\#$ return the same value for S_i. This means that ACG_i and $WACG_i$ satisfies the non-decreasing requirement of monotonicity.
   (b) In the case of adding such a function call to module m where $S_i(m)$ was empty, both $\#$ and χ will increase for $S_i(m)$, thus values of ACG_i and $WACG_i$ will be increased as well which means strict monotonicity.
4. We have to prove that $WACG_i(m) + WACG_i(n) \geq WACG_i(m+n)$ and $ACG_i(m) + ACG_i(n) \geq ACG_i(m+n)$. Since the proof is similar for both ACG_i and $WACG_i$, here we will only list it for $WACG_i$. We need to consider three possible cases.
   (a) *Disjoint modules.* In this case there exists no module p such that $\exists f \in p \wedge g \in m | p.f \rightarrow m.g$ and $\exists f \in p \wedge g \in n | p.f \rightarrow n.g$ and $\nexists f \in m \wedge g \in n | m.f \rightarrow n.g$ or $n.f \rightarrow m.g$: simply, there is no module that has a connection to both m and n and there are no calls between m and n. Merging such modules means that the merged module will have exactly the same calls as m and n, so $WACG_i(m) + WACG_i(n) = WACG_i(m+n)$.
   (b) *Call from a common module.* If there is a module p: $\exists f \in p \wedge g \in m | p.f \rightarrow m.g$ and $\exists f \in p \wedge g \in n | p.f \rightarrow n.g$, also $\nexists f \in m \wedge g \in n | m.f \rightarrow n.g$ or $n.f \rightarrow m.g$ meaning that there is one module that has a call to both m and n, but there is no call between m and n. The merged module will contain the call from p only once, so its weight will be accounted for only once, hence $WACG_i(m) + WACG_i(n) > WACG_i(m+n)$.
   (c) *Call between the modules.* If there is no module p in a way that $\exists f \in p \wedge g \in m | p.f \rightarrow m.g$ and $\exists f \in p \wedge g \in n | p.f \rightarrow n.g$ and $\exists f \in m \wedge g \in n | m.f \rightarrow n.g$ or $n.f \rightarrow m.g$. In this case there is a call from m to n (the proof is the same in the reverse order) and there are no common calls from outer modules. Merging such modules will have the same connections as the separate modules except for the call between m and n, which will be excluded since we don't consider self calls for $WACG$ and ACG. This leaves us with the same considerations as (4b), thus $WACG_i(m) + WACG_i(n) > WACG_i(m+n)$.
5. If m and n are disjoint, then the condition of 4.a. holds.

The coupling nature of $WACG$ follows from a more generic theorem.

Theorem 2. *The sum of coupling metrics is a coupling metric.*

Proof. Let M_1 and M_2 be coupling metrics. We have to prove that $M := M_1 + M_2$ is a coupling metric. We check the five properties of coupling metrics.

1. M is non-negative, since it is the sum of non-negative numbers.
2. If $M_1 = 0$ and $M_2 = 0$, then $M = 0$.
3. Let M_1 and M_2 be monotonously increasing functions on the domain set D. For all $x, y \in D, x \leq y$ we know that $M_1(x) \leq M_1(y)$ and $M_2(x) \leq M_2(y)$. Adding M_1 and M_2 together we have $M_1(x) + M_2(x) \leq M_1(y) + M_2(y)$ and that is equivalent to $(M_1 + M_2)(x) \leq (M_1 + M_2)(y)$.
4. Merging of two modules can also be derived back to the monotonicity of addition.
5. The equation derives from the monotonicity property as described in Theorem 1.

Since $WACG$ is the sum of two coupling metrics, it is also a coupling metric. We will use both $WACG$ and ACG to show that the degree distribution derived from these metrics shows a scale-free property.

4 Evaluation of the Metrics

In this section we provide a methodology and results that scale-free property of different software systems of different paradigms are preserved. First we provide the methodology of our measurements, then our expectations to these measurements and finally the data that supports our expectations.

4.1 Methodology

We used RefactorErl [21] for analyzing the Erlang [4] compiler and a Scala compiler plugin for analyzing the call-graph of the Scala [3] compiler. Both products are complex software systems usually written by experts who are familiar with the paradigms. With these tools we gathered the number of incoming function calls for each module or class (entity). We have investigated three consecutive major releases of Erlang OTP (R12B, R13B, R14B) [22]. The Erlang compiler is about 626.000 lines of code. RefactorErl loads the whole investigated software system into a semantic graph [23] and stores it into a database. We have written a plugin module for RefactorErl that queries the database to analyze all function calls and module graphs with incoming and outgoing edges deriving from the analyzed function calls. Erlang function calls can be dynamic, i.e. pure higher-order functions, or function and module names can be determined run-time. The dynamic function calls are not included in our results and their Scala counterparts are not analyzed either, and there are only a few of them in the analyzed Erlang systems.

We have investigated three consecutive major versions of the Scala compiler [24]: v2.10, v2.11, v2.12. The Scala compiler is about 430.000 lines of code.

The compiler plugin for Scala was inserted as the last compile phase traversing all method calls and registering incoming and outgoing edges for the corresponding classes. The last compiler phase receives the fully analyzed syntax tree.

The source code can be downloaded from https://github.com/olikasg/erlang-scala-metrics.

4.2 Hypotheses

Since several studies provided proof that real object-oriented software systems follow scale-free properties we expect that the Scala compiler will also show the same, despite the fact that it is written in a mixed, both functional and object-oriented paradigm. In other words, mixing the functional style (immutable data structures, higher-order functions, algebraic data types) has no (or insignificant) effect on the scale-free property.

Hypothesis 1. *The Scala compiler shows scale-free property for* $WACG_i$*,* $WACG_o$ *and* $WACG$*.*

Since the industrial AXD 311 product of Ericsson - which was written in Erlang - has scale-free behavior [10], we expect that the Erlang OTP will show similar properties. Although Erlang is not a pure functional programming language (more of a concurrent one), the base language elements are functional (except compound expressions and sequences). The lack of user-defined types (hence lack of classes) provides a different environment to our analysis. (One might argue that parametric modules and the actor model could be used to simulate object-orientation [25], but the existing systems rarely use parametric modules and Erlang OTP is not written using OOP.)

Hypothesis 2. *Erlang OTP shows scale-free properties for* $WACG_i$*,* $WACG_o$ *and* $WACG$*.*

The less complex ACG still grabs an interesting property of a software system. The lack of multiplicity of edges reveals a similar "coupling" order between nodes. We expect that this simpler metric also preserves the scale-free property of the systems under investigation.

Hypothesis 3. *Both the Scala compiler and the Erlang OTP preserves the scale-free property with* ACG_i*,* ACG_o *and* ACG*.*

We analyzed three consecutive major versions of the compilers to investigate whether the scale-free property changes over releases. Supposing Hypotheses 1–3 are true for the first analyzed version, the scale-free property remains and the average change of the metric values are significant (i.e. more than 5%) for all defined metrics.

Hypothesis 4. *The scale-free property can be observed for all analyzed versions of the Scala compiler and the Erlang OTP in all defined metrics.*

4.3 Our Findings

We used log-log plots to visualize the distributions of class dependencies. The charts can be read as the number of classes (y-axis) that have the given number of connections (x-axis). We have fitted a linear regression model (the red line in the charts) to visualize that the number of classes with a given number of connections is close to a straight line. The blue lines represent the average number of connections.

Figure 1 shows the results of the metrics for the Scala compiler v2.10. The number of Erlang modules analyzed is 1227, while the number of Scala classes is 2227. All of $WACG_i$ (Fig. 1a), $WACG_o$ (Fig. 1b) and $WACG$ (Fig. 1c) show a highly left-skewed distribution. This observation confirms Hypothesis 1, the distribution is very similar to ideal power-law distributions. It is common in all charts that the majority of the data points are below average and some of the modules are significantly higher than this average.

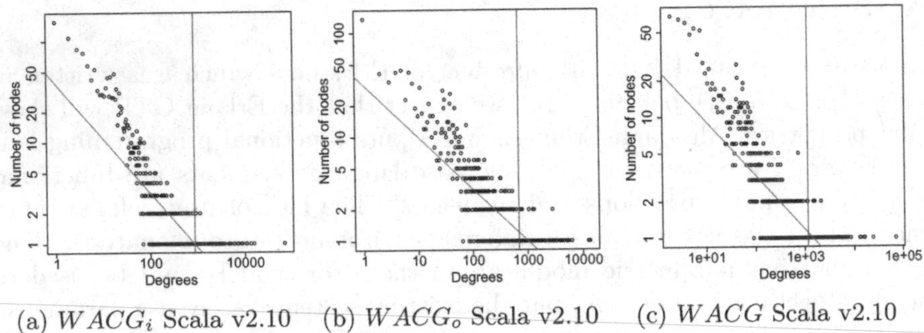

(a) $WACG_i$ Scala v2.10 (b) $WACG_o$ Scala v2.10 (c) $WACG$ Scala v2.10

Fig. 1. $WACG$ distributions for the Scala compiler. (Color figure online)

The same left-skewed distribution property is valid for Erlang OTP R12B in Fig. 2. Although the distribution shows a high number of outliers and is a bit scattered, but the majority of modules show below-average number of connections. We analyzed 993 modules, the majority of them are below-average and only a small number have significantly higher values than the average. We claim that Hypothesis 2 is also valid.

The ACG metrics show a cleaner distribution in the following way: with only a few outliers at the beginning, a steep decline and a long tail, the charts (Figs. 3 and 4) fit the regression lines nicely. Hence Hypothesis 3 also holds.

The main claim of our article, i.e. the scale-free property is independent from the programming paradigm, is supported by the observation that the charts of both the Scala and the Erlang systems show high levels of similarity.

As Hypothesis 4 suggests, the scale-free property is preserved throughout the different versions of both systems. We included only the distributions deriving from the ACG (Figs. 6 and 8) and $WACG$ (Figs. 5 and 7) metrics, but the incoming and outgoing distributions show similar results. The source code changes

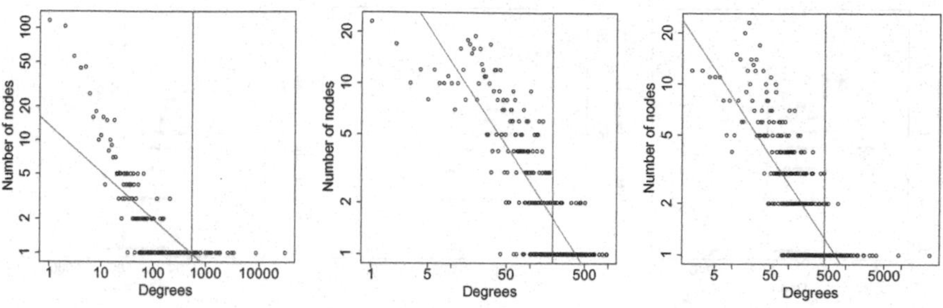

(a) $WACG_i$ Erlang R12B (b) $WACG_o$ Erlang R12B (c) $WACG$ Erlang R12B

Fig. 2. $WACG$ distributions for the Erlang OTP.

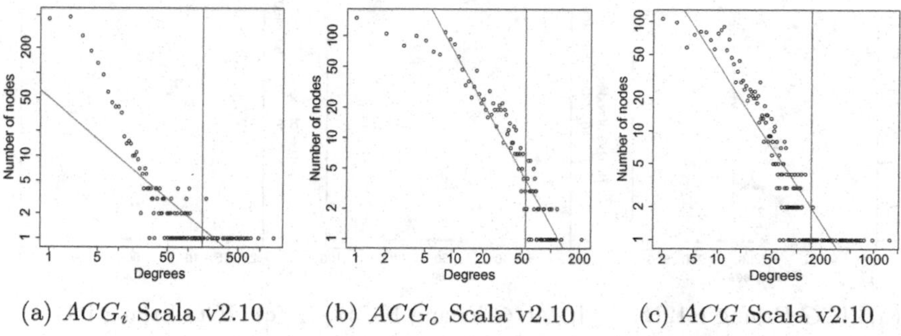

(a) ACG_i Scala v2.10 (b) ACG_o Scala v2.10 (c) ACG Scala v2.10

Fig. 3. ACG distributions for the Scala compiler.

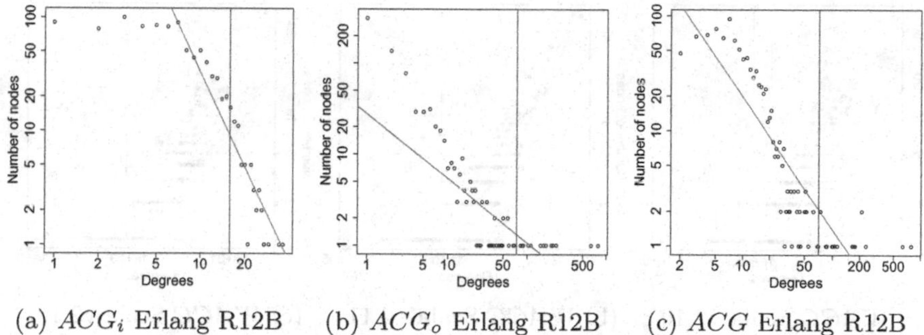

(a) ACG_i Erlang R12B (b) ACG_o Erlang R12B (c) ACG Erlang R12B

Fig. 4. ACG distributions for the Erlang OTP.

significantly: approximately 5% of the Erlang compiler changed, and approximately 50% of the code of the Scala compiler did. The changes in the values of the metrics are significant: for the Erlang compiler there is 9.93% increase in $WACG$ and 10.31% increase in ACG; for the Scala compiler there is 5.92% decrease in $WACG$ and 11.09% decrease in ACG. These numbers also support Hypothesis 4.

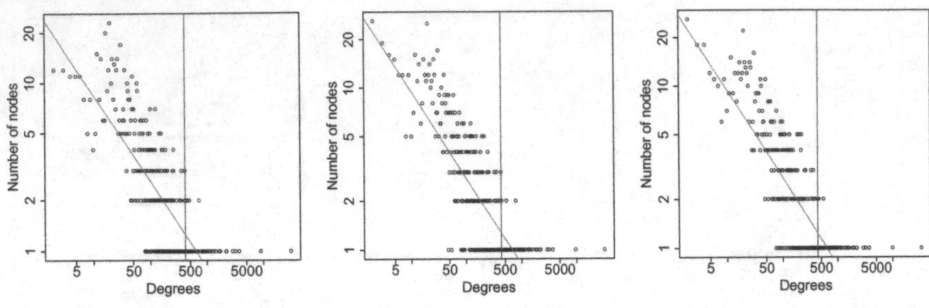

(a) *WACG* Erlang R12B (b) *WACG* Erlang R13B (c) *WACG* Erlang R14B

Fig. 5. *WACG* distributions for different versions of the Erlang OTP.

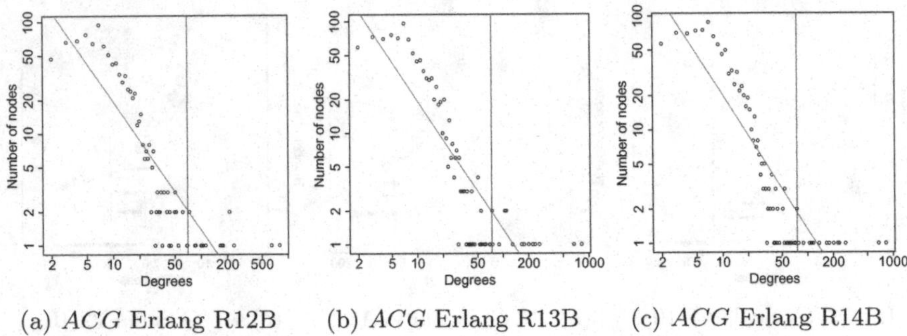

(a) *ACG* Erlang R12B (b) *ACG* Erlang R13B (c) *ACG* Erlang R14B

Fig. 6. *ACG* distributions for different versions of the Erlang OTP.

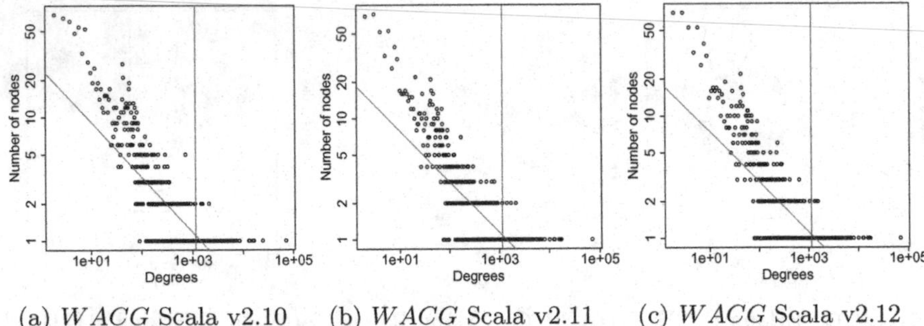

(a) *WACG* Scala v2.10 (b) *WACG* Scala v2.11 (c) *WACG* Scala v2.12

Fig. 7. *WACG* distributions for different versions of the Scala compiler.

Our conclusion is that both *ACG* and *WACG* are suitable to capture the scale-free property of the investigated systems. The scale-free property is preserved and significant source code modifications do not alter this property. Since scale-freeness means that some nodes (hubs) have above-average connections, both *ACG* and *WACG* are suitable to point out heavily dependent parts of software systems.

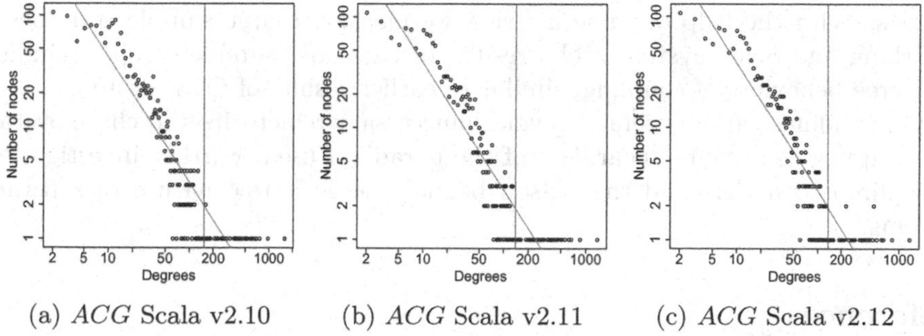

(a) *ACG* Scala v2.10 (b) *ACG* Scala v2.11 (c) *ACG* Scala v2.12

Fig. 8. *ACG* distributions for different versions of the Scala compiler.

Furthermore, the paradigm in which the system is written, is not relevant to the scale-free property.

5 Future Work

Our work can be extended to other functional languages like Haskell or Clojure. If a language lacks a module system then our definitions should be altered. Other paradigms such as logical programming (Prolog) or generic programming techniques (e.g. template meta-programming) may also be investigated.

The cause why large software systems tend to show a scale-free property should be further investigated. We see two possible explanations that are worth to consider. One reason can be that the developer's familiarity with classes or modules creates a preference resulting in the avoidance of other less-understood classes. Over time this creates hubs. The other reason can be that the chosen software architecture (e.g. layered architecture) creates artificial preference and hubs are inevitable.

6 Summary

In this paper we investigated the coupling behavior of programs written in multiple paradigms. Earlier research found that coupling level of object-oriented systems has a certain pattern, similar to scale-free networks. Thus overall coupling of systems cannot be decreased under a specific limit, i.e. there will always remain components that have significantly higher than average dependency.

As modern programming languages (like Scala) support multiple paradigms as opposed to purely object-oriented ones, it is important to understand whether the scale-free property is paradigm-agnostic, furthermore, whether functional programming languages (like Erlang) preserve the same property.

For this purpose we defined two metrics, Aggregated Coupling Metric (*ACG*) and Weighted Aggregated Coupling Metric (*WACG*) in a paradigm independent way. We have shown that both metrics fulfill all the requirements of coupling metrics. With the help of these metrics, we measured large sample code bases of Erlang and Scala systems. The results of these measurements show similar scale-free behaviors of coupling, similar to earlier results of OOP systems.

Our findings can be useful to avoid unnecessary refactorings to chase overall low coupling in systems regardless of the paradigm used. Further investigation is required to understand the reason behind the scale-free nature of software systems.

References

1. Stevens, W.P., Myers, G.J., Constantine, L.L.: Structured design. IBM Syst. J. **13**(2), 115–139 (1974)
2. Porkoláb, Z., Zsók, V.: Teaching multiparadigm programming based on object-oriented experiences. Teach. Math. Comput. Sci. **5**(1), 171–182 (2006)
3. Odersky, M., Spoon, L., Venners, B.: Scala (2011). http://blog.typesafe.com/why-scala. Accessed 28 Aug 2012
4. Armstrong, J.: Programming Erlang: Software for a Concurrent World. Pragmatic Bookshelf, Raleigh (2007)
5. Newman, M.E.J., Barabási, A., Watts, D.J.: The Structure and Dynamics of Networks. Princeton University Press, Princeton (2006)
6. Barabási, A.: Emergence of scaling in random networks. Science **286**(5439), 509–512 (1999)
7. Erdős, P., Rényi, A.: On the evolution of random graphs. Publ. Math. Inst. Hung. Acad. Sci. **5**, 17–61 (1960)
8. de Moura, A.P.S., Lai, Y.-C., Motter, A.E.: Signatures of small-world and scale-free properties in large computer programs. Phys. Rev. E **68**, 017102 (2003)
9. Yao, Y., Huang, S., Liu, X., Ren, Z.: Scale-free property in large scale object-oriented software and its significance on software engineering. In: Information and Computing Science, ICIC 2009 (2009)
10. Bokor, A., Burcsi, P., Kátai-Pál, G., Kovács, A., Nagy, P., Tátrai, A.: Complexity of the AXD301 software. ELTE eScience Regional Knowledge Center, ELTE CNL, Internal Research Report (personal communication) (2004)
11. Szabados, K.: Structural analysis of large TTCN-3 projects. In: Núñez, M., Baker, P., Merayo, M.G. (eds.) FATES/TestCom 2009. LNCS, vol. 5826, pp. 241–246. Springer, Heidelberg (2009). https://doi.org/10.1007/978-3-642-05031-2_19
12. Onnela, J.-P., et al.: Structure and tie strengths in mobile communication networks. Proc. Natl. Acad. Sci. **104**(18), 7332–7336 (2007)
13. Cohen, R., Erez, K., ben Avraham, D., Havlin, S.: Resilience of the internet to random breakdowns. Phys. Rev. Lett. **85**, 4626–4628 (2000)
14. Cohen, R., Erez, K., ben Avraham, D., Havlin, S.: Breakdown of the internet under intentional attack. Phys. Rev. Lett. **86**, 3682–3685 (2001)
15. Callaway, D.S., Newman, M.E.J., Strogatz, S.H., Watts, D.J.: Network robustness and fragility: percolation on random graphs. Phys. Rev. Lett. **85**, 5468–5471 (2000)
16. Taube-Schock, C., Walker, R.J., Witten, I.H.: Can we avoid high coupling? In: Mezini, M. (ed.) ECOOP 2011. LNCS, vol. 6813, pp. 204–228. Springer, Heidelberg (2011). https://doi.org/10.1007/978-3-642-22655-7_10
17. Clauset, A., Shalizi, C.R., Newman, M.E.J.: Power-law distributions in empirical data. SIAM Rev. **51**(4), 661–703 (2009)

18. McCabe, T.J.: A complexity measure. IEEE Trans. Softw. Eng. **2**(4), 308–320 (1976)
19. Weyuker, E.J.: Evaluating software complexity measures. IEEE Trans. Softw. Eng. **14**(9), 1357–1365 (1988)
20. Briand, L.C., Morasca, S., Basili, V.R.: Property-based software engineering measurement. IEEE Trans. Softw. Eng. **22**(1), 68–86 (1996). https://doi.org/10.1109/32.481535
21. RefactorErl webpage (2015). http://plc.inf.elte.hu/erlang/
22. Erlang OTP homepage (2015). http://www.erlang.org/download.html
23. Horpácsi, D., Kőszegi, J.: Static analysis of function calls in Erlang. Refining the static function call graph with dynamic call information by using data-flow analysis. e-Informatica Softw. Eng. J. **7**(1), 65–76 (2013)
24. Scala repository on GitHub (2015). https://github.com/scala/scala
25. Fehér, G., Békés, A.G.: ECT: an object-oriented extension to Erlang. In: Proceedings of the 8th ACM SIGPLAN Workshop on ERLANG, ERLANG 2009, pp. 51–62. ACM, New York (2009)

Author Index

Achten, Peter 341

Čukić, Ivan 42
Cunha, Jácome 1

Denuziere, Loic 137

Fernandes, João Paulo 1

Granicz, Adam 137
Grelck, Clemens 207
Grimm, Rainer 111

Koopman, Pieter 283
Korečko, Štefan 161

Nagy, Gergely 380

Oláh, Gábor 380

Pardo, Alberto 1
Plasmeijer, Rinus 283, 341
Porkoláb, Zoltán 75, 380

Saraiva, João 1
Stutterheim, Jurriën 341

Printed in the United States
By Bookmasters